Understanding Investments

Connel Fullenkamp, Ph.D.

THE
GREAT
COURSES®

PUBLISHED BY:

THE GREAT COURSES
Corporate Headquarters
4840 Westfields Boulevard, Suite 500
Chantilly, Virginia 20151-2299
Phone: 1-800-832-2412
Fax: 703-378-3819
www.thegreatcourses.com

Connel Fullenkamp, Ph.D.
Professor of the Practice,
Department of Economics
Duke University

Professor Connel Fullenkamp is Professor of the Practice and Director of Undergraduate Studies in the Department of Economics at Duke University. He teaches financial economics courses, such as corporate finance, as well as core courses, such as economic principles. In addition to teaching, he serves as a consultant for the Duke Center for International Development. Prior to joining the Duke faculty in 1999, Professor Fullenkamp was a faculty member in the Department of Finance within the Mendoza College of Business at the University of Notre Dame.

Originally from Sioux Falls, South Dakota, Professor Fullenkamp earned his undergraduate degree in Economics from Michigan State University. In addition to receiving the Harry S. Truman Scholarship, he was named one of the university's Alumni Distinguished Scholars. He earned his master's and doctorate degrees in Economics from Harvard University, where he was also awarded a National Science Foundation Graduate Research Fellowship.

Professor Fullenkamp's areas of interest include financial market development and regulation, economic policy, and immigrant remittances. His work has appeared in a number of prestigious academic journals, including the *Review of Economic Dynamics*, *The Cato Journal*, and the *Journal of Banking and Finance*. He also does consulting work for the IMF Institute at the International Monetary Fund, training government officials around the world. He is a member of the IMF Institute's finance team, whose purpose is to train central bankers and other officials in financial market regulation, focusing on derivatives and other new financial instruments.

In recognition of his teaching excellence, Professor Fullenkamp has received Duke University's Alumni Distinguished Undergraduate Teaching Award as well as the University of Notre Dame's Mendoza College of

Business Outstanding Teacher Award. Along with Sunil Sharma, Professor Fullenkamp won the third annual ICFR–Financial Times Research Prize for their paper on international financial regulation. ∎

Table of Contents

Table of Contents

Table of Contents

Understanding Investments

Scope:

Just about everyone can use some help when it comes to investing. There are thousands of different investments to choose from—with more appearing every day. The language of investing is full of technical terms and jargon that make it difficult to get straight answers to even the most basic questions. In addition, the financial markets often behave in ways that seem to defy common sense. Because of these reasons, it's not surprising that many people find the prospect of investing their hard-earned savings mysterious and intimidating.

This set of 24 lectures takes the mystery out of investing by giving simple and clear explanations of investments and the process of investing. You'll learn practical lessons about how to choose the best investments for your portfolio and how to plan for your financial goals. As you learn about investments, you'll also learn some of the most important lessons about how financial markets work. This course will help you make sense of the financial headlines so that you can make good investment decisions—or simply be better informed about what's happening in the financial markets.

In the first lecture, you'll learn about the important role that investing plays in the economy, and you'll encounter the main threats to investing success that keep many people from making the most of their investing opportunities. You'll also learn that there are sensible and effective ways to mitigate the main risks to your investments—even when one of the biggest threats to success is human nature.

The second lecture complements the first by asking one of the most important questions in all of investing: How do investors make money? In this lecture, you'll learn about the efficient markets hypothesis and its claim that it's impossible to beat the market. You'll learn why many believe that it is possible to earn market-beating returns, and you'll explore what it takes in order to achieve this. You'll also learn how to tailor your investing strategy, depending on whether you wish to match the market return—or try to do better.

Equipped with a better understanding of what you can achieve with investing, you will move on to learning about individual investments and investing strategies. The next set of lectures introduces the 4 most important investments that every individual investor should consider: stocks, bonds, mutual funds, and exchange-traded funds (ETFs). In these lectures, you will learn the basic characteristics of these instruments, how to invest in them, and why they deserve a place in your portfolio. After this introduction, you will take an in-depth look at how to choose the right stocks, bonds, mutual funds, and ETFs for you. You'll learn the main techniques—such as financial statement analysis and the method of comparables—that professional investors use to choose investments for their portfolios.

You won't just learn about the basic investments, however. Several additional lectures will introduce you to other opportunities that you'll want to consider. You'll learn why you should invest abroad, and you'll learn the safest ways to do so. Additionally, you'll learn several ways to invest in real estate without becoming a landlord, and you'll be enticed to consider investing in commodities like gold and oil. You'll even learn about derivatives and how call options can be used in surprisingly safe ways to increase the returns on your portfolio.

This course also introduces you to the most important investing strategies that all investors should understand, and it explains why some of these strategies should be avoided. For example, you'll learn how to use leverage and market-timing techniques, but you'll also learn why they are dangerous temptations best left to the professionals. You'll also learn why diversifying your portfolio is critical, and you'll discover how to make sure your investments are well diversified. Furthermore, you'll learn that selling off your investments can be difficult, but it's another essential skill that all investors should master.

In the final 3 lectures of the course, all the lectures will come together to focus on financial planning and taking charge of your investment portfolio. You'll learn the basics of time value of money, one of the most important tools in finance. Then, you'll put these ideas to work by learning how to do basic financial planning, focusing on saving for retirement. You'll learn why you'll need to keep investing even after you retire, and you'll learn the fundamentals of annuities.

This course draws on economic theory, expert advice, and hands-on examples to help you become a better informed and more confident investor. ∎

How to Stop Worrying and Start Investing
Lecture 1

In this course, you're going to learn the principles that successful investors rely on and how to use them to become a more confident investor. In this first lecture, you'll discover that the basic ideas behind investing are sensible and easy to understand. Understanding the main risks to investing is the first step toward managing them, and there are simple and effective ways to manage these risks. By the end of this lecture, any sense of frustration or dread that you associate with investing will hopefully start to fade—and may even be replaced with excitement.

What Is Investing?

- **Investing** is spending your money, time, or other resources to create or acquire assets. An **asset** is anything that holds onto its value over time. Buying an asset is a way to store resources you don't need now so that you can use them later. In other words, investing is a form of saving.

- **Financial assets** are documents that entitle their owners to receive something of value, generally a set of cash payments, from someone else. Another name for a financial asset is a **security**, which is written evidence of the extension of a loan.

- One of the distinguishing features of a financial asset is that it doesn't have any intrinsic value; it's either a piece of paper or, more likely, a collection of numbers stored on a computer.

- The value of financial assets comes from **real assets**, which are used directly in the production of goods and services. Some real assets are **storable commodities**, such as cotton or oil, but many real assets are what economists call **capital goods**—machines, buildings, factories, and the land that they sit on.

- Other real assets are invisible but are nonetheless real—such as ideas, knowledge, and skills. Economists call these assets **intangible assets**, and in the business world, they're often called intellectual property. What they all have in common is that their value comes from their ability to make goods and services, and when they're combined in new and creative ways, they can dramatically increase in value.

- Financial assets derive their value from real assets; however, the relationship is often complex. Financial assets are created whenever somebody borrows money in order to buy real assets.

- Financial assets make it possible for ordinary people to invest in real assets and enjoy the increase in value that can be associated with that investment. Additionally, financial assets can be divided into small amounts so that individuals can buy many different assets. Most real assets are so expensive that many households couldn't afford more than one—if any.

When a business borrows money to build a new factory, a financial asset is created.

- Furthermore, financial assets are extremely convenient to buy and sell. Real assets, such as factories, can sit idle for years until the right buyer comes along, but you can sell your stock in the company that owns the idle factory in a matter of seconds as a result of online trading.

- So the attraction of investing in financial assets is that it gives us a convenient way to participate—albeit indirectly—in the investment into real assets, which is where the value is created in our economy. This gives everyone the chance not only to store extra resources for later, but to have these resources grow significantly over time as well.

The Top 4 Threats to Investment Success

Market Downturns

- The danger that people most likely fear the most is the chance that an investment loses money because its value falls. The prices of financial assets typically move up and down frequently—sometimes almost violently—and these ups and downs are extremely difficult to predict, especially on a day-to-day basis.

- The first line of defense against losing money is simply to give your investment some more time. Even though financial prices constantly bounce up and down, the short-term bumps smooth out over longer periods of time and reveal a longer-term trend. If you invest in assets that really are creating value, the trend of prices will eventually show that value.

- The S&P 500 measures the stock prices of 500 of the largest companies in the United States. It's a pretty good indication of the overall value of the U.S. stock market, so most people use it to stand for the price of the entire stock market.

- During a market downturn, if you panic and sell off your investments, you'd lock in huge losses and miss out on the recovery. Time can be an effective defense against losses on your investments—but you have to be patient, and you have to have the time to spare.

- A critical part of investing involves gradually shifting riskier investments to safer ones well before you actually need cash, which will cushion the blow from a market downturn.

Bankruptcy

- Another risk of investing is the risk of bankruptcy of the issuer of one of your investments. The party who promises to give the owner of a financial asset something of value is called the **issuer**, which can be a firm, the government, or a person, and all of these parties can go bankrupt.

- When the issuer of a financial asset that you own declares bankruptcy, it almost always means that your asset will lose value. Fortunately, it doesn't necessarily mean that you will lose all of your investment. In general, if you hold a loan or a bond, you'll probably get something, but if you hold stock, you'll probably get nothing—even if the company survives the bankruptcy.

- Fortunately, in most cases, there are plenty of warning signs that an issuer is losing financial strength and may be sliding toward bankruptcy. Companies and governments—who are most likely to be the issuers of the investments you hold—are required to make their financial information publicly available.

- By being alert and proactive, investors can take effective steps to limit bankruptcy risk in their investments. You can simply avoid investing in financial assets that come from financially weak issuers. Additionally, you can monitor the financial strength of the issuers of the assets you do hold so that if an issuer starts to weaken, you can sell the asset before the issuer is in serious danger of bankruptcy.

Inflation

- **Inflation** is a general increase in prices. There are many ways to measure inflation, but most people are familiar with the consumer price index (CPI), which measures the price of a set of goods and services that a typical household consumes.

- Inflation is a danger to investing because it drives up the prices of the things we want to buy with our savings so that we may not be able to afford the type of college education, vacation home, or retirement that we wanted.

- Whereas financial prices go up and down—hopefully a bit more up than down on average—the prices of everything else only seem to go up steadily. If inflation is low, we hardly notice it. However, over time, a small increase in prices each year amounts to a huge increase in prices over decades as a result of compounding.

- The other aspect of inflation that makes it dangerous is that it can differ greatly across different types of products. Some products experience low rates of inflation. The prices of technology-related products, such as computers, can even fall for long periods of time.

- Other products, however, experience very high rates of inflation. High-inflation products and services include tuition and health care. Because these may be the very things you're saving for, you need to be aware that inflation can be a serious enemy of successful investing.

- To combat inflation, find investments that keep up with inflation. Many assets will keep up with inflation, and stocks seem to be one of them. However, the assets that tend to do better at keeping up with inflation also tend to be the riskier ones.

- Even if you load up on assets that keep up with the general rate of inflation, you may still be burned by inflation in the price of something that you are saving for. Again, the best strategy is to look for assets that keep up with the specific inflation you're worried about—but this can be a challenge.

- There is another way to protect against the ravages of inflation, but it's a difficult one: You could save more now—just to cover the amount of the increase in prices that you don't think your investments will match.

Human Nature

- The biggest threat to investing confidently and successfully is human nature. In many ways, our own psychology and emotions do far more damage to our investing success than market crashes do.

- Economists have noticed that investors tend to exhibit herd behavior, which involves joining the crowd and rushing into an investment without doing much, if any, research on it. The price gets pushed up by the herd but then plummets later.

- Another way that our unfamiliarity with financial instruments can lead to trouble is that it makes too many people easy victims for financial scams. We want to believe that there are some secret, surefire investing techniques waiting to be discovered, and this makes us easy to fool.

- **Behavioral economics** blends psychology and physiology with economics to gain a better understanding of how people's decision making goes wrong—especially in situations involving investing. Some of these behavioral quirks are fairly mild, but others can cause serious problems for your investments.

- An example of a mild type of behavioral impediment is called **confirmation bias**, which describes the tendency for people to only notice evidence that supports their beliefs and ignore evidence that contradicts it. A more serious type of behavioral impediment is our extreme aversion to losing and how it changes our behavior.

- Experiments that behavioral economists have done on gambling show that once people start to lose money, they become willing to try riskier gambles that have very little chance of winning—as long as the prize they get if they win will make up for previous losses. This applies to investors as well.

- The most interesting—and frightening—part of these behavioral quirks is that they are such a deeply ingrained part of us that most of the time we don't even realize that these are mistakes.

- The first step to making sure that we don't inadvertently sabotage our own investments is to become more familiar with investing, which includes learning some basic ideas about how the financial markets behave as well as learning how the main tools of investing really work. In addition, you'll need to learn some things about yourself so that you can figure out what kind of investing strategies and techniques you'll be comfortable with over the long term.

- The second step is making an **investment plan**, which is a set of decisions about how much to invest, which types of investments and strategies to try, and when to sell investments. All of the threats to investing will do the most damage to investors who haven't decided in advance how they want to handle these risks.

Important Terms

asset: Anything that holds onto its value over time.

behavioral economics: Blends psychology and physiology with economics to gain a better understanding of how people's decision making goes wrong—especially in situations involving investing.

capital good: A type of real asset that is involved in the production of goods, such as machines, buildings, factories, and the land that they sit on.

confirmation bias: Describes the tendency for people to only notice evidence that supports their beliefs and ignore evidence that contradicts it.

financial asset: A document that entitles its owner to receive something of value, generally a set of cash payments, from someone else.

inflation: A general increase in prices.

intangible asset: A type of real asset that is invisible but nonetheless real—such as ideas, knowledge, and skills.

investing: Spending your money, time, or other resources to create or acquire assets.

investment plan: A set of decisions about how much to invest, which types of investments and strategies to try, and when to sell investments.

issuer: The party who promises to give the owner of a financial asset something of value, including a firm, the government, or a person.

real asset: An asset that is used directly in the production of goods and services.

security: Written evidence of the extension of a loan.

storable commodity: A type of real asset that can be stored and retain value, such as cotton or oil.

Suggested Reading

Bodie, Kane, and Marcus, *Essentials of Investments*, chap. 1.

Browning, "A Long-Term Case for Stocks."

Shefrin, *Behavioral Corporate Finance*, chap. 1.

1. Go to the Bureau of Labor Statistics website and find their table on the annual Consumer Price Index and the associated annual inflation rates at ftp://ftp.bls.gov/pub/special.requests/cpi/cpiai.txt. Look at the final 2 columns, which present the annual inflation rates. What is the highest inflation rate that you've experienced during your lifetime? How likely do you think it is that inflation rates will be that high or higher during your investing career?

2. One additional behavioral quirk that is relevant to investing is identified by the term "illusion of control." Do an Internet search using this term and read about how it affects people's trading behavior. As an investor, what are the things that you truly have control over? What things do you have no control over?

How to Stop Worrying and Start Investing
Lecture 1—Transcript

Managing money, especially when it comes to investing, can be complicated and confusing. There are hundreds of investments to choose from, and it can be hard to tell them apart. For example, one mutual fund calls itself a "balanced fund" and another calls itself a "growth and income" fund. What's the difference between the two? And the language of investing is full of technical terms and jargon we aren't familiar with, like coupon yield, dividend yield, and yield to maturity. Do I have to be a rocket scientist to know what I'm doing?

And on top of that, investing can look pretty risky. Maybe you want to invest, but you're worried about making a big mistake and losing your savings. Maybe you already got burned by an investment that lost money. Given the ups and downs in the markets, investing might not seem a whole lot different than playing roulette at the casino. Is it really just a matter of luck?

For both of these reasons—both because investing looks complicated and because it looks risky—most people don't feel well prepared to make investment decisions. And when we don't feel prepared to make decisions, we put them off if we can. And it's so easy to put off investing decisions, because there's no real deadline. But putting off investing is one of the biggest mistakes that people make with their personal finances. It turns time, which can be one of your best allies, into your worst enemy. Have you put off investing?

Well, if you have, I'm here to help you get started. And if you're already out there investing, I'm here to help you invest with more confidence. In this course, I want to convince you that you don't have to be super smart, or super lucky, to be a successful investor. Investing well isn't about using fancy models or being foolhardy. Like many things in life, it's about mastering the fundamentals.

Not convinced? Well, let me tell you about one of the most brilliant investment decisions that I know of. You've probably heard of Warren Buffett, a self-made billionaire who's been a very successful investor for decades. In the late 1990s, while the dotcom boom was taking off and stock prices were soaring, Buffett refused to invest in any of these new companies. And what was the reason? He simply said, "I don't understand these companies. I don't understand what they do, and I don't understand why they have such high prices. And I won't invest in things I don't understand."

For a while, Buffett looked like an idiot, because stock prices kept going up. But eventually the stock market fell—dramatically. As the market fell, everyone else suffered big losses on their portfolios, but Buffett had plenty of cash to invest at much more attractive prices.

If you read about any great investor, and how they make decisions, you'll find similar stories. They can explain in one sentence exactly why they bought what they did—and their reasons always come down to basic, fundamental ideas that make sense.

Now, I'm not going to tell you that you can all be Warren Buffett. But in this course, we're going to learn the principles—the fundamental ideas—that Buffett and other successful investors rely on. And I'll show you how to use them to become a more confident investor. But I realize that your concerns about the complexity of investing, and the risk, aren't just going to disappear. That's why I want to deal with those concerns right away in this first lecture. First, I'm going to start making the case that the basic ideas behind investing are sensible and easy to understand.

Then I'm going to talk about the risks of investing. I'll tell you what I think are the most serious threats to your investments and explain why they're so bad. But I'll also show you that there are sensible and effective ways to protect your investments from these risks.

By the end of this lecture, I think you'll have a better picture of what you're getting yourself into when you invest—the good things as well as the bad. And hopefully, any sense of frustration or dread you associate with investing will start to fade, and may even be replaced with a little excitement.

So let's get started on learning those fundamentals that I keep talking about. What is investing in the first place? Well, basically investing is spending your money, time, or other resources in order to create or acquire assets. An asset is anything that holds onto its value over time. Buying an asset is a way to store resources that you don't need now, so that you can use them later. In other words, what we call investing is really a form of saving.

According to my very broad definition of assets, there are millions of potential investments out there. But when most of us think of investing, we're thinking of buying a certain type of asset—a financial asset. Financial assets are documents that entitle their owners to receive something of value, generally a set of cash payments, from someone else. Another name for a financial asset is a security, which is written evidence of the extension of a loan.

One of the distinguishing features of a financial asset is that it doesn't have any intrinsic value; it's either a piece of paper, or more likely a collection of digits stored on a computer. This fact leads to a lot of the interesting behavior of financial assets that we'll talk about later, and in future lectures. But for now, this fact leaves us with a couple of serious questions. How can something with no intrinsic value be a good place to store value? Where does the value of assets come from, anyway?

Well, the answer is that it comes from real assets. Real assets are used directly in the production of goods and services. Some real assets are storable commodities, like cotton or oil. Many real assets are what economists call capital goods—machines, buildings, factories, and the land that they sit on. Other real assets are actually invisible, but nonetheless real—like ideas, knowledge, and skills. Economists call these assets intangible assets, and in the business world they're often called intellectual property. What they all have in common is that their value comes from their ability to make goods and services. And when they're combined in new and creative ways, they can dramatically increase in value.

Financial assets derive their value from real assets, though the relationship is often quite complex. Financial assets are created whenever somebody borrows money in order to buy real assets. For example, when a business borrows money to build a new factory, a financial asset in the form of a bank loan, bond, stock, or other security is created. Later, the profits from operating that factory generate the cash that pays off the holder of the financial asset.

Financial assets make it possible for ordinary people to invest in real assets and enjoy the increase in value that can go with it. Financial assets can be divided into small amounts so that individuals can buy many different assets. Most real assets are so expensive that many households couldn't afford more than one, if any. For example, you probably can't afford to buy a factory—but you can afford to buy an investment that helps a company build a factory.

And financial assets are extremely convenient to buy and sell. Real assets, like factories, can sit idle for years until the right buyer comes along. But you can sell your stock in the company that owns the idle factory in a matter of seconds, thanks to online trading.

So the attraction of investing in financial assets is that it gives us a convenient way to participate—albeit indirectly—in the investment into real assets, which is where the value is created in our economy. This gives everyone the chance not only to store extra resources for later, but to have these resources grow significantly over time as well.

Sounds great, right? Well, before we rush out to find the next Google, we need to consider the threats to investment success. There are many, but I want to focus on the top four. It's important that you realize you can lose money even on the most well considered investment. At the same time, though, it's also important to know that you can take steps to protect your investments from all these threats.

Let's get right down to the danger that people probably fear the most. This is the chance that an investment loses money because its value falls. The prices of financial assets typically move up and down frequently—sometimes almost violently. And these ups and downs are extremely hard to predict, especially on a day-to-day basis. This situation makes new investors very uncomfortable, and for good reason. What if I buy a stock for $100 a share today and tomorrow its value falls to $80? Or, what if I was planning to retire next year and the value of my portfolio falls by 10%?

I think that questions like these keep a lot of people from investing in anything other than bank deposits. But what most people don't realize is that there are many ways to deal with the ups and downs of the market. I'm going to describe a few of them now, and I'll spend much more time on them in future lectures.

The first line of defense against losing money is simply to give your investment some more time. Even though financial prices bounce up and down minute to minute and day to day, over longer periods of time these short-term bumps smooth out and reveal a longer-term trend. If you invest in assets that really are creating value, the trend of prices will eventually show that value. The market is actually trying to discover the correct value for every investment, and though it makes mistakes, these mistakes do get corrected.

Let me give you a few examples to illustrate my point. I'm going to show you a few graphs of the daily closing value—the price, if you will—of the S&P 500 index. The S&P 500 measures the stock prices of 500 of the largest companies in the U.S. It's a pretty good indication of the overall value of the U.S. Stock Market, so most people use it to stand for the price of the entire stock market.

I'm going to show you some of the worst stock market drops in recent memory. As you look at these graphs, pay attention to how much stock prices fall, and how long it takes for the market price to rise back up to its previous level. The first drop I'll show you is the infamous crash of 1987. In this crash, the S&P 500 dropped by almost 20% on a single day! But as you can see from the prices after the crash, the market started to rise within a few months and was back up to its pre-crash price by the end of 1989—actually, it took less than two years to regain the losses. That's a fairly quick rebound, but the fact that the market came back is not unusual.

To help convince you of this point, let me show you another big market drop. This time, let's look at the so-called dotcom, or as I like to call it, dot-bomb, crash of 2000–2001. In this case, the market fell by over 40%, but the fall takes place over a period of years rather than days. And the recovery takes about three years in this case. But prices do recover.

Finally, let's look at how the S&P 500 behaved during the global financial crisis of late 2008. Again, market prices take a big dive over the course of about six months, but they start to rise again and nearly return to their previous value after about a year and a half. Then prices continue upwards and more than regain what they've lost, in less than three years after the start of the decline.

Just think what would happen if, during a market downturn like the ones I showed you, you panic and decide to sell off your investments? You'd lock in huge losses and miss out on the recovery. Time really can be an effective defense against losses on your investments, but you have to be patient.

And you also have to have the time to spare. Unfortunately, many of our investments run up against serious deadlines, such as the due date of your child's first college tuition payment, or the first day of your own retirement. If you leave all your investments in assets whose prices bounce up and down, you could suffer a serious loss on the day before you have to sell.

That's why a critical part of investing is selling off some of your risky investments well before you actually need the cash. The idea is to shift riskier investments into safer ones as you get closer to the time you need cash. But you should do it gradually, over a period of years, rather than doing it all at once. This will cushion the blow from a market downturn, because you won't be selling all of your investments at any given time, just a portion of them. In addition, the rest of your investments will get time to recover their value and hopefully even earn back enough to make up for any losses on the portion that you sold.

There are other ways to protect the value of your investments from large drops in market prices, such as diversification, and I'll discuss them in future lectures.

Now I'll move on to another risk of investing that everyone should be aware of. This is the risk of bankruptcy—not your own, but rather the bankruptcy of the issuer of one of your investments. Remember that a few minutes ago, I defined a financial asset as a document that entitles its owner to receive something of value from someone else. The party who promises to give the owner of the financial asset something of value is called the issuer of the instrument. Issuers of financial assets can be firms, governments, or people—and all three of these parties can go bankrupt.

When the issuer of a financial asset that you own declares bankruptcy, it almost always means that your asset will lose value. Fortunately, it doesn't necessarily mean that you will lose all of your investment. This depends on what kind of asset you hold, and how the bankruptcy is worked out. In general, if you hold a loan or a bond, you'll probably get something. But if you hold stock, you'll probably get nothing, even if the company survives the bankruptcy.

Bankruptcy is always a possibility, even for borrowers who look financially strong today. Fortunately, in most cases, there are plenty of warning signs that an issuer is losing financial strength and may be sliding towards bankruptcy. Companies and governments, who are most likely to be the issuers of the investments you'll hold, are required to make their financial information publicly available. You can examine that information for yourself or rely on the judgments of other market players who also frequently examine this information and make their opinions known.

There are some surprise bankruptcies now and then. You may recall the famous cases of Enron and WorldCom, which went bankrupt in the wake of the dotbomb crash. These firms had excellent reputations and huge market values, but each suddenly collapsed. In both cases, it was later discovered that massive accounting fraud was covering up big losses, so that the companies were not as solid as they seemed. The U.S. government passed a huge accounting reform in response to these cases, so another Enron seems fairly unlikely. But the fact remains that bankruptcy sometimes surprises the markets.

By being alert and proactive, investors can take effective steps to limit bankruptcy risk in their investments. First, you can simply avoid investing in financial assets that come from financially weak issuers. And you can monitor the financial strength of the issuers of the assets you do hold, so that if the issuer starts to weaken, you can sell off the asset well before the issuer is in serious danger of bankruptcy.

The two dangers I've just described are certainly serious threats to successful investing, and everyone who wants to invest should have a plan in place to deal with them. There are still more dangers out there, though. In fact, I think the two threats I'll talk about next are even more dangerous to individual investors than market crashes or bankruptcy.

The first of these is inflation. Are you surprised? Probably not, if you remember the 1970s! Inflation, of course, is simply a general increase in prices. There lots of ways we can measure inflation, but the one that most people are familiar with is probably the Consumer Price Index, or CPI. This index measures the price of a set of goods and services that a typical household consumes.

Why is inflation a danger to investing? As I mentioned earlier, one of the main reasons we invest is to set aside resources that we don't need now but we think we'll need later. We invest because we anticipate that, sometime in the future, we'll either want to buy something that costs a lot, like a college education or vacation home, or because our income will be lower than the amount we want to spend on living expenses, as is the case during retirement. Inflation drives up the prices of the things we want to buy with our savings, so that we may not be able to afford the type of college education, vacation home, or retirement that we wanted.

Of course, most of us are well aware of that. But what we don't seem to realize is how stealthy and relentless inflation is. Whereas financial prices go up and down, hopefully a bit more up than down on average, the prices of everything else only seem to go up, and steadily. And if inflation is low—say, 3% or less—we hardly notice it. But over time, a small increase in prices each year amounts to a huge increase in prices over decades, thanks to compounding.

Let me show you a couple of pictures to emphasize this point. What we're worried about is how much prices can change over the course of our investing. Suppose, just for the sake of argument, that we'll be investing for 40 years. I took the Consumer Price Index and calculated the total change in the index, measured in percent, over consecutive 40-year periods. This should give us an idea of how much prices could change, and how much they tend to change on average.

The graph shows that the price changes during these 40-year periods were 400 and even 500%—that means that something that cost $1 at the start of the period cost between $4 and $5 at the end!

By the way, these total increases in prices average out to annual inflation rates of just under 4% per year. So what I'm showing you is the damage that a moderate rate of inflation will do to the value of your investments.

The other aspect of inflation that makes it dangerous is that it can differ greatly across different types of products. Some products experience low rates of inflation—in the case of technology-related products, like computers, their prices can even fall for long periods of time. But other products experience very high rates of inflation. These inflation rates don't influence the average inflation rates, because these products make up a small share of the overall economy. But what if the products that experience high inflation are exactly the things that you're saving up for?

Here are a couple of examples that might get your attention. One of the reasons for investing I've mentioned is to save for a college education for your children. Well, if you've looked at the rate of inflation for college tuition, you'll realize that it's far higher than the average rate of inflation. In fact, a rule of thumb is that the rate of inflation of college costs runs about twice the rate of general inflation! According to statistics compiled by the College Board, the average annual rate of increase of college costs was just under 6% per year from 1989 through 2005.

And what about retirement? One of the retirement expenses that many people fail to anticipate is health care. Most of us think about spending our retirement savings on exotic vacations or a really nice set of golf clubs, but the reality is that our consumption of health care goods and services goes way up as we pass retirement age. Even though retirees have government-provided insurance programs, there are still many expenses that are only partly covered, and the coverage is likely to shrink over time, due to our government's long-term budget pressures.

Have you looked at numbers on the rate of inflation in health care? According to the Consumer Price Index data from the Bureau of Labor Statistics, the average annual rate of inflation in medical care has been about 5.9% per year over the last 50 years. It may make you feel a little better that the average inflation rate in medical care has fallen to only 4.3% over the last 20 years.

Hopefully, this helps convince you that inflation really is a serious enemy of successful investing. The question, then, is what can we do about it? Well, the main strategy is to find investments that keep up with inflation. Many assets will keep up with inflation, and stocks seem to be one of them. But the assets that tend to do better at keeping up with inflation also tend to be the riskier ones. For example, treasury bills are a very safe asset but tend to do a poor job of keeping up with inflation. On average, they just barely keep up, and over shorter periods of time, especially when inflation is increasing, they can seriously lag behind. There are some assets that are designed to keep up with inflation, and I'll devote some time to them in a future lecture.

Even if you load up on assets that keep up with the general rate of inflation, you may still be burned by inflation in the price of something you're saving for. Again, the best strategy is to look for assets that keep up with the specific inflation you're worried about. But this can be a really difficult challenge. For example, I don't really know of any private investment that keeps up with the price of college tuition.

There is another way to protect against the ravages of inflation, but it's a painful one—you could save more now, just to cover the amount of the increase in prices that you don't think your investments will match. But it's really hard to stay motivated to save more, just so you can keep up with inflation. Save this strategy to use as a last resort.

The word motivation brings me to my final threat to investment success. By far, the biggest threat to investing confidently and successfully is us. Well, to be more precise, it's human nature. In many ways, our own psychology and emotions do far more damage to our investing success than market crashes ever did.

Here's an example. Economists have noticed that investors tend to exhibit herd behavior. We see or hear about people buying, say, Internet stocks. We think that everyone else is buying and we need to buy it too, or else we'll be left behind. So we join the crowd, rush into an investment without doing much if any research on it, and then the price gets pushed up by the herd and then plummets later.

Another way that our unfamiliarity with financial instruments can lead to trouble is that it makes too many of us easy victims for financial scams. I think we want to believe that there are some secret, surefire investing techniques waiting to be discovered, and this makes us easy to fool. For example, one of the most celebrated financial scams of recent years was the fake investment fund operated by Bernard Madoff. It was a classic pyramid scheme, in which new investors' contributions were used to pay out earlier investors, and no real, actual investments were being made. Interestingly, Madoff was excessively secretive about the operations of the fund and actually used that fact as a marketing strategy. The fund was so popular that people had to compete to be allowed to invest in it.

There are so many ways that our own human nature interferes with our own success that economists recently invented a new branch of economics to describe and study them all. This new field of economics is called behavioral economics, and it blends psychology and physiology with economics to gain a better understanding of how people's decision making goes wrong—especially in situations involving investing. Some of these behavioral quirks are fairly mild, while others can cause serious problems for your investments.

An example of a mild type of behavioral impediment is called confirmation bias. People tend to only notice evidence that supports their beliefs and ignore evidence that contradicts it. So, if you get the idea that McDonalds is a great stock, then you would notice that their sales in China are booming, but you would ignore any evidence that their sales in the U.S. are declining.

A more serious type of behavioral impediment is our extreme aversion to losing and how it changes our behavior. Experiments that behavioral economists have done on gambling show that once people start to lose money, they become willing to try riskier and riskier gambles that actually have very little chance of winning as long as the prize they get if they win will make up for previous losses. If we apply this example to investing, it suggests that investors who lose money will tend to choose riskier investments that appear to have the potential to make up for previous losses. Believe me, this is not the way that you should be picking your next investment!

The most interesting, and frightening, part of these behavioral quirks is that they are such a deeply ingrained part of us that most of the time we don't even realize that these are mistakes. So if this is true, how do we make sure that we don't inadvertently sabotage our own investments? Well, the first step is to become more familiar with investing. This means learning some basic ideas about how the financial markets behave, as well as learning how the main tools of investing—all these financial assets—really work. In addition, you'll need to learn some things about yourself, so you can figure out what kind of investing strategies and techniques you'll be comfortable with over the long haul.

As you learn these things, you can go on to the second step, which is making an investment plan. You're most vulnerable to the behavioral problems I've just discussed if you're investing by the seat of your pants and making it up as you go along. In fact, all the threats that I've talked about so far will do the most damage to investors who haven't decided in advance how they want to handle these risks.

So you need to make a plan. It doesn't have to be a written document. An investment plan is simply a set of decisions about how much to invest, the types of investments and strategies you want to try, and when to sell off investments. We'll talk a lot about the details of financial planning in later lectures. But I just want to emphasize now that you should always have a plan that you can fall back on, when the markets, or life, throw something unexpected your way.

Well, I hope all this talk about risk makes you feel better about investing, because it should! Understanding the main risks to investing is the first step toward managing them. And we've learned that there are simple and effective ways to manage these risks. We've also already learned some of the fundamental ideas of investing. During the rest of this course we'll build on this foundation by learning about the different investments that are available and how to choose the ones that are best for you. We'll also learn about different investing strategies, so that you can protect yourself from risks and also take advantage of good opportunities. And we'll learn some financial planning tools that can help you reach your financial goals. If you take the time to learn the fundamentals of investing and make your own investment plan, then you'll feel prepared to make investing decisions and manage your investments. So you can stop worrying now and start investing!

How Investors Make Money
Lecture 2

D o you think markets are highly efficient and can't be beat, or do you think that investors can beat the market by exploiting inefficiencies? If you think markets are highly efficient, then you shouldn't try to beat the market; instead, you should join it. If you think that the market can be beaten, then you have another decision to make: Are you willing to put in the time and effort that it takes to find those market inefficiencies? It is important to remember that you can reach your investment goals no matter what your opinion is about market efficiency.

Beating the Market
- Can anyone beat the market? If you can beat the market, how do you do it? These 2 big questions get to the heart of one of the most important, and enduring, controversies in finance. Professors and investors have been arguing about these questions for decades, and this issue has direct relevance for your investing.

- Each investor needs to decide whether it's possible to beat the market. Your answer to this question will become one of the foundations of your investment strategy—deciding whether to join the investors who want to beat the market or those who don't really try.

The Efficient Markets Hypothesis
- To reach an informed decision, you'll first need to grasp the basic elements of the **efficient markets hypothesis (EMH)**. The economist who is credited with developing the EMH is Eugene Fama, who outlined this theory in a paper published in 1965. The driving force behind the EMH is the intense competition among investors to find and exploit any advantages that will help them earn high returns.

- The ultimate source of any investment advantage is information. Risk and uncertainty are an inescapable part of investing, so any information about an investment that reduces the uncertainty surrounding its future return is valuable. When new information about an investment is revealed to the market, this changes the price of the investment.

- You can potentially earn a big reward for being the first person to get a hold of some new information and then make an investment based on the information. This fact makes investors compete for information—but not just any information. Investors are only looking for information that would affect someone's decision over whether to invest in an asset.

- This highly desirable and profitable information is called **material information**, which affects the market price of an asset when it's revealed to the market. Because everyone wants to be the first one to find new material information and make an investment based on it, new information influences market prices very quickly—in fact, before most of the market knows the information.

- The United States and many other countries try to ensure that the competition for investment information is fair, and certain investors are explicitly forbidden from benefiting from material information they obtain as the result of an unfair advantage. Therefore, some countries, such as the United States, ban insider trading—even though some economists argue that this makes the market less efficient.

- The fierce competition to find material information and then make investments based on it leads to 2 consequences that are part of the efficient markets hypothesis. First, any material information about an asset that is known now is already incorporated into current asset prices. This includes anything you know or expect about the future because these things can also include material information. Second, new information is incorporated into asset prices extremely quickly, if not instantly.

- Often, people will summarize the EMH by stating a simple version of the first consequence: Market prices fully reflect all current information. However, many people object to the word "all" in this phrase. They agree that competition makes asset prices incorporate a lot of material information, but they disagree about the kinds of information that get incorporated into market prices.

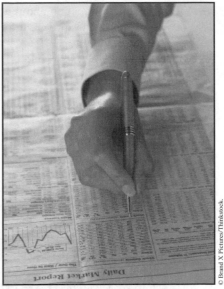

Every investor dreams about beating the market, but only some believe that it is actually possible.

- This disagreement has led to the creation of 3 different versions of the EMH. The weak version states that the EMH is correct with respect to past financial prices. The semistrong version states that current market prices reflect all publicly available material information. The strong version states that current market prices incorporate all material information—whether it's publicly available or private.

- **Private information** is information that is known only to a few people and isn't widely distributed or shared. Private information includes inside information—such as an executive's advanced knowledge of a merger deal—but it goes well beyond inside information.

- Private information that is not inside information usually combines observation with analysis. That is, investors often take publicly available information about a firm and perform their own analysis on it. This creates private information out of public information.

The EMH and Beating the Market

- If the EMH is correct—that market prices fully incorporate information that is known now and that new information is incorporated very quickly into market prices—then there's no way for anyone to predict future prices successfully or to benefit from the arrival of new information in the market.

- The unpredictability of future prices is devastating to your investment plans. How can you choose between different assets, let alone decide whether to buy or sell, if you can't predict prices? In this case, your best strategy is simply to buy a slice of the entire market and hold it. Some of the assets will be losers, but this is the only way to ensure that you also hold the winners. However, if you do buy a slice of the entire market, then your return on this investment will be the market return. You can't beat the market return.

- The EMH is controversial because if it's true, then anyone who is trying to beat the market is doomed to fail and there's no need for investment advisors, stock analysts, money managers, or anyone else who makes a living trying to forecast asset returns. As a result, most people in the financial services industry vehemently disagree with the EMH.

- Some of the most convincing evidence in favor of the EMH comes from simple statistics. Many studies have shown that less than 1/2 of all professional money managers beat the market over long stretches of time. In fact, from a statistical point of view, it may be difficult to judge whether the high returns that a money manager achieves in any given year are due to skill or to luck.

- People who don't believe in the EMH argue that there are at least a handful of money managers who did beat the markets for very long periods of time—if not over their entire investing careers.

For example, Warren Buffett, Bill Miller, and Peter Lynch earned above-market returns over decades rather than just a few years.

- People who don't believe that the EMH is true have found plenty of failings in the theory. For each version of the EMH, people have shown that there exist many different pieces of information that do help predict future market prices of stocks and other assets.

- Some of the most interesting evidence against the EMH comes in the form of anomalies, which are real-world examples of investment opportunities that shouldn't exist if the EMH is true. One of the most famous anomalies is the so-called January effect, which is a phenomenon in which stock prices tend to rise in January and is especially pronounced for small company stocks. Many professional investors have been able to earn good profits by purchasing stocks in early January and then selling at the end of the month.

- Defenders argue that even though some information does seem to be able to predict future prices, traders can't profit from these price changes because of trading costs and other frictions. Many people who support the EMH admit this but argue that the most important implication of the EMH holds true: You may be able to predict future prices a little, but you still can't use that information to beat the market.

- Supporters of the EMH argue that whenever anomalies are discovered, a large number of investors immediately try to exploit the anomaly. As they do this, their increased buying or selling will change market prices and will eventually drive the anomaly out of existence. Therefore, if the EMH is true, any anomalies will get weaker and will disappear as profit opportunities—and any meaningful violations of the theory, such as anomalies, will automatically be corrected by the market.

- Some people attack the EMH by taking a behavioral economics approach, arguing that the market can't be efficient because people aren't fully rational. People constantly make investment mistakes based on their emotions or on other psychological biases, and these mistakes end up affecting the behavior of market prices.

- An extreme version of the behaviorist approach reaches one of the main conclusions of the EMH—but for a completely different reason. The argument is that if people really are highly irrational, then this would also make market prices difficult to predict, meaning that price changes would be unpredictable—which is one of the main implications of the EMH.

- There's a paradox at the heart of the EMH because it relies on a balance between efficiency and inefficiency to make it work. For markets to be efficient, some investors have to believe that markets aren't efficient—so that every day, they go out into the markets and try to find inefficiencies that they can exploit for their own profits. By doing this, however, they make sure that the markets stay mostly efficient. Whenever these investors find an inefficiency, they buy or sell the mispriced asset, which changes the market price of the asset until the inefficiency disappears.

- If these investors find inefficiencies too well, the market becomes highly efficient and profit opportunities disappear. Then, these investors stop trying to find inefficiencies, and the inefficiencies creep back into the markets.

- No matter what you believe about market efficiency, there are good investment opportunities for you. If you think that markets are very efficient, then you can simply be a passive investor. When you invest, you should aim to buy your own slice of the entire market and earn whatever return the market delivers.

- On the other hand, you may think that the markets are inefficient enough so that you can actually earn a higher return than the market. If you want to try to beat the markets, you have to put in the time and effort it takes to learn about companies and decide whether their market prices are right. Anyone is capable of building up private information that they can use to become an active, market-beating investor.

Important Terms

efficient markets hypothesis (EMH): An economic theory that suggests that market prices fully incorporate information that is known now and that new information is incorporated very quickly into market prices.

material information: Highly desirable and profitable information that affects the market price of an asset when it's revealed to the market.

private information: Information that is known only to a few people and isn't widely distributed or shared.

Suggested Reading

Ball, "The Theory of Stock Market Efficiency."

Bodie, Kane, and Marcus, *Essentials of Investments*, chap. 8.

Lee and Verbrugge, "The Efficient Market Theory Thrives on Criticism."

Questions to Consider

1. Think about the effect of the rise of the Internet on market efficiency. In what ways could we argue that the Internet makes markets more efficient? In what ways might it make markets less efficient? What do you think the overall impact of the rise of the Internet has been on market efficiency—and why?

2. Do an Internet search using the term "stock market anomalies" and do some reading on the various stock behaviors that seem to violate the efficient markets hypothesis. Do any of them look like they may be a source of dependable investing profits? Why?

How Investors Make Money
Lecture 2—Transcript

In the first lecture, we learned about several threats to your investments, including the wild ups and downs of the market. But you know, where some people see threat, others see opportunity. Some people see dollar signs in those market swings, especially the upswings, and they're convinced they should be able make a fortune from them. Well, maybe not a fortune, that would be too greedy. All they really need to do is beat the market.

Ah, beating the market, what every investor dreams about. Or that's what it seems like, judging by all the books, magazines, TV shows, websites, blogs, podcasts, live seminars, and, of course, spam e-mails devoted to the subject.

For example, I did a quick search through the book section of Amazon.com and found over 100 books that have the phrase "beat the market" in their title, and that doesn't even count all the variations on that idea, like Peter Lynch's bestseller called *Beating the Street*.

If all these different authors claim that you can beat the market, can they all be right? If they are, then there must be hundreds of different ways to beat the market. That makes beating the market sound pretty easy. But if it's so easy, then why do we need all these books on investing to tell us how to do it?

These are the sorts of questions I'm going to discuss in this lecture. In fact, I'm going to take an in-depth look at the two really big questions that sum up all these smaller ones I've just raised. The first of these questions is simply: can anyone beat the market? The second one then, of course, is if you can beat the market, how do you do it? These two big questions get to the heart of one of the most important, and enduring, controversies in finance. Professors and investors have been arguing about these questions for decades.

And this controversy isn't just an academic issue—it has direct relevance for your own investing.

Each investor needs to decide where he or she stands on the issue of whether it's possible to beat the market, because your own answer to this question will become one of the foundations of your investment strategy. By the end of this lecture, you should be in a much better position to choose whether to join the investors who want to beat the market, or the investors who don't even try.

To reach an informed decision, though, you'll first need to grasp the basic elements of a theory called the efficient markets hypothesis. Many people also refer to this theory as Market Efficiency, or EMH for short. So in this lecture, I'll start by taking a look at what the efficient markets hypothesis claims, and I'll explain the economic reasoning behind it.

Then I'll spend some time explaining why the efficient markets hypothesis implies that it is very difficult, if not impossible, to beat the market. But I'll also summarize some of the evidence people use to suggest that there may be opportunities to earn market-beating returns after all, at least in theory.

I'll finish the lecture by discussing whether there are practical ways that individual investors can beat the market, and we'll talk about what this all means for your investment strategy.

So what is the efficient markets hypothesis? Well, its origin goes back to the 1950s and '60s, when economists began to apply the models of modern economic theory to a wide variety of subjects, including finance. The economist who is credited with developing the EMH is Eugene Fama, of the University of Chicago. He outlined this theory in a paper published in 1965. Now, if you've ever heard much about the various schools of thought in economics, you know that University of Chicago economists have been famous advocates of the free market and the power of competition. And the power of competition really is the main economic idea underlying the EMH. The driving force behind market efficiency is the intense competition among investors to find and exploit any advantages that help them to earn above-market returns.

The ultimate source of any investment advantage is information. Risk and uncertainty are an inescapable part of investing. So any information about an investment that reduces that uncertainty surrounding its future return is really valuable. When new information about an investment is revealed to the market, this changes the price of the investment. For example, think about Boeing's stock. If American Airlines suddenly announces that it intends to buy 100 new Boeing jets, this will make Boeing's stock price jump up, because the new order for jets implies that Boeing's future profits will be higher than we expected.

Of course, if you knew about this jet order before anyone else in the market did, you could make a nice profit by buying Boeing stock and waiting for the news to be released to the market. So you can potentially earn a big reward for being the first person to get a hold of some new information and then make an investment based on this information. This fact makes investors compete for the information, but not just any information.

Investors are looking only for information that would affect someone's decision over whether to invest in an asset. We use the term material information to describe this highly desirable and profitable information. We expect material information to affect the market price of an asset when it's revealed to the market.

Since everyone is in a hurry to find new, material information and be the first one to make an investment based on it, this means that the new information influences market prices very quickly. In fact, it may influence prices so quickly that the prices change before most of the market knows the information! Here's why I can make that statement.

Suppose I've noticed that whenever a particular investor buys Boeing stocks, some good news about Boeing is released to the market soon after that and the stock price goes up. I conclude that this other investor has some source of advanced information about Boeing—I don't know what the information is, but whenever I see this person buy Boeing shares, something good happens to Boeing. So whenever I see this other person buy Boeing shares, I buy the shares, too, hoping to profit from this person's information.

But if hundreds of other people are also watching this person's trades, then as soon as this person starts to buy Boeing shares, these other investors also buy—and that drives up the price of Boeing shares right away, even before the news about the sale is released to the public. It's as if the information had been released to everyone.

Before I move on to discussing the implications of this competition for information, I want to mention that the U.S. and many other countries try to ensure that the competition for investment information is fair. And certain investors are explicitly forbidden from benefiting from material information they obtain as the result of an unfair advantage. For example, if you work for Boeing, especially if you are a top executive, then you will probably know about the American Airlines contract before anyone else in the market does. So, you could easily benefit from buying Boeing shares before the news of the contract is released, at very low risk.

But the government makes the following argument. It says that you have this information only because you are a Boeing employee—an employee with privileged access to information. And this gives you an unfair advantage over other investors. Therefore, countries like the U.S. ban insider trading, even though some economists argue that this makes the market less efficient.

This fierce competition to find material information and then make investments based on it leads to two consequences that are part of the efficient markets hypothesis. First, any material information about an asset that is known now is already incorporated into current asset prices. This includes anything you know or expect about the future, since those things can also include material information. And second, new information is incorporated into asset prices extremely quickly, if not instantly. Often, people will summarize the EMH by stating a simple version of the first consequence: market prices fully reflect all current information.

Many people object to the word "all" in this phrase, because that seems pretty extreme. They agree that competition makes asset prices incorporate a lot of material information. But they disagree about the kinds of information that get incorporated into market prices. This disagreement has led to the creation of three different versions of the efficient markets hypothesis, and these versions differ based on what kind of information you believe is already built into asset prices.

One version is called the weak version of the EMH, and it states that the EMH is correct with respect to past financial prices. That is, current asset prices reflect all information about asset prices, but they don't necessarily reflect any other material information, even if it is known now.

A second version of the EMH is called the semistrong version, and it states that current market prices reflect all publicly available material information.

You've probably guessed that the third version of the efficient markets hypothesis is called the strong version. It states that current market prices incorporate all material information, whether it's publicly available or private. So the incorporation of private information is the big difference between semistrong and strong form market efficiency. This definition of strong form market efficiency begs the question, though, of exactly what is private information.

Private information, by definition, is known only to a few people and isn't widely distributed or shared. This is important because it means that this information is private property, and its owners can benefit from their exclusive access to it. Private information includes inside information, of course, such as an executive's advanced knowledge of a merger deal, but it goes well beyond inside information.

Anyone outside a firm can observe the firm's activities carefully and accumulate private information. For example, you could simply observe the number of trucks going into and out of Hershey's chocolate factories and build up advance information about increases or decreases in Hershey's sales from that.

Private information that is not inside information usually combines observation with analysis. That is, investors often take publicly available information about a firm and perform their own analysis on it. This creates private information out of public information. A good example of this is the firm's accounting information. Stock analysts love to tinker with companies' accounting numbers in order to reach their own conclusions about the companies' financial performance. Taking public information and using it to create private information is really how stock analysts try to add value in their jobs. In fact, in 2011, there was a fascinating insider trading case in which the defendants claimed that all they were doing was collecting bits of non-material public information about firms and putting them together in very clever ways.

So far, we've been discussing how information is incorporated into stock prices. But we haven't yet seen why the EMH has anything at all to say about beating the market. To see the connection, we need to go back to the two basic parts of the EMH and think about what they imply for the behavior of asset prices. Remember that the two parts of the efficient markets hypothesis are that market prices fully incorporate information that is known now, and that new information is incorporated very quickly into market prices.

Let's think about what it means for prices to reflect all available information, including our expectations about the future. This means that if we know or expect something about the future, then these expectations are already built into today's prices. This in turn means that changes in asset prices are literally unpredictable. Think back to my example of the Boeing contract. If I predict that Boeing shares are going to rise in value tomorrow, then I'll buy them today so that I can benefit from the increase in price—which helps drive the price up today. So today's price already reflects the expected increase in price tomorrow. That only leaves room for unexpected price changes in the future. By definition, an unexpected price change can't be predicted.

If I can't predict what future prices are going to be, how can I expect to earn high returns? I can't! Well, hold on, you might say. Instead of trying to guess what the prices will be tomorrow, why don't you just wait until new information comes to the market that nobody knew already? And then you can try to be the first person to invest, based on this brand new piece of information. Well, that sounds good, but then we run right into the second part of the EMH, which, again, says that new information is incorporated into the market prices extremely quickly. That means there's no time for me to follow this strategy. By the time I try to act on this new piece of information, it'll be too late—the price will already have moved.

So if the EMH is correct, there's no way for me to predict future prices successfully, and there's no way for me to benefit from the arrival of new information in the market. Notice how devastating the unpredictability of future prices is to your investment plans. How can you choose between different assets, let alone decide whether to buy or sell, if you can't predict prices?

In this case, your best strategy is simply to buy a slice of the entire market and hold it. Some of the assets will be losers, sure, but this is the only way to ensure that you also hold the winners, too. Again, if price changes are unpredictable, then there's no way to tell in advance which assets will be the winners and which assets will be the losers in the future. Now, if you do follow this advice and buy a slice of the entire market, then your return on this investment will be the market return. So we say that can't beat the market return.

Wow. Now you can see why the efficient markets hypothesis is so controversial. If it's true, then anyone out there trying to beat the market is doomed to fail. And there's no need for investment advisors, stock analysts, money managers, or anyone else who tries to make a living forecasting asset returns. So if only to save their jobs, most people in the financial services industry vehemently disagree with the efficient markets hypothesis.

But rather than taking anyone's word about the validity of the EMH, let's examine the evidence on both sides of the issue.

Some of the most convincing evidence in favor of the EMH comes from simple statistics. Of all the professional money managers out there, do you know how many actually beat the market? Well, study after study basically finds the same result—less than half of them manage to beat the market over long stretches of time, say, 10 to 20 years. Yes, many fund managers have an amazing year now and then. But most don't seem to be able to keep up that kind of performance year in and year out. Their low returns in other years more than offset the returns they get in really great years once in a while.

In fact, from a statistical point of view, it may be difficult to judge whether the high returns that a money manager achieves in any given year are due to skill or to luck. For example, suppose there are 5000 mutual funds all trying to beat the market. This is like buying 5000 scratch-off lottery tickets— if you buy that many, some are going to be winners. So even if investing returns are totally random, there will always be some managers who will win the lottery and earn really high returns. But it's just their lucky year.

People who don't believe in market efficiency are quick to argue in response that there are in fact at least a handful of money managers who did beat the markets for very long periods of time, if not over their entire investing careers. People like Warren Buffett, Bill Miller, and Peter Lynch did earn above-market returns for decades. And though it's possible that these super investors are just incredibly lucky, that argument is harder to believe if you examine these managers' investing strategies and their decisions.

For example, Peter Lynch looked for companies that did simple things but did them better than anyone else, like how Hanes made panty hose. He called one of his main investing strategies GARP, which stands for growth at a reasonable price. Lynch's investing ideas make sense, and they help explain the case that skilled and disciplined investors really can beat the market.

People who don't believe that the EMH is true have found plenty of failings in the theory, as well. One set of failings has to do with the implication that the EMH says that changes in market prices should be completely unpredictable. Researchers and market professionals have found lots of counterexamples to this prediction. For each version of the EMH, people have shown that there exist many different pieces of information that do help predict future market prices of stocks and other assets.

For example, researchers have shown that what goes down must come up in stock markets. When stock prices fall one day, especially if they fall a lot, this seems to increase the chance that the stock price will rise the next day. This would seem to contradict even the weakest version of the EMH—the one that says that past prices shouldn't be able to predict future prices. Other bits of information, like earnings announcements that companies make, also seem to predict future prices even a few days after they've been revealed to the market. This seems to contradict not only the idea that future prices are unpredictable, but also the idea that the information is quickly incorporated into asset prices.

But some of the most interesting evidence against the EMH comes in the form of so-called anomalies. These anomalies are real-world examples of investment opportunities that literally shouldn't exist, if the EMH is true. One of the most famous anomalies is the so-called January Effect. This is a phenomenon in which stock prices tend to rise in January, and it's especially pronounced for small company stocks. Many professional investors have been able to earn good profits by purchasing stocks in early January and then selling at the end of the month.

The defenders of the EMH, though, do have responses to these attacks. First, they argue, even though some information does seem to be able to predict future prices, traders can't profit from these price changes because of trading costs and other frictions. For example, if you know that the price of Ford Motor was going to rise by a penny per share tomorrow, but the trading commission was $0.02 per share, you couldn't actually make any money from this information. Many people who support the efficient markets hypothesis admit that the EMH is not strictly true because of transactions costs and other frictions. But they argue that the most important implication of EMH holds true—you may be able to predict future prices a little, but you still can't use that information to actually beat the market.

The supporters of the EMH also have a comeback for the anomalies, and the argument goes like this. Whenever anomalies like the January Effect are discovered, a large number of investors immediately tries to exploit the anomaly. But as they do this, their increased buying or selling will change market prices, and it will eventually drive the anomaly out of existence. So if the EMH is true, any anomalies will get weaker and they will disappear as profit opportunities. The January Effect is a case in point. Over time, the January Effect weakened, as investors shifted their purchases from January to late December, then mid-December, and so on. The earlier the buying started, the smaller the change in price was. So if the efficient markets hypothesis is true, any meaningful violations of the theory, such as anomalies, will automatically be corrected by the market.

Now, some people attack the EMH by taking a completely different approach—one that's based on ideas from behavioral economics, which you may remember me discussing in the introductory lecture. The argument is that the market can't be efficient, because people aren't fully rational. They make investment mistakes constantly, based on their emotions or on other psychological biases, and these mistakes end up affecting the behavior of market prices.

For example, behavioral economics has an explanation for what goes down must come up story I mentioned a few minutes ago. Behavioral economists think that markets overreact to new information, based on fear or other emotions. If a piece of bad news about a firm comes out, the share price is driven down far beyond what the news objectively implies for the firm's value. After this happens, investors realize their mistake, and the price rises back to a more reasonable value.

An extreme version of the behaviorist approach actually reaches one of the main conclusions of the EMH, but for a completely different reason. The argument goes like this. If people really are highly irrational, making mistakes and doing things that are not in their best interests, then this would also make market prices hard to predict. You don't know in advance what kind of odd behavior is going to drive the market next. This means that price changes would be unpredictable—which is one of the main implications of the EMH. So this behavioral economics story says that market inefficiency causes prices to be unpredictable.

The economist Robert Haugen uses this extreme behaviorist view to make a wonderful analogy about what we can say for sure about whether the markets are efficient. It's a sports analogy, and it uses American football. Imagine a football field where one end zone represents markets that are perfectly efficient and rational, and the other end zone represents totally irrational markets. Haugen says we can be pretty sure that we're on about the 20-yard line. We just don't know which end zone we're heading for.

I think this analogy really sums up well what we can truly say about market efficiency after looking at all this evidence. Remember that we've found some good evidence that prices are hard to predict, and that it's tough to beat the market. So we could be on the 20-yard line close to the market efficiency end zone, according to Haugen's analogy. This would be a market that is pretty efficient, though there are still some significant inefficiencies and irrationalities.

On the other hand, remember that the behavioral economics say that markets are hard to predict and it's still tough to beat the market. So we could also be on the 20-yard line that's closest to the irrationality end zone. That is, we could be in a mostly inefficient, irrational market that has just enough efficiency in it to correct the worst of the mistakes we make.

Another reason why I like that analogy is that it gives the sense of a balance between opposing forces in the markets. There's actually a bit of a paradox at the heart of the efficient markets hypothesis, in that it relies on a balance between efficiency and inefficiency to make it work. Here's what I mean. For markets to be efficient, some investors have to believe that markets aren't efficient—so that every day, they go out into the markets and try to find inefficiencies that they can exploit for their own profits. But by doing this, they make sure that the markets stay mostly efficient. Whenever these investors find an inefficiency, they buy or sell the mispriced asset, and this buying or selling changes the market price of the asset until the inefficiency disappears.

If they do too good of a job, the market gets highly efficient, and these profit opportunities go away. These investors stop trying to find inefficiencies, and the inefficiencies creep back into the markets. This picture of a dynamic balance between efficiency and inefficiency—sometimes the markets are more efficient, sometimes less—is surprising, but it's actually a satisfying explanation of market behavior. It does a good job of explaining the fact that irrationalities and exceptions to the EMH seem to pop up frequently, but they don't seem to last.

We're not even close to being able to prove whether this story is right or wrong, though. In fact, I don't think we'll ever be able to prove how efficient the markets are. What does seem true, though, is that there are good investment opportunities for you no matter what you believe about market efficiency. If you think that markets are very efficient, then you can simply be a passive investor. When you invest, you should aim to buy your own little slice of the entire market and earn whatever the market delivers. I'll have more to say about how to do this in future lectures, but it mainly involves buying into broad-based mutual funds that invest in the major stock and bond markets.

On the other hand, you may think that the markets are inefficient enough so that you can actually earn a higher return than the market. You may think this, for example, if you agree with the semistrong form of the EMH. You may believe that public information is incorporated into market prices, but private information isn't. That means that if you put some time and effort into creating your own private information, you can make good investments that beat the market.

You can produce your own private information by gathering publicly available information and analyzing it yourself. You literally put the pieces together to get a better understanding of a company so that you can tell whether its bonds or stocks are better investments than other people think they are.

Think you can't do that? Well, guess again. As a professor, I've had several students over the years who were outstanding individual investors. What they all had in common was a love of investing, and the willingness to read everything they could get their hands on about the firms they were interested in. These students didn't know a ton about fancy pricing models—after all, they were taking my courses to learn these things—but they were always able to tell me exactly what the value creation story behind their latest stock purchase. They were willing to put in the time and effort required to build up private information about firms, which they used to justify their investments.

I think my students' example helps show exactly what it takes to become an active investor who tries to beat the markets. If you want to do that, you'll have to put in the time and effort it takes to learn about companies and make up your own mind about whether their market price is right or not. I think that anyone is capable of building up private information that they can use to become an active, market-beating investor.

But if you're like me, you may not want to spend your spare time that way. Personally, I think the markets are pretty efficient, but there's plenty of room for people to find good investments that beat the market. But I also know that it's going to take a lot of my time and energy to find these investments. And frankly, I'd rather spend my time doing other things I really love, like spending time with my family, writing, and giving lectures. So in my own investing, I'm a pretty passive investor—I'm trying to hold my own little slice of the global market.

So in this lecture, we've learned about a big decision you have to make as an investor. Do you think markets are highly efficient and can't be beat? Or do you think that there's room for investors to beat the market, by exploiting inefficiencies or correcting irrational behavior? If you think markets are highly efficient, then your investing path is clear—don't try to beat the market, join it!

And if you think that the market can be beaten, then you still have another decision to make. Are you willing to put the time and effort in that it takes to find those market inefficiencies? You may find out that the answer is yes—after all, there's a great sense of satisfaction from being proven right, and making money in the process. But it's also okay if the answer is no. The main point to remember is that you can reach your investment goals no matter what your opinion is about market efficiency.

Starting with Stocks

Lecture 3

Although there are thousands of different financial products for you to invest in, most of them are made up of the same few basic types of financial instruments. This lecture serves as an introduction to the main building blocks of investments. You will learn some key facts about how stocks work and many important details about how stocks are traded. Some of these ideas will help you when learning about stock pricing in future lectures.

Stocks

- Stocks can be pretty risky investments, but they serve as a great model for learning about individual investments and how to use them because the basic ideas behind stock investing are clear and easy to understand. In addition, the stock contract itself is very simple. Furthermore, the details of stock investing are very similar to the details of other types of investing.

- Businesses are supposed to try risky but innovative and surprising new projects that have the chance to create valuable products and handsome profits. These projects always involve investments in real assets. To make something new, businesses need to buy machines, factories, land, ideas, and even entire companies.

- To do that, though, they need lots of money, and chances are, businesses don't have enough cash on hand to fund all the projects they want to pursue. They have to borrow the money from somewhere, and this is where financial assets come in.

- Financial assets are documents that describe the terms of a loan. The borrower gets money now, and the lender receives something of value in return. Usually, the thing of value is a promise from the borrower to make cash payments in the future—to whomever the owner of the document happens to be at the time.

- Additionally, there are other valuable things that a firm can offer in exchange for a lender's ready cash. One of them is an ownership stake in the business. There are several legal forms that this shared ownership can take, such as a partnership, but by far the most successful form of shared ownership has been the corporation, which uses stock.

- When a firm issues **stock**, it divides the ownership of the company into thousands—if not millions—of equal parts, which are the individual shares. Each **share** has an equal claim on the firm's profits and an equal say in the management of the firm. The more shares you buy, the bigger the slice of the company's profits you receive, and the more influence you have on company decisions.

- The basic skill of stock investing really boils down to finding companies that invest in successful projects. That's true when it comes to picking other types of investments as well.

Stocks in Practice

- When a company sells its shares to the public for the first time, in a special sale called the **initial public offering (IPO)**, it usually uses investors' money to expand its business and start new projects.

- Additionally, when one company buys another company, it often pays for this purchase by issuing new shares. Otherwise, firms are reluctant to sell shares; there are usually cheaper ways for firms to borrow from investors than selling shares of stock. Therefore, most investors buy their stock from other investors—not directly from firms.

- The term primary market describes the market for new assets that investors buy directly from the borrowers who issue them. The term secondary market describes the market for used—or, more accurately, preowned—assets. When you buy an investment in the secondary market, you're effectively taking over the loan from someone else.

- **Dividends** are the profits that companies pay out to their shareholders. While it's true that stockholders are entitled to a share of the company's profits, the company isn't under any obligation to actually pay them out.

- Many corporations—up to 40% or more, according to some estimates—don't pay any dividends. When a firm earns profits, it has a choice: It could pay the profits out to the shareholders or hold onto the profits and reinvest them into new projects. If the projects are really great and offer high returns, then shareholders should be glad to let the company keep the profits, reinvest them, and pay out even more profits later.

- If you buy a stock, you'll have to sell it sometime if you want to convert it to cash. A stock is technically a loan with infinite maturity, so the company won't actually ever pay back the loan. In reality, most companies come to an end eventually, but there are many companies that have lasted for 100 years or more. Furthermore, a stock may not ever pay out any cash dividends at all, so you may not get any interest on the loan either.

Trading Stocks

- Because firms don't sell much stock directly to investors and because you usually have to buy stock from someone else, trading is an essential part of investing in stocks.

- Stocks, and all other financial instruments, used to be physical documents that were traded in person. Today, we keep track of stock ownership through electronic records. Specialized financial institutions, called depositories, are the official storage places for most securities. The depository stores the shares electronically, keeps track of who owns the shares at all times, and effectively transfers ownership of shares when they change hands.

- Stocks, like most financial assets, tend to trade in organized markets. Most investors who buy and sell securities like stocks will have to go through an intermediary. There are 2 types of intermediaries in the financial markets. One type is a **broker**, who simply helps buyers locate sellers—and vice versa—and arranges the sale.

Most investors buy their stock from other investors—not directly from firms.

- A broker may also help buyers and sellers agree on a price. The buyer or seller (or both) pay a fee, or commission, to the broker for these services. One type of broker that most people have experience with is a realtor, who helps bring buyers and sellers of homes or other properties together, facilitates the sale, and collects a commission for doing all of that.

- If you want to invest in individual stocks, you'll need to set up an account with a broker. A brokerage account operates a lot like an ordinary bank account—except that in addition to cash, your account also contains the securities that you buy.

- When you buy stocks through a broker, technically the broker is registered as the owner of the shares in the securities depository, but the broker's internal accounts will show that you have a claim on your broker for those shares. This is done so that shares can be transferred very quickly, and brokers have to comply with many regulations that make sure they can't misuse the customers' money and securities.

- The main differences between brokers boil down to 2 questions. The first question is how much human contact you want from your broker. There are human brokers, and there are online brokers that will let you do almost everything yourself, at your convenience—or you can have some kind of mixture.

- Besides the amount of human contact you want, you also need to consider the amount of services you want from a broker. All brokers provide the basic services of maintaining your accounts and executing the trades that you pay them to make on your behalf, but some brokers will provide additional services.

- The other type of intermediary is a **dealer**, who also connects buyers and sellers but does so indirectly. Dealers announce to the market that they'll sell a specified security to anyone who is willing to pay the dealer's asking price, or the **ask price** for short. At the same time, dealers also announce that they will buy a certain security from anyone who is willing to sell at the dealer's offering price, or the **bid price**.

- Because dealers are always ready to sell to you or buy from you, this method of trading stocks is more convenient than waiting for a broker to find someone for you to trade with. When the dealer buys a share of stock from someone and then sells it to you, he or she earns the difference between the ask price and the bid price, which is called the **bid-ask spread**.

- When you use a dealer to sell shares, the dealer pays you right away, but he or she may not be able to find a buyer for the shares very quickly. When you use a broker to sell shares, even though you may be paying less, you bear the risk of not being able to find a buyer as quickly as you want.

- Traditionally, brokers have been associated with **stock exchanges**, which are organized markets where people can meet and trade shares. However, you have to be a member of the exchange in order to be able to trade on the exchange, and to become a member, you have to pay a large fee.

- The members of the exchange earn money not only by trading their own shares, but also by trading shares on behalf of people who are willing to pay a fee for this service. Thus, the members of stock exchanges become stockbrokers.

- Not all stocks are traded on exchanges; many stocks trade in a dealer market, such as NASDAQ or the dozens of other online trading systems. Fortunately, stock trading has remained relatively simple and dependable for investors despite the increasing complexity of the stock market—mostly because you pay your broker to handle the trading for you.

Lot Sizes and Types of Orders
- We tend to buy things in standard quantities, called lots, and most financial investments have standardized lot sizes. For stocks, the size of a round lot is 100 shares. You'll get the best price, and the fastest trade, if you buy or sell in multiples of 100 shares.

- Additionally, there are several different types of orders you can submit to the market. A market order is an order to buy or sell at whatever the current market price is. The basic problem with market orders is that market prices can move very quickly. Electronic trading allows orders to be placed very quickly, but it also enables prices to move much faster.

- A limit order places an upper limit on the price you're willing to pay or a lower limit on the price you're willing to receive. Placing limit orders may mean that you don't end up buying or selling those shares. In addition, limit orders cost more than market orders, so you should be aware of the cost difference.

- A stop-loss order is an order to sell shares that is triggered once the price of the shares falls below a certain level. The problem with stop-loss orders is that once the price goes below the stop-loss level and the order is submitted, the price can keep falling quickly. Many traders think of a stop-loss order as a type of insurance, but it's not.

Important Terms

ask price: The price at which the dealer will sell a share of stock to you, or the asking price.

bid price: The price at which the dealer will buy the stock from you, or the offering price.

bid-ask spread: The difference between the ask price and the bid price.

broker: A type of intermediary in the financial markets who simply helps buyers locate sellers—and vice versa—and arranges the sale.

dealer: A type of intermediary in the financial markets who connects buyers and sellers indirectly.

dividend: The profit that a company pays out to its shareholders.

initial public offering (IPO): A special sale in which a company first sells its shares to the public; marks the transition from being a privately held company that only 500 or fewer people can own to becoming a publicly held company that anyone can own a part of.

share: An equal portion of a company's stock.

stock: A form of ownership that a firm issues that divides the ownership of the company into thousands—if not millions—of equal parts, or shares.

stock exchange: An organized market where people can meet and trade shares.

Suggested Reading

Bodie, Kane, and Marcus, *Essentials of Investments*, chap. 3.

Brealey, Myers, and Allen, *Principles of Corporate Finance*, chap. 1.

Swensen, *Unconventional Success*, chap. 2.

Questions to Consider

1. Go to the website of an online brokerage such as E*TRADE, TD Ameritrade, or Scottrade. Compare the price of the trading commission for a market order through this broker with the trading commission for a limit order. When do you think it's worth paying the extra money to use a limit order?

2. Do an Internet search on the term "shareholder activism" and read up on articles that describe how these market players attempt to improve the performance of companies. Why don't shareholder activists simply try to take over poorly performing companies?

Starting with Stocks
Lecture 3—Transcript

Welcome back. In this lecture, I'm going to start to take an in-depth look at different types of investments. Although there are literally thousands of different financial products for you to invest in, most of them are made up of the same few basic few types of financial instruments. So you can consider this lecture, and the next three that follow, your introduction to the main building blocks of investments. Later in the course, I'll also introduce a few more building blocks that you might want to add to your set—but the ones I'll show you now are what I consider the essentials.

The investment I want to start with is stocks. This may come as a big surprise to you. After all, stocks can be pretty risky investments. So, isn't starting to invest by picking stocks like learning to swim by jumping into the deep end of the swimming pool? Absolutely—so let me be very clear that I'm not saying that stocks are the investments you should buy first.

But I am convinced that stocks are the best place to start learning about investing. There are several reasons why I say this. First, the basic ideas behind stock investing are clear and easy to understand. The ideas behind stock investing are really the same ideas behind all the investing we do.

Also, the stock contract itself is very simple. Other investment contracts are more complex, and sometimes those details get in the way of understanding the big picture.

And finally, the details of stock investing—the nuts and bolts of buying and selling stocks, should you ever want to do that—are very similar to the details of other types of investing as well. So although stocks are not necessarily the best starter investment, they are a great model for learning about individual investments and how to use them.

The way to start thinking about stocks is to think about what companies do, and why they need stocks to achieve their goals.

Every day, the media is full of reports about companies who have just announced bold new projects. For example, in August of 2011, Google announced that it had made a deal to buy Motorola Mobility. This was a surprising deal—Google was a provider of Internet services and software, while Motorola Mobility was primarily a maker of mobile phones. And even though Google produces the operating system that makes mobile phones work, this is still a risky combination of businesses. It's an expensive deal, too—Google agreed to pay $12.5 billion. But it could pay off tremendously, making the money spent on the deal seem like a real bargain.

This example shows what businesses are supposed to do—try risky but innovative and surprising new projects that have the chance to create valuable products and handsome profits. These projects always involve investments in real assets. To make something new, businesses need to buy machines, factories, land, ideas, and in the case of Google and Motorola Mobility, entire companies.

To do that, though, they need money, lots of money. And chances are, businesses don't have enough cash on hand to fund all the projects they want to pursue. They have to borrow the money from somewhere, and this is where financial assets come in. Financial assets are documents that describe the terms of a loan. The borrower gets money now, and the lender receives something of value in return. Usually, the thing of value is a promise from the borrower to make cash payments in the future, to whoever the owner of the document happens to be at the time.

But there are other valuable things that a firm can offer in exchange for a lender's ready cash. One of them is an ownership stake in the business. There are several legal forms that this shared ownership can take, such as a partnership, but by far the most successful form of shared ownership has been the corporation, which uses stock.

When a firm issues stock, it divides up the ownership of the company into thousands if not millions of equal parts, which are the individual shares. Each share has an equal claim on the firm's profits, and an equal say in the management of the firm. The more shares you buy, the bigger the slice of the company's profits you receive, and the more influence you have on company decisions.

This is one of the reasons that I wanted to start with stocks. I think all of us can understand and identify with—maybe even fantasize about—becoming the owner of a company. If you own a company, then your investment increases in value when you make good decisions and invest in successful projects that increase your company's profits.

I'll have a lot more to say about picking stocks in future lectures, but the basic skill of stock investing really boils down to finding companies that invest in successful projects. That's true when it comes to picking other types of investments as well.

The story I've told so far about stocks is basically right, but it's highly stylized. I'm going to add a dose of reality now, and explain how the stock contract tends to work in practice. This will help distinguish stocks from other financial instruments, and it'll give us a few tips along the way about stock investing.

First off, the story I've told makes it sound like whenever a company has a good project it wants to fund, it just sells some shares to investors. In reality, companies don't sell shares all that often, and they don't fund most of their projects through selling shares. When a company sells shares to the public for the first time, in a special sale called the initial public offering, or IPO, it usually does use investors' money to expand its business and start new projects.

And when one company buys another one, it often pays for this purchase by issuing new shares. But otherwise, firms are reluctant to sell shares. There is a long and interesting explanation why, but the short version is that there are usually cheaper ways for firms to borrow other than selling shares of stock to investors.

What this means is that most investors buy their stock from other investors, not directly from firms. By the way, we use the term primary market to describe the market for new assets that investors buy directly from the borrowers who issue them. So when Facebook has its IPO, and sells shares directly to the public, this takes place in the primary market for stocks.

We use the term *secondary market* to describe the market for used—or more accurately, pre-owned—assets. When one investor buys a share of Citigroup stock from another investor, we say that this takes place in the secondary market for stocks. The primary and secondary markets aren't actually different markets, or different places, just different types of transactions.

Just because you're buying an investment in the secondary market, it doesn't mean that you're not really lending the company money. What you're effectively doing is taking over the loan from someone else. Your objective as an investor is still the same, whether you're buying in the primary or secondary market—find those good companies that will make your investment increase in value.

Another way that the real story of stocks differs significantly from the simple version is in terms of control. The simple story of stock investing makes it sound like corporate decisions are made in town hall meetings, where all the shareholders get a chance to make their voice heard. The reality is that most investors hold such a small piece of the company that they have little if any impact on its decisions.

Corporations are a type of representative democracy, in which shareholders elect the Board of Directors, who represent their interests. But the Board of Directors then turns around and hires a professional management team, which runs the firm day to day. For large companies such as IBM or Exxon-Mobil, only shareholders who own millions of shares have the potential to affect the decisions of the firm, and even then it's fairly difficult for them to do that.

Despite this reality, the power of ownership that goes along with stocks does still matter. If the managers of a company make a string of bad decisions that threaten the value of the shares, stockholders will start to put pressure on the firm to improve. You may have heard of so-called activist investors such as William Ackman or Carl Icahn, who amass large blocks of stock in poorly performing companies and then pressure the managers to change the way that they run their business.

Because of activist investors—and other mechanisms that I don't have time to get into—bad managers eventually get punished, and their firms get reformed, while good managers eventually get rewarded, and their firms get more valuable. So even though you probably can't exercise much control over a firm you invest in, you can still benefit from the power of ownership by looking for companies that are run by good managers whose firms haven't yet been adequately rewarded.

Yet another way that reality differs from the simple stories we tell about stocks has to do with dividends, which are the profits that companies pay out to their shareholders. While it's true that stockholders are entitled to a share of the company's profits, the company isn't under any obligation to actually pay them out. Many corporations—up to 40% or more, according to some estimates—don't pay any dividends.

There's actually a good reason for this, though. When a firm earns profits, it has a choice—it could pay the profits out to shareholders, or it could hold onto the profits and reinvest them into new projects. If the projects are really great, and offer high returns, then shareholders should be glad to let the company keep the profits, reinvest them now, and pay out even more profits later.

A company like Microsoft is a good example of this. For many years, Microsoft didn't pay any dividends to its shareholders—and its stock still rose like a rocket. That's because the market for personal computers was exploding, and Microsoft's sales of software were exploding along with it. Microsoft had great investment opportunities in the form of new versions of its Windows operating system and its Office software, among many others. Investors were happy to let Microsoft hold onto its profits so that it could continue to invest in these projects. But eventually, Microsoft found that it was making more profits than it had good investments to spend them on, so it started to pay a small dividend in 2003, and has been paying one ever since.

The final reality of the stock contract I want to mention is that if you buy a stock, you'll have to sell it sometime if you want to convert it to cash. A stock is technically a loan with infinite maturity, so the company won't actually ever pay back the loan. In reality, of course, most companies come to an end eventually, but there are some companies out there that have lasted for 100 years or more, such as AT&T. And, as I just mentioned, a stock may not ever pay out any cash dividends at all, so you may not get any interest on the loan either.

Why is it important that you have to sell your shares to cash out your stock investment? Well, combine this fact with one I mentioned a few minutes ago: firms don't sell much stock directly to investors. You usually have to buy stock from someone else. Together, these two facts imply that trading is an essential part of investing in stocks. You may not trade very often, but you should know how to do it safely, and you should know what your options are in terms of trading services.

Let's start to think about trading stocks by making clear what it is you're trading. Stocks, and all other financial instruments, used to be physical documents. Companies had special certificates made for their stocks, which often had designs on them that were as elaborate as the designs on money. When people traded stock, they had to physically deliver these certificates to each other to complete the sale.

Needless to say, this can get a little cumbersome, and it isn't all that secure, either. That's why stocks and other securities have been largely dematerialized over time. That's a fancy, almost "science-fictiony" term, but all it really means is that we keep track of stock ownership through electronic records rather than possession of physical documents. Specialized financial institutions, called depositories, are the official storage places for most securities these days. The depository stores the shares electronically, keeps track of who owns the shares at all times, and effectively transfers ownership of shares when they change hands. It's an essential part of the financial market, but not one you hear about all that much.

Stocks, like most financial assets, tend to trade in organized markets. Most investors who buy and sell securities like stocks will have to go through an intermediary—a middleman, if you'll pardon the gender bias there. There are two types of intermediaries in the financial markets. How they differ, and the way they earn a living, is important to keep in mind.

One type of intermediary is a broker. A broker simply helps buyers locate sellers, and vice versa, and arranges the sale. A broker may also help buyers and sellers agree on a price. The buyer or seller (or both) pay a fee, or commission, to the broker for these services. One type of broker that most people have experience with is a realtor. A realtor helps bring buyers and sellers of homes or other properties together, facilitates the sale, and collects a commission for doing all that.

Generally speaking, if you want to invest in individual stocks, you'll need to set up an account with a broker. A brokerage account operates a lot like an ordinary bank account, except that in addition to cash, your account also contains the securities that you buy.

When you buy stocks through a broker, technically the broker is registered as the owner of the shares in the securities depository. But the broker's internal accounts will show that you have a claim on your broker for those shares. This is done so that shares can be transferred very quickly, and this practice is known as holding the shares "in street." You don't have to worry about holding your shares this way with a reputable broker. Brokers have to comply with a lot of regulations that make sure they can't misuse the customers' money and securities. And there is a fund, like the FDIC, that protects the value of your account if the brokerage firm goes bankrupt. It's called the SIPC, or Securities Investor Protection Corporation.

You have lots of choices among brokers these days, but the main differences between brokers boil down to two questions. The first question is how much human contact you want from your broker. There are still lots of human brokers out there, and they would be glad to take you on as a new client.

On the other hand, there are online brokers that will let you do almost everything yourself, at your convenience. And you can have some kind of mixture of the two. Keep in mind that human brokers can be great resources—their knowledge and experience can go well beyond stocks into all areas of investment and financial planning. In fact, many brokers these days double as financial planners. But that human touch, and the advice, does come at a price. And brokers are people, too, with their own biases and incentives. If you do choose to use a live person, make sure you know how the broker is earning money by working with you.

Brokers earn fees by providing services, and they earn commissions from selling products. Good brokers will always be honest with you about what's in it for them, when they offer you any advice or product.

With online brokers, the big issue is how good their customer service and technical assistance are. Most online brokers will let you poke around their websites without having to open an account, and I strongly encourage you to do that before you settle on a particular online broker.

Besides the amount of human contact you want, you also need to consider the amount of services you want from a broker. All brokers provide the basic services of maintaining your accounts and executing the trades that you pay them to make on your behalf. But some brokers will provide additional services. For example, a full service broker will give you investing advice, as well as access to the firm's own research on different companies and on different investment opportunities. And some brokers will give you access to online stock screening programs that search for stocks according to certain criteria that you specify, like stocks that pay high dividends.

Before you sign up for extra services, though, you should take a good look at what is available for free. You may well find that, for the type of investor you want to be, there's plenty of good data, analysis, and advice to be had for the price of your monthly Internet service.

Now let's talk about the other type of intermediary—the dealer. A dealer also connects buyers and sellers, but does so indirectly. That's because dealers are traders themselves. Dealers announce to the market that they will sell a specified security to anyone who is willing to pay the dealer's asking price; we call this the ask price for short.

At the same time, dealers also announce that they will buy this security from anyone who is willing to sell at the dealer's offering price. We call this one the bid price. So a dealer is always ready to sell to you at a price called the ask price or buy from you at a price called the bid price. This makes life convenient, because you don't have to wait for a broker to find someone for you to trade with. You can go to a dealer and buy or sell immediately.

The dealer earns a living from this by setting the ask price—the price at which the dealer will sell a share of stock to you—higher than the bid price, which is the price at which the dealer will buy a share of stock from you. So when the dealer buys a share of stock from someone and turns around and sells it to you, he or she earns the difference between the bid price and the ask price, which is called the bid–ask spread.

It may seem unfair at first that you have to pay a higher price to buy than you will get from selling. But the fact of the matter is that when you buy or sell most financial instruments, you have to pay something. When you use a broker, you have to pay a commission. I will say, on the other hand, that commissions tend to be smaller than bid–ask spreads on the same security. That is, a broker charges less. But there's a good reason for that—a dealer takes on a lot more risk than a broker does. When you use a dealer to sell shares, the dealer pays you right away, but he or she may not be able to find a buyer for them very quickly. Well, that's the dealer's problem. When you use a broker to sell shares, you bear the risk of not being able to find a buyer as quickly as you want.

In some financial markets, you'll mostly find dealers bringing buyers and sellers together, while in other markets, you'll find mostly brokers. But in the case of stock markets, there are lots of both. And not only are there both brokers and dealers, but many people wear both hats—that is, they're broker–dealers.

Traditionally, brokers have been associated with stock exchanges, like the New York Stock Exchange. A stock exchange is an organized market where people can meet and trade shares. But they're not open to everyone. You have to be a member of the exchange in order to trade shares on the exchange. And to become a member, you have to pay a fee—a big fee.

The members of the exchange earn money not only by trading their own shares, but by trading shares on behalf of people who are willing to pay a fee—a commission—for this service. And thus, the members of stock exchanges become stockbrokers.

But not all stocks are traded on exchanges. Many stocks trade in a dealer market. Traditionally this was called the over-the-counter, or OTC, market. Now it's usually referred to as NASDAQ, after the name of the electronic trading system for the OTC market that was introduced in the 1970s. For years, the stock market was roughly divided up into the exchanges on one side, and NASDAQ on the other. Since the advent of the Internet, however, dozens of online trading systems have been created that compete with NASDAQ as well as the traditional exchanges. Now there is a large and, frankly, confusing array of stock markets, and almost any company's shares can be traded on any of these systems.

Fortunately, though, stock trading has remained relatively simple and dependable for investors despite the increasingly complex stock market. This is mostly because you're paying your broker to handle the trading for you. In addition, the SEC (Securities and Exchange Commission) requires trading systems to show each other their prices, and it requires brokers and dealers to send their customers' orders to the market that has the best price that can be executed immediately. So, when you submit an order through your broker, the broker has to find the best price for your shares. If that price is found on an exchange, the broker trades on the exchange. If the best price is found in a dealer-dominated market like NASDAQ, the broker trades with one of the dealers on your behalf. In some cases, your broker will also trade with you directly, acting in their capacity as a dealer. In the end, all you see is that your trade gets executed.

Let's say you open an account with a broker, you spend some time crunching numbers and reading up on companies, and you find a stock that really excites you. Before you plunge into your first—or next—stock investment, you need to know a few things about lot sizes and types of orders.

First, there's lot size. We tend to buy things in standard quantities, called lots. We buy eggs by the dozen, shoelaces by the pair, and copy paper by the ream. You could buy a single egg, a single shoelace, or a single sheet of paper, but it's hard to do and more expensive. In the same way, financial investments have standardized lot sizes.

For stocks, the size of a round lot is 100 shares. You'll get the best price, and the fastest trade, if you buy or sell in multiples of 100 shares. Now, I realize that this may put that stock investment out of reach, at least for now. After all, 100 shares of Google are about the price of a new car. But the higher price you'll pay per share for an odd lot makes it harder to profit from the shares. Why put yourself at a disadvantage like that, right off the bat?

Now let's turn to orders. We may think that stock trading is just a matter of hitting the "buy" or "sell" button on a trading screen, but there are several different types of orders you can submit to the market. Using the right language can set conditions on your order that help protect you from adverse market movements.

First, let's start with a market order. A market order is an order to buy or sell at whatever the current market price is. This is the type of order that most of us have in mind when we think of trading stocks. The basic problem with market orders is that market prices can move very, very quickly. You may have heard a friend complain that they hit the "buy" button when the price on the screen said $25, but they got a trade confirmation for buying 100 shares at $27 or $30 each. Electronic trading allows orders to be placed very quickly, but it also enables prices to move that much faster.

You also may have heard of the infamous "flash crash" of 2010, when the Dow Jones lost 1000 points in just over 10 minutes. That's an extreme example, of course, but it shows what kinds of price changes are possible these days.

You can protect yourself from nasty surprises like this by using a different type of order—the limit order. A limit order places an upper limit on the price you're willing to pay, or a lower limit on the price you're willing to receive. In the above example, if you submitted a limit order at $25 per share, you would ensure that you wouldn't end up paying any more than $25 for the shares, and you might actually end up paying less.

If the price moves up above your limit order, the order won't be filled. But limit orders are customarily valid for an entire trading day, so if you put in a limit order in the morning, the price may bounce down below your limit and enable you to buy at the price you want. Technically, what happens is that your limit order is entered into what is called a limit order book, which is maintained by the electronic trading system. The limit order book basically shows the demand and supply curves for shares. As an economist, I just had to mention that.

Placing limit orders may mean that you don't end up buying or selling those shares. In addition, limit orders do cost more than market orders, so you should be aware of the cost difference and think about whether it's worth paying the extra money for the trade. But the protection that limit orders provide may be well worth the cost.

One more order that you should know something about is the stop-loss order. A stop-loss order is an order to sell shares that is triggered once the price of the shares falls below a certain level. So if you set a stop-loss order for 100 shares of Verizon Wireless at $80 per share, the sell order is placed as soon as Verizon Wireless' price goes to $79.99 or less.

The problem with stop-loss orders is the same problem with market orders. Once the price goes below the stop-loss level and the order is submitted, the price can keep falling dramatically. Even though the stop-loss was set at $80, the order may not have been filled before the price fell to, say, $71 per share. The point is that many traders think of stop-loss orders as a type of insurance, but it's not. If you think you need to use a stop-loss order, you should think carefully about where you should set the stop-loss level. You should probably also ask yourself why you're holding this stock in the first place.

At this point, I think we've covered just about everything you need to know about stock investing, except which stocks to pick. We learned some key facts about how stocks actually work, and some of these ideas will help us later when we learn about stock pricing. We also learned a lot of important details about how stocks are traded.

I hope that this introduction to stocks has helped you feel more comfortable with the idea of investing in stocks, and other financial assets as well. As I said in the beginning of this lecture, I really don't expect you to want to start your investing career here. But I hope that at this point, you're not ruling out the possibility that you might find a great company that you want to own a piece of.

In future lectures, I'll be giving you a lot of information about how to find a great company or two. But in the next lecture, I'd like to go over the basics of another popular investment—bonds. See you then.

The Basics of Bonds
Lecture 4

In this lecture, you will learn the key features of bonds that make their returns more predictable and dependable than the returns on stocks. This lecture focuses specifically on how to pursue a buy-and-hold investment strategy in bonds. Although the returns on bonds might seem boring, bonds are actually very interesting. There is a diverse set of bonds that nonetheless has a high degree of safety and competitive returns. If you shop carefully among the many options, you'll find the right set of bonds that fit your desired mix of safety and yield.

Bonds

- The variety and dependability of bonds can make them a very useful investment to have in your portfolio. Bonds also enable governments to borrow, and they're the tool that central banks like the Federal Reserve use when they want to expand or shrink the money supply.

- Bonds are contracts in which a borrower—the issuer of the bond—promises to make a set of payments to the buyer of the bond. This sounds like a pretty simple arrangement, but bond contracts are actually extremely complex documents, running to dozens if not hundreds of pages.

- The buyer of the bond lends money to the issuer of the bond and wants to prevent the borrower from defaulting. Naturally, the buyer of the bond can't completely prevent the issuer from defaulting, but the buyer can make the issuer of the bond agree to a large set of terms and conditions, which are called **restrictive covenants**.

- Some of the covenants require the borrower to do things that make the borrower financially stronger and less likely to default. For example, covenants may require the borrower to keep a certain amount of cash in a reserve fund that can be used to pay off part of the loan.

- Other covenants require the borrower not to do things that make them financially weaker and more likely to default. An example of this type of negative covenant is one stipulating that the borrower can't take on any more debt.

Features of Bonds

- There are 3 main types of features that distinguish bonds from each other in ways that should matter to you as an investor: who issued the bond, whether the bonds are secured, and the timing of the payments.

- There are 3 main types of bond issuers: governments, companies, and individuals. Government bonds make up the largest share of the bond markets and are usually considered the safest types of bonds because governments have the ability to raise taxes in order to pay off the bonds.

- Each level of government—national, state, and local—can generally issue its own bonds. Bonds that come from local government units are called municipal bonds. A general term for foreign government bonds is sovereign bonds.

- Technically, the words "bonds" and "debt" can be used interchangeably. The term "debt" includes all borrowing that doesn't involve selling stock. Therefore, debt includes bank loans as well as bonds. However, when you sign a bank loan, you are issuing a bond to your bank.

- In addition to governments, companies issue large amounts of bonds, which we generally call corporate bonds, or private debt. The private bond markets are much smaller than the government bond markets.

- Finally, individuals can also issue bonds—though, generally, these investments are far too risky to be considered an attractive part of your portfolio.

- In addition to the issuer of the bond, the second feature that investors care about is whether a bond is **secured**, which means it is backed up by specific collateral. For example, a company may secure a bond by pledging a factory or perhaps a portfolio of valuable

© Creatas/Thinkstock.

Bonds enable governments to borrow and central banks to expand or shrink the money supply.

patents. If the company defaults on a secured bond, the lender gets to claim the specific assets that were pledged as collateral.

- On the other hand, the owners of unsecured bonds have to stand in line with all the other lenders and sort out who gets what from the bankrupt issuer. This process takes a long time, and generally the bond buyers receive a lot less than they would have received if they had held a bond that was secured by some specific asset.

- The final characteristic of bonds that you should be aware of is the immense variety in the timing of bond payments. **Maturity** is the length of time until the final payment on the bond. The standard range of maturity available in the market runs from 1 day to 30 years or more. The wide range of maturities gives you the possibility of investing in a bond that will mature very close to the day you need to receive the cash from your investment.

- There are 3 terms that categorize bonds by their maturity. **Bills** are bonds that mature in less than 1 year. **Notes** are bonds that mature in 1 to 10 years. An instrument known as the **medium-term note (MTN)** typically has 1 to 5 years of maturity.

- The fact that you can buy bonds on the secondary market, the market for preowned securities, greatly adds to the range of maturities of bonds that are available. On the secondary market, you'll find bonds with maturities of only 4 months, for example, which had been issued with much longer maturities but have many fewer months remaining to maturity.

- Another way that the timing of bond payments varies is in the number of payments and the sizes of the payments. Some bonds make a single payment, and these are called **zero-coupon bonds** because you get no interest payments, or **coupons**, between the time you buy the bond and the time that the borrower makes the payment to you.

- The downside of zero-coupon bonds is that you have to wait until the maturity of the bond to receive your interest. The benefit of zero-coupon bonds is that the price you pay for them is much lower than the payment they make to you at maturity.

- Most bonds make multiple payments to their holders between the purchase date and the bond's maturity. Generally, bonds make regular payments, but this depends on the agreement between the borrower and lender. Additionally, the payments may all be of a single size, or the size of the individual payments may vary.

- In the borrowing arrangement of a standard bond, which is also referred to as a straight bond, the lender gives the borrower a sum of money called the **principal**, or the par value of the bond. In return, the borrower pays interest on the principal every 6 months and then returns the principal to the lender at maturity.

Investing in Bonds

- At least in the United States, bonds are mostly a dealer market because there are so many different bonds that it would be difficult to support a large enough pool of active traders in an exchange. In some developing economies, the governments force all bond trading to go through exchanges.

- Due to pressure from the U.S. Securities and Exchange Commission (SEC), as well as the development of the online discount brokerage business, information about bond prices has become widely available, so you can be confident that the price you pay for a bond represents a true market price.

- Going through a broker is the main way to buy a bond on the secondary market, but you will have to pay a commission to the broker and possibly a markup to a dealer that the brokerage works with.

- You can also buy many primary market bonds through a brokerage, including both private bonds and government bonds, but there is also a direct market in many bonds that may be cheaper and more convenient than using a broker.

- In addition, many large corporations sell notes and bonds directly to the public because it's a cheap way for them to borrow, and many investors like it because they earn higher interest than on their bank deposits, from a company they regard as safe.

- Bonds tend to have large lot sizes. That is, they have minimum investments that tend to be large. For example, most corporate bonds tend to have a minimum par value of $10,000 and are only available in increments of $10,000.

- The lumpiness of bonds potentially ties up a lot of money for a long period of time. If you buy a bond that matures in 20 years, for example, you won't get that $10,000 back for 2 decades—though you will receive the interest every 6 months. The liquidity risk—the risk that you will have a sudden need for cash—leads most buy-and-hold bond investors to pursue a strategy called laddering.

- A **bond ladder** is a set of bonds that has one bond maturing every year, every quarter, or maybe even every month. As one bond matures, you can use the cash from the bond if you need to, but you can also buy a new bond to replace it. If you always buy the same maturity of bond, then you end up with a self-replenishing set of bonds that generates a steady stream of cash.

- One of the main risks of buy-and-hold bond investing is what economists call reinvestment risk. When you build your bond ladder, your bonds may pay an average interest rate of 5% per year, for example. Every 6 months, you'll get a set of coupons from your bonds and have to decide where to reinvest this money, but by this time, market interest rates may have fallen to 4%, for example, so you'll have to reinvest your interest at a lower rate, which will drag down the average return on your total bond investment.

- Reinvestment risk is usually more of an annoyance than a real risk of loss, and sometimes interest rates will rise, so the risk can work in your favor. However, if interest rates fall dramatically and stay there for long periods of time, then you may want to reevaluate your investment plan.

- One of the more serious risks to the buy-and-hold bond investor is inflation. If you are holding a bond with long maturity and inflation starts to rise, then the purchasing power of your investment will fall dramatically by the time you collect your final payment. Fortunately, the bond laddering strategy helps to mitigate the damage that inflation can do to your bond portfolio.

- If the price level falls, the purchasing power of the future payments on the bonds increases, but deflation is incredibly damaging to business. Significant deflation leads firms into bankruptcy because the prices they receive for their goods and services may fall below the costs of production.

- If you are holding corporate bonds, the likelihood of default increases dramatically when deflation occurs. However, deflation is usually associated with recessions, and during recessions, government revenues at all levels decline, so deflation can also cause governments to default.

Important Terms

bill: A bond that matures in less than 1 year.

bond ladder: A set of bonds that has one bond maturing every year, every quarter, or maybe even every month. As one bond matures, you can use the cash from the bond if you need to, but you can also buy a new bond to replace it. If you always buy the same maturity of bond, then you end up with a self-replenishing set of bonds that generates a steady stream of cash.

coupon: An interest payment.

maturity: The length of time until the final payment on a bond.

medium-term note (MTN): A bond that typically matures in 1 to 5 years.

note: A bond that matures in 1 to 10 years.

principal: The par value of a bond.

restrictive covenant: A large set of terms and conditions that the buyer of a bond can make the issuer of the bond agree to.

secured: Refers to a bond that is backed up by specific collateral.

zero-coupon bond: A bond that makes a single payment and that gives no interest payments, or coupons, between the time the bond is bought and the time that the borrower makes the payment to the buyer.

Suggested Reading

Bodie, Kane, and Marcus, *Essentials of Investments*, chap. 2.

Swensen, *Unconventional Success*, chap. 2.

Questions to Consider

1. Go to the TreasuryDirect website at www.treasurydirect.gov and view the auction calendar, which shows when different government bonds are available for purchase. When is your next chance to buy a 10-year U.S. Treasury note? When is your next chance to buy a 30-year U.S. Treasury bond?

2. Go to an online brokerage website and look for corporate bonds rated A or higher that are available in the secondary market. What is a typical ask yield for a high-rated corporate bond that matures in the next year— or in 5 years?

The Basics of Bonds
Lecture 4—Transcript

In the previous lecture, I introduced stocks by pointing out how stocks are risky but fascinating. In this lecture, I'm turning to bonds. Now, bonds don't have quite the same reputation as stocks. In fact, they might seem boring. It's true that bonds are not necessarily the sexiest investments out there, but they are extremely important. And, if you get to know them a bit better, you'll see that the variety and dependability of bonds can make them a very useful investment to have in your portfolio.

Bonds also play a starring role in economic policy. Bonds enable governments to borrow, and they're also the tool that central banks like the Federal Reserve use when they want to expand or shrink the money supply. The bond market has become so large that governments have to worry about how it will react to their decisions. In fact, an adviser to President Bill Clinton remarked early in the Clinton presidency that he would like to be reincarnated as the bond market, because it was the only person who could tell a president what to do.

In this lecture, we'll learn the key features of bonds that make their returns more predictable and dependable than the returns on stocks. I'm going to focus this lecture on how to pursue a buy-and-hold bond investment strategy in bonds, but I'll come back to active bond investing in a future lecture. Although the returns on bonds might seem boring, I think you'll see that bonds themselves are really very interesting. And besides, when it comes to investment returns, a little bit of boring is not such a bad thing.

As we did with stocks, let's begin learning about bonds by thinking about what bonds are. I've mentioned before that bonds are contracts in which a borrower—the issuer of the bond—promises to make a set of payments to the buyer of the bond. This sounds like a pretty simple arrangement, and you may suspect that the bond contract is just as simple as the stock contract, which we learned about in the last lecture. But bond contracts are actually extremely complex documents, running to dozens if not hundreds of pages. Why is this the case?

It's about how much risk the buyer of the bond wants to take on—and the answer is, not much. The buyer of the bond is lending money to the issuer of the bond and wants to prevent the borrower from defaulting. Naturally, the buyer of the bond can't completely prevent the issuer from defaulting. But, what the buyer can do is make the issuer of the bond agree to a large set of terms and conditions—which are called restrictive covenants. So a bond contract is long and complex because it's full of restrictive covenants.

Some of the covenants require the borrower to do things that make the borrower financially stronger and less likely to default. For example, covenants may require the borrower to keep a certain amount of cash in a reserve fund that can be used to pay off part of the loan. Other covenants require the borrower not to do things that make them financially weaker and more likely to default. An example of this type of negative covenant is one stipulating that the borrower can't take on any more debt.

Covenants effectively give bond investors some say over what the borrower can and can't do. You may recall from the previous lecture that stocks also give their owners at least a little bit of control over the borrowers' activities. In both cases, having some control helps investors ensure that they get good returns on their investments. And in the case of bonds, the restrictive covenants significantly reduce the risk of loss to the investors.

Fortunately, most bonds will have a standard set of restrictive covenants written into their contracts, so you generally don't have to worry about reading through all the fine print yourself. That way, you can focus your attention on choosing among other features that matter to you as an investor. There are really three types of features that distinguish bonds from each other in ways that should matter to you as an investor: who issued the bond, whether the bonds are secured, and the timing of the payments.

First, let's consider who issued the bond. There are three main types of bond issuers: governments, companies, and individuals. Government bonds make up the largest share of the bond markets. Their size has a lot to do with the fact that government bonds are usually considered the safest types of bonds, because governments have the ability to raise taxes in order to pay off the bonds. We know that there are many levels of government—national, state, and local—and each level can generally issue its own bonds. Bonds that come from local government units are often called municipal bonds, or munis, for short.

Of course, foreign governments can and do issue bonds as well. A general term for foreign government bonds is sovereign bonds, or sovereign debt, which hearkens back to the days when foreign governments were kings and queens. Many of the most popular government bonds have their own special names. For example, everyone around the world calls U.S. government bonds *treasuries*, or *U.S. treasuries*. People use the term *gilts* for British government bonds, which goes back to the days when the bond certificates had gold leaf on the edges—true gilt-edged securities! And German government bonds are called *bunds*.

Foreign government bonds are usually issued in the government's home country, and of course the governments are borrowing in their home currencies, like British pounds for the British government and euros for the German government. But increasingly, governments and even companies will borrow in other countries by issuing bonds in the foreign country's home currency. For example, many foreign governments and companies borrow U.S. dollars by issuing their own bonds in the U.S., but the bonds are priced in U.S. dollars. These bonds are called Yankee bonds. In fact, there is a whole set of nicknames for bonds that are issued in foreign countries. A Chinese bond issued in Hong Kong, for example, is called a dim-sum bond.

Also, in many countries, governments own one or more large companies, or big stakes in these large companies. For example, one of the largest owners of Volkswagen is the German state of Lower Saxony. When government-owned companies issue bonds, these companies usually have the implicit support of their governments, so many investors treat these bonds as if they were government bonds.

Yet another type of bond that is treated just like a government bond is a bond issued by an international financial institution, or IFI for short. There are many large international institutions that function like banks, but specialize in funding economic development projects in different areas of the world. These organizations are owned by groups of national governments, so the bonds issued by them are treated like government bonds. Many of these organizations issue debt in the U.S. on a regular basis. As a matter of fact, I was looking at an online brokerage website recently and found several bonds available from the European Bank for Reconstruction and Development, which is one of these IFIs. These bonds can be attractive because they offer good yields and the major IFIs are considered quite safe borrowers.

By the way, you'll notice that I go back and forth between using the words bonds and debt as if they were the same thing. Technically, they are. The term debt includes all borrowing that doesn't involve selling stock—we use the term *equity* as a synonym for stock. Therefore, debt includes bank loans as well as bonds. But if you think carefully about it, when you sign the papers on a bank loan, you've just issued a bond to your bank. So debt and bonds really are the same thing.

Companies issue large amounts of bonds, too, which we generally call corporate bonds or private debt. But by and large, the private bond markets are much smaller than the government bond markets. This is because in many parts of the world, private bonds are just beginning to take off because most lending has traditionally been done through banks. With corporate bonds, the danger of default is a major concern and so this also limits the appeal of private bonds relative to government bonds, which keeps the markets smaller.

Finally, individuals can also issue bonds—though generally, these investments are far too risky to be considered an attractive part of your portfolio. Of course, to every rule, there's an exception, and here's one. The singer David Bowie issued his own bonds in the 1990s. The payments on the bonds came directly from the royalties on Bowie's previous recordings, so investors were happy to buy these bonds.

So far we've been looking at the first feature you need to think about when investing in bonds: who is the issuer of the bond?

The second feature that investors care about is whether a bond is secured or not. A bond is secured if it is backed up by specific collateral. For example, a company may secure a bond by pledging a factory, or perhaps even a portfolio of valuable patents. If the company defaults on a secured bond, the lender gets to claim the specific assets that were pledged as collateral. The bond owner literally gets to take the factory, patents, or other assets that were being used as collateral.

If a bond is unsecured, on the other hand, this doesn't mean that a lender comes up empty-handed if the borrower goes bankrupt. Instead, it means that the owners of unsecured bonds have to stand in line with all the other lenders and sort out who gets what from the bankrupt issuer. This process takes a long time, and generally the bond buyers get a lot less than they would if they had held a bond that was secured by some specific asset.

Now, one thing I should also mention is that defaults don't even occur until the stockholders lose the entire value of their investment. So, in a very real sense, the equity in a company which is owned by the shareholders provides a cushion that shields the bondholders from losses. This is another reason why out-and-out defaults are fairly uncommon in corporate bonds, which again means that bonds are a much safer investment than stocks.

The final characteristic of bonds that you should be aware of is the immense variety in the timing of bond payments. Let's start with maturity, which is the length of time until the final payment on the bond. The standard range of maturity available in the market runs from one day—technically, one night—all the way out to 30 years, though in many markets around the world the maximum maturity is closer to 10 or 20 years. And some lenders, including the government of Mexico and the University of Southern California, have even issued bonds with maturity of 100 years, which is called century debt. The wide range of maturities gives you the possibility of investing in a bond that will mature very close to the day you need to receive the cash from your investment.

By the way, some people still use three terms that categorize bonds by their maturity. *Bills* are bonds that mature in less than one year. Some people also call bonds that mature in less than one year *money market instruments*—so when you hear the term *money market*, you should think that this is the market for very short-term bonds of less than one year of maturity. The word *note* is often used for bonds that mature in 1 to 10 years. And some people only use the term *bond* for maturities of 10 years or more. When people refer to *t-bills*, for example, they're referring to government bonds that have less than one year of maturity. And, there is an instrument known as the *medium-term note*, or MTN, that typically has 1–5 years of maturity. Of course, the term bond is completely general, so it's not improper to call a three-month t-bill a three-month government bond.

The fact that you can buy bonds on the secondary market greatly adds to the range of maturities of bonds that are available. You may remember the distinction I drew in the previous lecture between the primary market, or the market for newly issued securities, and the secondary market, which is the market for pre-owned securities. On the secondary market, you'll find bonds with maturities of, say, 4 months, 17 months, 2 years and 2 months, and so on. All of these bonds had been issued with much longer maturities, but time has passed and now they have many fewer months remaining to maturity. The rates of return on these bonds are dictated by the current market for similar bonds, so that the original maturity of the bond doesn't affect the rate of return on the bond nearly as much as the remaining maturity does. For example, a 30-year bond issued 29 years ago—which has one year remaining until maturity—will be priced so that it gives an investor virtually the same yield as a comparable, newly issued one year bill.

Another way that the timing of bond payments varies is in the number of payments, and the sizes of the payments. Some bonds make a single payment, and these are called zero-coupon bonds because you get no interest payments, or coupons, between the time you buy the bond and the time that the borrower makes the payment to you. The downside of zero-coupon bonds is that you have to wait until the maturity of the bond to receive your interest. The nice part of zero-coupon bonds is that the price you pay for them is much lower than the payment that you receive at maturity. For both of these reasons, zero-coupon bonds are very similar to certificates of deposit.

Most bonds make multiple payments to their holders between the purchase date and the bond's maturity. Generally, bonds make regular payments, but of course it's up to whatever the borrower and lender can agree on. And the payments may all be of the same size, or the size of the individual payments may vary. Recurring payments consist of accumulated interest, and possibly some principal as well. When a bond payment contains interest only, the payment is called a coupon payment and the bond makes a set of unequal payments, because at maturity the borrower will have to make a big payment to repay the principal of the loan. Bonds whose payments include both interest and repayment of principal are called amortizing bonds, and they generally have equal payments, though of course they don't have to.

The vast majority of bonds that are available to investors have a common payment pattern, no matter who issues them or whether the bond is secured. So let me describe this standard bond, which is also referred to as a straight bond. The borrowing arrangement on a straight bond goes like this. The lender gives the borrower a sum of money today, called the principal or the par value of the bond. In return, the borrower pays interest on the principal every six months, and then returns the principal or par value back to the lender at maturity. So at maturity, the bondholder gets the final interest payment and the principal back as well.

That's a brief introduction to the variety of bonds out there. Now I'd like to turn to the practical issues of investing in bonds. In this lecture, I'll only be talking about pursuing a buy-and-hold investment strategy—that is, I'll talk about buying bonds and holding them to maturity. I'll get into more active trading strategies in a future lecture.

As we learned in the previous lecture, there is a distinction between broker markets and dealer markets in most investments. And bonds, at least in the United States, are mostly a dealer market. In some developing economies, the governments are forcing all bond trading to go through exchanges. And there are bond exchanges in the U.S. as well—but they don't handle very much of the trading of bonds. One of the reasons why the bond market in the U.S. tends to be a dealer market is that there are so many different bonds out there. Each bond has its own relatively small market. That fact alone makes it hard to build a large enough pool of active traders to support an exchange for bonds, especially when you consider that many investors plan to hold their bonds to maturity.

The downside of the dealer market for bonds used to be that information about current market prices was hard to come by. The lack of information about bond prices meant that it was too easy for individual investors to overpay for bonds—which of course lowers the overall return on your investment. Fortunately, due to pressure from the SEC, as well as the development of the online discount brokerage business, information about bond prices has become much more widely available, so you can be confident that the price you pay for a bond represents a true market price.

Going through your broker is the main way to buy a bond on the secondary market. Most brokers will have access to an inventory of corporate bonds, municipal bonds, and government bonds from the U.S., Canada, perhaps other foreign countries, and international financial institutions as well. When you buy a bond on the secondary market through a broker, you will have to pay a commission to the broker and you may also have to pay a markup to a dealer that the brokerage works with. Generally, bond trading commissions have come down just like the commissions on stocks, but in many cases there are minimum commissions that you will have to pay. So for example, a brokerage may charge you a one-dollar per bond trading commission, but have a $10 minimum commission.

You can also buy many primary market bonds through a brokerage, including both private bonds and government bonds. But there is also a direct over-the-counter market in many bonds that you should be aware of, and you may find this way of buying bonds cheaper and more convenient than using a broker. For example, Treasury Direct is a service provided by the U.S. Department of the Treasury that enables you to purchase U.S. Treasury bonds as well as savings bonds. You open the account directly through TreasuryDirect.gov.

In addition, many large corporations sell notes and bonds directly to the public. Companies do this because it's a cheap way for them to borrow, and many investors like it because they earn higher interest than on their bank deposits from a company they regard as safe. For example, in one of my recent electric bills, my power company included a flyer about their retail notes. As you can see from this example, many companies market their notes to their current customers or employees. But you can also get access to these programs yourself, if you're willing to look for them, and many brokers offer access to these retail programs as well.

So I hope I've shown that it's more convenient to find bonds to buy than you might have thought. But there are some other convenience issues with buying bonds that you should be aware of. Bonds tend to have large lot sizes. That is, they have minimum investments that tend to be big. For example, most corporate bonds tend to have a minimum par value of $10,000, and are only available in increments of $10,000. U.S. Treasury bonds, on the other hand, are available in lot sizes as small as $1000. Some corporate retail note and bond programs have minimum investments in the hundreds of dollars, but many of them also tend to have minimum required investments of $1000, and to get a really attractive interest rate, you need to invest tens of thousands of dollars.

The lumpiness of bonds ties up a lot of money for potentially a long period of time. If you buy a bond that matures in 20 years, for example, you won't get that $10,000 back for two decades—though you will receive the interest every six months. So it's not usually a great idea to run out and buy a set of 10 bonds that all mature 5, 10, or 20 years from now—you may have an emergency between now and then and need access to cash in a hurry. This liquidity risk—the risk that you will have a sudden need for cash—leads most buy-and-hold bond investors to pursue a strategy called *laddering*.

The idea behind laddering is really simple. A bond ladder is a set of bonds that has one bond maturing every year, every quarter, or maybe even every month. As one bond matures, you can use the cash from the bond if you need to, but you can also turn around and buy a new bond to replace it as well. If you always buy the same maturity of bond, then what you end up with is a self-replenishing set of bonds that generates a steady stream of cash. And you're always close to the maturity of one of your bonds, meaning that you'll have cash coming in if you need it.

Setting up a ladder of bonds is a little bit of a hassle at first, but once you build your ladder, it's easy to maintain. Suppose you want to build a bond ladder with 10-year bonds, so that each year one of the 10-year bonds matures. To set your ladder up, you can buy bonds with maturities equal to one year, two years, and so on up to 10 years. In the case of U.S. Treasury bonds, you can buy almost all of your bonds on the primary market. The Treasury offers one-year bills, and notes with maturities of 2, 3, 5, 7, and

10 years. So you would then need to go to the secondary market and buy Treasury bonds with maturities of 4, 6, 8, and 9 years to complete your set. Once you have the ladder in place, you only need to buy the new 10-year Treasury bond or bonds once each year. And of course, you can also add to your ladder using the interest payments you'll be collecting.

Speaking of what to do with the interest, one of the main risks of buy-and-hold bond investing is what economists call reinvestment risk. When you build your bond ladder, your bonds may pay an average interest rate of, say, 5% per year. Every 6 months, you'll get a set of coupons from your bonds and have to decide where to reinvest this money. But by the time you get the coupons, market interest rates may have fallen to, say, 4%. So you'll have to reinvest your interest at a lower rate, which will drag down the average rate of return on your total bond investment.

Reinvestment risk is usually more of an annoyance than a real risk of loss. And sometimes interest rates will rise, so this risk can work in your favor. But if interest rates fall dramatically, and stay there for long periods of time, then you may want to reevaluate whether you want to continue to reinvest your interest payments into bonds, and maybe you'll want to reconsider whether you want to continue with the entire bond ladder. Of course, that also depends on what your other investment opportunities are.

There are certainly other more serious risks to the buy-and-hold bond investor. And one of them is inflation. Bonds are often called *fixed-income securities* by investment professionals. In fact I think I hear the term *fixed income* more often than the word bonds when I talk to people who work with bonds for a living. The term *fixed income*, of course, comes from the fact that once you buy a bond, the income you earn from it is indeed fixed—it won't change. This means that the payments on a standard bond are especially vulnerable to inflation. If you are holding a bond with long maturity and inflation starts to rise, then the purchasing power of your investment will fall dramatically, by the time you collect your final payment. For example, the final payment on a 10-year bond will lose over a quarter of its purchasing power if inflation is 3% per year.

Fortunately, the bond laddering strategy helps to mitigate the damage that inflation can do to your bond portfolio. In general, the market interest rate on bonds will rise and fall with inflation. So if you are buying new bonds each year to replace maturing bonds in your ladder, then the interest rate on the new bond will be higher than the interest rate on the bond that it is replacing, if inflation is rising. This won't completely shield you from inflation, but it will help.

The other adjustment you can make to your bond ladder is to shorten the overall maturity of the ladder. The example I started with was a 10-year bond ladder, but this has a high vulnerability to inflation. If you change to a five-year bond ladder, so your maximum maturity is five years, then this will again help to minimize the loss of purchasing power on your bonds. If inflation rises and falls more gradually, then a five-year ladder could give adequate protection against inflation and still enable you to take advantage of higher rates that you can earn for lending over longer periods of time.

Of course, we've seen that the price level can fall as well as rise. If inflation is bad for the value of your bond portfolio, does this mean that deflation is good for it? Well, yes and no. It's true that if the price level falls, the purchasing power of the future payments on the bonds increases. But the problem is that deflation is incredibly damaging to business. Significant deflation leads firms into bankruptcy, because the prices they receive for their goods and services may fall below the costs of production. So if you are holding corporate bonds, the likelihood of default on these bonds increases dramatically.

But don't think that you're necessarily shielded from deflation-driven default risk if you are holding government bonds. Deflation is usually associated with recessions, and during recessions, government revenues at all levels decline. So deflation can also make it difficult for governments to make ends meet—so much so that they may also default. Now, it's true that nobody expects the U.S. government to ever default, and no U.S. state has defaulted on its bonds since the Great Depression. But every now and then, a local government or authority does default on its municipal bonds.

Deflation is not the only cause of default. And default risk is increased when you pursue a buy-and-hold investment strategy, because the longer you intend to hold any given bond, the greater your exposure to default risk. So we should discuss default risk in more detail; but, this is such an important issue that we should take our time and learn about it in a future lecture on bonds.

For now, let's review what we've learned. We made a good start on exploring the huge variety of bond investments that are available to you, and we learned that bond investing has become much more accessible, cheap, and convenient, thanks to the Internet. Hopefully, I've helped you realize that there is a very diverse set of bonds out there that nonetheless has a high degree of safety and competitive returns. If you shop carefully among the many options, you'll find the right set of bonds that fit your desired mix of safety and yield.

I focused on being a buy-and-hold bond investor in this lecture. If you're going to follow this strategy, you'll face increased default risk, inflation risk, and liquidity risk. You can shrink the default risk by holding U.S. Treasuries or other government bonds, and you can mitigate the effects of inflation and the liquidity risk as well by laddering your bonds.

If you follow these steps, then the biggest risk that you'll have to live with is probably reinvestment risk. That means that you'll always be looking for good opportunities to invest the coupon payments that you'll receive. Finding a good place to invest all that cash coming in—not a bad problem to have. Sometimes, boring looks pretty good.

Introduction to Mutual Funds
Lecture 5

In this lecture, you'll learn that mutual funds are one of several different types of pooled investments, or packages of instruments such as stocks and bonds. Mutual funds make stock and bond investing more convenient and affordable than buying and holding these instruments directly. For beginning investors, at least 2 types of pooled investments are worth considering: unit investment trusts and open-end mutual funds. Most of the lecture will be devoted to the most popular type of pooled investment, which is the open-end mutual fund.

Mutual Funds as Pooled Investments

- On the surface, **mutual funds** aren't very attractive investments because they're really nothing more than pools or packages of stocks, bonds, and perhaps other instruments. However, some people consider mutual funds to be the best starter investment because they offer a tremendous variety of products, low trading costs, and a high level of transparency.

- Mutual funds are just one type of investment from a broader category of pooled investments called collective investment schemes. In the United States, collective investment schemes are called registered investment companies by the SEC.

- Another type of collective investment scheme is a **unit investment trust**, which buys and then holds a fixed portfolio of assets. The portfolio could hold many types of securities, but usually the investments are stocks or bonds. The assets are held by a **trust**, which is a legal vehicle for holding property on behalf of someone. The trust divides the ownership of this large portfolio of assets into many small shares and sells these shares to the public—so it works like stock, in that respect. The shares are technically called redeemable trust certificates but are commonly called units.

- The holders of the units can sell them back to the trust at any time. The trust pays the holder of the unit the **net asset value (NAV)** of the unit, which is the market value of the portfolio on that day minus any liabilities of the fund divided by the total number of units. Unit investment trusts also have a set termination date on which the assets in the fund are liquidated and the proceeds of the sale are paid out to the shareholders.

- Unit investment trusts hold a static portfolio, which means that the assets in the portfolio don't change. Once the assets are purchased, they stay in the trust until they need to be sold off to pay off the unit holders, and no new assets are added. Unit investment trusts tend to be small, but they are still popular.

- The main difference between mutual funds and unit investment trusts is that mutual funds have dynamic portfolios, which means that the portfolios can and do change. Someone has to make these changes, and that job rests with a fund manager. The SEC refers to mutual funds as managed investment companies.

- An **open-end mutual fund** is always ready to issue new shares by selling them to investors and to redeem shares from investors. As with a unit investment trust, an open-end fund pays the holder of the shares the net asset value of the shares on the day they are sold. In fact, in the United States, the NAV is always determined by the market prices as of 4 pm Eastern time.

- The other type of mutual fund is called a **closed-end mutual fund**, which only issues shares once and doesn't redeem shares unless the entire fund is liquidated. Closed-end mutual fund shares are traded—just like stocks. In fact, shares in closed-end funds are usually traded on exchanges.

- Additionally, just like stocks, the shares of closed-end mutual funds can take on some fairly strange values. Closed-end fund shares tend to be above their net asset values when the shares are first issued, and then they tend to fall below their NAVs and stay there. Because of this, closed-end funds only make up a very small part of the mutual fund market.

Open-End Mutual Funds

- Open-end mutual funds are by far the most popular type of pooled investment. An open-end mutual fund is an actual company with shareholders and a board of directors. The mutual fund investors are the shareholders, and the board of directors hires a team of advisers, who are the ones that make the investment decisions for the mutual fund.

- The sole purpose of the mutual fund company is to hold the investments selected by the advisers. A separate company, called a sponsor, sets up the mutual fund, takes care of all the administrative details, and handles the task of selling and redeeming shares. Mutual fund sponsors can be stand-alone companies like Fidelity or Vanguard, or they can be other types of financial institutions as well—commercial banks like Wells Fargo or brokerage firms like Merrill Lynch.

Mutual funds divide a large pool of stocks or bonds into smaller chunks that individual investors can afford.

© Comstock/Thinkstock.

- Generally, you buy and redeem shares of a mutual fund directly through the sponsor, but some mutual funds also sell their shares through brokers and pay the broker a commission.

- To protect shareholders, the SEC places a large set of restrictions and requirements on open-end mutual funds. Most importantly, mutual funds are restricted to holding securities. Generally, they hold stocks, bonds, or a mixture of the 2 in their investment portfolios, and they also hold cash or other highly liquid assets.

- Mutual funds have a lot of restrictions on the concentrations of their portfolios; the tax laws for mutual funds require a minimum amount of diversification. In addition, open-end funds are prohibited from borrowing unless they set aside more than enough assets to cover the debt—approximately 2 to 3 times the amount borrowed.

- One of the most important requirements that the government imposes on mutual funds is that they issue detailed prospectuses to their investors. A **prospectus** is a document describing the objectives, operation, and risks of the mutual fund. It's the best source of information on the mutual fund for prospective investors.

- In 2009, the SEC simplified the format and language of the mutual fund prospectus that investment companies are required to distribute. Mutual funds are now allowed to distribute an abridged version of the prospectus, called the summary prospectus, that contains only the most essential information for investors.

Standard Sections in a Summary Prospectus

Investment Objectives and Primary Investment Strategies
- The investment objectives statement is the first thing the summary prospectus tells you, and it is a general statement about what the fund is trying to accomplish.

- The primary investment strategies is the third piece of information that the fund is required to list, and it's a more detailed statement about how the fund will actually go about reaching its investment objective.

- Both the investment objective and the primary investment strategy statements are legally binding on the mutual fund. In addition, a mutual fund can't change its objective or strategy without the approval of the shareholders. Together, these 2 statements give you most of the information about what the fund is going to do with your money.

- In the primary investment strategy section, you'll discover whether the fund is actively or passively managed. Actively managed funds buy and sell investments in an attempt to beat some kind of benchmark return or simply to earn the highest return possible. Passively managed funds buy and sell investments in order to match the return on some benchmark, such as the S&P 500 index, and are often called index funds for this reason.

- Another piece of information the fund must give you in the summary prospectus is a list of the fees the fund charges. One of the main fees that mutual funds charge are sales fees, which are also called **loads**. Some mutual funds charge a fee when you buy shares—usually a few percent of the value—called a front-end load. In addition, some funds also charge you a fee to redeem the shares, called a back-end load.

- Front-end and back-end loads directly reduce the value of your investment, which means that the managers need to earn even higher returns in order to make paying for the sales loads worthwhile.

- Since the early 1970s, investment companies have offered no-load mutual funds to American investors. In these mutual funds, you pay the net asset value and no more when you buy shares, and you receive the net asset value when you sell. There are hundreds of no-load funds, and they include both actively managed and passively managed funds.

- Unfortunately, managers of no-load mutual funds make up for the fact that there are no sales fees by deducting their expenses right from the value of your shares. The expenses that may be claimed and deducted include all the costs of operating the portfolio.

- Another type of expense that mutual funds are allowed to deduct from assets are 12b-1 fees, which are named after the SEC rule that allows firms to charge them. These expenses are associated with the costs of marketing and distributing the mutual fund. However, rather than being unhappy that these costs exist at all, you should be looking for funds that deliver the best performance relative to the fees they charge.

- Investment companies offer different classes of shares. Although every share in a mutual fund owns an equal fraction of the assets in the fund, they don't share the expenses of the fund equally. Most mutual funds divide the shares into several classes, and each class pays a different mixture of expenses.

- Different classes of shares may have different front-end and back-end loads and different expense ratios. In general, larger investments are eligible to be put into classes with lower overall expenses. Having different classes of shares is good for the investment companies because it gives them a way to incentivize investors to invest more and keep their money in the fund longer.

- You should plan to grow one or more of your mutual fund investments quickly so that you can move it into a favorable share class as soon as possible.

The Risk and Return of the Fund
- The next 2 pieces of information in the prospectus that appear after the fee table and the primary investment strategy are the risk and return of the fund. The mutual fund must describe the main reasons that the fund might lose money or not perform as well as the managers expect it to, and it has to tell you that the fund is not FDIC insured.

- Additionally, the fund must present the past 10 years of returns in a bar chart, and it has to present the average annual total returns over the most recent 1-year, 5-year, and 10-year periods. This, on the other hand, is specific enough to be very helpful as you make decisions.

- The remaining information in the prospectus is good to have, but it isn't extremely important. It includes the name of the fund advisory company as well as the name of the portfolio manager. Then, the fund must tell you about the tax consequences of any trades that it does, followed by a statement of whether the mutual fund company makes payments to brokers and other intermediaries.

Important Terms

closed-end mutual fund: A type of mutual fund that only issues shares once and doesn't redeem shares unless the entire fund is liquidated.

load: A sales fee that a mutual fund charges.

mutual fund: A package of stocks, bonds, and perhaps other instruments.

net asset value (NAV): The market value of a portfolio on a particular day minus any liabilities of the fund divided by the total number of units.

open-end mutual fund: A type of mutual fund that is always ready to issue new shares by selling them to investors and to redeem shares from investors.

prospectus: A document describing the objectives, operation, and risks of a mutual fund.

trust: A legal vehicle for holding property on behalf of someone.

unit investment trust: A type of collective investment scheme that buys and then holds a fixed portfolio of assets.

Suggested Reading

Bodie, Kane, and Marcus, *Essentials of Investments*, chap. 4.

Bogle, *Common Sense on Mutual Funds*, chaps. 4 and 5.

1. Go to the site of a mutual fund company such as Fidelity, Vanguard, or T. Rowe Price and find the summary prospectus of any mutual fund the company offers. Read the fund's investment objectives and primary investment strategies. Then, try to find a fund that seems as different as possible from the first one you picked—judging only by the names of the funds—and find the same information from its prospectus. Do the 2 funds really seem very different in terms of what they tell you about their investment objectives and strategies?

2. Suppose you are comparing 2 mutual funds you are interested in. You are currently comparing the returns each fund has earned during the past 10 years. One fund has earned returns of 12% during 3 years, but it also lost 5% during 3 years and earned returns of 4% during the other 4 years. The other fund earns a low but consistent return. How high would that low but consistent return need to be to convince you to buy that fund instead of the riskier one?

Introduction to Mutual Funds
Lecture 5—Transcript

For the last two lectures, we've been learning about the essential investments that belong in every investor's portfolio. We started with stocks, moved on to bonds, and now we'll learn about mutual funds. On the surface, mutual funds shouldn't be very attractive investments—after all, they're really nothing more than pools or packages of stocks, bonds, and perhaps some other instruments as well. Someone might look at a mutual fund and say, "All you've done is bought a bunch of assets and repackaged them to make them look different. Where's the value in that?"

Actually when we combine and repackage financial instruments in new ways, we're not just selling old wine in new bottles. These new combinations of assets take on characteristics that are fundamentally different from the characteristics of the individual assets that go into them. For example, we'll learn in a future lecture exactly how diversification works to literally reduce the amount of risk in a portfolio of assets. So the risk profile of a diversified mutual fund can be very different from the risk profiles of the individual assets in it. Investors value that ready-made diversification.

Repackaging assets in a mutual fund adds value in other ways as well. If I wanted to buy my own diversified portfolio of bonds or stocks, I'd need to have a ton of money saved up. But a mutual fund divides up a large pool of stocks or bonds into bite-sized chunks that even small investors can afford. So even if I only have $50 to invest, I can still buy into a globally diversified stock index or a pool of emerging-market bonds. So mutual funds give us access to all kinds of investments that we couldn't dream of holding otherwise.

And finally, repackaging takes advantage of economies of scale in management and advising. I suppose that if I wanted to, I could hire a money manager to look after my personal portfolio. But that would be somewhere between sort of expensive and absurdly expensive—it's probably not worth it unless I have a very large portfolio, and I don't. But if I pool my savings with thousands of other investors to buy millions of dollars worth of assets, we could hire a money manager to look after our portfolio, and hardly notice the cost.

So repackaging assets, and the payments that flow from them, really can add significant value for the economy. Mutual funds are a prime example of this. They make stock and bond investing more convenient and affordable than buying and holding these instruments directly. This benefits households, who get improved choice and safety in their investments. But it also benefits companies as well. They get improved access to the savings of households, which reduces their cost of borrowing and makes it possible to invest in more projects.

In case you haven't guessed already, we've finally found what I consider to be the best starter investment. In addition to the benefits I've just mentioned, mutual funds also offer a tremendous variety of products, low trading costs, and a high level of transparency. It's possible to be a very successful investor and never hold anything other than mutual funds—in fact, in these days of 401-Ks and other defined benefit retirement plans, it can actually be hard to hold anything other than mutual funds.

In this lecture, we'll learn that mutual funds are one of several types of pooled investments available to you. I'll explain how each of them works, so you can decide which ones are attractive to you. I'll devote most of the lecture, though, to the most popular type of pooled investment—the open-end mutual fund.

Pooled investments similar to mutual funds originated in the European markets as early as the 18th century, and they made it to the U.S. by the late 19th century. The modern mutual fund didn't take shape until the 1920s, and although the industry grew quickly in the 1960s, it really didn't come into its own until the '80s and '90s. Two forces have driven the growth in mutual funds. One of them is the rise in the value of the financial markets, especially the stock market, which attracts new funds and managers, as well as investors. The U.S. stock market started on a long-term upward trend in the early '80s and only had one longer-term downturn before the year 2000. That in itself attracted lots of money into mutual funds.

The other force was a change in pensions that took place beginning in the 1980s and accelerated through the 1990s. Companies replaced their defined benefit pension plans with defined contribution plans. Instead of being promised a fixed salary after retirement, which is what a traditional pension delivers, employees were switched to saving plans.

The saving plans are called defined contribution plans, because employees typically set aside a fixed proportion of their wages, like 5%, or a set dollar amount, which is then invested into various instruments, usually mutual funds. These defined contribution plans, of course, are the 401-K, 403-B, individual retirement accounts (or IRAs), and various other plans that we all know about today.

Just to give you an indication of how dramatically the defined contribution retirement plans have changed the financial markets, the share of Americans who owned stocks before 1990 was less than one quarter of the population. But by the year 2000, over half of Americans owned stocks. Much of that increase was driven by the switch to defined contribution retirement plans and investments in mutual funds.

I've been using the term *mutual fund* as if it were a generic term that includes all pooled investments. Actually, mutual funds are just one type of investment from a broader category of pooled investments called collective investment schemes. In the United States, the SEC calls collective investment schemes *registered investment companies*.

I want to tell you about at least one other type of collective investment scheme, because it does exist in the United States, and in many countries it is a much more common investment tool. In addition, this other scheme is simpler than a mutual fund, and I want to use this simpler structure to explain some of the basics about how most kinds of collective investment schemes work. This other type of investment scheme is called the *unit investment trust*.

A unit investment trust buys and then holds a fixed portfolio of assets. The portfolio could hold many types of securities, but usually the investments are stocks or bonds. The assets are held by a trust, which is a legal vehicle for holding property on behalf of someone. The trust divides the ownership of this big portfolio of assets into many small shares and then sells these shares to the public—so it works like stock, in that respect. The shares are technically called redeemable trust certificates, but are commonly called "units," hence the name unit investment trust.

As the word redeemable suggests, the holders of the trust certificates, or units, can sell them back to the trust at any time. The trust pays the holder of the unit the net asset value, or NAV, of the unit, which is basically the market value of the portfolio on that day minus any liabilities of the fund, divided by the total number of units. Unit investment trusts also have a set termination date, on which the assets in the fund are liquidated and the proceeds of the sale are paid out to the shareholders.

Unit investment trusts hold what we call a static portfolio—which means that the assets in the portfolio don't change. Once the assets are purchased, they stay in the trust until they need to be sold off to pay off the unit holders, and no new assets are added. Some people also say that unit investment trusts are unmanaged, by which they mean that nobody tinkers with or manages the portfolio. But unit investment trusts are managed, in the sense that a trustee looks after them and takes care of redemptions and so on. So I prefer to use the term *static* or *fixed* portfolio to characterize unit investment trusts.

In the United States unit investment trusts only held about $51 billion in total assets in 2010—which is a drop in the bucket, compared to the $13.1 trillion in total assets held in all registered investment companies that year. But there were almost 6000 different unit investment trusts, which is over a third of the total number of registered investment companies. So unit investment trusts tend to be small, but they are still popular.

Now we can move on to mutual funds. The big difference between mutual funds and unit investment trusts is that mutual funds have dynamic portfolios, which means that the portfolios can and do change. Someone has to make these changes, and that job rests with a fund manager. So the SEC uses the term *managed investment company* to describe a mutual fund. Again, though, the word "managed" can be a bit misleading and I'd rather use this idea of a dynamic or changing portfolio to distinguish mutual funds from unit investment trusts.

There are actually two different types of mutual funds that you need to be aware of. One type is called an open-end mutual fund, and this is the type that most people have in mind when they use the term mutual fund. An open-end fund is always ready to issue new shares by selling them to investors, and it's always ready to redeem shares from investors. As with a unit investment trust, an open-end fund pays the holder of the shares the net asset value, or NAV, of the shares on the day they are sold.

In fact, in the United States the NAV is always determined by the market prices as of 4:00 pm Eastern time. So effectively, you can only buy or sell shares in your mutual fund at the end of the day. If I want to buy shares on Tuesday morning, I have to pay the NAV per share as of the end of the day on Tuesday. If I submit my order after 4:00 pm, then the price I'll get is the NAV at 4:00 pm on the next trading day.

There was actually a scandal at a handful of mutual funds back in 2003 in which some big traders were allowed to buy and sell mutual funds after 4:00 pm, say at 8:00 am the next morning, but they got the 4:00 pm price from the previous day. Naturally, that gave these traders an unfair advantage over everyone else, because they got to see more information that came in overnight that might have influenced how the markets performed the next day.

You probably guessed the other type of mutual fund is called a closed-end fund. A closed-end fund is really different from an open-end fund. Closed-end funds only issue shares once, and they don't redeem shares unless the entire fund is liquidated.

Buying a share in a closed-end mutual fund is like buying a share of stock in a company whose sole purpose is to hold and manage a portfolio of assets. In addition, you know that this company will never issue any more shares. If you want to cash out your investment, then you'll have to find another investor to sell your shares to. In other words, closed-end mutual fund shares are traded, just like stocks. In fact, shares in closed-end funds are usually traded on exchanges.

And this means that, just like stocks, the shares of closed-end mutual funds can take on some fairly strange values. We can calculate the NAV for closed-end mutual funds just like we do for unit trusts and open-end mutual funds. And you'd think that the price of a share in a closed-end fund should be pretty darn close to its NAV. Well, guess again. The prices of shares in closed-end mutual funds leave most researchers—and investors—scratching their heads. Closed-end fund shares tend to be above their NAV when the shares are first issued, and then they tend to fall below NAV and stay there afterwards. Because of these reasons, closed-end funds only make up a very small part of the mutual fund market—just a few percent of the total.

Closed-end funds have experienced some popularity despite the puzzling behavior of their share prices, because they traditionally offered focused investments in industries like energy, or in certain geographical regions like Latin America. They're also very popular for municipal bonds. But other less-puzzling investments like open-end mutual funds have increased their offerings of focused investments, so there really isn't a compelling reason for most investors to use closed-end funds. And so my advice for beginning investors is to leave them alone.

We've delved into the different types of collective investment schemes, and now we can focus on open-end mutual funds. As I mentioned at the beginning of the lecture, open-end mutual funds are by far the most popular type of pooled investment. At the end of 2010, there were over 8500 open-end mutual funds holding over $11.8 trillion of assets. They held nearly one quarter of all U.S. corporate equity and at least 10% of each major category of bonds.

An open end mutual fund is an actual company, with shareholders and a board of directors. The mutual fund investors are the shareholders, naturally, and so if you hold mutual fund shares, you will occasionally get ballots so that you can vote in company elections. The board of directors of the mutual fund hires a team of advisers, who are the ones who make the investment decisions for the mutual fund.

The sole purpose of the mutual fund company is to hold the investments selected by the advisers. A separate company, called a sponsor, actually sets up the mutual fund, takes care of all the administrative details, and handles the task of selling and redeeming shares. Mutual fund sponsors can be stand-alone companies, like Fidelity or Vanguard, or they can be other types of financial institutions as well—commercial banks like Wells Fargo or brokerage firms like Merrill Lynch.

Generally, you buy and redeem shares of a mutual fund directly through the sponsor. In other words, if you want to buy shares in one of Fidelity's mutual funds, you have to set up an account directly with Fidelity. But some mutual funds also sell their shares through brokers and pay the broker a commission.

To protect shareholders, the SEC places a big set of restrictions and requirements on open-end mutual funds. The ones that are most important for you to be aware of are the restrictions on the assets that mutual funds can hold. Mutual funds are restricted to holding securities, so you won't find open-end mutual funds that hold commodities or other real assets. Generally, they hold stocks, bonds, or a mixture of the two in their investment portfolios, and of course they also hold cash or other highly liquid assets in order to meet demands for share redemptions. Mutual funds are required to hold 85% of their investments in liquid assets that can be sold for their full value within seven days.

Mutual funds have a lot of restrictions on the concentrations of their portfolios—the tax laws for mutual funds actually require a minimum amount of diversification. Most mutual funds must hold securities from at least 12 different issuers. And that's really just a lower bound.

Mutual funds can elect to call themselves diversified, and if they do, they're not allowed to invest more than 5% of their portfolio in any one security. In addition, diversified mutual funds are not allowed to hold more than 10% of the total amount of any issuer's voting securities. As a result of these regulations, mutual funds tend to be very well diversified. The median number of different companies held by stock mutual funds in 2010, for example, was 101.

Mutual funds are also highly restricted in terms of taking on leverage. Basically, open-end funds are prohibited from borrowing unless they set aside more than enough assets to cover the debt—we're talking two to three times the amount borrowed. This tends to seriously discourage mutual fund borrowing, which is good news for investors. You can be confident that there isn't some kind of leverage time bomb in your mutual fund waiting to go off. Similarly, mutual funds aren't allowed to do any kind of short selling or buying on margin.

They are permitted to hold derivatives, however. But because some mutual funds have been using derivatives in a way that effectively mimics the use of leverage, the SEC will probably narrow and refine the approved uses of derivatives in mutual funds over time. Like the restrictions on leverage, this is a good development for investors.

One of the more important requirements that the government imposes on mutual funds is that they issue detailed prospectuses to their investors. A prospectus is a document describing the objectives, operation, and risks of the mutual fund. It's really the best source of information on the mutual fund for prospective investors, so it's crucial that you read the prospectus before you invest in any mutual fund. And after you've invested you should review the prospectus annually.

Fortunately, in 2009 the SEC simplified the format and the language of the mutual fund prospectus that investment companies are required to distribute. Mutual funds are now allowed to distribute an abridged version of the prospectus, called the summary prospectus, which contains only the most essential information for investors. The big advantage of the summary prospectus is that all of the most important information is included, in a standard order, which enables you to compare information between mutual funds very easily. The only drawback is that some very useful information is only found in the full prospectus, which you'll have to look up online or request from the investment company.

Now, what I'd like to do next is highlight some of the standard sections in a summary prospectus and tell you why each of these sections should matter to you as a potential mutual-fund investor.

Let's start with the fund's investment objectives and primary investment strategies. The investment objectives statement is the first thing the summary prospectus tells you. This is a general statement about what the fund is trying to accomplish. The primary investment strategies is the third piece of information that the fund is required to list, and it's a more detailed statement about how the fund will actually go about reaching its investment objective.

Both the investment objective and the primary investment strategy statements are legally binding on the mutual fund—they actually have to do what they promise in these statements. In addition, a mutual fund can't change its objective or strategy without the approval of the shareholders. Together, these two statements give you most of the information about what the fund is going to do with your money.

Why should you care about this? Well, these statements really help you tell different mutual funds apart. For example, one fund's investment objectives might tell you that its managers invest in companies with high growth potential. Meanwhile, another fund's objective may be to invest in companies that pay high and stable dividends. These are very different investing strategies.

Another thing you'll find in the primary investment strategy section is whether the fund is actively or passively managed. Actively managed funds buy and sell investments in an attempt to beat some kind of benchmark return, or simply to earn the highest return possible. Passively managed funds, on the other hand, buy and sell investments in order to match the return on some benchmark, such as the S&P 500 index. Passively managed mutual funds are often called index funds for this reason, because the benchmark returns are almost always the return on some index.

You may be wondering, why do index funds need to be managed? Don't the organizers of the funds buy all the assets in the index, and that's that? Well, the assets in the indices do actually change. The firms in the S&P 500, for example, are selected by a committee, and every so often the committee drops a company or two from the index and replaces them with other companies. When that happens, passive mutual fund managers have to sell their shares in the outgoing companies and buy shares in the incoming companies. In any case, choosing an actively or a passively managed fund depends on your beliefs about how efficient the markets are. There's a lot more to learn about the choice between active and passively managed funds, and we'll get into more details a bit later in the course.

Another piece of information the fund must give you in the summary prospectus is a list of the fees the fund charges. As I mentioned in my lecture on stocks, whenever you invest in something, you're going to have to pay some kind of transaction cost. Mutual funds aren't any different from other investments in this respect. But some of these transaction costs are hard to understand. I want to make sure that you are aware of all these different costs, so you can choose carefully.

One of the main fees that mutual funds charge is the sales fee, also called a load. Some mutual funds charge a fee when you buy shares, usually a few percent of the value, called a front-end load. In addition, some funds also charge you a fee to redeem the shares, called a back-end load.

Back-end loads do two things—they earn money for the management and operation of the fund, and they give investors an incentive to leave the money in for longer periods of time. That gives the managers more breathing room to pursue their investment plans. In many cases, mutual funds that charge back-end loads will reduce the loads the longer you wait to redeem the shares. When this is the case, the back-end loads tend to start high, say about 5 or 6%, and then decline by something like 1% per year.

There's nothing intrinsically wrong with front-end and back-end loads. But they do directly reduce the value of your investment, which means that the managers need to earn even higher returns in order to make paying for all these sales loads worthwhile. All I can say on that score is that some funds are worth it, and some aren't.

Since the early 1970s, though, investment companies have offered no-load mutual funds to American investors. In these mutual funds, you pay the net asset value and no more when you buy shares, and you receive the net asset value when you sell. These days, there are hundreds of no-load funds, and they include both actively managed and passively managed mutual funds.

Hopefully, this idea makes you a little skeptical. If the funds don't charge sales fees, then they must make up the money somewhere, since it takes a lot of resources to run a mutual fund and manage the portfolio. You're right. And the way that fund managers make a living is to deduct their expenses right from the value of your shares.

The expenses that may be claimed and deducted include all the costs of operating the portfolio, in other words, things like paying the fund manager. Expenses typically run from 0.2% to 2% of assets, so it's a nontrivial charge that can seriously reduce your returns if the expenses are high enough.

One more type of expense that mutual funds are allowed to deduct from assets is the so-called 12B-1 fee. These fees are named after the SEC rule that allows firms to charge them. These expenses are associated with the costs of marketing and distributing the mutual fund—things like advertising, printing the prospectuses, and paying commissions to brokers who sell the funds to investors.

A lot of investors are unhappy about this rule, since they don't want to have to pay the marketing costs of funds that they've already bought. But on the other hand, the expenses are limited to 1% of assets in the fund. Also, part of the price of every product goes to cover the producer's marketing costs.

And finally, if the fund can't attract enough investors, it will have to liquidate, be folded into another fund, or otherwise cease to exist. So rather than be unhappy that these costs exist at all, you should be looking for funds that deliver the best performance relative to the fees they do charge.

Sales loads and expenses are confusing enough, but investment companies make your choice even more complicated by offering different classes of shares. Although every share in a mutual fund owns an equal fraction of the assets in the fund, they don't share the expenses of the fund equally. Most mutual funds divide up the shares into several classes, and each class pays a different mixture of expenses.

Different classes of shares may have different front-end and back-end loads, and different expense ratios. Generally speaking, larger investments are eligible to be put into classes with lower overall expenses.

Share classes go by different names, and many funds just use alphabet names like class A, B, C, and so on. But other firms get creative. For example, Vanguard uses designations like Admiral class shares to denote share classes that pay lower expenses.

Having different classes of shares is good for the investment companies, because it gives them a way to incentivize investors to invest more and keep their money in the fund longer. For example, many mutual funds with sales loads will move your shares into classes with lower sales loads if you leave the money in the fund long enough. Similarly, if your investment in a no-load mutual fund grows to a high enough value, the company can move your shares into a class with lower expenses.

Some 401-K plans offered by big companies are able to negotiate favorable deals with mutual fund companies so that all the employees of the company are able to buy mutual fund shares in the classes with the lowest expenses, even though their individual investments are very small. This is something worth looking for if you're participating in a 401-K plan at work.

Another possibility is to plan to grow one or more of your mutual fund investments quickly, so that you can move it into a favorable share class as soon as possible. For example, if you are a passive mutual fund investor and you are planning to hold a global stock index fund as one of your main investments, it might be worthwhile to focus your investing into this global stock index fund so that it qualifies for the higher share class. The savings from the reduced expenses, accumulated over decades, can be significant. And if the investment is in a well-diversified mutual fund, you really aren't putting all your eggs in one basket.

The next two pieces of information in the prospectus that appear after the fee table and the primary investment strategy are the risk and return of the fund. Unfortunately, the discussion of risk probably won't be very specific or enlightening. The mutual fund must describe the main reasons for why the fund might lose money or not perform as well as the managers expect it to, and it has to tell you that the fund is not FDIC insured. This information is worth knowing, but in a future lecture I'll tell you about the risk you really want to know, and how to measure it.

As far as returns go, the fund must present the past 10 years of returns in a bar chart, and it has to present the average annual total returns over the most recent 1-, 5-, and 10-year periods. This, on the other hand, is specific enough to be very helpful as you make choices. In particular, look at the last 10 years of returns to see how consistent the fund has been at earning good returns. A mutual fund that delivers a 4% return year in and year out is going to look a lot different than a fund that earns a 10% return one year and loses 2% the next.

The remaining information in the prospectus is good to have, but it isn't nearly as important as the information we've already highlighted. It includes the name of the fund advisory company as well as the name of the actual portfolio manager. Then the fund must tell you about the tax consequences of any trades that it does, followed by a statement of whether the mutual fund company makes payments like commissions to brokers and other intermediaries.

That wraps up the prospectus, and it's time to wrap up this lecture as well. We've learned that there are several types of pooled investments to choose from, and at least two of them are worth considering for the beginning investor—unit investment trusts and open-end mutual funds.

We've also learned that, thanks to all the rules that mutual funds have to comply with, what you see is what you get. That's great, but it means that the burden is on you to look at the prospectus and see what the mutual fund is actually offering you. If you get in the habit of doing this, then it will be much easier to tell the thousands of investments apart and pick the right mutual funds for you. We'll have a lot more to say about that in a future lecture.

What Are Exchange-Traded Funds?
Lecture 6

In this lecture, you will learn how exchange-traded funds (ETFs) differ from mutual funds and how that gives them certain advantages over other investments. ETFs are especially attractive to investors who are making taxable investments and to investors who are looking for a broader set of investment opportunities than they can find in standard mutual funds. ETFs also come with a different set of potential risks, but the low cost and tax efficiency of ETFs make them great candidates for long-term buy-and-hold investments.

Exchange-Traded Funds

- In addition to stocks, bonds, and mutual funds, there's another investment that you need to be familiar with: **exchange-traded funds (ETFs)**, a relative newcomer to the world of investing. Even though this investment does share some of the features of mutual funds, it's completely different.

- The first ETF was introduced in 1993, and this type of investment has grown at an astonishing rate since then, making them the second largest type of pooled investment after open-end mutual funds. There are about 1000 different ETFs in the market, investing in stocks, bonds, commodities, currencies, and even futures contracts. Some people think that ETFs will eventually overtake standard open-end mutual funds as the most popular pooled investment.

- As the name suggests, exchange-traded funds combine some of the features of mutual funds with some of the features of individual stocks. The main feature they take from stocks is being listed and traded on an exchange.

- **Depository receipts** have been around for a long time, and until ETFs were created, the most common use for depository receipts was in trading shares of foreign stocks. The structure of a depository receipt is simple: Somebody deposits an asset in a specialized bank that offers depository services. The asset stays in the depository, but the bank issues receipts—documents proving ownership of these assets—to the original depositor of the assets.

- The depositor can hold the receipts, of course, but the real reason to make this transaction is for the depositor to sell these receipts to other investors. Whoever holds the receipts are the legal owners of the assets. Depository receipts look and feel just like shares of stock—and they're traded just like stocks.

- Depository receipts are convenient for a few reasons: They are priced in local currency, so they make it easy to trade foreign assets outside their home country, and they allow the original depositor to divide the value of the deposited asset any way he or she wishes, which enables the depositor to choose a size for the depository receipt that will make it attractive to small investors.

ETFs versus Mutual Funds

- Relative to mutual funds, the main source of attraction for ETFs is trading. ETFs can be traded at any time the markets are open, which is all the time (as a result of the Internet), instead of only at 4 pm Eastern time, which is the only time you can buy or sell mutual funds. An even bigger reason to like the flexible trading of ETFs is taxes; ETFs give you much more flexibility when it comes to incurring taxable income or capital gains.

- The U.S. tax code taxes the capital gains that investors make on their investments. A **short-term capital gain** is a trading profit that you make on an investment that you've held for 1 year or less. Short-term capital gains are taxed as ordinary income, so your rate depends on your marginal tax bracket.

- On the other hand, **long-term capital gains** are trading profits you make on investments you've held for longer than 1 year. Long-term capital gains are taxed at a rate that is generally much lower than the income tax rate.

- Because you choose when you're going to sell an ETF, you get to determine whether you make a short-term capital gain or a long-term capital gain. Additionally, you can choose which year you want to realize any capital gains on your ETF shares.

- Many investors don't realize that if you hold open-end mutual funds as a taxable investment, you will almost certainly owe capital gains taxes—courtesy of your mutual fund manager.

- Most open-end mutual fund companies don't pay taxes—which is good because it keeps expenses low—but, unfortunately, they pass all the dividend income and capital gains on to the investors. With this system, even if your mutual fund loses value during the year, you still might have to pay capital gains taxes.

- If you are going to hold open-end mutual funds in a taxable account, you need to pay attention to the turnover rate of the mutual funds you're considering. The **turnover rate** is the fraction of the total value of the mutual fund that the portfolio manager trades, or turns over, during the year. The higher the turnover rate, the more capital gains the shares are likely to report at the end of the year, so try to look for funds with lower turnover rates.

- There's a big difference between mutual funds and ETFs in terms of when you have to pay capital gains taxes. Because of the flexibility that ETFs offer, people say that ETFs are tax efficient relative to open-end mutual funds. This tax efficiency doesn't matter if you are talking about tax-deferred investments, such as IRAs and 401(k)s. In these cases, you don't pay any taxes until you withdraw money, so there's really no tax difference between having an open-end mutual fund or an ETF in your IRA.

- Another advantage of ETFs over mutual funds is that they generally have lower expenses and higher returns than identical mutual funds would. ETFs pay far fewer brokerage fees than mutual funds because technically the ETF isn't buying the assets that get put into the depository—some very wealthy investor is.

- Furthermore, mutual fund companies have to maintain individual accounts for their shareholders, but people hold ETF shares in their brokerage accounts, so there's no record keeping or account maintenance for ETFs, which also cuts down on expenses.

- Additionally, mutual funds always have to have some amount of cash on hand so that they can cash out investors who want to sell their shares on any given day. They try to minimize the amount they need, but holding cash necessarily delivers a lower expected return than the rest of the assets the mutual fund holds. By contrast, ETFs don't redeem shares. You cash out your ETF shares by selling them to another investor at their current market price—just as you would a share of stock.

- A final advantage of ETFs is that ETFs invest where open-end mutual funds either cannot go or don't go in as much depth. Also, because ETFs were limited to indexes for the first 15 years of their existence, they specialized in global, regional, and even country-by-country indexes. ETFs generally offer more opportunities to invest in foreign stock indexes than mutual funds do.

Disadvantages of ETFs
- The first potential drawback of ETFs is trading costs. Although you're free to trade ETFs at any time, trading isn't free. You'll have to pay commissions similar to those you pay for trading stocks, and the more you trade, the more these commissions will pile up and lower your return from investing in ETFs. Investors have to find some happy medium between not trading at all and trading too much.

- The next potential drawback of ETFs is their pricing. ETFs represent a particular pool of assets that is held by some depository, and the price of each ETF share should reflect the market value of the underlying pool of assets. The correspondence between the price of the ETF and the market price of the underlying assets is enforced by a process known as arbitrage.

- Although the price of a depository receipt could differ from the market value of the underlying assets, arbitrage should drive the prices together. For example, consider an ETF that invests in an equity index made up of the BRIC country stocks—that is,

The ticker symbol for one of the largest exchange-traded funds is GLD, which stands for gold.

the stocks of Brazil, Russia, India, and China. If there's a sudden surge of demand for ETF shares in this BRIC equity index, then the demand could temporarily outstrip supply, sending the price of ETF shares up. The price of the ETF shares could potentially rise above the index value.

- However, if this happens, then the process of arbitrage should come to the rescue. Other traders would notice that the ETF shares are more expensive than the index shares, and they would step into the market. They would buy the shares of the stocks that make up the BRIC index, deposit these shares with the ETF depository, and then take the depository receipts from the depository and sell them to the ETF investors.

- This increase in demand for the shares would drive up the prices of the shares in the BRIC index, sending the BRIC index up in value. Additionally, this increase in supply of the depository receipts or ETF shares would make the price of the ETF shares decline. Ideally, the prices of both the underlying stock shares and the ETF shares would change quickly and enable them to meet in the middle, and the prices would agree again.

- Even though the process of arbitrage generally works very well in financial markets, occasionally it will fail and allow the price of the ETF shares to differ significantly from the value of the underlying assets held in the depository—meaning that you run the risk of selling for less than full value when it comes time to sell or buying for more than the true value when you buy. For an open-end mutual fund, this is not an issue because they only buy and sell shares at the net asset value, which is based on the fair market value of their holdings.

- The next potential disadvantage of ETFs is leverage. The SEC doesn't allow open-end mutual funds to take on much leverage, but it does allow ETFs to use derivatives to effectively leverage up their portfolios through a process of financial engineering. ETFs that pursue this investment strategy usually promise to deliver 2 or 3 times the gains (or the losses) on some underlying index, such as the Dow Jones index.

- Fortunately, these ETFs always identify themselves as leveraged ETFs. In addition, ETFs are required to reveal the entire list of assets that they hold on a daily basis, so you can see whether they are in fact using financial engineering. In general, beginning investors should stay away from leveraged ETFs.

- One final potential disadvantage of ETFs is taxes, depending on the type of ETF that you buy. Although it's true that most ETFs will be more tax efficient than mutual funds, ETFs that hold alternative investments, such as commodities, still have tax issues. If you want to invest in an alternative-asset ETF—that is, one that isn't investing in stocks or bonds—then you should seek some advice about the tax consequences first.

Important Terms

depository receipt: A document that proves ownership of an asset that is in a bank's depository and is issued to the original depositor of the asset by the bank.

exchange-traded fund (ETF): A fund that combines some of the features of mutual funds with some of the features of individual stocks, including being listed and traded on an exchange.

long-term capital gain: A trading profit that you make on an investment that you've held for longer than 1 year.

short-term capital gain: A trading profit that you make on an investment that you've held for 1 year or less.

turnover rate: The fraction of the total value of a mutual fund that a portfolio manager trades, or turns over, during a year.

Suggested Reading

Malkiel, "Investors Shouldn't Fear 'Spiders.'"

Motley Fool Staff, "Exchange-Traded Funds."

U.S. Securities and Exchange Commission, "Exchange-Traded Funds (ETFs)."

Questions to Consider

1. Because ETFs are traded on exchanges, they have ticker symbols just like stocks do. Go to a free website that gives information about stocks and find a BRIC index ETF, such as the iShares MSCI BRIC Index Fund. You should be able to enter "BRIC" into the website's search window and find several ETFs. Find the ticker symbol for one of these ETFs and use it to look up the ETF. What exactly does the ETF invest in? What is the current price of the ETF, and what is the return on this ETF so far this year?

2. One of the drawbacks of ETFs is the commissions, or trading fees, associated with buying and selling ETF shares. However, some online brokerages offer commission-free ETFs. Go to one of the online brokers that offers commission-free ETFs and look at their offerings. Do you find the selection of commission-free ETFs offered by this broker

attractive? Which ones would you consider investing in if you were investing for a taxable investment account?

What Are Exchange-Traded Funds?

Lecture 6—Transcript

In the previous lecture, we learned about mutual funds, and I talked about how these products are the perfect starter investment. You might think, then, that our basic set of essential investments is complete—stocks, bonds, and mutual funds. But wait—there's one more investment that you really need to be familiar with. It's a relative newcomer to the world of investing, and you may not even know it exists. Or you may have mistaken this investment for an ordinary mutual fund. But even though this investment does share some of the features of mutual funds, it's a different character altogether. The general name of this investment is an exchange-traded fund, but people mostly call it by its initials, ETF.

To give you some idea of how different ETFs are from mutual funds, consider one of the largest ETFs. Its ticker symbol is GLD—which, as you might guess, stands for gold. For the price of a share in this fund—which is only a fraction of the price of an ounce of gold—the average investor can invest in gold bullion without any of the hassles of storage or the big transactions costs and commissions associated with buying gold coins or bars.

If you remember my previous lecture, where I discussed the regulations on mutual fund portfolios, you'll realize that there's no way a standard, open-end mutual fund can invest in gold bullion. So ETFs really are quite different from open-end mutual funds.

People like these differences, judging by their incredible rise in popularity over the years. The first ETF was introduced in 1993, and this type of investment has grown at an astonishing rate since then. Here's a chart I made that shows the total assets held by ETFs from 1995 through 2010. Notice that ETFs come from out of nowhere—just $1 billion in 1995—and by 2010 they are just a hair short of $1 trillion in total assets. That makes them the second largest type of pooled investment, after open-end mutual funds.

There are about 1000 different ETFs in the market these days, investing in stocks, bonds, commodities, currencies, and even futures contracts. And there are lots more to come. Some people even think that eventually,

ETFs will overtake standard open-end mutual funds as the most popular pooled investment.

I'm not sure about when that would happen, if ever, but one thing I do know is that there are some very good reasons for investing in ETFs in addition to, or even in place of, other instruments like mutual funds. In this lecture, we'll learn about exactly how ETFs differ from mutual funds, and we'll see how that gives them certain advantages over other investments. We'll see that ETFs are especially attractive to investors who are making taxable investments, and to investors who are looking for a broader set of investment opportunities than they can find in standard mutual funds. Of course, ETFs also come with a different set of potential risks, and we'll learn about what those are as well. But by the end of the lecture, you may find yourself agreeing that ETFs are part of your investing future.

As the name suggests, exchange traded funds combine some of the features of mutual funds with some of the features of individual stocks. The main feature they take from stocks is being listed and traded on an exchange. To understand how ETFs work, I should start by telling you about a related instrument called a depository receipt.

Depository receipts have been around for a long time, and until ETFs were created, the most common use for depository receipts was in trading shares of foreign stocks. The structure of a depository receipt is simple, and it basically works like its name suggests. Somebody deposits an asset, like a share of stock in the Japanese company Canon, Inc., into a specialized bank that offers depository services. The asset stays in the depository, but the bank issues receipts—documents proving ownership of these assets—to the original depositor of the assets.

The depositor can hold the receipts, of course, but the real reason to make this transaction is for the depositor to sell these receipts to other investors. Whoever holds the receipts, of course, are the legal owners of the assets. So the depository receipts look and feel just like shares of stock—and they're traded just like stocks. Depository receipts are listed on stock exchanges and you can buy, hold, and trade them in the same ways that I described in my previous lecture on stocks.

Why do investors go through all this? Depository receipts are convenient for a couple of reasons. One is that they're priced in local currency. In our example, the Canon shares are actually priced in Yen, the currency used in Japan where the shares are issued. But the depository receipts are going to be traded in the United States, so they will be priced in U.S. dollars. That's much easier to deal with. So depository receipts make it easy to trade foreign assets outside their home country.

The other convenient feature of depository receipts is that they can divide up the value of the deposited asset any way that the original depositor wishes. This enables the depositor to choose a size for the depository receipt that will make it very attractive to small investors. For example, let's go back to our gold ETF example. Did you know that the standard size of a bar of gold bullion is a petite 400 ounces? And with gold priced in the multiple hundreds of dollars per ounce, a single bar is pretty expensive. But suppose I take a 400-ounce gold bar and put it in a depository and have the depository issue receipts that are each good for one tenth of an ounce of gold. Now I have 4000 depository receipts that individual investors can afford—and they'll want to buy these depository receipts from me instead of having the hassle and expense of seeing a coin dealer and storing the gold themselves.

So depository receipts are a great way to convert a foreign asset, or a very expensive asset, into a form that is convenient and attractive for trading by all investors, even individuals. Back in the early 1990s, executives at the American Stock Exchange made that connection, and basically created an investment company that issued depository receipts against the S&P 500 index.

The investment company literally bought multiple sets of all 500 shares that make up this index, placed them in a depository, and then issued depository receipts against these shares. This was simply called Standard and Poor's Depository Receipts. The ticker symbol used was SPY, but the acronym based on its initials was SPDR, so the investment came to be known as spiders.

The spiders took off immediately. And in finance, whenever somebody has a successful idea, it's almost immediately copied. So the race to create ETFs was on. My favorite imitation was the creation of ETFs that held foreign stock indexes. These were called World Equity Benchmark shares, or WEBs for short. So first came the spiders, and then came the webs!

Now, the first generation of ETFs—and the vast majority of ETFs that exist today—are still investment companies registered with the SEC under the same law that governs the operation of open-end mutual funds. ETFs get a special exemption from the SEC that allows them as investment companies to issue depository receipts. The SEC granted this exemption, but imposed an additional condition on ETFs that they could only offer passively managed, indexed products. This restriction remained in place until 2008.

Actively managed ETFs have been in the market ever since that time. They potentially offer the best of both the mutual fund and the stock worlds. On the one hand, you get the possibility of buying shares in a diversified fund run by an expert asset manager who may generate above-market returns. But you can also trade your shares in this fund at any time, just like a stock. The details of actively managed ETFs are a bit trickier, because the fund's assets may be changing at the exact time that you're buying and selling the shares in the fund. This requires some extra caution and effort on the part of investors to make sure that they know what is actually in the fund, especially when they're about to buy shares.

Over the years, as people have become more creative with ETFs, and the SEC has also become more comfortable with them as well, new types of ETFs have been created that are not actually investment companies. For example, all the ETFs that hold physical commodities are not technically investment companies and are not regulated under the Investment Company Act of 1940. But they are still regulated by the SEC under its other main law, the Securities Exchange Act of 1933.

In addition, some ETFs also invest in futures contracts of various kinds. These ETFs are actually regulated by the Commodity Futures Trading Commission, or CFTC. All ETFs that are available to individual investors are regulated in ways that try to protect the interests of individual investors. That's the good news. The only bad news is that the regulations that ETFs must follow do differ, depending on what they hold. I'll come back to a few of the most important differences later on.

So what's the main source of attraction for ETFs, relative to mutual funds? Well, I've actually mentioned it already: trading. You probably remember from the previous lecture that you can only buy or sell mutual funds one time per day, generally at 4:00 pm Eastern time. But ETFs can be traded any time the markets are open, which you may have realized is all the time. In addition to the standard opening hours of major exchanges, there's a thriving after-hours trading market on the Internet that never closes.

This ability to trade ETFs at any time comes as a big relief to some investors, who worry about being locked into once-a-day trading of mutual funds. For example, suppose you get news early in the morning that may disturb the markets—like the outbreak of a war, or a market crash on the Shanghai exchange overnight. If you're holding mutual funds, you can place your order to sell shares of your funds, but you'll get the 4:00 pm price, which will probably fully reflect the bad news. On the other hand, if you're holding ETFs, you may be able to sell your shares before the bad news drives their price down by nearly as much. Of course, this example presumes that you think that you can time the market—and a lot of people think they can.

An even bigger reason to like the flexible trading of ETFs, though, is taxes. Don't get your hopes up—I'm not saying that ETFs are tax free. But I am saying that ETFs give you much more flexibility when it comes to incurring taxable income or capital gains.

The context of this discussion is someone who is investing outside of a tax-deferred saving plan like a 401-K, IRA, 529 college saving plan, or other similar plan. Those plans aren't affected by the tax issues I'll discuss next. I'm talking about someone who holds additional savings in taxable accounts. For example, if you max out your tax-deferred saving options and still want to save even more—and believe me, you do—then you'll have to pay taxes on income and capital gains from these savings, even if they are held in bank accounts.

You may be familiar with the U.S. tax code, which taxes the capital gains that investors make on their investments. A short-term capital gain is a trading profit that you make on an investment that you've held for one year or less. Short-term capital gains are taxed as ordinary income, so your rate depends on your marginal tax bracket. On the other hand, long-term capital gains are trading profits you make on investments you've held for longer than one year. Long-term capital gains are taxed at a rate that is generally much lower than the income tax rate.

Since you choose when you're going to sell an ETF, you get to determine whether you make a short-term capital gain or a long-term capital gain. For example, if your ETF shares have gone up 10% after 10 months, then you can sell the ETF shares now and have a 10%, short-term capital gain. But you could hold the ETF for two more months and try to realize a long-term capital gain on the ETF. Even if the share price falls a little, because of the lower tax rate on long-term capital gains, you may still come out ahead by waiting.

The other aspect is that you can choose which year you want to realize any capital gains on your ETF shares. Again, for example, suppose you are holding ETF shares you've held for, say, 10 years, and the share prices have doubled in that time. You know that you'll pay a long-term capital gain when you sell the shares, but you may want to realize that capital gain in a year when it's convenient for you.

What many investors do, actually, is try to liquidate some of their winning positions when they also have some losing positions that they want to get rid of. The tax code allows investors to use the losses on some investments to offset the capital gains on others, so that they can reduce their overall tax bill using this strategy. But you have to have the flexibility to choose when to sell shares and realize those gains and losses.

The reason why I'm going into these details is because I'm going to contrast the tax flexibility of ETFs with the tax inflexibility of open-end mutual funds. A lot of investors don't realize this, but if you hold open-end mutual funds as a taxable investment, you will almost certainly owe capital gains taxes—courtesy of your mutual fund manager.

Most open-end mutual fund companies don't pay taxes, which is good, because it keeps expenses low. But the reason they don't pay taxes is that they pass all the dividend income and capital gains on to the investors. So every year, the mutual fund managers have to look over all their trades and calculate the capital gains and losses on them. They have to calculate the dividends, too, by the way. The mutual fund manager basically divides up the total capital gain over all the shares and then reports a capital gain on your shares to the IRS. So if you hold mutual funds in a taxable account, you'll get a notice about the capital gains on your mutual fund shares, and you'll owe capital gains taxes on them.

And to make matters worse, it can actually be the case that your mutual fund loses value during the year, and you still have to pay capital gains taxes. This happens when the market value of the assets held in the mutual fund falls from one year to the next, but the mutual fund manager has sold some of the assets in the fund for more than he originally paid for them. In the eyes of the tax authority, your losses only exist on paper, but your gains are real. Of course, that's not how we see it when we get our statements from the mutual fund. This is one of the nasty surprises that mutual fund investors hate the most. Imagine that you have to sell your mutual fund shares at a loss, and then you get a capital gains bill on top of that the next April. Talk about adding insult to injury.

As a note, if you are going to hold open-end mutual funds in a taxable account, you need to pay attention to the turnover rate of the mutual funds you're considering. The turnover rate is the fraction of the total value of the mutual fund that the portfolio manager trades, or turns over, during the year. The higher the turnover rate, the more capital gains the shares are likely to report at the end of the year. So if you do hold open-end mutual funds, try to look for funds with lower turnover rates, all else equal. You can find this information, by the way, right after the fee tables in the summary prospectus. Ah, yet another reason to read that prospectus.

Now you can see the reason why I've gone into all this tax information. There's a big difference between mutual funds and ETFs, in terms of when you have to pay capital gains taxes. Because of the flexibility that ETFs offer, people say that ETFs are tax efficient, relative to open-end mutual funds. Now again, keep in mind that this tax efficiency doesn't matter at all if we are talking about tax-deferred investments like IRAs and 401-Ks. In these cases, you don't pay any taxes until you withdraw money, so there's really no tax difference between having an open-end mutual fund or an ETF in your IRA. This difference only matters if you are investing outside of one of these plans.

Another advantage of ETFs over mutual funds is that they generally have lower expenses and higher returns than identical mutual funds would. First, the lower expenses. ETFs pay far fewer brokerage fees than mutual funds, because technically the ETF isn't buying the assets that get put in the depository—some very wealthy investor is. Also, ETFs don't have to deal with individual investors, like mutual funds do. Mutual fund companies have to maintain individual accounts for their shareholders, but people hold ETF shares in their brokerage accounts. So there's no need for record keeping or account maintenance for ETFs. That also cuts down on expenses.

Turning to returns, the returns on ETFs are influenced by the fact that they don't have to redeem shares. Mutual funds always have to have some amount of cash on hand, so they can cash out investors who want to redeem their shares on any given day. They try to minimize the amount they need, but holding cash necessarily delivers a lower expected return than the rest of the assets the mutual fund holds. By contrast, ETFs don't redeem shares. You cash out your ETF shares by selling them to another investor at their current market price, just as you would a share of stock.

A final advantage of ETFs, which I've already hinted at a couple of times, is that ETFs invest where open-end mutual funds either can't go or don't go in as much depth. For example, commodity ETFs are some of the larger ETFs out there. In fact, the ETF that goes by the ticker symbol GLD—which refers to the SPDR Gold Trust—has on occasion been the largest ETF by asset value, even larger than the largest S&P 500 ETFs. Also, because ETFs were limited to indexes for the first 15 years of their existence, they specialized in global, regional, and even country-by-country indexes. ETFs generally offer more opportunities to invest in foreign stock indexes than mutual funds do.

So there are several big reasons behind the surge in popularity of ETFs among many investors, and it's hard to deny that ETFs bring something to the table that is different from stocks, bonds, and open-end mutual funds. Of course, ETFs aren't perfect. They have their own set of tricky issues and potential problems that you need to be aware of.

As you've probably figured out by now, there is no such thing as a one-size-fits-all investment or investment plan. You may well believe that ETFs suit your needs better than any other investments despite these costs and problems, and you're willing to put up with the shortcomings of ETFs in order to take advantage of their benefits. Other people will disagree, and choose a mutual fund substitute, or something else altogether for their investment portfolios.

The first potential drawback of the ETF is trading costs. Although you're free to trade ETFs any time you like, trading itself isn't free. You'll have to pay commissions similar to those you pay for trading stocks, and the more you trade, the more these commissions will pile up and lower your all-in return from investing in ETFs. Everyone has to find some happy medium between not trading at all and trading too much. But if behavioral economics is any indication, it's harder to strike that balance than you might think. You may either put too much weight on the trading commission and trade too seldom, or ignore the trading commission and trade too much. This is one of those places where you really need to have an investment plan in place and stick with it.

The next potential drawback of ETFs is their pricing. Remember that ETFs represent a particular pool of assets that is held by some depository. We know that the price of each ETF share should reflect the market value of the underlying pool of assets. For example, if we are trading a gold ETF, where one share represents one tenth of an ounce of gold, then the price of each ETF share should be very close to one tenth of the market price of an ounce of gold. But how is this correspondence between the price of the ETF and the market price of the underlying assets enforced?

The answer is every financial economist's favorite concept: arbitrage. Although the price of a depository receipt could differ from the market value of the underlying assets, arbitrage should drive the prices together. For example, consider an ETF that invests in an equity index made up of the so-called BRIC country stocks—that is, the stocks of Brazil, Russia, India, and China. If there's a sudden surge of demand for ETF shares in this BRIC equity index, then the demand could temporarily outstrip supply, sending the price of the ETF shares up. And the price of the ETF shares could actually rise above the index value.

But if this happens, then the process of arbitrage should come to the rescue in a hurry. Other traders would notice that the ETF shares are more expensive than the index shares, and they would step into the market. What they would do is they would buy up the shares of the stocks that make up the BRIC index, deposit these shares with the ETF depository, and then take the depository receipts from the depository and sell them to the ETF investors. This would do two things. First, this increase in demand for the shares would drive up the prices of the shares in the BRIC index, sending the BRIC index up in value. And second, this increase in supply of the depository receipts or ETF shares would make the price of the ETF shares decline. Ideally, the prices of both the underlying stock shares and the ETF shares would change quickly and enable them to meet in the middle, where the prices would agree again.

This process is actually a very common one in financial markets, and it's one that traders rely on daily. For example, there is a very strong arbitrage between the shares of the S&P 500 index and the S&P 500 index futures contract, which is traded in Chicago's so-called "pits" or commodity exchanges. Traders called index arbitrageurs, or index arbs for short, simply watch the markets for significant gaps to open up between the S&P 500 index and the futures contract based on the S&P 500. Whenever a significant gap opens up, they do what arbs always do—they buy whichever asset is cheaper and sell whichever is more expensive, until the gap goes away. Their trading keeps the two markets—which otherwise have absolutely nothing to do with each other—in synch. In fact, part of what caused the great stock market crash of 1987, which I mentioned in my first lecture, is that these two markets became disconnected because of computer problems.

The reason I bring up the crash of 1987 is to point out that even though the process of arbitrage generally works very well in financial markets, occasionally it will fail and allow the price of the ETF shares to differ significantly from the value of the underlying assets held in the depository. That means you run the risk of selling for less than full value when it comes time to sell, or buying for more than the true value when you buy. You'll have to expend a little more effort to make sure that the ETF shares are close to their true market value when you buy or sell. For an open-end mutual fund, of course, this is not an issue, since they only buy and sell shares at the NAV, which is based on the fair market value of their holdings.

The next potential disadvantage of ETFs is leverage. This is a case where too much choice might not be such a good thing. We learned in the previous lecture that the SEC doesn't allow open-end mutual funds to take on much leverage at all. But it does allow ETFs to use derivatives to effectively leverage up their portfolios through a process of financial engineering. ETFs that pursue this investment strategy usually promise to deliver twice or even three times the gain on some underlying index, like the Dow. Of course, they can also deliver two or three times the losses.

Fortunately, these ETFs always identify themselves as leveraged ETFs. In addition, ETFs are required to reveal the entire list of assets that they hold on a daily basis, so you can see whether they are in fact using financial engineering. One of the best indications to me that beginning investors should stay away from leveraged ETFs is that experienced investors can't agree over the best way to use them. Some believe that they're really only tools for sophisticated day traders, while others maintain that they can also be good investments if held for longer periods, like months. So far, though, nothing I've seen has praised leveraged ETFs as being a good long-term, buy-and-hold investment.

One final potential disadvantage of ETFs is taxes, depending on the type of ETF that you buy. Although it's true that most ETFs will be more tax-efficient than mutual funds, ETFs that hold alternative investments such as commodities still have tax issues. Specifically, capital gains on commodities are taxed at a higher rate than other securities, and this applies to commodity ETFs as well.

In addition, if you invest in an ETF that uses derivatives, 40% of capital gains will be taxed at the short-term capital gains rate. This can also be an issue for commodity ETFs, because many commodity ETFs invest in futures contracts rather than the actual commodity. So if you want to invest in an alternative-asset ETF—that is, one that doesn't invest in stocks or bonds— then you should definitely seek some advice about the tax consequences first.

That's a fairly complete rundown of all that ETFs have to offer, and the main things to watch out for. If you didn't know about ETFs before this lecture, then hopefully you've learned about a relatively new investment that could have a role to play in your portfolio. If you already knew about ETFs, then hopefully you learned more about how they work and what their strengths and weaknesses are.

In my opinion, ETFs definitely have a place in your portfolio, if you're going to be making taxable investments. As I mentioned earlier, if you haven't maxed out your allowances for tax-deferred investing—especially if your employer matches your contributions—then you should do that first. But if you do that and still wish to invest, then ETFs may make a lot of sense for your portfolio. The low cost and tax efficiency of ETFs, especially the broad index ETFs, make them great candidates for long-term, buy-and-hold investments.

If you do plan to include ETFs as part of your overall portfolio, then you may have some tough decisions to make about what assets to hold in your tax-advantaged saving plans and what assets to hold in taxable accounts. The answer is going to depend in part on the specific menu of investments available to you in your tax-deferred or tax-advantaged saving plans. This is one of those places where a financial planner, who can sit down with you and look over the details of the investment options you have in your 401K, can really help you make better decisions.

Overall, ETFs are another case that shows how financial innovation that adds real value for investors becomes a permanent part of the financial landscape. I expect that in the not too distant future, ETFs will be mentioned in the same breath as stocks, bonds, and mutual funds when we give a list of all the standard investments we expect everyone to own, or at least know about. Of course, having one more type of investment to choose from isn't necessarily great news if you're already overwhelmed by the choices out there. Fortunately, in the next lecture I'm going to start discussing issues that ought to help you narrow down your search.

Financial Statement Analysis

Lecture 7

I n this lecture, you're going to learn some skills that can help you choose the best investments from among the thousands of options through financial statement analysis. In order to do this, you'll have to learn some definitions from accounting. You'll also need to learn the overall structure of every company's financial statements, including what information is presented where. Then, you'll learn some of the most important ratios and what these numbers tell you about the condition or performance of the company—and of other similar companies—which will be helpful when selecting stocks or bonds.

Analyzing Financial Statements

- **Financial statement analysis** is the practice of forming ratios and other statistics using the numbers presented in a set of financial statements—that is, the firm's official accounts.

- Although the numbers in a borrower's financial statements already tell us a lot of information, we can learn even more about a borrower's financial condition and performance if we combine or compare these numbers in creative ways. This information will hopefully give us a clearer picture of which firms are more attractive investment opportunities.

- A company's financial statements try to show a concise yet complete picture of a company's finances. They consist of 4 main parts—3 different tables that correspond to the main financial activities of the firm plus a set of notes that explains many of the details that are omitted from the 3 tables for the sake of brevity. The 3 tables, or statements, are the income statement, the statement of cash flows, and the balance sheet.

The Income Statement

- The income statement, also called the statement of earnings or the statement of operations, gives an overview of how much revenue the company brings in, how much it pays out as various expenses, and how much profit is left over—if any.

- As an example, let's analyze the financial statements of the Campbell Soup Company, which goes by the stock ticker CPB. To get this statement, go to the company's website and look for links to company information or investor relations so that you end up at the latest annual report.

- On the top of Campbell's income statement is **net sales**, which is sales minus returns. Campbell's sold nearly $7.7 billion worth of products in 2010. Below the sales come all the expenses of running the company, including expenses for production, marketing, research and development, and administration.

- After subtracting those expenses, we have a rough statement of earnings, which goes by 2 names: operating income or **earnings before interest and taxes (EBIT)**. For Campbell's, the EBIT is about $1.3 billion.

- If we take EBIT and subtract interest and then corporate income taxes, we get **net income** or net earnings. For Campbell's, this number was $844 million in 2010. Net income tells a stock investor all the profits that could be paid out to the shareholders.

- The last thing an income statement does is calculate the earnings per share (EPS) of the firm. Campbell's earned $2.42 per share in 2010. The income statement tells you what the accounting measures of profit are, but accounting measures of profit are not equal to cash. This is because most accounting is done under the principle of **accrual**, which refers to one particular set of procedures for recognizing revenue and expenses.

- Accrual is the most popular way to make sense of these transactions, but one of the costs of its flexibility and simplicity is that accrual-based measures of income and expenses are not equal to the actual cash payments going into and coming out of the firm.

The Statement of Cash Flows

- The purpose of the statement of cash flows is simply to give investors a clearer picture of how much cash the company is taking in and how it is using cash. Investors use the statement of cash flows primarily to see whether the company is bringing in more cash than it is spending.

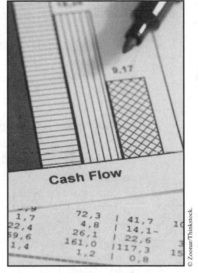

Investors use a company's statement of cash flows to determine whether it earns more cash than it spends.

- On the statement of cash flows, the company's use of cash is broken down into operations, investing, and financing. One thing that is always worth checking is to see whether the company's operations—the things it is in business to do—are bringing in more cash than they use.

- For Campbell's, this cash flow from operations, or net cash provided by operating activities, is just over $1 billion. Also, at the bottom of the statement, we can see whether the company as a whole increased or decreased its holdings of cash.

- Nearly all investors find 2 pieces of information particularly useful in the statement of cash flows. Depreciation and amortization attempt to keep every company honest about the fact that its factories and equipment are wearing out and will have to be replaced sometime.

Using up these real assets is a real economic cost—but not one that causes any money to change hands. Therefore, if a company reports a depreciation expense, its earnings fall, but its cash isn't actually affected.

- The second item on the statement of cash flows that most investors like to know is called free cash flow, which measures how much cash the firm could be returning to shareholders; it's the cash flow analog to net earnings on the income statement.

- Different analysts calculate free cash flow in different ways, but nearly everyone starts with cash flow from operations and subtracts **capital expenditures**, which is usually the first item in the section on cash flows from investing activities. Capital expenditures are purchases of real assets, such as equipment and factories.

- For Campbell's, cash flow from operations is $1.057 billion, and just below it is an item for purchases of plant assets, which is $315 million. Therefore, free cash flow for Campbell's is $1057 − $315, or $742 million.

The Balance Sheet
- The balance sheet is a snapshot of the company's assets, liabilities, and equity at a point in time. Assets are anything the firm owns, and **liabilities** are what the firm owes to other parties. **Equity**, or net worth, is the difference between assets and liabilities. Equity tells you what the entire company is worth.

- On Campbell's balance sheet, it had about $6.3 billion in assets and just over $5.3 billion in liabilities (as of August 1, 2010), which implies that Campbell's equity was $929 million. Many investors refer to balance sheet equity as "book" equity—where the book in question is the company's accounting books.

Financial Ratios
- Liquidity ratios measure whether a company has enough money to pay all the bills that are coming due. A standard liquidity ratio

is the current ratio, which is defined as current assets divided by current liabilities. (The word "current" is an accounting term that means that it comes due within the next 12 months.) The current ratio determines how many dollars a company thinks it will receive in payment over the next year divided by the number of dollars of bills it will have to pay during the next year.

- Campbell's had current assets of $1687 million and current liabilities of $2065 million, which give a current ratio of about 81.7 cents. This means that Campbell's currently has about $0.82 in short-term assets for each dollar of liabilities that it expects to have to pay during the next year.

- For manufacturing firms like Campbell's, the current ratio can be misleading because inventories make up much of the firm's current assets. Therefore, for many manufacturing companies, analysts also calculate a related liquidity ratio called the quick ratio, which is cash, securities, and accounts receivable divided by current liabilities.

- For Campbell's, cash and investments are $254 million and accounts receivable are $512 million for a total of $766 million. Then, we divide $766 million by the total current liabilities of $2065 million, which gives us a quick ratio of 0.371 (37.1 cents) in cash, securities, and accounts receivable for every dollar in current liabilities.

- **Leverage** determines how much the firm is borrowing and is often expressed as total assets divided by total equity. Campbell's total assets are $6276 million and their equity is $929 million, which means that leverage is equal to $6.76. This means that every dollar of equity supports $6.76 of assets. In other words, for every dollar of equity the shareholders have contributed, the managers have borrowed another $6.76.

- The next category of ratios is the profitability ratios. One of the profitability ratios that most investors look at is the operating margin, which is defined as EBIT divided by sales. This ratio simply tells us what fraction of each dollar of sales goes to operating income, so it's clear that this is a profit margin. Campbell's EBIT is $1348 million and its sales are $7676 million, so the operating margin is 0.176. This means that 17.6 cents of every dollar of sales is operating profit.

- Efficiency describes how well a company utilizes its assets. One of the main efficiency ratios is called the asset turnover ratio, which is defined as sales divided by total assets. Many financial analysts use average total assets in the denominator of this ratio; using total assets is just simpler.

- Campbell's sales, which we just used in the margin calculation, were $7676 million. The total assets, which we found in the leverage calculation, were $6276 million. The asset turnover ratio, then, is equal to 1.24, which means that every dollar of Campbell's assets produces $1.24 of sales per year.

- Finally, the ratios that every investor wants to know are return on assets and return on equity. These are performance ratios that attempt to measure the return that different investors would get by lending a dollar to the company.

- **Return on assets (ROA)** is defined as (EBIT − taxes)/total assets. The numerator measures the profits that are available to be distributed to both the bondholders and the stockholders of the company. In fact, ROA calculates the return you would earn if you finance a dollar's worth of the company's assets by buying both the company's bonds and its stock. Moreover, ROA assumes that you finance the company by buying its stock and bonds in the same proportions as the ones the company has listed on its balance sheet.

- For Campbell's, you are buying about $5.76 of bonds for every dollar of stock. EBIT was $1348 million, and taxes paid were $398 million. This makes the numerator equal to $950 million. Then, total assets were \$6276 million, so the ROA ratio is 950/6276, which is 0.154, or 15.4%.

- **Return on equity (ROE)** is defined as net income divided by equity. Campbell Soup's net income was \$844 million, and its equity was \$929 million, which makes the ROE ratio 844/929, which gives 0.909, or 90.9%.

- By themselves, these ratios have very little meaning; they're really meant to be used in comparison with other firms' ratios. In order to use financial statement analysis to help you choose stocks, you need to select a set of similar firms (in terms of industry and size) and then compare ratios. You should also do research on how Campbell's is currently valued and is projected to be valued in the market.

Important Terms

accrual: One particular set of procedures for recognizing revenue and expenses.

capital expenditure: A purchase of real assets, such as equipment and factories.

earnings before interest and taxes (EBIT): Net sales minus the expenses of running a company.

equity: The difference between assets and liabilities, which tells you what a company is worth.

financial statement analysis: The practice of forming ratios and other statistics using the numbers presented in a set of financial statements.

leverage: Determines how much a firm is borrowing and is often expressed as total assets divided by total equity.

liability: What a firm owes to other parties.

net income: EBIT minus interest and corporate income taxes.

net sales: Sales minus returns.

return on assets (ROA): (EBIT − taxes)/total assets.

return on equity (ROE): Net income divided by equity.

Suggested Reading

Bodie, Kane, and Marcus, *Essentials of Investments*, chap. 14.

Ittelson, *Financial Statements*.

Questions to Consider

1. Find and download the most recent annual financial statements from a company you might be interested in as an investment. You can usually find them by going to the company's website and then following links to information about the company that usually have labels such as "about the company" or "investor relations." On the financial statements, find the company's net income and equity for the most recent year. Using the numbers you find, calculate the return on equity (ROE) for this company.

2. DuPont analysis is a way of showing that a company's ROE is driven by profitability, efficiency, and leverage. For a firm you are interested in, calculate the net margin (net income/sales), asset turnover (sales/assets) and leverage (assets/equity) ratios. Multiply your numbers together and compare to the ROE you found in the first question.

Financial Statement Analysis
Lecture 7—Transcript

In this lecture, we're going to move on to some advanced topics in investing. We've just finished learning the basics about the four instruments that every investor should consider: stocks, bonds, mutual funds, and ETFs. Now we're going to move on to the next step. We're going to learn some ideas and skills that can help you choose the best investments for you from among the thousands of options out there.

I'm going to follow the same general order that I did when I introduced the four main investments—so again I'll start with stocks. If you want to pick your own stocks, then you'll need a stockpicker's toolkit. The next three lectures are going to build up a standard set of tools that make up the core of every stock analyst's toolbox. But even though I'm calling this a stockpicking toolkit, the ideas and techniques I'm going to discuss will be useful for analyzing just about every possible investment.

This is certainly true of the stockpicking tool we'll learn about in this lecture—financial statement analysis. Although we tend to associate financial statement analysis with picking stocks, it's actually just as important for bond investors. And it doesn't really matter who is issuing the securities, either. Sovereign debt investors do financial statement analysis on governments, and retail lenders do financial statement analysis on households. What do you think goes into your credit score? Well, financial statement analysis, among other things.

Financial statement analysis is the practice of forming ratios and other statistics using the numbers presented in a set of financial statements, that is, the firm's official accounts. The idea is that, although the numbers in a borrower's financial statements already tell us a lot of good information, we can learn even more about a borrower's financial condition and performance if we combine or compare these numbers in creative ways. This information will hopefully give us a clearer picture of which firms are more attractive investment opportunities.

In this lecture, we're going to learn some basic financial statement analysis. In order to do this, we'll first have to learn a little bit of accounting—mostly just some definitions, but ones that are used all the time. We'll also need to take a brief look at the overall structure of every company's financial statements, and learn what information is presented where. Once we've done that, we'll learn some of the most important ratios and other statistics, and I'll explain what these numbers are trying to tell us about the condition or performance of the company.

As we learn about the ratios themselves, we'll also learn how to use these numbers when you select stocks or bonds. Beyond selecting investments, however, this information is also useful for gaining a better understanding of your employer's financial condition and performance—which, these days, is not a bad thing to know. In addition, if you ever want to start your own business, you'll need to put together a set of financial statements for your venture, as well as project the values of certain financial ratios into the future. Hopefully, this lecture will help you understand financial statements so that this task doesn't seem quite as daunting as it otherwise might.

The obvious place to start learning about financial statement analysis is a company's financial statements. The financial statements try to show a concise yet complete picture of a company's finances. They consist of four main parts—three different tables that correspond to the main financial activities of the firm, plus a set of notes that explains a lot of the details that are omitted from the three tables for the sake of brevity. The three tables, or statements are the income statement, the statement of cash flows, and the balance sheet. What I'm going to do next is go through these tables, or statements, and discuss what they tell investors.

I'll start with the financial statement containing the information that stock investors seem to pay the most attention to—the income statement. If you stop and think about what you'd most like to know about the financial condition of a company, it's probably whether the company is making any money. The income statement, also called the statement of earnings or the statement of operations, presents a detailed answer to that question. It gives an overview of how much revenue the company brings in, how much it pays out as various expenses, and then how much profit is left over, if any.

Because it's much easier to understand financial statements and financial statement analysis with an example in front of you, I'm going to introduce my example now. I'm going to work with the financial statements of the Campbell Soup Company, which goes by stock ticker CPB. I picked this company mainly because I've noticed that they always present a very simple and clean set of financial statements, so they're great for people just starting to learn financial statement analysis. And besides, soup is good for you. Actually, Campbell's has diversified its line of products well beyond canned soup, so if you don't care for soup, they have plenty of other snacks and prepared foods to think about as well.

I suppose the first question is, where did I get this statement? I like to go right to the source—the company website, and look for links to company information or investor relations. Eventually, I find my way to the latest annual report, and the annual financial statements are always in the annual report. Publicly traded companies are required to report their financial results quarterly, so you can get more up-to-date information by viewing the quarterly financial statements, and most companies these days do link to these on their websites as well. But the SEC also has this data as part of their so-called EDGAR database, and many financial websites, including free ones, also post financial statements from publicly traded companies.

My only complaint about the financial websites is that they take the companies' actual financial statements and then move the information into a one-size-fits-all financial statement template. After you get some experience looking at different companies' statements, you'll realize that there's actually a lot of variation in how information gets reported. Unfortunately, when these financial websites translate the financial statements into their templates, sometimes good information is lost in translation.

So let's have a look at Campbell's income statement, which they call a consolidated statement of earnings. *Earnings* is the finance word for profit, and as we'll see, the income statement shows fairly clearly how Campbell's calculates its profits.

The top of the income statement is net sales, which is sales minus returns. Other companies will just have a number for sales, or even revenues.

Campbell's sold nearly $7.7 billion worth of products in 2010. Then below the sales come all the expenses of running the company, including production costs, marketing costs, R&D, and administrative expenses. After we subtract those expenses, we have a rough statement of earnings, which goes by two names. One name is operating income, and the other is EBIT, which is an acronym that stands for earnings before interest and taxes. For Campbell's, this turned out to be about $1.3 billion.

You may have also heard of EBIT's cousin, EBITDA, which stands for earnings before interest, taxes, depreciation, and amortization. You'll notice that you don't see depreciation and amortization listed on the income statement, and you'll have to find that somewhere else. I'll tell you where in a little bit.

If we take EBIT and subtract off interest, and then income taxes—well, we call them corporate income taxes but they're actually taxes on corporate profits—then we get to net income, or net earnings. This is our so-called bottom line on the income statement. For Campbell's, this number was $844 million in 2010. Net income tells a stock investor all the profits that could be paid out to the shareholders. You may recall, though, that most firms don't pay out all of these earnings as dividends. I'll have more to say about that in a future lecture.

The last thing that an income statement typically does is it calculates the earnings per share, or EPS, of the firm. This is done as a convenience, since so many investors want to see the profits on a per-share basis, and otherwise investors would have to dig up the information on the number of shares that the firm has outstanding. So Campbell's earned $2.42 per share in 2010.

It's tempting to think that as a Campbell's shareholder you have a claim to $2.42 in cash for each share you hold. But you actually don't. The income statement tells you what the accounting measures of profit are, but the truth is that accounting measures of profit are not equal to cash. This is because most accounting is done under the principle of accrual.

Accrual refers to one particular set of procedures for recognizing revenue and expenses. Business transactions get pretty complicated, and we need a set of simple rules for making sense of these transactions. Accrual is the most popular way to do this—but one of the costs of its flexibility and simplicity is that accrual-based measures of income and expenses are not equal to the actual cash payments going into and coming out of the firm.

For example, suppose Campbell's makes a deal to sell $1 million of snack food over the next three years to a company that operates vending machines on college campuses—talk about a solid business. Under the principle of accrual, Campbell's can record the entire $1 million in sales now—as soon as it has the signed sales agreement. The accountants at Campbell's don't have to recognize the revenues immediately, but they can if they want to. So the sales numbers don't necessarily tell you about the money flowing into and out of the company.

Needless to say, investors are really interested in knowing how much cash is being generated by the company. Veteran business owners, and anyone who has ever started a business, knows that firms generally go out of business because they run out of cash, not because they don't make accounting profits.

Fortunately, there's another financial statement that addresses the need to know about cash—and not surprisingly, it's called the statement of cash flows. The purpose of this statement is simply to give investors a clearer picture of how much cash the company is taking in, and how it is using cash. Investors use the statement of cash flows primarily to see whether the company is bringing in more cash than it is spending—happiness is positive cash flow.

First, note that on the statement of cash flows, the company's use of cash is broken down among operations, investing, and financing. One thing that is always worth checking is to see whether the company's operations— the things it is actually in business to do—are bringing in more cash than they use. For Campbell's, this cash flow from operations, or net cash provided by operating activities, is just over $1 billion. Also, at the bottom of the statement, we can see whether the company as a whole increased or decreased its holdings of cash.

Some investors use the statement of cash flows quite intensively, but nearly all investors find two pieces of information particularly useful. The first piece of information is the depreciation and amortization expense, which is counted as a production expense on the income statement. Depreciation and amortization attempt to keep every company honest about the fact that its factories and equipment are wearing out and will have to be replaced sometime. Using up these real assets is a real economic cost, but not one that causes any money to change hands. So if a company reports a depreciation expense, its earnings fall but its cash isn't actually affected.

The second item on the statement of cash flows that most investors like to know is called free cash flow. Now there's an exciting name. This doesn't appear directly on the statement of cash flows, but it can be calculated directly and easily from it. Free cash flow measures how much cash the firm could be returning to shareholders—so it's the cash flow analog to net earnings on the income statement.

Different analysts like to calculate free cash flow in different ways, but nearly everyone starts with cash flow from operations and subtracts off capital expenditures, which is usually the first item in the section on cash flows from investing activities. Capital expenditures are purchases of real assets, like equipment and factories. Given how most financial statements are laid out, cash flow from operations and capital expenditures are almost always next to, or at least very close to, each other. For Campbell's, we know that cash flow from operations is $1.057 billion, and just below it is an item for purchases of plant assets, which is $315 million. The number is in parentheses, too, to indicate that it's an expense. So our basic measure of free cash flow for Campbell's is 1057 − 315, or $742 million.

Notice that for Campbell's, there is a fairly close correspondence between the accounting measure of profit, net earnings, and the cash flow measure of profit, free cash flow. But again, given the differences between accounting earnings and cash flow, this isn't necessarily the case for any given company. Many investors will do all the same things to free cash flow that they do with earnings—especially they'll divide it by the number of shares in the firm to get the free cash flow per share.

The income and cash flows of the firm are important, but if we stop there, we leave out an essential part of the firm's financial story. You may recall that in the very first lecture of this course, we learned that firms issue financial assets in order to borrow money from investors so they can buy real assets. The final financial statement that's last—the balance sheet—tells part of this story.

The balance sheet is a snapshot of the company's assets, liabilities, and equity at a point in time. We use the term *assets* for anything the firm owns, and *liabilities* for what the firm owes to other parties. Equity, or net worth, is the difference between assets and liabilities. It tells you, in accounting terms, what the entire company is worth. On Campbell's balance sheet, it had about $6.3 billion in assets and just over $5.3 billion in liabilities, as of August 1, 2010. That implied that Campbell's equity was $929 million. Many investors, including me, also refer to balance sheet equity as *book equity*— where the book in question is the company's accounting books. I like the term *book value* of the company because it makes it clear that I'm talking about the accounting value of a firm's equity, from the balance sheet, rather than the market value of the company.

Now we've seen the financial statements, and learned about the basic information they contain. The financial statements already contain a lot of information about the firm's performance. Numbers such as EBIT, free cash flow, net earnings, and net worth all tell essential information that helps us understand a company.

But there's a lot more we can do with these numbers. In fact, there are entire university courses and entire books on financial statement analysis. My goal is to give you what I consider to be the most important financial ratios that nearly all investors know and use to help them pick stocks. Each ratio we'll learn about represents an entire category of ratios that are designed to measure some crucial aspect of a company's financial performance.

The first category of financial ratios we'll look at is called liquidity ratios. Liquidity ratios measure whether a company has enough money to pay all the bills coming due. A standard liquidity ratio is the current ratio, which is defined as current assets over current liabilities. The word current here is an accounting term that means that it comes due within the next 12 months.

So the current ratio says how many dollars of current assets a company has for each dollar of current liabilities, or in other words, how many dollars a company thinks it will receive in payment over the next year, divided by the number of dollars of bills it will have to pay during the next year. Campbell's had current assets of $1687 million and current liabilities of $2065 million. These numbers give a current ratio of about 81.7 cents. This means that Campbell's currently has about $0.82 in short-term assets for each dollar of liabilities that it expects to have to pay during the next year. These short-term assets should be converted to cash within the next 12 months.

For manufacturing firms like Campbell's, the current ratio can be a bit misleading because inventories make up a lot of the firm's current assets. For example, Campbell's has $724 million in inventories, which is almost half of its current assets. But it may be hard to liquidate inventories in a hurry, and if the company is forced to do that, it may have to sell the inventories of soup and snacks at very low prices. So for many manufacturing companies, analysts also calculate a related liquidity ratio called the quick ratio. The quick ratio still puts current liabilities in the denominator, but the numerator only includes cash, securities, and accounts receivable. Accounts receivable, by the way, is the amount of money that Campbell's customers owe it for soup and snacks they have purchased.

So, for Campbell's, we calculate the quick ratio this way. Cash and investments are $254 million, and accounts receivable are $512 million, for a total of $766 million. Then we divide $766 million by the total current liabilities of $2065 million and this gives us a quick ratio of 0.371 or 37.1 cents in cash, securities, and accounts receivable for every dollar in current liabilities.

We've calculated a couple of financial ratios. What do they mean? Taken by themselves, we don't really know whether these ratios are good, bad, or indifferent. That's because these ratios have very little meaning by themselves. They're really meant to be used in comparison with other firms' ratios. We'll get to the comparisons in a little bit. For now, though, I want to show you what ratios are important and how you can calculate them.

So, at this point we've learned how to find two liquidity ratios—the current ratio and the quick ratio. The next set of ratios is leverage ratios. Leverage measures how much the firm is borrowing. I'll discuss leverage in much more detail in a future lecture, but for now I'll just say that leverage is a two-edged sword. A bit of leverage can do you good, but too much leverage is just plain dangerous. That goes for companies as well as individual investors.

There are lots of ways to measure leverage. Although some investors like to use debt-to-equity ratios, I tend to prefer leverage ratios expressed as total assets over total equity. Campbell's total assets are $6276 million and their equity is $929 million. This means that total assets over total equity is equal to 6276/929 or 6.76. This means that every dollar of equity supports $6.76 of assets. I think this view gives you a very clear idea of the extent of the leverage, and what it's being used for. And, you can still take this number and deduce that for every dollar of equity that the shareholders have contributed, the managers have borrowed another $5.76.

The next category of ratios is the profitability ratios. One of the profitability ratios that most investors look at is the operating margin, which is defined as EBIT/sales. You may remember that we also call EBIT "operating income," which is the connection to operating margin. This ratio simply tells us what fraction of each dollar of sales goes to operating income, so it's clear that this is a profit margin. Campbell's EBIT, which we've seen before, is $1348 million. Its sales are $7676 million, so the operating margin is 1348/7676, which gives 0.176. This means that 17.6 cents of every dollar of sales is operating profit.

Now we'll move on to efficiency ratios. Efficiency describes how well a company utilizes its assets. One of the main efficiency ratios is called the asset turnover ratio, which is defined as sales/total assets. Note that many financial analysts use average total assets in the denominator of this ratio, but I'm using total assets for simplicity.

Campbell's sales, which we just used in the margin calculation, were $7676 million. And the total assets, which we saw in the leverage calculation, were $6276 million. This makes the asset turnover ratio equal to 7676/6276 or 1.24. This is literally saying that every dollar of Campbell's assets produces $1.24 of sales per year.

And finally, I've saved the best financial ratios for last. The ratios that every investor wants to know right off the bat are ROA and ROE—which are return on assets and return on equity. These are so-called performance ratios, and they try to measure, in an accounting sense, the return that different investors would get by lending a dollar to the company. First, let's start with ROA. This is defined as EBIT − taxes/total assets.

The numerator measures the profits that are available to be distributed to both the bondholders and the stockholders of the company. In fact, ROA calculates the return you would earn, again measured in accounting terms and not market terms, if you finance a dollar's worth of the company's assets by buying both the company's bonds and its stock. ROA assumes, moreover, that you finance the company by buying its stock and bonds in the same proportions as the ones the company has listed on its balance sheet. So, for Campbell's, you are buying about $5.76 of bonds for every dollar of stock. EBIT, once again, was $1348 million, and taxes paid were $398 million. This makes the numerator equal to $950 million. Then total assets, once again, were $6276 million. So the ROA ratio is 950/6276, which gives 0.154, or 15.4%.

Finally, let's do ROE. ROE is defined as net income/equity. Campbell Soup's net income was $844 million, and its equity was $929 million. This makes the ROE ratio 844/929, which gives 0.909, or 90.9%. Wow! That seems really high. Is it realistic?

To answer that we really need to compare Campbell's ROE to the ROEs from a set of similar companies, such as an industry group or subgroup. As I said a moment ago, Campbell's financial ratios have very little meaning by themselves. They're really meant to be compared with other firms' ratios. In order to use financial statement analysis to help you pick stocks, you need to select a set of similar firms and then compare ratios. If one firm's ratios are impressive relative to its peers, then it's probably worth doing further analysis on it to see whether it is worth adding to your portfolio.

Let's do this comparison on ROE for Campbell's Soup Company. If you go to about any financial website and look up Campbell's, which has stock ticker CPB, the site will probably list that Campbell's is in the Consumer

Goods sector and the Processed and Packaged Goods industry. What we can do is look up several firms from this industry that seem like they would be similar to Campbell's Soup and compare their ratios to Campbell's.

One way that I like to choose similar firms is to find a list of companies in the industry, sorted by market capitalization. Market capitalization is a measure of market value equal to the current stock price times the number of shares outstanding. Most financial websites will list companies in order of market capitalization, which will also help you choose firms that are similar in size. I think this is useful, because I don't want to compare Campbell's either with a company that is many times larger or smaller; it doesn't seem like the firms would have much in common.

When I went to the list of firms in the Processed and Packaged Goods industry, on one financial website, and I constructed this list. I've included more companies than I really think are comparable, just to give you an idea of what you might find when you look on these websites. Note that Campbell's is a pretty big firm, but by no means the biggest. There are several firms on the list that are about the same size as Campbell's, and also seem to be in about the same line of business. For example, Heinz, Sara Lee, J. M. Smucker, ConAgra, and McCormick all make packaged foods like Campbell's does. So I'll compare Campbell's to these five companies.

Once I get my list of companies, I gather the information on their financial ratios and do a simple comparison. For ROE, here's what a comparison among the five firms that seem most closely related to Campbell's Soup shows: We see that among the firms that are Campbell Soup's peers, there are certainly some healthy ROEs. But Campbell's, by far, has a much higher ROE than these firms. Should I buy 100 shares and see what happens?

Well, maybe. But first I should do a whole lot more research. I'd start by comparing all the other ratios we learned about in this lecture to Campbell Soup's peers. For example, based on my experience looking at companies, Campbells' leverage ratio seems pretty high. I'd have to find out why Campbell's uses so much debt, and how the firm has been able to support that debt so far.

The next step would be going on to doing more research to measure how Campbell's is currently valued in the market. It could be that Campbell's soup already has a price that reflects its relatively high ROE. I'd also have to learn a lot more about the products that Campbell's and its subsidiaries intend to roll out in the coming months and years. So in other words, I've made a good start on finding an interesting company, but I'm nowhere near the point where I'm confident enough in its future success to put my money on the line.

I hope this lecture helps you feel more comfortable around a company's financial statements. We've learned the basic financial ratios that help us judge the performance of different companies and seen that the way to use ratios is to compare one firm to a group of its peers. Though there's no one single ratio that identifies good companies, ROE is a good starting point for noticing strong performers.

Once you find a company that interests you, look over all the major ratios to really get a feel for its financial performance. And don't forget to look into the stories behind the numbers—like why Campbell's uses so much leverage and what kinds of new products it will bring to market in the coming years. These stories are really where you'll discover the information that will convince you to invest or not invest.

P/E Ratios and the Method of Comparables
Lecture 8

I n this lecture, you'll learn how to use the method of comparables, a type of valuation model, to price stocks. You can use the information from the 4 main ratios that you will learn about—P/E, price-to-book, price-to-sales, and PEG ratios—to help find stocks that seem undervalued. However, once you find a potentially undervalued stock, you still need to gather more information about the company to see whether it deserves its low ratio because of lackluster performance or whether it really is an overlooked and underappreciated company that has the potential to surprise the market.

Valuation Models

- **Valuation models** are extremely important to stock picking. Valuation models simply help us figure out what something is worth. Whenever we buy any product, we compare the price of the product to what it's actually worth to us. If we think something is worth the price, we buy it.

- Investing works the same way. By figuring out what we think a stock is worth, we can pick the stocks that we think are worth at least as much—and hopefully a lot more—than their current prices, and we can avoid buying stocks that are overpriced.

- In general, there's constant disagreement in the markets about what any given investment is worth, which is actually a good thing. It gives each of us the opportunity to pick stocks and try to beat the market.

- Your mission in using valuation models is to use them to help you find companies that you think most people have overlooked or underestimated; you want to find companies that you think are worth more than the market says they are.

- The **method of comparables** is a valuation method that is based on using ratios, such as the price-to-earnings (P/E) ratio, to value stocks. This model is widely used in all kinds of financial markets—not just the stock market. In addition, it's the model that professionals overwhelmingly prefer to use because it's simple, fast, and reliable.

- The method of comparables starts with a very simple idea: Every asset has some features or characteristics that indicate or influence its value. These characteristics are called value drivers because they drive the value of an asset. Every asset has a different set of value drivers, and some are easy to measure, such as a company's earnings, while others are difficult to measure.

- The second idea behind the method of comparables is that if 2 assets are truly comparable, then they'll have a similar relationship between their price and any given value driver. The relationship between the price of some asset and its value drivers can be complex, so we allow the ratio between the price of the asset and its value to represent the relationship.

- Let's let P stand for the price of some asset and V stand for the value of some value driver that we think affects P. In addition, let's consider 2 comparable assets, asset A and asset B. The method of comparables says that if asset A and asset B really are comparable, then the ratio of each asset's price to its value driver should be the same for both assets: $P_A/V_A = P_B/V_B$.

- We use the ratio of one asset's price to its value driver, called a **valuation multiple**, to estimate the price of other assets. For example, if we were using the price-to-earnings ratio, then V_A would be the earnings per share for Company A and P_A/V_A would be the earnings multiple. We would multiply Company A's earnings multiple by Company B's earnings to get an estimate of Company B's price. Then, if the market price of Company B's stock is less than the predicted price, we would want to look deeper into Company B to see whether there is more information about Company B that indicates it would be a good investment.

- The 3 most popular value drivers for stocks are earnings per share, book value per share—which is balance sheet equity divided by the number of shares outstanding—and sales per share. Therefore, the 3 most popular ratios that analysts look at are the price-to-earnings ratio, the price-to-book ratio, and the price-to-sales ratio.

In choosing stocks, you want to find companies that you think are worth more than the market says they are.

- All kinds of other value drivers are possible, and the choice of value driver depends on the industry as well as on the state of development of the firms in the industry.

- The accuracy and reliability of the method of comparables relies heavily on finding truly comparable assets to compare to each other. When it comes to applying the method of comparables to stocks, we usually use companies in the same industry or subindustry as comparable companies.

- Of course, just because a company is listed as being in the industry, this doesn't necessarily make it comparable to the company that you are interested in. Other considerations are whether to include foreign stocks or companies of very different sizes in your list of comparable companies. Your choice will depend on the specifics of the company you're investigating and whether you can find many companies that are good matches for it.

- Using The Cheesecake Factory as an example, we will include other American casual-dining chains that also have fairly large total market values—about $1 billion or more.

- In practice, valuation multiples are averages of the multiples for many different firms, so to value The Cheesecake Factory using the price-to-earnings ratio, form the earnings ratios for all the comparable firms on your list and then take a simple average of these multiples. Most free financial websites have several pages of summary statistics on each company where you can find all the prices and various company statistics that you need.

- Start by finding the prices of all the companies on your list. Then, find the earnings per share for each company. To find the P/E multiples for each company, divide each company's price by its EPS. Don't include the multiple for The Cheesecake Factory because you want to use the information from the rest of the market to price that company, but you should still collect The Cheesecake Factory's price and EPS.

- Calculate the average P/E ratio for the companies on your list, which is the average valuation multiple. For example, let's say that the value of the average multiple for a sample of 8 companies is 14.55. Now you can use this valuation multiple and the actual value of The Cheesecake Factory's EPS to estimate the price of the stock.

- To find a price for The Cheesecake Factory, take its earnings, which are $1.67 per share, and multiply by the average earnings multiple for the comparable firms, which is 14.55. The answer, which is the estimated price of The Cheesecake Factory, is $24.29. Then, compare this estimated price to the actual market price of The Cheesecake Factory. If the actual price is $26.14, then the comparables estimate based on an earnings multiple is less than $2 below the current market price of the shares.

- For The Cheesecake Factory, the method of comparables produces estimates of the price that are fairly close together. The earnings multiple gives a value of $24.29, the book value multiple gives a value of $28.67, and the sales multiple gives a value of $26.17. These estimates are not only close together, they're also pretty close to The Cheesecake Factory's actual stock price of $26.14.

- For many other companies, however, there may be a large variation in estimated prices; this is true of Cracker Barrel. The valuation ratios are really saying that The Cheesecake Factory's multiples are about average—relative to these peer firms. This may indicate that the company is more or less fairly valued, and it doesn't look like there are any big opportunities for investors to profit from buying this firm.

- However, if you analyze Cracker Barrel in a similar manner, the variation in prices shows that Cracker Barrel looks undervalued according to EPS and sales—but overvalued according to book value. Further investigation will hopefully help you come to some conclusion about whether the company would be a good investment.

- One of the ways you can do this investigation is by digging deeper into the ratios. For example, stock analysts think that the P/E ratio is driven by the expected growth rate of the company's earnings. To understand this relationship, analysts take the P/E ratio for a stock, which is usually some number greater than 1 but less than 100, for example, and then divide this number by the forecast earnings growth rate, as expressed as a percentage. This is called the **PEG ratio** because it takes the P/E ratio and divides by the growth rate of earnings.

- According to investors, a fairly priced stock would have a PEG ratio of 1. An underpriced stock would have a PEG ratio less than 1, and an overpriced stock would have a PEG ratio of greater than 1.

- There's not necessarily any reason that a company's P/E ratio should be equal to its EPS growth rate, but it only matters what the people in the market think. The investors in the market have established that the benchmark for the PEG ratio is 1, and people are making investment decisions based on this benchmark.

- This phenomenon points out a potential problem with the method of comparables: This method has been so successful that it has become more prescriptive than descriptive in many cases. For example, the P/E ratio is often used in a prescriptive way to talk about the overall value of the stock market. Investors pay a lot of attention to historic P/E ratios, and they use average P/E ratios to judge whether the entire market is overvalued or undervalued.

- One of the reasons that professionals like to use the method of comparables is their confidence that this method can't be easily manipulated; however, it's possible to bias a method of comparables valuation fairly easily.

- The key step in the method of comparables is to select the appropriate set of comparable firms to include in your valuation multiple. In general, the number of companies that you'll be using to estimate valuation multiples isn't very big—perhaps you'll use 15 to 20 firms in a large industry. Choosing the firms you include in a careful way can distort the valuation multiple that you end up with.

- Another matter of choice is the value drivers that you choose to use in your estimates. In many cases, companies will try to direct investors to modified measures of earnings or other value drivers in the hopes that the investors will plug these modified versions into their standard valuation multiples and be willing to pay higher prices for a company's shares.

- The other side of this problem of understating the P/E ratios is that the accounting rules that firms are supposed to follow require some investments to be counted as expenses. This lowers the amount of recorded earnings and, therefore, raises the P/E ratio, making firms look overvalued. One of the investments that is accounted for in this way is research and development costs.

method of comparables: A valuation method that is based on using ratios to value stocks.

PEG ratio: A ratio found by taking a company's price-to-earnings (P/E) ratio and dividing by the growth rate of earnings.

price-to-earnings (P/E) ratio: A ratio of a company's price to its earnings per share (EPS).

valuation model: A model that helps us figure out what something is worth.

valuation multiple: The ratio of one asset's price to its value driver.

Suggested Reading

Bodie, Kane, and Marcus, *Essentials of Investments*, chap. 13.

English, *Applied Equity Analysis*, chap. 15.

Hough, "Peeling Back the Market's P/E."

Questions to Consider

1. General Electric (GE) is known as a conglomerate, meaning that it participates in many different lines of business that are not necessarily related. For example, GE makes and sells appliances, jet aircraft engines, nuclear reactors, and plastics among other things. What are some possible ways to find a company comparable to GE that you can use to base an earnings multiple on?

2. Many free financial websites report average P/E and PEG ratios for a company and also for the industry it is in. Choose a stock you are interested in and find its current P/E ratio and the average P/E ratio for the company's industry. Use the industry P/E ratio as a P/E multiple to value the company you are interested in.

P/E Ratios and the Method of Comparables
Lecture 8—Transcript

In the previous lecture, we started the unit on stockpicking tools. We learned some basic financial statement analysis, and saw how to use it to identify companies that are worth looking at in more depth. In this lecture, we'll start learning how to actually drill down into a company and its stock, using valuation models.

Valuation models are extremely important to stockpicking. In fact, any time you're investing, you should be using some kind of valuation model, even if it's very simple. Valuation models simply help us figure out what something is worth. Whenever we buy any product, whether it's a cup of coffee at Starbuck's or a new car, we compare the price of the product to what it's actually worth to us. If we think something is worth the price, we buy it.

Investing really works the same way. By figuring out what we think a stock is worth, we can pick the stocks that we think are worth at least as much, and hopefully a lot more, than their current prices. And, we can avoid buying stocks that are overpriced.

Notice that I keep emphasizing that we're going to use valuation models to think about what we think an investment is worth. As I keep telling my students, there's no absolute truth about value waiting to be discovered out there. Generally speaking, there's constant disagreement in the markets about what any given investment is worth. These disagreements arise for several good reasons.

First, the value of any investment depends on what will happen in the future—and everybody has different ideas about that. Second, you have to make tons of judgment calls when you apply any valuation model to the real world. Different people will apply the same model in different ways, and get different answers. And finally, there are many different valuation models, and they often disagree.

When I first tell people that there's no such thing as the true value of an investment, they get a little panicked. Isn't it a bad thing that we don't know for sure what an investment is worth?

No. It's actually good that there's a lot of disagreement about value. That's exactly what gives each of us the opportunity to pick stocks and beat the market. So as you take these valuation models and start applying them to interesting stocks, keep in mind that your mission is to use these models to help you find companies that you think most people have overlooked or underestimated. You want to find companies that you think are worth more than the market says they are.

So, with these ideas about valuation in mind, let's look at our first stock-picking model. The general name for this valuation method is the method of comparables, and it's based on using ratios, like the price-to-earnings or P/E ratio, to value stocks.

This model is widely used in all kinds of financial markets, not just the stock market. In addition, I'd say that it's the model that professionals prefer to use, by far. The reason why professionals prefer this method is that it's simple, fast, and reliable. In fact, most professionals will tell you that this method lets the market speak directly about what an asset should be worth. What's not to like, right? In this lecture, we'll learn how to use the method of comparables to price stocks. And we'll see whether it's really all it's cracked up to be.

The method of comparables starts with a very simple idea. Every asset has some features or characteristics that indicate or influence its value. For example, one of the characteristics of a company that most influences its value is its earnings. We call these characteristics value drivers, because they literally drive the value of an asset. Every asset has a different set of value drivers. Some are easy to measure, like a company's earnings, while others are hard to measure. For example, we know that in real estate, the big value driver is location, but it's hard to capture that in a simple number. So we have to use other value drivers for real estate and try to hold the location constant when we apply this method.

The second big idea behind the method of comparables is that if two assets are truly comparable, then they'll have a similar relationship between their prices and any given value driver. Now, we know that the relationship between the price of some asset and its value drivers can be complex, maybe even nonlinear. But we don't assume that we know anything about the specific form that this relationship takes. Instead, we simply form the ratio between the price of the asset and its value driver, and let this ratio represent the relationship.

To make this concrete, let's let P stand for the price of some asset, and V stand for the value of some value driver that we think affects P. In addition, let's consider two comparable assets, asset A and asset B. Now, the method of comparables says that if asset A and asset B really are comparable, then the ratio of each asset's price to its value driver should be the same for both assets. Here it is in an equation:

$$P_A/V_A = P_B/V_B.$$

And that's it. The method of comparables is simply a use of ratios and proportions. We use the ratio of one asset's price to its value driver, which we call a valuation multiple, to estimate the prices of other assets.

For example, if we were using the price-to-earnings ratio, then V_A would be the earnings per share for Company A and P_A/V_A would be called the earnings multiple. We multiply Company A's earnings multiple times Company B's earnings to get an estimate of Company B's price. Then, if the market price of Company B's stock was less than the predicted price, we'd want to look deeper into Company B to see whether there is more information about Company B that indicates it would be a good investment.

This method seems pretty simple. So let's think more carefully about actually using it to estimate some stock prices, and see if it really is as easy to use as it appears to be.

The first issue is, what value driver should we pick? You can literally choose any characteristic you want. The three most popular value drivers for stocks are earnings per share, or EPS; book value per share; which is balance sheet equity divided by the number of shares outstanding; and sales or revenues per share. So the three big ratios that analysts look at are called the price-to-earnings or P/E ratio, the price-to-book ratio, and the price-to-sales ratio. I'll be giving examples with all three of these.

But all kinds of other value drivers are possible, and the choice of value driver depends on the industry, as well as on the state of development of the firms in the industry. One of my favorite valuation multiples comes from the days of the dotcom boom. You may remember that there were hundreds of firms trying to go public at the time that didn't even have positive earnings. But that didn't stop the analysts from finding a value driver.

Since these firms were mostly Internet startups—you may remember, for example, Pets.com, Webvan, and other famous or notorious examples—the analysts figured that the number of clicks on the websites of these companies should be related to the price of the companies. After all, the more clicks there are on a site like Pets.com, the more sales there should be. So the valuation multiple "price-to-clicks" or even "price-to-eyeballs," where "eyeballs" was a distinct new visitor to a website, briefly became valuation multiples that investors used to price these companies.

This example helps to show one of the strengths of the method of comparables—you can always find some value driver to base a multiple on. If a company's earnings are negative, no problem—try the price-to-book ratio. If the company doesn't have a lot of equity, no problem—try the price-to-sales ratio. And so on, until you find some ratio that works.

The next issue is finding comparable companies. The accuracy and reliability of the method of comparables relies heavily on finding truly comparable assets to compare to each other. For example, if you're trying to find the price for your home when you want to sell it, you'd like to find the selling price of the same-sized house in your own neighborhood. The price of a smaller house in a neighborhood across town wouldn't generally be very comparable, and it would give an unreliable estimate of the value of your house.

When it comes to applying the method of comparables to stocks, we usually use companies in the same industry or sub-industry as our comparable companies. For example, suppose you were interested in the stock of The Cheesecake Factory, a chain of casual dining restaurants. When you look up information on this stock on most financial websites, they will tell you what industry this company is in, and probably link you to information about the industry. The industry that The Cheesecake Factory belongs to is restaurants.

Of course, just because a company is listed as being in the industry, this doesn't necessarily make it comparable to the company that you are interested in. For example, the restaurants industry includes fast food places, like McDonalds Corporation, in addition to sit-down casual dining restaurants like The Cheesecake Factory. On the other end, the restaurants industry also includes higher-end chains like Morton's and Ruth's Chris Steakhouses. You probably wouldn't want to include either end of the spectrum of restaurants in with your set of casual-dining companies; they're just not the same.

Other considerations are whether to include foreign stocks as comparable companies, or companies of very different sizes in your list of comparable companies. Again, your choice will depend on the specifics of the company you're investigating and whether you can find many companies that are good matches for it.

In the case of The Cheesecake Factory, I'm going to include other American casual-dining chains that also have fairly large total market values—about $1 billion or more. So, as a first cut of companies, I would include these on my list: Darden Restaurants, Inc. (DRI); Brinker International, Inc. (EAT); Ruby Tuesday, Inc. (RT); Panera Bread Co. (PNRA); Cracker Barrel Old Country Store, Inc. (CBRL); Bob Evans Farms, Inc. (BOBE); Texas Roadhouse Inc. (TXRH); and Buffalo Wild Wings, Inc. (BWLD).

Most of these companies' names are self-explanatory, but you may not recognize Darden Restaurants until I tell you that it operates Red Lobster and The Olive Garden, among other restaurants. Likewise, Brinker International is the company behind Chili's Bar and Grille, and several other restaurant chains as well.

Generating a list like this leads to a related question: How should we use the information from all of the different firms? In practice, valuation multiples are averages of the multiples for many different firms. So if I wanted to value The Cheesecake Factory using a price-to-earnings ratio, I would form the earnings ratios for all the comparable firms on my list and then take a simple average of these multiples. Doing this is actually fairly easy, since most free financial websites have several pages of summary statistics on each company where you can find all the prices and various company statistics that I'm using in this lecture.

So I went out and found the prices of all the companies on my list, and I put them in a column that I've labeled P, for Price. Then I found the earnings per share, or EPS, for each company and put them in a column labeled EPS on the spreadsheet. Then to find the P/E multiples for each company, I divide each company's price by its EPS, and then I put the result in another column called P/EPS.

Notice that I'm not including the multiple for The Cheesecake Factory, because I want to use the information from the rest of the market to price that company. I collected The Cheesecake Factory's earnings per share and put that information in my table, but notice that I skipped a line to keep it separate.

Underneath the P/EPS column, I calculated the average P/E ratio for my eight companies and I've labeled this the average valuation multiple. The value of this average multiple was 14.55. Now I'll use this valuation multiple, and the actual value of The Cheesecake Factory's EPS, to estimate the price of the stock.

To find a price for The Cheesecake Factory, I take its earnings, which are $1.67 per share, and then multiply by the average earnings multiple for the comparable firms that I selected, that is 14.55. So when I multiply the two numbers together, the answer is $24.29. I put this in the table and labeled it the estimated price of CAKE, using the stock ticker symbol for The Cheesecake Factory, CAKE.

Now I compare this estimated price to the actual market price of The Cheesecake Factory. I put the actual price in a line just below the estimated price. The actual price when I did this exercise was $26.14. So my comparables estimate based on an earnings multiple is less than $2 below the current market price of the shares. Not too bad.

One question you may have is whether there is a minimum number of comparable firms you should use. Generally, the answer is that there isn't a minimum number. Sometimes industries are relatively small, and you only have a few firms to compare. In other cases, you may know that one or two firms are extremely similar to the company you want to investigate, so that adding other less similar companies to your multiple will only water down the quality of the comparison. It's fine to use only one or two companies in your valuation multiple, as long as you have a sensible reason for doing that. If you don't, though, then more is generally better, since you don't want to base your analysis on one firm that may turn out to be an extreme case.

For the sake of comparison, here's what we get for the value of The Cheesecake Factory using a price-to-book multiple, in the same way that I used the price-to-earnings multiple before. And then, here's what we get for the value of The Cheesecake Factory when we use a price-to-sales multiple to value the company. Wow! Notice that for The Cheesecake Factory, the method of comparables produced estimates of the price that were fairly close together and in fact in one case was almost exactly equal to the current market price. The earnings multiple gave a value of $24.29, the book value multiple gave a value of $28.67, and the sales multiple gave a value of $26.17. These estimates are not only close together, they're all pretty close to The Cheesecake Factory's actual stock price of $26.14.

Before we get too excited about the reliability of this method, though, let me show you what would have happened if I would have used the same set of total firms to value Cracker Barrel instead. What I'll show you next is a similar set of comparables tables just like the ones I used to value The Cheesecake Factory. But in these tables, I took Cracker Barrel out of the set of comparable firms and replaced it with The Cheesecake Factory. So now I'm using The Cheesecake Factory, and the other seven comparable companies, to price Cracker Barrel.

I went through the same steps as I did with The Cheesecake Factory. For example, here is the P/E analysis for Cracker Barrel. On the table, you can see that I've separated Cracker Barrel out from the list of comparable firms and added The Cheesecake Factory to it. I calculate an average P/E ratio for the eight companies, which is 15.27, and then multiply this by Cracker Barrel's earnings per share of $4. This gives an estimated price of $61.08.

Similarly, here's the analysis for the price-to-book ratio. The average price-to-book ratio is 2.79 for the eight comparable companies, and this is multiplied by Cracker Barrel's book value per share of $11.32 to get an estimated price of $31.54. And finally, repeating this analysis for the price-to-sales ratio, we get an average price-to-sales ratio for the eight comparable companies of 0.97. We multiply this sales multiple by Cracker Barrel's sales per share of $105.43 and get an estimated price of $101.87.

This time, the multiples didn't do so well. There's a big variation in the estimated prices. And while the predicted price based on the book multiple is somewhat close to the current market value, it's still about $9 lower than the current market price. The other two predicted prices are far higher than the current market price. What investing decision should we make, based on this evidence?

Notice what the valuation ratios are really saying about the two companies. On one hand, they're saying that The Cheesecake Factory's multiples are about average, relative to these peer firms. This may indicate that the company is more or less fairly valued, and it doesn't look like there are any big opportunities for investors to profit from buying this company. But if we look at Cracker Barrel, the variation in the prices is saying that for at least two of the value drivers, Cracker Barrel looks seriously undervalued. Should we believe the evidence from these high multiples? Well, not at face value. We need to investigate why Cracker Barrel looks undervalued according to EPS and sales, but overvalued according to book value. Our further investigation will hopefully help us come to some conclusion about whether the company would be a good investment.

One of the ways we can do this investigation is by digging deeper into the ratios. For example, stock analysts think that the P/E ratio is itself driven by the expected growth rate of the company's earnings. This positive relationship between the P/E ratio and the earnings growth rate is well known, and many analysts have tried to understand it. And of course, they understand it by making another ratio. In this case, what analysts do is they take the P/E ratio for a stock, which is usually some number greater than one but less than, say, 100, and then they divide this number by the forecast earnings growth rate, expressed in whole percent. This is called the PEG ratio, since it takes P/E and divides it by g, the growth rate of earnings.

For example, in the case of The Cheesecake Factory, the price was $26.14 when I looked it up, and the current year's EPS estimate was $1.67. So the P/E ratio was 26.14/1.67 = 15.65. I take this P/E ratio of 15.65 and divide it by the estimated long-term growth rate forecast of EPS, which was 14.34% on the day I looked it up. So the PEG ratio for The Cheesecake Factory is 15.65/14.34 = 1.09.

What does this PEG mean? According to investing folklore, a fairly priced stock would have a PEG ratio of one, an underpriced stock would have a PEG ratio less than one, and an overpriced stock would have a PEG ratio of greater than one. Since The Cheesecake Factory's PEG is a little over one, this would be taken as evidence that this company is a little bit overpriced. For Cracker Barrel, on the other hand, the PEG ratio is about 0.93, which indicates that it's a bit underpriced.

The benchmark of one for the PEG ratio has been around for a long time, and it was popularized as a part of Peter Lynch's investing philosophy called GARP or "growth at a reasonable price." But, if we think about it, there's not necessarily any reason why a company's P/E ratio should naturally be equal to its EPS growth rate. In fact, an academic paper I read a few years ago, that used a ton of algebra and assumptions, came up with some incredibly complicated formula relating the PEG ratio to a stock's return.

But who cares? This is a case in which it doesn't matter what the truth is, it matters what the people in the market think. The investors in the market have established that the benchmark for the PEG ratio is one, and people are making investment decisions based on this benchmark—so reality is being shaped by that idea. A firm with a PEG ratio of, say, 0.6 will attract investors, who will buy the stock, and that pushes up its price. The P/E rises, and with it the PEG ratio of the stock, until the PEG gets close to one. When that happens, investors stop buying the stock because they think it's not a bargain anymore, so the PEG comes to rest at one.

This phenomenon points out a potential problem with the method of comparables. This method has been so successful that it has become more prescriptive than descriptive in many cases.

For example, we often hear the P/E ratio being used in a prescriptive way to talk about the overall value of the stock market. Investors pay a lot of attention to historic P/E ratios, and they use average P/E ratios to judge whether the entire market is over- or undervalued. For example, at the height of the dotcom boom in 2001 the P/E ratio for the S&P 500 was about 26, when historically it had been at about 14. Over the decade of 2001–2010, the average P/E ratio for the S&P 500 was about 18 and the range was between about 15 and 20.

Statistically, it's possible that there is some kind of long-run average P/E ratio that the stock market should return to over time. But the P/E ratio itself is going to depend, as we've seen, on the underlying growth rate of earnings, and all the economic forces that we know are responsible for that. We know that the economy is always changing and evolving. So why shouldn't this long-run average P/E ratio change and evolve over time as well? The answer is probably that it does. But what we see in the market, in my opinion, is that people don't change their minds about the long-run average P/E ratio very quickly. So we continue to use long-run P/E ratios that may actually be outdated. But even though it may be outdated, this number still has a big influence on the prices that people are willing to pay for stocks.

The tendency of the P/E ratio and other valuation multiples to be used prescriptively is only one possible drawback of the method of comparables. There are several others that you should understand as well.

As I mentioned at the start of this lecture, one of the reasons why professionals like to use the method of comparables is their confidence that this method can't be easily manipulated. But if you've been paying attention to some of the assumptions that I've had to make in order to implement this method, then you'll realize that this claim doesn't stand up. It's possible to bias a method of comparables valuation fairly easily.

As we've learned, the key step in the method of comparables is to select the appropriate set of comparable firms to include in your valuation multiple. In general, the number of companies that you'll be using to estimate valuation multiples isn't all that big—maybe you'll use 15 to 20 firms in a really big industry. Choosing the firms you include in a careful way can distort the valuation multiple that you end up with.

Another matter of choice is the value drivers that you choose to use in your estimates. In many cases, companies will try to direct investors to modified measures of earnings or other value drivers, in the hopes that the investors will plug these modified versions into their standard valuation multiples and be willing to pay higher prices for a company's shares.

For example, during and immediately after the dotcom boom and bust, many companies started to get very aggressive in presenting what they called pro-forma earnings. Pro-forma means *as if*, so firms were presenting their own versions of earnings that left out many expenses, as if they didn't occur. The companies who did this claimed that the expenses were one-time expenses or extraordinary events, and that the pro-forma earnings gave a clearer picture of what the firm's true earnings were. Of course, firms got really creative about what they termed "extraordinary" expenses. One waste-disposal firm, for example, called it an extraordinary expense when it had its fleet of garbage trucks repainted. After a while, pro-forma earnings took on the alternative definition of "earnings before bad stuff" and firms began to emphasize their pro-forma earnings more than their true earnings.

This raised a big concern at the SEC that individual investors would accept the pro-forma earnings as the firm's true earnings, and use them as the basis of their P/E valuations. Naturally, if a company excludes all kinds of expenses from earnings, they look a lot bigger, so the company doesn't look overvalued. This problem became such an issue that the SEC actually created a regulation in 2003, called Regulation G, that strongly regulated the practice of using pro-forma earnings and forced companies to de-emphasize them in their press releases and other filings.

Fast forward to 2011, and the case of Groupon, a web-based company that markets group coupons for discounts at restaurants and other retailers. Groupon came under fire from the SEC for pursuing exactly this type of practice with respect to its earnings.

Groupon constructed a measure of earnings called "Adjusted Consolidated Segment Operating Income," or adjusted CSOI, which basically excluded any marketing expenses from the calculation of earnings. In the case of Groupon's business model, these marketing expenses were one of the largest expenses faced by the company. So, it seemed that Groupon was also trying to focus on an earnings number that made the company's P/E ratio look small, so that people wouldn't think the company was overvalued.

The flip side of this problem of understating the P/E ratios is that the accounting rules that firms are supposed to follow require some investments to be counted as expenses. This lowers the amount of recorded earnings and hence raises the P/E ratio, making firms look overvalued. One of the investments that is accounted for in this way is research and development costs, or R&D.

Under the U.S. generally accepted accounting principles, any money spent on research and development must be counted as an expense, which directly lowers earnings. But these R&D costs lead to the creation of knowledge and other assets that create future profits, leading to increases in the companies' stock values. Because the R&D costs are expensed, this makes earnings look very low, so the P/E ratio looks far too high and the shares look overvalued.

In fact, Federal Reserve economist Leonard Nakamura has studied this effect and he has taken the time to construct an economy-wide measure of the P/E ratio that adjusts for R&D. He basically found that once R&D is accounted for, the P/E ratio for the 1990s and after is almost exactly the same as in the 1960s. His findings only reinforce to me the point that I made a few minutes ago that we should expect the P/E ratio to evolve with the economy, and take these age-old P/E benchmarks with a grain of salt. It's far better to judge the value of each company on its own merits.

There's an overview of the method of comparables. You can use the information from the four main ratios we learned about in this lecture—P/E, price-to-book, price-to-sales, and the PEG ratio—to help find stocks that seem undervalued. But keep in mind that once you find a potentially undervalued stock, your work is just starting. You need to get more information on the company to see whether it deserves its low ratio because of lackluster performance, or whether it really is one of these overlooked and underappreciated companies that has the potential to surprise the market. In the next lecture, we'll learn another valuation method that can provide some of the additional information we need.

Fundamentals-Based Analysis of Stocks
Lecture 9

In the last lecture, you learned about the main model that most professional investors use to help them pick stocks: the method of comparables. Once you identify a company that looks good, however, you still need more information about it. One way to do this is to use other stock-pricing models, such as the dividend discount model (DDM), which can offer insights into a company that help explain why it looks undervalued based on its valuation ratios. Models like the DDM are sources of additional evidence that help to confirm or contradict the information gained through the method of comparables.

The Dividend Discount Model

- In addition to the method of comparables, the **dividend discount model (DDM)** is a fundamentals-based stock-pricing model. Fundamentals-based models rest on 2 simple ideas: The price of any investment should depend only on the cash that it's going to pay you, and cash paid to you in the future is worth less to you than cash you receive now.

- The cash flows that investors receive from stock are the dividends, so fundamentals-based models of stock price note that the current price of a share of stock is equal to the present discounted value of the sum of all its future dividends. Technically, this represents an infinite number of future dividends.

- There's a surprisingly simple formula for the present value of the sum of all future dividends: $D/(r - g)$, where D is the next year's dividend, r is the expected return on the stock, and g is the growth rate of the dividend. This formula is called the dividend discount model.

- There are other fundamentals-based stock pricing models, but this one is the simplest and by far the most common. The main assumption that this model makes is that companies try to make their dividends grow at a low, constant rate. In reality, dividends don't necessarily grow at a constant rate, so the g in the formula really represents the long-run, average growth rate of the dividend.

- In order to get a sensible number from the DDM, we have to assume that g is less than r. If g is greater than r, then not only does the formula imply a negative price for the stock, which is unrealistic, but a negative value would be the exact opposite of the true value.

Applying the DDM
- Let's apply the dividend discount model to the stock of AT&T, whose stock ticker symbol is T on the New York Stock Exchange. Applying the DDM is a matter of getting the 3 numbers you need for the formula: the amount of the next annual dividend, the expected return on the stock, and the growth rate of the dividend.

- Next year's dividend, the D in the formula, is the easiest number to find. Just about any free financial website that covers stocks will have an information page about the stock that lists the annual dividend, among many other pieces of information. AT&T's annual dividend is currently given as $1.72 per share, for example.

- The next number is the expected rate of return on the stock, r. In the case of stocks, most people use a model of expected returns called the **capital asset pricing model (CAPM)** in order to estimate expected rates of return. When you look on most free financial websites, you'll find the information you need to use the CAPM to estimate a discount rate for a stock.

- The number you need in order to use the CAPM is called beta, and most financial websites list the stock's beta as well. **Beta** is a measure of the riskiness, or return variation, of a stock; in fact, it's supposed to be the number of units of risk in the stock, where one unit of risk is equivalent to the amount of risk, or return variation, in the overall stock market.

- According to the CAPM, the expected return on a stock rises about 7% for every unit of risk it contains, and if a stock has zero units of risk, then it's risk-free and should earn the risk-free rate of return, which is usually based on the rate of return of government bonds because they're as close to risk-free as any asset gets.

- To use the CAPM to estimate the expected return, or discount rate, on a stock, we use the following formula: $E(r_i) = r_f + \beta_i \times (E(r_m) - r_f)$, in which $E(r_i)$ is the expected return we want to find. The r_f is the risk-free rate, which we usually take to be the return on a 10-year Treasury bond, and β_i is the beta. The final term is the difference between the expected return on the entire market and the risk-free rate—called the market risk premium, or the compensation for bearing one unit of risk.

- We use 7% for the market risk premium, and we find the beta from the financial website. For AT&T, the current beta is 0.52, for example, which means that there is just over 1/2 a unit of risk in AT&T stock. To find the risk-free rate, we could just take the current market rate on the 10-year Treasury rate, but this rate fluctuates. A normal level for the 10-year Treasury rate, based on decades of experience, is around 4% to 6%. Let's use 4% in our example.

- When you plug all the numbers into the CAPM, you get $E(r_i) = 0.04 + 0.52 \times 0.07 = 0.0764$. Therefore, the expected return on AT&T stock is 7.64%. You can also interpret this as the discount rate used to find the present value of the dividends.

- We now have numbers for the dividend and the discount rate, so this just leaves g, which is supposed to be the average, long-term growth rate of dividends on the stock from now until eternity.

Calculating the Growth Rate
- There are many ways to calculate g, but there are 3 ways that capture the various ways of thinking about where the growth of a firm comes from. These different ways may lead to very different

price estimates, or only one estimate of g may give you a sensible answer for the price of the stock.

- The simplest way to estimate the long-term average growth rate of dividends is to look at past dividend growth and use that as your estimate. In fact, on most financial websites, you can find a link to statistics on the dividends a firm pays, and one of the statistics most sites list is the average dividend growth rate over the past 5 years. For example, you might find that this number for AT&T is 5.39%.

- Plugging in the numbers we have obtained thus far for AT&T, we get $D/(r - g) = 1.72/(0.0764 - 0.0539) = \$76.44$. In other words, the DDM suggests that a share of AT&T should be priced at \$76.44, assuming that the historical growth rate of dividends will continue into the indefinite future.

- Stock analysts are able to forecast the earnings growth rate, and we are able to use this as an estimate of the growth rate of dividends. One of the implications of the DDM is that both earnings per share and dividends grow at the same rate: g. Therefore, we can assume that the dividend growth rate will be the same as the growth rate of earnings per share, or EPS.

- For AT&T, you might find that the mean of the analysts' long-term EPS growth rate forecast is 4.27%, which is not much different from the historical average growth rate of dividends. When you plug this estimate of the dividend growth rate into the formula with the same numbers for dividend (1.72) and expected return (0.0764) as before, you will get a price estimate equal to $1.72/(0.0764 - 0.0427) = \$51.04$.

- This second estimate changed the dividend growth rate estimate by only a little over 1%, but it changed the estimate of the price by over \$20. This illustrates one of the main complaints about the DDM: The price estimates are very sensitive to small changes in the estimated dividend growth rate and to changes in the discount rate.

- The final method of estimating g depends on accounting data and allows us to think about where the company's growth comes from. If corporations want to, they can retain their earnings and reinvest them into new projects, creating growth for the firm.

- If a company takes all of its earnings and reinvests 100% of EPS back into the company, then the net earnings and EPS will grow at a rate given by ROE. However, in reality, only a part of EPS is reinvested; the rest is paid out to the shareholders as dividends.

- Analysts refer to the fraction of EPS that is paid out to shareholders as the **payout ratio** and to the share of EPS that is reinvested in the company as the **plowback ratio**, which is $(EPS - D)/EPS$, or $1 - (D/EPS)$. The payout ratio is D/EPS so that the payout ratio and the plowback ratio sum to 1.

- The fraction of EPS that is reinvested into the company makes net earnings grow at a rate given by ROE, but the fraction of EPS that is paid out doesn't cause any earnings growth for the company at all. Therefore, we can form a weighted average to find the implied growth rate of net earnings: g = plowback ratio × ROE, where the plowback ratio is $1 - (D/EPS)$.

- We need 3 numbers to implement this estimate of g: the dividend, some measure of EPS, and ROE. The EPS forecast you might find for AT&T, for example, is $2.38, which together with the dividend of $1.72 implies that the plowback ratio is $1 - (1.72/2.38) = 27.23\%$. You might find that the ROE is 12.39%, for example, so the estimate of g is $0.2723 \times 0.1239 = 3.44\%$. This gives an even lower estimate of price than the other 2 methods. When we plug this g into the DDM formula, we get that the price is equal to $1.72/(0.0764 - 0.0344) = \$40.91$.

Conceptual Shortcomings
- There are several issues with all 3 models that make the estimates seem less reliable than we'd like them to be. First, the numbers on past dividend growth don't tell us anything about why dividends

were growing the way they did, so we have no idea whether the company can sustain this growth rate or whether it intends to maintain it in the future.

- Next, stock analysts are notoriously biased in the positive direction when forecasting future EPS growth, overstating the future growth of the companies they follow.

- With the accounting method of finding g, the main issue is that both the plowback ratio and a company's ROE are subject to change, and as they change, the estimated growth rate of dividends will change. Furthermore, in addition to the information in the DDM, specific information about a company's investment plans—which they do openly share—is what you need.

- In addition to these problems, there's an even larger practical problem with the DDM: Often, you can't apply the DDM at all. Many companies simply don't pay dividends. Additionally, many times, g will be greater than r.

- Despite the criticisms of the DDM, it is useful because it focuses our attention on information about dividend growth and its sustainability. However, the full explanation of dividend growth and sustainability has to come from in-depth information about a company's investment projects.

Important Terms

beta: A measure of the riskiness, or return variation, of a stock; the number of units of risk in a stock, where one unit of risk is equivalent to the amount of risk, or return variation, in the overall stock market.

capital asset pricing model (CAPM): A model that is used to estimate expected rates of return for stocks.

dividend discount model (DDM): A fundamentals-based stock-pricing model that is represented by $D/(r - g)$, where D is the next year's dividend, r is the expected return on the stock, and g is the growth rate of the dividend.

payout ratio: The fraction of earnings per share (EPS) that is paid out to a company's shareholders: D/EPS.

plowback ratio: The fraction of earnings per share (EPS) that is reinvested in a company: $(\text{EPS} - D)/\text{EPS}$, or $1 - (D/\text{EPS})$.

Suggested Reading

Bodie, Kane, and Marcus, *Essentials of Investments*, chap. 13.

English, *Applied Equity Analysis*, chap. 14.

Questions to Consider

1. Choose a stock you are interested in that pays dividends and look it up on a free financial website. Find the dividend that the company is expected to pay this year. Then, find the company's beta and estimate the expected return r for the stock using a risk-free rate of .04 and an expected return to the market of .10. Then, find the analyst forecasts for earnings per share growth of this stock and use this as your estimate of g, the growth rate of dividends. Does your estimate of this company's price using the dividend discount model formula, $P = D/(r - g)$, agree with the current market price?

2. Choose a stock you are interested in that pays dividends and find its average dividend growth rate during the past 5 years. Then, compare this to the company's expected growth of earnings per share, which should also be equal to the dividend growth rate. Do the 2 numbers agree? If they are different, what do you think is responsible for the difference you observe?

Fundamentals-Based Analysis of Stocks
Lecture 9—Transcript

In the last lecture, we learned about the main model that most professional investors use to help them pick stocks—the method of comparables. But remember, at the end of the lecture I said that once we identify a company that looks good, based on its P/E or other ratios, we'll still want to get more information about it. We want to know as much as we can about that company, and especially how it creates value for its shareholders, before we invest.

A great way to get this additional information is to see what other stock pricing models can tell us about the value of the company. Other models can give us insights into a company that help explain why it looks undervalued, based on its valuation ratios. In other words, these models are sources of additional evidence that helps to confirm or contradict the story that the method of comparables is telling us. If all the information we gather tells a consistent story saying that a company is creating a lot of value, then we can feel a lot more confident that it's really a good investment.

So with this in mind, let's introduce our next big stockpricing model. It's called the Dividend Discount Model, or DDM for short. The DDM is a fundamentals-based model. And what does that mean? Fundamentals-based models rest on two simple ideas. First, the price of any investment should depend only on the cash that it's going to pay you. And second, cash paid to you in the future is worth less to you than cash you receive now.

Any cash promised to you in the future has to be discounted—that is, reduced in value—to reflect the fact that if you would have received the cash today, you could have invested it and earned some kind of positive return on it. Because of their focus on cash and discounting, fundamentals-based models are also called discounted cash flow, or DCF, models.

What does a fundamentals-based, or discounted cash flow model say specifically about the value of a stock? Well, the cash flows that investors receive from stock are the dividends. So fundamentals-based models of stock prices say that the current price of a share of stock is equal to the present discounted value of the sum of all its future dividends.

Now, all future dividends sounds like a whole lot of dividends—and it is. Technically, it's an infinite number of future dividends. So this sounds like it might be a complicated, if not impossible task to find the present discounted value of all these dividends. Actually, there's a surprisingly simple formula for the present value of the sum of all future dividends: $D/(r - g)$, where D is the next year's dividend, r is the expected rate of return on the stock, and g is the growth rate of the dividend.

This formula is called the Dividend Discount Model. When you hear someone say that they're using a fundamentals-based model to value a stock, this formula should pop into your head. There are other fundamentals-based stock pricing models, but this one is the simplest and by far the most common. The main assumption that this model makes is that companies try to make their dividends grow at a low, constant rate. In reality, dividends don't necessarily grow at a constant rate, but we can think that the little g in the formula represents the long-run, average growth rate of the dividend. So g is a small number like 3% per year—though of course it can be higher.

If you look at the formula carefully, you can see immediately that we need to make one more assumption. In order to get a sensible number from the DDM, we have to assume that g, the dividend growth rate, is less than r, the expected return on the stock. If g is greater than r, then we get an absurd result from the formula. In that case, not only does the formula imply a negative price for the stock, which is silly, but a negative value in this case would be the exact opposite of the true value. If a firm's dividend grew at a rate faster than the expected rate of return on the stock, then the present value of all the future dividends would literally be infinity. You should be willing to pay all the money in the world for a stock like that. So it's very important to keep in mind that this formula only works for the case where g is less than r.

$D/(r - g)$: Hopefully, you'll find the DDM easy to remember. But the more important issue is whether it's easy to apply in real life. Fortunately, the answer is yes—with a few conditions, of course. What I'm going to do next is to show you the ropes of applying the DDM to real companies, so you can see how to do it and what the conditions are.

To make this easier to follow, I'm going to apply the dividend discount model to the stock of AT&T. AT&T's stock ticker symbol is simply T, and it's listed on the New York Stock Exchange.

Applying the DDM is a matter of getting the three numbers you need to work the formula: the amount of the next annual dividend, D; the expected return on the stock, r; and the growth rate of the dividend, g.

Next year's dividend, the D in the formula, is the easiest number to find. Just about any free financial website that covers stocks will have an information page about the stock that lists the annual dividend, among many other pieces of information. When I looked up AT&T's information, the annual dividend was given as $1.72 per share.

The next number I need is the expected rate of return on the stock, that's the little r. In the case of stocks, most people use a model of expected returns called the CAPM in order to estimate expected rates of return. CAPM is an acronym that stands for Capital Asset Pricing Model. Even though many people don't believe the CAPM is true, or accurate, most people still use the CAPM as if it were. Interestingly, the reason why people who don't believe the CAPM is true still want to use it is that they probably want to know what everyone else is thinking, so they can know what prices other traders have in mind. Either way, when you look on most free financial websites, you'll find the information you need to use the CAPM to estimate a discount rate for a stock.

The number you need in order to use the CAPM is called beta, and indeed most financial websites list the stock's beta. Beta is a measure of the riskiness, or return variation, of a stock, and in fact it's supposed to be the number of units of risk in the stock, where one unit of risk is equivalent to the amount of risk, or return variation, in the overall stock market.

According to the CAPM, the expected return on a stock rises about 7% for every unit of risk it contains. And if a stock has 0 units of risk, then it's risk free, and should earn the risk-free rate of return. The risk-free rate is the rate of return that human beings demand simply because they're impatient, and need to be compensated for waiting for a loan to be paid back, even if it's a sure thing that the loan will be repaid. We usually use the rate of return earned on government bonds as a measure of the risk-free rate, because they're about as close to risk free as any asset gets!

To use the CAPM to estimate the expected return, or discount rate on a stock, we use the following formula: $E(r_i) = r_f + \beta_i \times (E(r_m) - r_f)$. Now, in the formula, $E(r_i)$ is the expected return we want to find. The r_f is the risk-free rate, which we usually take to be the return on a 10-year Treasury bond. I've explained what the beta is, and then the final term in the brackets is the difference between the expected return on the entire market and the risk-free rate. This is called the market risk premium, and it's also called the compensation for bearing one unit of risk. In other words, that's the 7% I just mentioned.

So we take 7% for the market risk premium, and we find the beta from the financial website. For AT&T, the beta I found was 0.52, which means that there's just over half a unit of risk in AT&T stock. That just leaves the risk-free rate. Here, there's a bit of a judgment call to make. We could just take the current market rate on the 10-year Treasury bond, but this rate does fluctuate and sometimes it takes on levels that are much higher and much lower than normal. A normal level for the 10-year Treasury rate, based on decades of experience, seems to be around 4 to 6%. I'll use 4% for the risk-free rate in my calculations.

When I plug all my numbers into the CAPM expected return formula, I get $E(r_i) = 0.04 + 0.52 \times 0.07 = 0.0764$. Therefore, my expected return on AT&T stock is 7.64%. As I've mentioned a couple of times already, we can also interpret this as the discount rate used to find the present value of the dividends.

We've found numbers for the dividend and the discount rate, so this just leaves g. And now the fun really begins. You see, g is supposed to be the average, long-term growth rate of dividends on the stock from here until, well, eternity. How do we find that number?

There are lots of ways we could do it, but I'll show you the three ways that I think make the most sense. I want to show you three different ways to estimate g because they capture different ways of thinking about where the growth of the firm comes from. And frankly, at any given time, these different ways may lead to very different price estimates, or only one estimate of g may give you a sensible answer for the price of the stock.

Let's try the simplest thing you can think of to estimate the long-term average growth rate of dividends—well, besides a pure guess. You'd probably want to look at past dividend growth and see what it looked like, and use that as your estimate. That's perfectly fine, and in fact on most financial websites, you can find a link to statistics on the dividends that a firm pays, and one of the statistics most sites list is the average dividend growth rate over the past five years. On the site I looked at, the average dividend growth rate for AT&T over the past five years was 5.39%.

Before we move on, let's see what kind of price this implies for AT&T. To remind ourselves, the dividend is $1.72, the discount rate is 7.64%, and the growth rate of the dividend is 5.39%. The growth rate of dividends is less than the discount rate, so the price estimate won't be absurd. Plugging in the numbers, we get $D/(r - g) = 1.72/(0.0764 - 0.0539) = \$76.44$. In other words, the DDM suggests that a share of AT&T should be priced at $76.44, assuming that the historical growth rate of dividends will continue into the indefinite future. In the interest of time, I'll move on to the other methods of estimating g, and then we can compare outcomes.

The first method of estimating g used past data, and so we could call it backward looking. Can we find a forward-looking estimate of g that tries to project growth into the future? Sure—there are lots of people whose job it is to forecast all kinds of information about companies into the future. These are stock analysts, and one of the main things they do is forecast the earnings of a company. They forecast both the dollar value of earnings as well as the growth rate of earnings, and over short-run as well as long-run horizons. So let's use these analysts' forecasts somehow.

Now, you may be wondering why we can use earnings growth rate forecasts as an estimate of the growth rate of dividends. Well, it turns out that one of the implications of the DDM is that both earnings per share and dividends grow at the same rate—g. I'll show you why that's the case later, but for now we can assume that the dividend growth rate will be the same as the growth rate of earnings per share or EPS.

Most financial websites will list analyst forecast numbers at several different horizons. Since g is supposed to be a long-term average growth rate, you'll want to use the forecast of long-term EPS growth. On the websites, look for the mean of the analysts' forecasts of long-term EPS growth, and this will be an estimate of the long-term dividend growth rate.

For AT&T, the mean of the analysts' long-term EPS growth rate forecast was 4.27%. That's not all that different from the historical average growth rate of dividends. When I plug this estimate of the dividend growth rate into the formula with the same numbers for dividend ($1.72) and expected return (0.0764%) as before, I get a price estimate equal to $1.72/(0.0764 - 0.0427)$ = $51.04.

Wow! This second estimate changed the dividend growth rate estimate by a little bit—only a little over 1%—and this changed the estimate of the price by over $20! This illustrates one of the main complaints about the DDM—the price estimates are very sensitive to small changes in the estimated dividend growth rate, and to changes in the discount rate as well, for that matter. And of course, the variable in the DDM that we're least sure of is the dividend growth rate. So this uncertainty about the actual rate of dividend growth leads to a very large amount of uncertainty about the correct price of the stock.

We're not through estimating the dividend growth rate yet, though. There's one more method of estimating it, which depends on accounting data. This method actually gets us to think about where the company's growth comes from. If you recall my earlier lecture about stocks, then you might remember that we learned a little about this already. In that lecture, I explained that corporations are under no obligation to pay out their earnings as dividends. If they want to, they can retain their earnings and reinvest them into new projects. It's this process of reinvesting earnings into new projects that creates growth for the firm. So the third method of estimating g assigns some numbers to this reinvestment process.

In the previous lecture on financial statement analysis, we learned that some of the terminology and ratios that will help us understand this method of estimating the growth rate of dividends. When a company retains a dollar of earnings, this dollar is added to assets but no liabilities are added. Therefore, this adds a dollar to the equity of the company. You may remember from the lecture on financial statement analysis that we learned how total equity was both assets minus liabilities as well as the sum total of all paid-in capital and retained earnings over the entire history of the company.

When a dollar is added to equity, what does the company earn from this extra dollar? Well, we learned the answer in the previous lecture—it earns the return on equity, or ROE. Most free financial websites will report the ROE of a company, often in several places, so it's easy to find.

So if a company takes all of its earnings and reinvests 100% of EPS back into the company, then net earnings and EPS will grow at a rate given by ROE. But in reality, only a part of EPS is reinvested—the rest is paid out to the shareholders as dividends. Analysts refer to the fraction of EPS paid out to shareholders as the payout ratio, and they refer to the share of EPS that is reinvested in the company as the plowback ratio, the plowback ratio because it is plowed back into the firm. The plowback ratio is given by (EPS − D)/EPS, or 1 − D/EPS. The payout ratio, of course, would then be D/EPS so that the payout ratio and the plowback ratio sum to one.

The fraction of EPS that is reinvested into the company makes net earnings grow at a rate given by ROE. But the fraction of EPS that is paid out doesn't cause any earnings growth for the company at all. So we can form a weighted average to find the implied growth rate of net earnings. Here's the equation: g = plowback ratio × ROE + payout ratio × 0, and of course we drop the term that is zero and simply say that the growth rate of net earnings is equal to the plowback ratio times ROE.

But what about dividend growth? Well, we're almost there. If we assume that companies maintain a constant plowback ratio, then dividends will grow at the same rate as net earnings and EPS. This is important, so let me show you how it works.

For example, let's say the plowback ratio is fixed at one third of EPS, and EPS is equal to $3. So one dollar is plowed back into the company and $2 per share are paid out as dividends. Now let EPS grow by 10%, to $3.30.

With a fixed plowback ratio of 1/3, the company reinvests $1.10, and pays out the remaining $2.20 as dividends. So the fixed plowback ratio means that the EPS growth rate of 10% is going to be the growth rate of dividends as well. Whew! Now you can understand better why it was okay to use the EPS growth rate forecasts to estimate g, the growth rate of dividends. As long as we assume that the plowback ratio stays the same, dividends will grow at the same rate as earnings, which as we've learned is given by plowback times ROE.

Actually, just to draw one more connection here that you may find useful, the DDM not only implies that dividends and earnings grow at the same rate, but the price of the stock does, too. That is, the price of the stock will also grow at rate g, according to the DDM. That's because the price of the shares is proportional to the dividend, and the dividend grows at rate g, so the price of the stock must grow at rate g as well. This means that g is the rate of capital gains you should expect each year on your stock, if the DDM is correct. I always tell my students that in the DDM, everything grows at rate g—earnings, dividends, and the stock price.

Let's get back to our price estimate using the accounting numbers. So, remember that g is equal to the plowback ratio times ROE, where the plowback ratio is $1 - D/EPS$. Therefore, we need three numbers to implement this estimate of g: the dividend, some measure of ROE, and EPS. As I mentioned a minute ago, many free financial sites carry all these numbers. Let's take a look at AT&T once again and see what this method of applying the DDM has to say about AT&T's price.

The EPS forecast I found for AT&T was $2.38, which together with the dividend of $1.72, implies that the plowback ratio is $1 - \$1.72/\$2.38 = 27.23\%$. The ROE was 12.39%. So, when I take the plowback ratio times ROE, I find that the estimate of g is $0.2723 \times 0.1239 = 3.44\%$. This gives an even lower estimate of price than the other two methods. When we plug this g into the DDM formula, we get that the price is equal to $D/(r-g)$: $1.72/(0.0764 - 0.0344) = \$40.91$.

Now we've gone through a basic DDM analysis and showed how to use all three methods of estimating the dividend growth rate to implement this valuation model. What have we seen so far? Well, confusion for one thing.

Let's quickly review the three prices we came up with. When we used historical dividend growth to get g the share price we came up with was $76.44. When we used analysts' forecasts of EPS growth, we estimated a price of $51.04. And using accounting numbers, we formed an estimate of $40.91.

The prices we calculated disagree by fairly wide margins, and moreover none are all that close to the actual market price of AT&T when I obtained these numbers. For the record, the value of the stock at the time was only about $28, which was much lower than all of these estimates. I mentioned part of the reason for the disagreement, which is that the DDM's prices are very sensitive to small changes in the discount rate and the dividend growth rate estimates.

But another part of the problem comes from conceptual shortcomings in all three methods. First, let's start with historic dividends. These numbers on past dividend growth don't tell us anything about why dividends were growing the way that they did. So we have no idea whether the company can sustain this growth rate, or whether it even intends to maintain it into the future.

Next, let's think about analysts' forecasts of future EPS growth. Although stock analysts have access to much better data than the typical individual investor does, and although it's literally their job to forecast how a company will perform into the future, there's a big problem that offsets these advantages. Stock analysts are notoriously biased in the positive direction.

It's been well documented that analysts' buy recommendations outnumber their sell recommendations by a huge margin, and that analysts typically overstate the future growth of the companies they follow. Now, as an economist, all I can say is that it must be in their best interests to do so, because these people are generally pretty smart and pretty well informed. And if you look carefully, you'll discover a lot of possible incentives for analysts to be biased, ranging from their own compensation packages to maintaining a good working relationship with the firms that they follow.

Finally, the accounting method of finding g also has its problems. The main problem with this method is that both the plowback ratio and a company's ROE are subject to change, and as they change, the estimated growth rate of dividends will change. In addition, numbers like ROE are summary statistics that just don't tell us what we really want to know about a company. What we really want to know about are the actual projects that the company hopes to use to create the dividend growth in the future. Specific information about a company's plans—which they do share with the rest of the world—is what you need to get in addition to the information in the DDM.

For example, let's think about the case of AT&T for a moment. I mentioned that the DDM estimates not only disagreed, but they overstated the current market price of AT&T by quite a bit. At the time that I gathered the numbers that I showed you, AT&T had just received some bad news about a major investment project. AT&T had offered to buy T-Mobile's American wireless communication business, and the offer was accepted. This is a huge project for AT&T that could re-shape the entire U.S. communications market into a two-company market, meaning good things for AT&T's future profits. But the U.S. Department of Justice blocked the acquisition, which at the very least would mean that the entire deal would have to be scaled back. It could even mean that the deal is off.

If you know these facts about AT&T, then you're in a much better position to use the information from the dividend discount model. For example, you may believe that the company will be able to go through with its acquisition and sustain a dividend growth rate close to the ones that are implied by its plowback ratio or previous dividend growth rates. If this really is the case, then you'd think that at its current low price, AT&T is a great buy. Of course, the market must not be thinking that AT&T will be able to support the dividend growth rates we calculated, because it's assigning a low price to the stock. So in order to profit from buying AT&T, not only do you have to be smarter than the market, the market also has to change its mind eventually and come to agree with you.

So, all three ways of estimating the growth rate of dividends for the DDM have some serious issues that make the estimates seem less reliable than we'd like them to be. In addition to these problems, there's an even larger practical problem with the DDM, which I mentioned earlier in this lecture. Often, you can't apply the dividend discount model at all.

One reason for this is that many companies simply don't pay dividends. This problem is actually easier to deal with than you might think. You may remember from the lecture on financial statement analysis that I discussed an alternative measure of earnings called free cash flow. Free cash flow is the cash that could be paid out to the shareholders as dividends. Many analysts use free cash flow per share in place of the dividend in the DDM, and you can use this method as well.

Another reason why we can't apply the DDM is that many times, g will be greater than r. This condition implies that the company is worth an infinite amount, if the dividend continues to grow this quickly forever. But there's the problem—the assumption of constant dividend growth. Usually, firms that experience very high dividend growth can't sustain it for long periods of time, or at least not forever. Even the fastest-growing startup companies eventually mature and slow down. Happens to all of us, I know.

Relaxing the assumption that g stays constant can be done, but it requires more intensive math than we have time to get into. But when you encounter a stock that has g greater than r, you can still ask questions about why g is so high for the firm right now, and how long you can expect the high-growth period to last. The higher the growth is, and the longer it lasts, the greater the potential value of the company.

Despite all these criticisms of the DDM, it really is doing something useful for us. It's focusing our attention on information about dividend growth and its sustainability—which are very good issues to look into. But the full explanation of dividend growth and sustainability has to come from in-depth information about a company's investment projects, which can't be neatly summarized in numbers like ROE and plowback.

You'll have to supplement your number crunching with lots of reading about the companies you're considering adding to your portfolio. As you read, let the DDM guide the questions you ask and the directions that your research takes. Why did the company grow its dividend as quickly—or as slowly—as it did over the past five years? What objective reasons are analysts offering for their long-term EPS growth forecasts? What range of ROE can the company really expect from the projects they are disclosing to the media?

All of these questions are great—and they are motivated directly by the DDM and one of the three methods of estimating the dividend growth rate that we learned about in this lecture.

At the end of the day, I think these are the kinds of questions that successful stockpickers like Warren Buffett, Bill Miller, and others typically ask. So even though the fundamentals-based models won't win the Wall Street popularity contest, and they don't necessarily provide all the answers, they do point us to key information about a company's value. What you need to do as you consider different companies is to use the DDM's estimates of dividend growth rates, and stock prices, to drive your search for the stories behind the numbers. Again, look for companies that tell a value creation story that is consistent across their financial statements, their valuation ratios, and the dividends they pay out over time.

Start-Up Companies and IPOs
Lecture 10

In the last few lectures, you've learned how to pick the stocks of established companies that have solid financial statements, long track records of paying dividends, and healthy earnings. However, one of the most exciting types of stocks comes from companies that often don't have those things—companies that are about to have their initial public offerings, or IPOs. There might be money to be made in IPOs, but the facts about who really makes the money and what that means for individual investors will surprise you. In addition, not every new company is going to be the next Google.

Initial Public Offerings

- The **initial public offering (IPO)** marks the transition from being a privately held company that only 500 or fewer people can own to becoming a publicly held company that anyone can own a part of.

- In most IPOs, the company hires an investment bank to underwrite the public offering of stock. On the day of the IPO, the company sells the entire public offering to the investment bank, and then the investment bank sells the shares to the general public.

- When they underwrite IPOs, investment banks are taking a big risk. If the company that is going public turns out not to be very interesting to investors, the investment bank will be stuck with a ton of shares that it can't sell, and it will probably end up taking a loss on the deal. Therefore, the investment bank's top priority is to make sure that it finds enough investors to sell out the IPO shares.

- Institutional investors—including pension funds and especially the big mutual fund companies—are the ones investing in IPOs. If they choose to participate in an IPO, the shares will be fully subscribed and the IPO will be a success, but if they don't, the investment bank may call off the IPO or at least scale it back severely.

- As a result, institutional investors have market power in the IPO process, and they use it. Before each underwritten IPO, the investment bank contacts big institutional investors and asks them about their interest in the IPO. Basically, the investment bank builds up a demand curve for the company's shares—a process called building an IPO book or **book building**.

- The institutional investors use their market power by understating their true interest in the IPO—that is, they underbid. They want to hold the IPO price down because this will increase the chance that any shares they buy will increase in value after the company's shares start trading. Furthermore, because the mutual funds and other institutions make up such a large fraction of the demand for shares, they almost always succeed in holding the IPO price down.

- The result of this behavior is the famous first-day pop, in which the price of the firm's shares rise by 10% or more on the first day of market trading. The IPO pop is the result of the systematic underpricing of IPO shares.

Implications of the Book-Building Process
- The investment banks control who gets the shares of hot IPOs, and they use these shares to reward their best retail customers. As a result, it's almost impossible for the average individual investor to get an allocation of a popular IPO from a brokerage firm.

- Additionally, institutional investors end up with a huge portion of the new company's shares, which means that your mutual fund company probably ends up with a lot of IPO shares, so you may be getting indirect access to a lot of IPOs without knowing it. Unfortunately, mutual fund managers make all the decisions about which IPOs to buy and what to do with the shares.

- After the IPO, the shares don't tend to earn very good returns over longer holding periods—on average. If everyone knows the IPO is underpriced, then people are eager to trade the shares on the first day to participate in the first-day pop. They keep buying on that first day of trading and push the price even higher. However, after a while, somebody finally asks whether the company is really worth all this money, and the share price will tend to languish.

- Of course, for some firms, the pop lasts for quite a while, and in some cases, firms get a new burst of energy when lock-up periods expire. The lock-up period refers to a length of time after the IPO—usually about 90 days—during which the employees of the company are not allowed to trade their shares. In fact, the sum of employee shares and friends and family shares represents a significant fraction of the company.

- When the lock-up expires, there's a new supply of shares that comes into the secondary market, so in some cases, the arrival of these shares drives

Only about 100 IPOs come to market in the United States in an average year.

the price down. In other cases, the arrival of these shares presents a chance for those people who missed out on the IPO to buy shares, and some firms experience a revival of interest in their shares.

The Dutch Auction Method
- In the open IPO method, or the **Dutch auction method**, everyone who is interested in the IPO submits a bid for shares that tells what price they will pay and how many shares they'll buy at that price. The bids are then ranked by price offered, starting from the highest and running to the lowest.

- Each price also has a number of shares associated with the bid, so the shares that each bidder wants are then added. When the sum of the shares the bidders offer to buy is greater than or equal to the number of shares the firm is offering to sell, anyone who bid at least the price offered by the last person whose bid was included gets shares, and everyone pays the last winning bidder's price. Therefore, everyone pays the lowest winning bid.

- For a while, Dutch auction IPOs were popular because they seemed more fair and promised to remove underbidding and first-day pops. However, investment banks enjoy the profits from book building and companies going public are averse to bearing the risk that their IPO won't raise much money, so the Dutch auction IPO remains a very small portion of the IPO market.

Evaluating Start-Up Companies

- The secret of trying to put a value on a start-up company is to project into the future and work backward. In the future, one of several things can happen: The company could be wildly successful and dominate its market; it could survive and be minimally to moderately successful, but nothing special; or it could collapse.

- In finance, this type of analysis is known as **scenario analysis**, in which a complex future is simplified to just a few possibilities that are regarded as the most likely ones. First, each scenario needs its own value. Then, choose a probability for each scenario, which should reflect your best guess about how likely each scenario is. To get the value of the company, multiply the value of the company in each scenario by the probability of that scenario and then add all these values.

- In order to construct these scenarios, you need to do your homework so that you can put numbers on these scenarios—and you'll have to make a lot of assumptions.

- For example, Skype was acquired by eBay in 2005 for $2.6 billion. At the time, Skype was the main pioneer in the world of VoIP, or voice over Internet protocol, and millions were already using Skype's products. However, the company was still making losses in 2005, so how could it be worth $2.6 billion?

- Using scenario analysis, you can start by simply thinking about the evolution of the market for voice over Internet and what the profit potential was. In 2005, there were about 200 million users of broadband Internet worldwide—mostly in the United States and Europe. Basically, the market consisted of all the broadband Internet users.

- Next, you can project the market into the future by estimating that by 2015, there might be about 1 billion users of broadband Internet worldwide. You could guess that broadband penetration would grow very quickly over the decade after 2005, especially in developed countries. After the year 2015, you might assume that the number of broadband subscribers would continue to grow at about the general rate of population growth, which is about 3%.

- Then, you should think about the profit potential of the market. In 2005, Skype was earning less than $2 per user per year, and you might assume that this number is valid for all voice over Internet users. In addition, you might assume that this number would grow over the following decade—perhaps growing from $2 per user per year to $6 per user per year.

- The global profit market for voice over Internet in 2005 was only $400 million, which is 200 million users multiplied by $2 per user per year. However, this would grow to a market worth $6 billion in the following decade—1 billion users multiplied by $6 per user.

- Using scenario analysis, you could imagine 3 basic scenarios. In the first one, Skype became the dominant firm in voice over Internet and claimed 80% of the market, earning $4.8 billion per year by the end of 2015.

- In the second scenario, competition would drive Skype to be a big player in the market but not dominant. If they held 35% of the market, they would earn $2.1 billion in 2015.

- Finally, Skype could simply fade within the market or even fold—perhaps due to some technological innovation that could make the entire market disappear.

- In each scenario, how much would Skype be worth? One way to calculate this is to use the dividend discount model, $D/(r - g)$, by treating all of Skype's earnings as if they are one dividend—using the total value of earnings for D so that you can value the entire company.

- Assuming a discount rate, which is the r in the formula, of 20%, and assuming a growth rate of 3% after 2015, which is the g in the formula, Skype earns 4.8 billion per year in the first scenario, growing at 3% and being discounted at 20% each year. The DDM formula for this is $4.8/(0.2 - 0.03) = \$28.24$ billion, as of the year 2015. If Skype earns only $2.1 billion as one of a few big players, we can apply the DDM formula to this and get $2.1/(0.20 - 0.03) = \$12.35$ billion. Of course, in the third scenario, Skype is worth zero by 2015.

Assigning Probabilities
- Using your best judgment, assign probabilities to each scenario. For example, you can use 30%, 50%, and 20% to the first, second, and third scenarios, respectively, which sum up to 100%.

- You can find the value of Skype as of 2015 by multiplying the value of Skype in each scenario by the probability assigned to each scenario. When you do the multiplication and add the products, you find that Skype's value in 2015 would be $14.65 billion.

- Because you want this number to reflect 2005's terms, you might discount $14.65 billion by 20%—as an example of a high rate—for 10 years, which results in $2.35 billion. Remember that eBay paid $2.6 billion for Skype in 2005, but it sold Skype to private equity investors in 2009 for $1.9 billion. By that time, however, Skype was actually making money.

book building: The process of building up a demand curve for a company's shares that is carried out by an investment bank.

Dutch auction method: A method in which everyone who is interested in a particular IPO submits a bid for shares that tells what price they will pay and how many shares they'll buy at that price. The bids are then ranked by price offered, starting from the highest and running to the lowest.

scenario analysis: A type of financial analysis in which a complex future is simplified to just a few possibilities that are regarded as the most likely ones.

Suggested Reading

Benveniste and Wilhelm, Jr., "Initial Public Offerings."

Perkins, "IPOs Go Dutch, and Small Investors Gain."

Questions to Consider

1. Go to a free financial website and find the stock of one company that has had its IPO within the past year. Look at the graph of its price since the IPO. What has happened to the company's shares since the IPO? Why do you think this has happened?

2. Some companies are experimenting with alternative ways to attract investors, and one method has become known as crowd funding. Search for the term "crowd funding" on the Internet and read some of the articles you find. Would you participate in crowd funding as an investor? Why or why not?

Start-Up Companies and IPOs
Lecture 10—Transcript

In the last few lectures, we've learned how to pick the stocks of established companies that have solid financial statements, long track records of paying dividends, and healthy earnings. But one of the most exciting types of stocks comes from companies that don't have any of those things—companies that are about to have their initial public offerings, or IPOs.

Even though the dotcom bubble showed the downside to being overly optimistic about high-tech start-up companies, investors still get very excited about the possibility of becoming a shareholder in the next Amazon or Google. And they'll go to great lengths to be one of the lucky ones who buys into these firms at, or even before, the IPO.

When you think that these days only about 100 IPOs come to market in the U.S. in an average year, it's not surprising that people are competing harder than ever to invest in them.

But let's take a step back for a second and ask whether it's really worth all the hassle to try to participate in IPOs. People tell a lot of stories about the money to be made in IPOs, but the facts about who really makes the money and what that means for individual investors will surprise you. In addition, not every new company is going to be the next Google—many turn out to be the next Pets.com. Never heard of them? Exactly—they were the poster child of the dotcom bubble. The only thing that remains of the company today is the sock puppet that was their spokesperson.

In this lecture, we're going to sort out fact from legend about IPOs, so you can make up your own mind if you want to pursue them. We'll also take a look at valuing the high-tech, start-up companies that generate the most interest from IPO investors.

The initial public offering, or IPO, marks the transition from being a privately held company that only 500 or fewer people can own, to becoming a publicly held company that literally anyone can own a part of. In order to make this transition, a company must write a prospectus for a public offering and have this prospectus approved by the SEC. Once the SEC approves the prospectus, the firm has permission to solicit investors to buy the shares that it will offer in the IPO.

It's important to understand the details of how IPOs work, because so many of the positive and negative aspects of IPOs are the result of the particular way that most of them are conducted. So let's take a closer look at the process.

In most IPOs, the company hires an investment bank to underwrite the public offering of stock. What this means is that on the day of the IPO, the company literally sells the entire public offering to the investment bank, and then the investment bank turns around and sells the shares to the general public. So the investment bank or banks that underwrite the IPO are really in charge of distributing the shares.

It's important to realize that when they underwrite IPOs, investment banks are taking on a big risk. If the company that is going public turns out not to be very interesting to investors, the investment bank will be stuck with a ton of shares that it can't sell, and it will probably end up taking a loss on the deal. So the investment bank's number one priority is to make sure that it finds enough investors to sell out the IPO shares.

And which investors have the ability to make that happen? Well, it's institutional investors—pension funds and especially the big mutual fund companies. If they choose to participate in an IPO, the shares will be fully subscribed and the IPO will be a success. But if they don't, the investment bank may call off the whole IPO, or at least scale it back severely.

So the institutional investors have market power in the IPO process, and they use it. Before each underwritten IPO, the investment bank contacts big institutional investors, called a road show, and it asks them about their interest in the IPO. The investment bank says, if we priced the shares at $20 per share, how many would you like to buy? What if we priced the shares at $25? And so on. Basically, the investment bank is building up a demand curve for the company's shares. This process is called building an IPO book or simply book-building.

The institutional investors use their market power by understating their true interest in the IPO—that is, they underbid. They want to hold the IPO price down, because this will increase the chance that any shares they buy will increase in value after the company's shares start trading. And because the mutual funds and other institutions make up such a large fraction of the demand for shares, they almost always succeed in holding the IPO price down.

You're probably familiar with the result of this behavior—the famous first-day pop, as it's called, in which the price of the firm's shares rise by 10% or more on the first day of market trading. The IPO pop is the result of the systematic underpricing of IPO shares.

There are several implications of this story that you need to keep in mind as an individual investor. First, the investment banks control whom gets the shares of hot IPOs, and they use these shares to reward their best retail customers. The best customers are the people who generate big profits for the investment banks by maintaining large brokerage accounts, buying high-commission investment products, and trading a lot. This means that it's really tough if not almost impossible for the average individual investor to get an allocation of a popular IPO from a brokerage firm.

Unfortunately, this problem is only getting worse over time, not better. One of the big differences between IPOs now and the ones of the dotcom era is the portion of the company that is sold to the public in the IPO. In the dotcom era, it was typical for the IPO to distribute at least half of the outstanding shares of the company. These days, however, it's much more typical for a company to distribute 30% or less of its outstanding shares in the IPO. Several of the biggest IPOs in 2011, for example, offered less than 10% of the outstanding shares of the companies. This further reduces the supply of shares that investment banks have to dole out to their customers.

The second big implication of the book-building model of IPOs is that institutional investors end up with a huge proportion of the new company's shares. Now, that means that your mutual fund company is probably ending up with a lot of IPO shares. So you may be getting indirect access to a lot of IPOs without knowing it, if you own mutual funds.

The good news about this is that you can brag to all your friends that you're actually getting those hard-to-come-by IPO shares. The bad news, of course, is that the mutual fund managers make all the decisions about what IPOs to buy and what to do with the shares. Perhaps the mutual fund manager has even already flipped them by the time you find out that one of your mutual funds bought the IPO shares. Yeah, there's something that just isn't as satisfying about that. Part of the fun of getting a hold of IPO shares and then selling them for a big profit is being able to say to your friends, "I flipped those shares!"

Let's hope that somebody flipped them, because this brings me to the third consequence of the book-building process. What do you suppose generally happens after that fantastic first day of trading? The answer is something that financial economists call "subsequent underperformance." In other words, after the IPO, the shares don't tend to earn very good returns over longer holding periods, on average.

This phenomenon has been well documented by financial economists, and you can see why it might be the case. If everyone knows the IPO is underpriced, then people are eager to trade the shares on the first day to participate in the first-day pop. We don't know how big the first day pop is going to be, so it's easy for traders to get carried away. They keep buying on that first day of trading and push the price even higher. But after a while somebody finally asks whether the company is really worth all this money. And the share price will tend to languish. So if you buy into the firm after the IPO, hoping that the party will keep on going, you're generally going to be disappointed.

Of course, for some firms, the party lasts for quite a while. And in some cases, it gets a new burst of energy when so-called lock-up periods expire. The lock-up period refers to a length of time after the IPO, usually on the order of 90 days, during which the employees of the company are not allowed to trade their shares.

In many if not nearly every startup firm, a large portion of employee compensation takes the form of stock in the company. In addition to these shares, there are so-called "friends and family shares," and for many startup firms, the sum of these two types of shares represents a significant fraction of the company. The purpose of the lock-up, as you can probably guess, is to prevent employees from flooding the market with their shares and driving the share price down inadvertently on the first day of trading.

When the lock-up expires, there's a new supply of shares that comes into the secondary market. So in some cases, the arrival of these shares drives the price down. But for other companies, the arrival of these shares presents a chance for those people who missed out on the IPO to get in on the fun. Some firms experience a revival of interest in their shares around the expiration of the lock-up date. So if you are holding employee shares in a firm that is about to go public, it's really hard to predict whether your shares will still be rising in value by the end of the lock-up, or whether they'll have already peaked. And if you missed the IPO and are still sitting on the sidelines thinking about investing, you may want to wait until the lockout expiration to see how this event affects the value of the shares.

Now, after this discussion of the consequences of the book-building method of conducting IPOs, you may be wondering, Isn't there a different way to do this?

There is, and it's called the open IPO or the Dutch auction method. A Dutch auction is a type of auction where the bids on the item for sale start at a high price and then fall until all the units of the item are sold. It works well whenever there are many, many units of something for sale—like flowers, for example.

For IPOs, a Dutch auction method works this way. Everyone who is interested in the IPO submits a bid for shares that tells what price they will pay and how many shares they want to buy at that price. The person running the auction collects all the bids, and then ranks them by price, starting from the highest and then going to the lowest price offered.

Each price also has a number of shares associated with the bid, so the auctioneer adds up the shares that each bidder wants, again starting with the high bidders and working her way down. When the sum of the shares the bidders offer to buy is greater than or equal to the number of shares the firm is offering to sell, the auctioneer looks at the price offered by the last person whose bid was included, and says that anyone who bid at least this price will get shares, but everyone pays the last bidder's price. So everyone pays the lowest winning bid.

A few IPOs have been conducted in this way over the years, and in fact Google's IPO was supposed to have been conducted in this way. But there were a bunch of changes in the auction format that were made to ensure that a minimum price was paid by all the winning bids, so I really wouldn't say that Google used a true Dutch auction method in their IPO. For a while, Dutch auction IPOs were considered the wave of the future, because they seemed more fair, and they promised to remove the problem of underbidding and first-day pops.

But the advocates of the Dutch auction method failed to realize that the investment banks really like the profits from book building, and the companies going public are really averse to bearing the risk that their IPOs won't raise very much money. So the Dutch auction IPO remains a very small portion of the IPO market. Nonetheless, you may be interested in participating in them, since they really are more open than traditional IPOs.

So far I think I'm raining on the IPO parade a bit. It's really hard to get your own allocation of shares from the traditional book-building IPOs, and your mutual funds may already get the shares anyway—not that it does you all that much good. The long-term performance of IPO shares isn't very impressive on average. So why would anyone still be interested in IPOs?

Hopefully, you're thinking to yourself—or maybe you're shouting at the screen at this point—that there's still the chance that one of these stocks will be the next Microsoft, or Dell Computer, or any number of game-changing companies that went on to deliver amazing returns for shareholders, over years or even decades. Okay, fair enough. So the question then becomes, how do I find the next Amazon or Google out of all the IPO candidates that come to market?

That's a tough question—because, as I mentioned at the beginning of the lecture, the firms that are being taken public don't have any of the things that we've been using to value companies—earnings, dividends, or even reliable financial ratios. But what they do have is potential. The whole reason we're interested in them is that they could generate lots of profits and lots of dividends in the future.

So if you're really going to invest in IPOs or startup firms, you need to find a way to put a price tag on potential. Wow—that sounds like a pretty tall order. And in fact it is. But you can actually use some of the ideas that we've already learned about during the past few lectures to think about the value of startup companies. You have to adapt them to the special circumstances that characterize these young, high-growth, high-risk firms, though. That's what we'll learn about now.

The big secret of trying to put a value on a startup company is to project into the future and work backwards. In the future, one of several things can happen to this company. First, it could be wildly successful and dominate the market. Second, it can survive and be minimally to moderately successful, but nothing really special. And finally, the company could just go belly up.

What I've just done here is use a common technique in finance known as scenario analysis. In scenario analysis, we simplify a terribly complex future down to just a few possibilities that we regard as the most likely ones. Each scenario is going to imply a different value for the company. Then we choose a probability for each scenario, which should reflect our best guess about how likely each scenario really is. To get the value of the company today, I multiply the value of the company in each scenario by the probability of that scenario, and then add all these values up.

So the real skill required to value a start-up company is the ability to put together scenarios that are as realistic as you can make them, yet simple enough so that you can easily work with them. And in order to construct these scenarios, you need to do your homework so that you can put numbers on these scenarios. For example, you need to be able to think about things like the size of the market, the profit potential of the market, the market share of the firm, and so on. You'll have to make a lot of assumptions—but that's simply how this works. Everyone who is going to get a handle on the value of a startup company has to make their own set of assumptions.

To make this whole process more concrete, let me show you a valuation exercise I did for Skype back in 2005. That's when Skype was acquired by eBay for $2.6 billion. At the time, Skype was the main pioneer in the world of VOIP, which stands for voice-over-Internet-protocol, and millions were already using Skype's products. But in 2005 the company was still making losses—in fact, its first operating profit wasn't even expected until 2007. How could Skype be worth $2.6 billion back then?

I used scenario analysis to find out. The first thing I did was to simply think about the evolution of the market for voice-over-Internet, and what the profit potential was. In 2005, there were about 200 million users of broadband Internet worldwide, mostly in the United States and Europe. Since services like Skype only work well with very fast Internet, I assumed that only broadband Internet users would use Skype. But since Skype is so handy, and I noticed that just about everyone I knew who had a broadband connection had at least tried Skype, I assumed that everyone with a broadband connection would in fact use some kind of voice-over-Internet service. So the market consisted of all broadband Internet users.

Next, I projected the market out into the future. I thought that by the end of 2015, there would be about one billion users of broadband Internet worldwide. Two things made me choose the number one billion—well, besides the fact that it's a nice big, round number. First, I thought that broadband penetration would grow very quickly over the coming decade after 2005, especially in developed countries. But I noticed that in other developing countries, a lot of their communication development was taking place in terms of mobile phones not computers. So that made me not want to push the number of broadband subscribers into the billions, but to leave it at one billion. After the year 2015, I assumed that the number of broadband subscribers would continue to grow at about the general rate of population growth, which is about 3%. So there's the size of the market—200 million rising to one billion over about 10 years, then growing at a much slower rate of 3% thereafter.

Next, I thought about the profit potential of the market. In 2005, I found a statistic that Skype was earning less than $2.00 per user per year, mostly because the predominant users of Skype were individuals. Individuals mostly use Skype for computer-to-computer calls, which are free, and only occasionally for calls to mobile phones and landlines, which are the services that you have to pay for. So I assumed that this $2 per user per year number was valid for all voice-over-Internet users at the time. In addition, I also assumed that this number would grow over the next decade.

It would grow because first, companies like Skype would try to get more businesses to replace their traditional phone services with voice over Internet, which would generate higher revenues per user. Second, I also thought that any company in the VOIP business would simply become more clever at inducing individuals to use more services that they would have to pay for. So between these two considerations, I assumed that the amount of revenue per year would grow from $2.00 per user per year to $6.00 per user per year during the following decade.

Since the average cost of providing voice-over-Internet services was minimal—that's one of those great features about the Internet economy, by the way—I assumed that all revenues more or less went to the bottom line. In other words, I assumed that, even after figuring in the costs of producing the services, VOIP companies would be making annual profits of $6.00 per user per year.

With all those assumptions, I have my projection of the profits at stake. The global profit pie for voice over internet in 2005 was a measly $400 million, that's 200 million users times two bucks per user per year. But this would grow to a $6 billion market in a decade—that's one billion users times $6 per user. And I assumed that the growth over that decade was more or less constant.

Now comes the scenario analysis part. How much of that global profit pie was Skype going to claim? Well, I laid out three basic scenarios. In the first one, Skype became the dominant firm in voice over Internet and claimed 80% of the market. So that means that Skype earned $4.8 billion per year by the end of 2015. Again, that's 80% of that $6 billion market.

In the second scenario, I imagined that other big telecom or Internet or even software firms could easily jump into this market and compete actively with Skype. In a strongly contested market, I figured that Skype would have a first-mover advantage and that would make it a big player but not dominant—so I thought a 35% market share would reflect that. That would mean Skype would earn $2.1 billion in 2015 in this scenario.

And finally, I thought that it's entirely possible that Skype would fade to being a bit player in this market who earned next to nothing. I used to call that the Netscape scenario until people started asking me, "Who's Netscape?" Another reason why Skype could fold is that some technological innovation could come along that makes the entire market go away. Or the market could become completely commoditized, meaning that prices on the premium services all drop down to near 0 or at least down to their costs of production, which would leave no profits for anyone.

So now I have my three scenarios. How much would Skype be worth in each scenario? Well, we can calculate this in two ways, based on what we've learned in previous lectures. One way is to use the dividend discount model, treating all of Skype's earnings like one big dividend. Remember that the DDM says that the value of a company's stock is given by the formula $D/(r - g)$, where D is the dividend, r is the discount rate, and g is the growth rate of dividends. Here, I'm using the total value of earnings for D, so I can value the entire company.

I assumed a discount rate, which is the r in the formula, of 20% for Skype. This reflects the high risk of the firm. I assumed a growth rate of 3% after 2015, which is the g in the formula. So in the market domination scenario, the good one, Skype earns $4.8 billion per year, growing at 3%, and I discount it at 20% per year. The DDM formula for this is $4.8/(0.2 - 0.03) = \$28.24$ billion, as of the year 2015. If Skype earns only $2.1 billion as one of a few big players, we can apply the DDM formula to this and get $2.1 /(0.20 - 0.03) = \$12.35$ billion, again as of the year 2015. And of course, in the third scenario, Skype is nothing more than a pleasant memory, unfortunately worth 0 by 2015.

Those are the scenarios, and I assigned probabilities to each one like this. First, I thought that Skype had such a big lead on other firms that there was a 30% chance of market domination. On the other hand, the large number of possible competitors and the low costs of entering this market made me think that there was about a 50% chance that Skype would be only one of a few major players in this market. And finally, I thought that there was also a nontrivial chance, about of 20%, that Skype, or the entire market, could crash and burn.

Notice that my probabilities—30%, 50%, and 20%—all sum up to 100, so I'm okay there. These probabilities are subjective, of course, because I was simply making my best guesses at the time. If I could have found better information about the intentions of competitors, or any of the hidden vulnerabilities of Skype, I would have used that information to adjust my probabilities for these different scenarios.

Now we can find the value of Skype as of 2015, by multiplying the value of Skype in each scenario by the probability I assigned to each scenario. Remember, my calculations implied that Skype would be worth $28.24 billion with probability of 30% in the market domination scenario. It would be worth $12.35 billion with a probability of 50% in the market-sharing scenario. And it would be worth 0 with probability of 20% in the bust scenario. When I do the multiplication and add the products up, I get that Skype's value in 2015 would be, drumroll please, $14.65 billion.

Well, that's as of 2015, so I need to put that in 2005's terms. I do that by discounting this $14.65 billion price tag 10 years, back to 2005. I picked a high discount rate, 20%, which implies that one dollar in 2015 is only worth one-sixth as much in 2005. So the price that I calculated as of 2005 was about one-sixth of $14.65 billion, or $2.35 billion. Now, remember that eBay paid $2.6 billion for Skype in 2005. So, did eBay get a bargain?

Well, not if you know the rest of that story. EBay was actually disappointed with Skype, and ended up selling Skype to private equity investors in 2009 for $1.9 billion. But by that time, Skype was actually making money—it had revenues that year of over half a billion dollars and was expected to have net income of $90 million.

I wanted to show you this example for a couple of reasons. First, I think this gives you the flavor of what you need to go through in order to value a start-up company. And second, I wanted you to see just how many assumptions you need to make in order to get to an answer. So, on the one hand, it's very hard to take this estimate seriously—there's no way I'd bet on the accuracy of this specific estimate of a company's value.

But on the other hand, going through this exercise makes me think systematically and clearly about all the important issues that really do influence a startup company's value. I had to think about the size and growth of the voice-over-Internet market, Skype's actual and potential competitors, and the amount of profits to be made. These are exactly the sorts of questions you should be asking if you're looking at a start-up. And after you make your estimates, you should stop and ask whether these estimates are reasonable. How fast does Skype really have to grow between 2005 and 2015 to reach a revenue level of $4.8 billion? Well, it's about 28% per year. Is this growth rate really reasonable?

In short, scenario analysis makes you take a serious look at how a start-up company really creates value. If you can better understand how a start-up firm intends to create and maintain value, then you're in a much better position to decide whether you buy into their story. And at the end of the day, it's more about whether you buy into a start-up firm's long-term value creation story, and their ability to realize it, than the specific numbers. Remember, when venture capitalists decide whom they want to back, the quality of a company's management is at least as important as the company's products and ideas.

Well, I hope I haven't spoiled the fun of trying to get in on some hot IPOs. But I really do think that in most cases, it's not worth the effort to pursue them. The exception would be if you have the chance to participate in some Dutch-auction IPOs, where you do your homework on the firm and are able to name the price you'd want to pay for the shares.

One final thing that I hope you've realized over the course of this lecture is that if a firm really is the next Google, it will still be the next Google six months after the IPO. In other words, a great start-up company is simply a great company that's out there creating value for shareholders. If you focus on finding those types of firms, perhaps by using some of the scenario analysis that we've learned, then you'll have plenty of time to identify them after the IPO and still enjoy great returns.

Why Should You Care about Dividends?
Lecture 11

Y ou may think of dividends as outdated, but in this lecture, you're
going to learn why you should care about dividends. You may care
about them for their own sake, but you'll also learn that there are
plenty of other reasons to pay attention to dividends. In general, when you
pick stocks, you should look for companies that maintain a high-dividend
yield, that consistently increase their dividends over time, and that pay out a
high proportion of their earnings in dividends.

Dividends

- As mentioned previously, a dividend is a part of the profits of a
  company that are paid out to the shareholders. The company doesn't
  have to pay out any dividends, and in fact, many companies don't.

- Companies that do pay dividends try to keep on paying them,
  year after year, and they try to make the dividends grow at a low
  but steady rate. If a company doesn't pay dividends, it's because
  the managers are reinvesting the company's profits on behalf of
  the shareholders.

- One of the reasons you should care about dividends is that they
  can give you a solid return in their own right. The statistic to pay
  attention to with a dividend-paying stock is the **dividend yield**,
  which is the annual dividend on the stock divided by its price.

- You can always be on the lookout for high-dividend-yield shares,
  but one of the best times to shop for them is during a stock market
  downturn. When share prices fall, this boosts the value of the
  dividend yield for many shares, giving you many more firms to
  choose from.

- Many people use the yield on the long-term government bond—
  for example, the 10-year note—as the hurdle rate, or the minimum

acceptable rate of return on an investment. To use the 10-year bond to choose stocks, find the stocks that pay a dividend yield higher than the interest rate on the 10-year note and choose from these stocks.

- One danger of selecting firms with high-dividend yields is that you may select firms whose share prices are falling for good reason. These firms have a high-dividend yield because they're not doing well but haven't cut the dividend yet. Even if the company doesn't cut its dividend if it runs into hard times, the share price may fall so much that the loss would offset the dividend yield if you had to sell the shares.

The low interest rates that bonds yielded after the financial crisis of 2008 reawakened many investors to the value of dividends.

- Once you do your homework and find a high-dividend-yield company you'd like to own, however, you shouldn't hesitate to buy the shares. Typically, high-dividend-yield firms attract dividend shoppers very quickly and experience rapid price increases that drive the dividend yield down.

- If you're really interested in collecting dividends, then an alternative you should consider is **preferred shares**, which are stocks that have a higher priority claim on the company's profits than the common shares do. A company can't pay a dividend on its common shares unless its dividend payments on its preferred shares are up to date.

- Additionally, preferred shares promise an explicit dividend; it's written into the stock contract. Therefore, preferred shares don't run the risk of a dividend cut; however, they of course still run the risk of company bankruptcy.

- There are many variations on preferred shares, especially in terms of their maturity. Although there are many perpetual preferred shares, which the company intends to pay dividends on forever, other types of preferred shares have provisions allowing them to be repurchased by the firm at specific dates.

- The weakness of preferred shares is that the dividends are usually fixed, but the price of the shares can rise and effectively lower the dividend yield on them. Therefore, it's still important to not put off making a decision about whether to buy high-yielding preferred shares once you've identified an interesting candidate.

- If you're a long-term, buy-and-hold investor, then there's another reason to be interested in dividends: the **dividend reinvestment program (DRiP)**, which is a stockholding plan in which any dividends earned on the shares are automatically reinvested in the shares. Many companies offer DRiPs for their shares as a way to develop a solid base of long-term shareholders, and DRiPs can be great wealth builders.

Dividend Cuts and Increases

- A company's **dividend policy**—that is, the way a company chooses to pay out dividends and how it changes these payouts over time—reveal a wealth of information about the company. This information can be used by investors to improve their stock picking.

- Companies, and most investors, regard dividends as a long-term commitment. There seems to be an unwritten agreement—what economists call an implicit contract—that firms will only pay dividends that they think they can sustain for the indefinite future. Companies will do everything they can to preserve their dividends and to make them grow over time in a sustainable way.

- This agreement means that companies put off cutting their dividends, even after their earnings fall significantly. Companies that do cut their dividends generally do so only after they've exhausted all the cost-cutting possibilities—and maybe even only after they've run out of credit.

- The implication of all this is that a dividend cut is usually a strong signal that a firm is in big financial trouble. A company that has to cut its dividend will usually see its stock price fall by more than the dividend discount model would predict, for example, because of the very powerful negative signal that a dividend cut conveys to the market.

- On the other hand, a large dividend increase is a way that the managers of a company signal that the projects that the company will be undertaking in the future are going to generate great returns.

- The information contained in dividend increases is so reliable that there are investors and entire mutual funds devoted to finding firms that repeatedly increase their dividends by large proportions and to investing in those firms.

- Dividends don't necessarily have to be money payments. Anything of value that the company gives to its shareholders is a dividend. Sometimes these in-kind dividends are called shareholder benefits programs.

- One of the most common types of noncash dividend is the **stock dividend**, or stock split. When a company issues a stock dividend, it pays out part of a share instead of cash for each share that an investor holds. A company can pay out whatever amount it chooses as a stock dividend.

- Just like a significant increase in a cash dividend, a stock dividend is a signal from the managers of the firm to the general public that they expect high growth of earnings in the future. In most cases, these signals are followed by good news about successful projects and increasing profits, so the prices of stocks that split start rising as soon as the split occurs.

- A company that has seen its share price fall may be in danger of getting kicked off a stock exchange, which leads to continued declines in value. It turns out that many stock exchanges have rules about the minimum price at which listed companies can trade, so a company that has experienced a big drop in its share price might resort to a reverse split, in which it issues one new share to replace several existing shares. This will distribute the market value of the company over a smaller number of shares and raise the price of the shares in the opposite effect of a stock split.

Dividends as a Form of Discipline
- In addition to sending strong messages to the markets about a company's future performance, dividends also send a strong signal to investors about a company's dedication to creating value by imposing discipline on managers' spending.

- Most companies prefer to pay for their new projects out of their current earnings, but companies have to be careful when they have high earnings because it's very difficult to find the few projects that will create real value for a company.

- When a company has plenty of cash flowing in, managers find that it's easier just to fund a bunch of new projects than it is to take the time to sort through them all carefully In addition, there's also the danger that managers will waste earnings on pet projects, which are projects that boost the manager's status and image but don't really boost profits.

- For some companies, the answer to both of these problems is to pay out a high proportion of their earnings in dividends. This reduces the supply of earnings that could be reinvested in the firm, and that's the source of discipline. With less earnings to go around, managers have to put in the effort to choose only the very best projects to receive these scarce funds. In fact, this can set up a beneficial competition for resources in the firm that leads to better choices for new projects, and managers' pet projects generally lose that competition.

- Several academic studies show that the higher the fraction of earnings a company pays out as dividends, the higher the growth rate of earnings tends to be over the next 10 years.

Stock Buybacks

- A **stock buyback**, or share repurchase, is a transaction in which a company goes into the stock market and repurchases, or buys back, some of its outstanding shares. This is a substitute for a dividend because the company has to pay cash for these repurchased shares, which returns cash to the company's shareholders.

- Stock buybacks have gone from being almost unknown to being one of the things that companies spend the most money on each year. One of the main reasons that buybacks have become a popular alternative to dividends is that, for companies, buybacks are more flexible than dividends. Buybacks give companies a way to pay out a short-term windfall to shareholders without creating any expectations.

- Another reason that repurchases have become more popular is the different tax consequences of buybacks versus dividends. When a company pays a dividend, the company chooses when the investor pays taxes, but in the case of a buyback, the investor chooses when to sell the shares and incur the tax liability for the capital gains.

- A third reason behind the surge in popularity of buybacks is the rise of stock-option compensation at many companies. Starting in the 1990s, companies issued billions of stock options, and they bought back billions of shares to sell to the option holders.

- The last reason that buybacks have become so popular is because the quality of the signal in stock buybacks seriously deteriorated over time. If the managers of a company signal to the market that shares are undervalued, then investors may come running to buy the shares—which helps drive the price of the shares up. However, over time, this undervaluation story lost credibility, and companies that announced buyback programs often didn't follow through with them.

Important Terms

dividend policy: The way a company chooses to pay out dividends and how it changes these payouts over time

dividend reinvestment program (DRiP): A stockholding plan in which any dividends earned on the shares are automatically reinvested in the shares.

dividend yield: The annual dividend on a stock divided by its price.

preferred share: A stock that has a higher priority claim on a company's profits than a common share does.

stock buyback: A transaction in which a company goes into the stock market and repurchases, or buys back, some of its outstanding shares.

stock dividend: A common type of noncash dividend in which a company pays out part of a share instead of cash for each share that an investor holds.

Suggested Reading

Brealey, Myers, and Allen, *Principles of Corporate Finance*, chap. 16.

Hough, "Dividends."

Levinsohn, "It's Payback Time!"

1. Go to a free financial website and find the list of firms that have recently undergone stock splits. These are often found on links labeled "market calendar" or "events" that are posted on the websites. Take one of the companies that has undergone a stock split and look at a graph of its stock price over the past 2 or 3 years. Do you think it is worth investigating the company further—based on its recent stock price?

2. McDonald's has a dividend reinvestment program (DRiP) called McDirect Shares (http://www.aboutmcdonalds.com/mcd/investors/ mcdirect_shares.html). Visit this website—or the site of another company that offers a dividend reinvestment program—and look over the prospectus materials for this program. As an investor, what features of the program do you find attractive? Are there any features that you don't like?

Why Should You Care about Dividends?
Lecture 11—Transcript

In the last lecture, we learned about the exciting and challenging opportunity of investing in IPOs. If IPOs are new and hip, then the subject of this lecture—dividends—is decidedly old school. You may even think of dividends as outdated and dowdy, something only grandma could get excited about.

In this lecture, I'm going to change your mind about dividends. You should care about dividends, and in fact, you should care a lot. You may care about them for their own sake, but you'll also learn that there are plenty of other reasons to pay attention to dividends as well.

I mentioned dividends in my lecture on stock market basics, but let me refresh our memory. A dividend is a part of the profits of a company that are paid out to the shareholders. The company doesn't have to pay out any dividends, and in fact many companies don't. Companies that do pay dividends try to keep on paying them year after year, and they try to make the dividends grow at a low but steady rate. If a company doesn't pay dividends, it's because the managers are reinvesting the company's profits on behalf of the shareholders.

I can understand why dividends fell out of favor with many stock investors over the years. Starting in the 1950s, firms became less generous about paying out dividends, and this behavior persisted for decades. Also, since dividends used to be taxed as ordinary income, the tax rate on dividends was a lot higher than the tax rate on capital gains. So, given a choice, investors wanted to receive their returns in capital gains instead of dividends, and therefore they stopped pressing companies to pay out as many dividends.

In 2003, though, the tax laws were changed and now dividends are placed on almost an equal footing with capital gains. This helped renew investor interest in dividends. In addition, the low interest rates that bonds yielded for several years after the financial crisis of 2008 also reawakened many investors to the value of dividends. The financial crisis also reminded stock investors that capital gains can go way down as well as way up, which in turn reminded investors of the value of having a reliable dividend to fall back on.

So one of the reasons you should care about dividends is that they can give you a solid return in their own right. The statistic to pay attention to with a dividend-paying stock is the dividend yield, which is the annual dividend on the stock divided by its price. For example, International Paper was paying an annual dividend of $1.05 per share the last time I checked. And the market price of its shares was $27.22. If we divide the annual dividend of $1.05 by the stock price of $27.22, we get a dividend yield of just over 3.85%. That's not too bad!

Now, if I were to buy the shares of International Paper in order to earn that dividend yield of 3.85%, then I'd stop caring about the current price of the shares when I calculated the dividend yield. Once I buy a stock, I've essentially locked in the value of the denominator of the dividend yield that I am going to earn on those shares. So as long as International Paper continues to pay that $1.05 per share dividend, I'm continuing to earn the same dividend yield of 3.85%. Of course, if the company increases the dividend, then my dividend yield will rise, too.

So let's think about shopping for high-dividend-yield shares. This is something you can always be on the lookout for, though one of the best times to do this is during a stock market downturn. When share prices fall, this boosts the value of the dividend yield for many shares, giving you more firms to choose from.

What value for a dividend yield should you look for? Many people use the yield on the long-term government bond, say the 10-year note, as the hurdle rate. The idea is that collecting the dividend on a stock is similar to collecting the coupon on a long-term bond, so you should buy whichever instrument offers a higher yield. To use the 10-year note to choose stocks, simply find the stocks that pay a dividend yield higher than the interest rate on the 10-year note, and choose from these stocks. You should set your own hurdle rate wherever you feel comfortable as an investor, but this idea of considering the income you could earn on an alternative investment like a bond is a good one.

One danger of selecting firms with high dividend yields is that you may select firms whose share prices are falling for good reason. These companies have a high dividend yield now because they're not doing well but haven't gotten around to cutting the dividend yet. As we'll see later in the lecture, firms try to avoid cutting their dividend as long as they can, so this is a distinct possibility. Even if the company doesn't cut its dividend if it runs into hard times, the share price may fall so much that the loss would offset the dividend yield if you had to sell the shares. So it's a good idea to do your homework on a firm that you're about to buy because of its high dividend yield. For example, after the financial crisis of 2008, personal finance advisors warned investors to be wary of banks and other financial firms even though some were paying dividend rates above 5%.

Once you do your homework and find a high-dividend-yield company you'd like to own, you shouldn't hesitate to buy the shares. Typically, high-dividend-yield firms attract dividend shoppers very quickly and experience rapid price increases that drive the dividend yield down to more ho-hum levels. Most free financial websites and online brokers have the ability to do at least some sorting of shares by dividend yield, so it's relatively easy to find high-dividend-yielding stocks.

If you're really interested in collecting dividends, then an alternative you should consider is preferred shares. Preferred shares are stocks that have a higher priority claim on the company's profits than the common shares do. A company can't pay a dividend on its common shares unless its dividend payments on its preferred shares are up to date. Also, preferred shares promise an explicit dividend—it's written into the stock contract. So preferred shares don't run the risk of a dividend cut, though of course they still run the risk of company bankruptcy.

There are lots of different variations on preferred shares, especially in terms of their maturity. Although there are many perpetual preferred shares out there, which the company intends to pay dividends on forever, other types of preferred shares have provisions allowing them to be repurchased by the firm on specific dates. Some preferred shares look even more like bonds, in the sense that they have more or less fixed maturities.

The weakness of preferred shares is that the dividends are usually fixed in money terms, but the price of the shares can rise and effectively lower the dividend yield on them. Therefore, it's still important to do your homework fairly quickly and not put off making a decision about whether to buy high-yielding preferred shares, once you've identified an interesting candidate.

If you're a long-term, buy-and-hold investor, then there's another reason to cheer for dividends. It's called the Dividend Reinvestment Program, or DRiP for short. Many companies offer DRiPs for their shares, as a way to develop a solid base of long-term shareholders. A DRiP is a stockholding plan in which any dividends earned on the shares are automatically reinvested in the shares.

Suppose you hold 100 shares of International Paper in a DRiP, and it pays the $105 in annual dividends that it promised. This $105 in dividends will buy approximately four more shares of International Paper during the year. That's assuming that the price I quoted earlier of $27.22 is an average price for the year. At the end of the year, you'll have almost four more shares, which means more dividends, which means more shares, and so on. DRiPs can be great wealth builders, and the best part is that once you make the initial purchase of shares, they're on automatic pilot until you want to cash out your investment.

So dividends can be attractive for their own sake—they can boost the overall return on a stock investment, they can be the main source of return of your stock investment, and they can build wealth over time. But there's another reason entirely to be interested in dividends, and it has to do with information. A company's dividend policy—that is, the way a company chooses to pay out dividends, and how it changes these payouts over time—reveal a wealth of information about the company. Investors can use this information to improve their stockpicking. It can help you identify firms that are worth looking into, as well as some that are worth avoiding.

First, let's look into dividend cuts and dividend increases. The main thing to keep in mind regarding dividend policy is that companies, and most investors, regard dividends as a long-term commitment. There seems to be an unwritten agreement—what economists call an implicit contract—that firms will only pay dividends that they think they can sustain for the indefinite future. The understanding is that companies will do everything they can to preserve their dividends, and to make them grow over time in a sustainable way.

This agreement means that companies put off cutting their dividends, even after their earnings fall significantly. And companies that do cut their dividends generally do so only after they've exhausted all the cost-cutting possibilities and maybe even only after they've run out of credit. The implication of all this is that a dividend cut is usually a strong signal that a firm is in big financial trouble. A company that has to cut its dividend will usually see its stock price fall by more than, say, the dividend discount model would predict, because of the very powerful negative signal that a dividend cut conveys to the market.

Of course, investors follow some companies more closely than others, and they anticipate when companies will cut their dividends. For example, before the financial crisis of 2008, General Motors was forced to cut its dividend, and the markets hardly reacted to the announcement. But that was because by the time that GM got around to actually cutting the dividend, the market had already beaten the shares down in anticipation of this. Again, this shows the value of doing your homework on a high-dividend-yielding stock.

On the other hand, a large dividend increase is also a strong signal from the company about its future financial performance. Remember, all companies try to increase their dividends year to year, but only at a low rate, like a couple of percent per year. But a big dividend increase of, say, 5% or more, is a signal of long-term strength. The company managers are saying to the markets, we are so confident about our future profits that we're committing to a big dividend increase that we think we can sustain permanently. So these big dividend increases are actually a way that the managers of the company signal that the projects that the company will be undertaking in the future are going to generate great returns.

The information contained in dividend increases is so reliable that there are investors and entire mutual funds devoted to finding firms that repeatedly increase their dividends by large proportions, and they invest in those firms. Instead of searching for serial dividend increasers yourself, you could buy into one of these funds and let the fund managers do the searching for you.

One thing that I haven't mentioned about dividends is that they don't necessarily have to be money payments. Anything of value that the company gives to its shareholders is a dividend. Sometimes these in-kind dividends are called shareholder benefits programs. For example, until it was taken private, Wrigley used to send its shareholders 20 packs of gum once a year. Most of these in-kind dividends have fallen victim to cost cutting, but a few companies still do it.

One of the most common types of non-cash dividend is the stock dividend; this is also known to most investors as a stock split. When a company issues a stock dividend, it pays out part of a share instead of cash for each share that an investor holds. The most common stock dividends are one share per outstanding share, and one-half of a share per outstanding share.

When a company pays out a one-share dividend per outstanding share, an investor will receive one additional share for each share she already owns. After this stock dividend, the investor has twice as many shares as she did before, so this is commonly called a 2-for-1 split. Similarly, when a company pays a stock dividend of one-half of a share per outstanding share, an investor who had two shares before the dividend will have three shares after it. So this stock dividend is also called a 3-for-2 split. But a company can pay out whatever amount it chooses as a stock dividend.

What happens when a company pays out a stock dividend? Let's take a 2-for-1 split as an example. Suppose a company has one million shares outstanding, with a current market price of $100 per share, so the total market value of the company is $100 million. If the company issues a 2-for-1 stock split, suddenly there are two million shares outstanding. But the market value of the company hasn't really changed, since the only thing that has happened is the number of shares doubled. So what should happen is that the price of each share falls by half, to $50 per share. Well, so what?

The answer has to do with signaling. A lot of companies like to maintain their share price in what they consider an affordable range for individual investors. These companies know that in order to make a stock investment, you need to buy at least 100 shares at a time, and so they will try to keep their share price in a range that enables individuals to afford to buy 100 share lots of their firms. This usually means keeping the share price under $100, and in many cases under $50 per share.

When a company issues a stock dividend, one of the things it effectively is saying to the market is, "We think that the value of our shares will keep growing in the future. So we'll cut the price down now to keep it affordable even as it grows."

Just like a significant increase in a cash dividend, a stock dividend is a signal from the managers of the firm to the general public that they expect high growth of earnings in the future. And in most cases, these signals are followed by good news about successful projects and increasing profits. So the prices of stocks that start to split start to rise as soon as the split occurs. In fact, many young firms that are growing very quickly will find themselves splitting their shares multiple times within a few years. So stock splits are highly credible signals that the company managers expect strong growth, and many investors take stock splits as strong buy signals.

Of course, there is such a thing as a reverse split. A company that has seen its share price fall may be in danger of getting kicked off a stock exchange. It turns out that many stock exchanges have rules about the minimum price at which listed companies can trade, and usually this price ranges from one dollar to a few dollars per share. So a company that has experienced a big drop in its share price might resort to a reverse split, in which it issues one new share to replace several existing shares. This will distribute the market value of the company over a smaller number of shares and raise the price of the shares in the opposite effect of a stock split.

The reason why companies would want to do reverse splits is that getting kicked off an exchange would lead to continued declines in value. When a company is forced to leave an exchange, it basically disappears from most investors' radar. So this loss in investor interest can further damage the value of a company.

In the aftermath of the Financial Crisis of 2008, several firms underwent reverse splits so that they could remain listed on the New York Stock Exchange. For example, Citigroup underwent a 1-for-10 reverse split in May

2011. Every 10 shares held by investors before the split were replaced by one share.

These examples show that dividend changes, and certain types of dividends like stock dividends, can send strong messages to the markets about a company's future performance. But there's another use for dividends that also sends a strong signal to investors about a company's dedication to creating value. Dividends are used in some companies as a way to impose discipline on the managers' spending.

The idea behind this strategy is pretty simple. I've mentioned in previous lectures that most companies prefer to pay for their new projects out of their current earnings. So in general, having a lot of earnings is good for a company, because that means it can afford to start new investments, like developing a new product. But companies also have to be careful when they have high earnings, because really good projects don't exactly grow on trees. It's easy to think of things to invest in, but it's actually very difficult to find the few projects that will create real value for a company. When a company has plenty of cash flowing in, managers find that it's easier just to fund a bunch of new projects than it is to take the time to sort through them carefully. Who cares if a few of them turn out to be duds?

And on top of that, there's also the danger that managers will waste earnings on pet projects—these are projects that boost the manager's status and image, but don't really boost profits. The higher the company's earnings are, the more managers will be tempted to channel some of these earnings to their pet projects. As I like to tell my students, idle cash is the devil's workshop.

So for some companies, the answer to both of these problems is to pay out high dividends—or rather, to pay out a high proportion of their earnings in dividends. This reduces the supply of earnings that could be reinvested in the firm, and that's the source of discipline. With fewer earnings to go around, managers have to put in the effort to choose only the very best projects to receive these scarce funds. In fact, this can set up a beneficial competition for resources inside the firm that leads to better choices for new projects. And managers' pet projects are generally going to lose that competition.

Several academic studies show that the higher the fraction of earnings a company pays out as dividends, the higher the growth rate of earnings tends to be over the next 10 years. This is a pretty robust finding, too—it's worked since the Second World War. And let me just drop a name or two of companies that pay out a very high fraction of their earnings—close to half. One is 3M, and another is Abbot Labs. Now, of course I'm not saying that all companies that pay out a large fraction of their earnings as dividends are all going to be innovative and successful—but experience suggests that these firms are worth looking into.

That gives a pretty good overview of why you should care about dividends, even if you're not in it for the dividends. What I want to do next is talk about a substitute for paying dividends that has become incredibly popular since the early 1990s. This substitute is share repurchases, also known as stock buybacks.

As the name suggests, a share repurchase or stock buyback is simply a transaction in which a company goes into the stock market and repurchases, or buys back, some of its outstanding shares. This is a substitute for a dividend because the company has to pay cash for these repurchased shares. So stock buybacks return cash to the company's shareholders—which is exactly what dividends also accomplish.

Stock buybacks have gone from being almost unknown to being one of the things that companies spend the most money on each year. In 1995, for example, there were about $100 billion of share repurchases for the year. By 2005, there were more than $100 billion of share repurchases each quarter that year. And in 2007, the amount that companies spent on share repurchases was almost as large as the amount of money they spent on new physical capital, like factories and equipment. This was significant because buying new capital is typically the main investment that companies make. Although share repurchases fell after the financial crisis of 2008, they bounced back fairly quickly and were back above $75 billion per quarter by 2010.

The basic similarity between dividends and stock buybacks might make you think that all the great things we've been learning about dividends also apply to buybacks. But in fact, they don't. I'm going to get into the details of why buybacks have become so popular, and whether you should pay as much attention to them as you should to dividends.

One of the main reasons why buybacks have become a popular alternative to dividends is that, for companies, buybacks are more flexible than dividends. If a company has a short-term windfall—a really good quarter where earnings are unusually high—then it can use the windfall to repurchase shares. Remember that dividends are regarded as long-term commitments. If a company increases its dividend, it's expected to maintain that higher dividend forever. But if the windfall is temporary, as in this example, then the company won't want to increase the dividend. Buybacks give companies a way to pay out that windfall to shareholders without creating any expectations.

Another reason why repurchases have become more popular is the different tax consequences of buybacks versus dividends. Before the tax code was changed to equalize the tax treatment of capital gains and dividends, investors preferred buybacks because they led to capital gains, which carried a lower tax rate. But even today, investors still prefer buybacks because the investor gets to choose whether to sell their shares back to the company. In other words, when a company pays a dividend, the company chooses when the investor pays taxes. But in the case of a buyback, the investor chooses when to sell the shares and incur the tax liability for the capital gains.

A third reason behind the surge in the popularity of buybacks is the rise of stock option compensation at many companies. Starting in the 1990s, more and more companies began to award incentive options to their managers and other employees. These incentive options gave the employees the right to buy shares in the company in the future, but at today's price. So if the company's stock increased in value, the employees would exercise the options and buy the shares from the company. Well, where did the company get all the shares it needed?

The answer is that the companies didn't issue new shares. Issuing new shares is expensive, and it involves a huge regulatory hassle. Instead, they bought back their own shares and held them in case they needed to sell them to the option holders. When shares are repurchased by the company, they don't disappear. Instead, we say that the company holds them as so-called treasury shares.

Imagine the company buying its own shares and stashing them in a safe inside company headquarters—that's basically what happens. The treasury shares don't collect dividends, because it's kind of silly for the company to pay dividends to itself, but otherwise, they're real shares that can be put back on the market at any time. So part of the story behind the rise of share repurchases is that companies issued billions of stock options, and so they bought back billions of shares to sell to the option holders.

Now, the last reason why buybacks have become so popular is the most interesting. It's based on a signaling story. A few minutes ago, we learned about the signals that dividend cuts and stock dividends send to investors The idea here is that stock buybacks, like dividends, can send a strong positive signal about the value of the company. The argument in this case goes like this. The managers of a company know a lot more than investors do about the company's true value, because they have access to much more information about how the company is actually performing. So if the managers of the company go out into the market and buy back stock on behalf of the company, they could be indicating to the market that they think the shares of the company are undervalued.

In fact, if you read any quotes from company managers who announce buyback programs, they typically describe the rationale for the buyback in terms of buying a dollar bill for $0.50, and some say exactly that.

If the managers of the company signal to the market that the shares are undervalued, then investors may come running to buy the shares. And of course, this helps drive the price of the shares up. In the early days of buybacks, before they were very widespread, some academic studies found that buyback program announcements were associated with 10% increases in share price. Wow! That's a nice improvement in share price for not much effort.

With results like this, word got out pretty fast that announcing share buyback programs was a surefire way to boost the share price. So as you can probably guess, companies large and small started to announce all kinds of share repurchase programs. Everyone wanted to signal to the market that their shares were undervalued.

If everyone claims that their shares are undervalued, they can't all be right, can they? Also, the timing didn't look so great. Companies kept announcing more and more buyback programs as the economy boomed and the stock markets rose to new highs. So companies were in the odd position of arguing that their shares were undervalued when the prices of their shares were higher than ever.

So the short story is that the quality of the signal in stock buybacks seriously deteriorated over time. If you know some engineering, then you could say that the signal-to-noise ratio in share buybacks fell dramatically, as the amount of noise in the market increased. The main reason companies were giving to investors for their buybacks—this undervaluation story—simply lost credibility. It also didn't help that companies who announced buyback programs didn't actually follow through on them. Many firms announced multiyear buyback programs and quit after the first one or two repurchases.

There are plenty of reasons why buybacks remain popular today—investors like the tax flexibility, and companies like the lack of a long-term commitment. In addition, companies are still using a lot of stock-based compensation, and so they need to repurchase shares in order to make good on these commitments. But you should think twice before believing a firm's claim that its shares are undervalued when it announces its latest buyback program.

At the end of the day, the fundamental difference between share buybacks and dividends is that dividends force a company to put its money where its mouth is. So when you pick stocks, you should look for companies that do just that with their dividends. These are companies that maintain a high dividend yield, companies that consistently increase their dividends over time, and companies that pay out a high proportion of their earnings in dividends. Growing firms that like to engage in stock splits are good investments, too, though they can be harder to find.

Dividends literally show you the money. Are you a dividend believer now?

Using Leverage
Lecture 12

I n the last lecture, you learned that dividends and dividend information are tools that every investor should understand and use. In this lecture, you'll learn about a tool that every investor should understand, but not necessarily use. You're going to learn about using leverage—both the tempting rewards of using it as well as the potentially harsh punishments. Individual investors, and companies, can use leverage to turn otherwise boring and predictable investments into more exciting ones, but perhaps the best way for individuals to use leverage is to invest in the companies that use it wisely.

Leverage
- Leverage is a term that we use to describe how much of the money used to buy an investment has been borrowed. We often calculate leverage by dividing the total cost of the investment by the amount that the investor pays out of pocket. The higher this number is, the more highly leveraged the investor is.

- If you have a mortgage, then you're a leveraged investor. Excessive leverage was one of the main culprits behind the global financial crisis of 2008. However, when used wisely, leverage is an important—if not essential—part of our investments. Leverage enables us to control and enjoy assets that we don't fully own and to enhance our investment returns as well.

- The main reason any investor would want to take on a leveraged investment in a financial asset is that leverage is a return multiplier; in other words, you can greatly increase your returns on investments by using leverage.

- Your leverage ratio tells you how many times the gross returns on the investment are multiplied when you use this amount of leverage. If your leverage ratio is 4 to 1, for instance, your gross returns will be quadrupled. Your actual return will be less when you also factor in the interest and any fees you have to pay on the loan.

© iStockphoto/Thinkstock.

Leverage is calculated by dividing the total cost of an investment by the amount that an investor pays for it.

- The real danger of leverage is that a change in price can more than wipe out your investment. You could actually end up losing more than what you paid out of pocket. However, most of the ways that investors are allowed to use leverage are set up so that it's very unlikely that the investor will lose more than the value of their investment. This protects both the investor and the institution that loaned the money to the investor.

Using Leverage

- There are 2 ways that investors can use leverage directly. One of them is buying assets on margin, which involves borrowing part of the money you use to buy the assets.

- In order to buy shares on margin, you generally have to go through a broker, who will be lending you the money that you use to buy assets. Because the broker is also handling the asset purchase transaction, he or she can handle the leverage in a pretty seamless way so that it looks like a normal asset purchase to you.

- Brokers refuse to make margin loans on some types of highly risky assets, so not every asset is available for leveraged investing. The broker will also tell you the minimum stake that they will require you to hold in the asset, expressed as a percentage of the value of the asset.

- The government establishes limits for margin buying that also specify the minimum ownership stake that an investor must take in the assets they buy on margin. There are 2 types of minimum required ownership stakes, which are referred to as **margin requirements**. The word "margin" refers to the share of the asset owned by the leveraged investor.

- The first margin requirement is called **initial margin**, and it's the minimum ownership stake you have to take in order to start a leveraged investment. For stocks, the Federal Reserve has currently set the minimum initial margin requirement at 50%, so when you buy stocks on margin, the most you will be able to borrow is 1/2 the value of the shares.

- If you borrow from a broker and buy assets on margin, then the margin will fluctuate with the market price of the asset. If the asset price rises, then your margin increases, and if the market price falls, your margin decreases.

- Your **margin** in an investment at any time is given by the value of your equity stake in the asset divided by the total value of the asset. The value of your equity stake is the net value of what you own, and it is calculated by taking the current value of the asset and subtracting the amount of the loan you took out to buy the asset.

- The second type of margin requirement is **maintenance margin**, which is the minimum level of equity that you have to maintain at all times after you make the initial leveraged purchase. Maintenance margin is usually set below the level of initial margin, and this allows the price of the asset to fall a bit without requiring the borrower to take any action, but it also protects the lender if the price falls too much.

- Generally, brokers will require a maintenance margin of 30% on leveraged purchases of stocks, so if the price of the stock falls so much that your equity in the shares—your margin—goes below 30%, you get a **margin call**, which is a request from your broker to deposit cash or securities into your brokerage account in order to bring your equity in the shares at least back up to the maintenance margin level. If you don't make your margin call, the broker has the right to liquidate your position—that is, sell your shares—in order to pay off the loan.

- If you can't make the margin call and the broker liquidates your position, you may or may not still owe money, depending on how quickly the price of the asset continues to fall once you get your margin call. Suppose the broker liquidates your position, and by the time the broker is able to sell the shares, they've fallen in value to $70 per share. The broker sells your 100 shares at $70 each, raising $7000, so there is enough to pay back the $5000 loan principal—and probably enough to pay back the interest and any fees on the loan as well.

- This example clarifies why brokers want you to keep a fairly high level of maintenance margin on many of the assets that you can use leverage to buy: The maintenance margin gives the broker a cushion to protect their interests in case you can't meet your margin call, and it also protects you from having to come up with even more cash to repay the broker.

- A simpler way to make leveraged investments is to buy the shares of leveraged companies. Many high-achieving companies use fair amounts of leverage to maintain their high returns.

Borrowing Securities and Short Selling

- The main reason you'd want to borrow securities is to engage in what's called a short sale—in which an investor borrows securities, sells the borrowed securities immediately, and then hopes to buy them back later at a lower price. Investors borrow securities when they believe that their value will fall.

- When you borrow securities, the lender doesn't want to be repaid in money—the lender wants the securities back. This makes borrowing securities and short selling especially interesting and risky.

- The first step in borrowing stocks and selling them short is locating someone who is willing to lend you the stocks. Because of the extra risk involved in short sales, securities lenders are extremely particular about who they lend to.

- Short selling any security without having borrowed it first is illegal. This transaction is called a naked short sale, and in most markets around the world, it's prohibited.

- Once you borrow the shares, you still may not be allowed to sell them because many markets have special rules called **uptick rules**, which are regulations aimed directly at limiting the practice of short selling. It says that a short sale cannot take place while the price of the asset is falling. In other words, the last tick, or price movement, must be in the upward direction before a short sale can take place.

- If you manage to sell the shares you borrow, then you have to remember that if the shares pay a dividend, you have to pay any dividends earned on the shares to the person you borrowed the shares from. That person is the true owner of the shares, but you borrowed the shares and sold them to someone else. You have to pay those dividends to the lender out of your own pocket, and that further adds to the cost of short selling.

- Furthermore, the lender of the shares has the right to ask for them back at any time—so you can sell them short one day, and the lender may ask for them back the next day. If that happens, you either have to quickly arrange another loan of securities, or you have to go out into the market and buy the shares back. That transaction is known as covering your short position. The danger is that you'll have to cover your short position well before you're ready to, and in particular, before you've made any money.

- Additionally, because you're using leverage, you'll need to post margin to your broker. Your broker will hold on to all the cash generated by the short sale, and you'll also have to deposit more cash or government securities in order to put your own skin in the game.

- Just as in the case of buying on margin, when you sell something short, you have to establish an equity position in the trade. The margin requirements for short selling stocks are usually the same for short sales as they are for leveraged purchases—50% initial margin and 30% maintenance margin—but you calculate the equity in your account differently for a short sale than you do for a leveraged purchase.

- For a short sale, your equity in the trade at any time, as a percent of the value of the shares, is the ratio of the net value of what you own divided by the current value of the shares. The net value of what you own is the total cash held by the broker minus the current value of the shares you sold short. The total cash held by the broker is equal to the proceeds from the short sale plus the cash that you deposit for your initial margin.

- Just as with buying on margin, your margin will go up and down as the price of the shares does. Your big fear is that the price of the shares rises after you sell them short, which will lead to losses.

- You'll also want to know the price of the shares that will trigger a margin call from your broker. Again, if you get that call and don't have the resources to bring the equity in your account back up above 30%, then the broker will cover the short position and end the transaction.

- Our financial markets are skewed toward buying and holding—not short selling. Therefore unless you really know what you're doing, you should stay away from short selling. Those who make money by short selling are willing to take risks, and they do their homework.

Important Terms

initial margin: A margin requirement that is the minimum ownership stake you have to take in order to start a leveraged investment.

maintenance margin: A margin requirement that is the minimum level of equity that you have to maintain at all times after you make an initial leveraged purchase.

margin: The share of an asset owned by a leveraged investor; the value of an equity stake in an asset divided by the total value of the asset.

margin call: A request from your broker to deposit cash or securities into your brokerage account in order to bring your equity in the shares at least back up to the maintenance margin level.

margin requirement: A minimum required ownership stake.

uptick rule: A regulation that is aimed directly at limiting the practice of short selling.

Suggested Reading

Bodie, Kane, and Marcus, *Investments*, chap. 3.

Fasciocco, "Buying on Margin is a Double-Edged Sword."

Questions to Consider

1. Visit the website of an online brokerage and find the interest rate that the brokerage charges when you purchase shares on margin. Do you think the interest rate charged on margin loans is commensurate with the risk of these loans?

2. Suppose that you purchased 500 shares of a $30 stock on margin where the initial margin requirement was 50%. If the maintenance margin requirement is 30%, at what price of the share would you get a margin call?

Using Leverage
Lecture 12—Transcript

In the last lecture, we learned that dividends and dividend information are tools that every investor should understand and use. In this lecture, we'll learn about a tool that every investor should understand, but not necessarily use—at least, not all the time. We're going to learn about using leverage.

Leverage is a term that we use to describe how much of the money used to buy an investment has been borrowed. You may remember the leverage ratio from the lecture on financial statement analysis, and we usually express leverage in terms of ratios. For example, we often calculate leverage by dividing the total cost of the investment by the amount the investor pays out of pocket. The higher this number is, the more highly leveraged the investor is.

Leverage has become one of those emotionally charged words in finance, especially in the wake of the financial crisis of 2008. After the financial crisis, it was uncovered that some American banks were leveraged 30 to 1 or more, which means that for every dollar of equity the firm owned free and clear, the managers had borrowed $29. And if you think that's bad, there were some European banks that were leveraged at 70 to 1 on the eve of the financial crisis.

Excessive leverage, of course, was indeed one of the main culprits behind this global financial crisis. It's also behind millions of small, private financial crises as well. But leverage, when used wisely, is an important if not essential part of our investments. Leverage enables us to control and enjoy assets that we don't fully own, and it enables us to enhance our investment returns as well.

And besides, chances are that you're a leveraged investor already. Don't think so? Well, if you have a mortgage, then you're a leveraged investor. In fact, if you have a typical American mortgage, then you're a highly leveraged investor. For example, suppose you buy a $250,000 home with a typical American mortgage. These usually call for a 10% down payment, so you put down $25,000 and you borrow the other $225,000. Well, congratulations—you've just borrowed $9 for every one that you've contributed out of your own pocket. So you're leveraged 10 to 1.

True, you might respond, but somehow, using a high amount of leverage to buy a home just doesn't seem all that dangerous. Using leverage to buy other assets, like stocks, is a lot more risky. Well, you have a point. Houses tend to have much more stable values than other financial assets, so it's not as likely that the value of your investment will be completely wiped out by a fall in the price of your home. Many financial investments have prices that bounce up and down much more, which dramatically increases the danger that a drop in prices will leave you with nothing—or possibly less than nothing.

In addition, we use leverage to buy our homes because we have to. It would take decades to save up enough money so that you could buy a house without having to borrow anything. If you want to have enough time to get your money's worth of enjoyment out of the house while you're still alive, you need to take out a mortgage to buy a house. What's the benefit of borrowing money just to invest in stocks or bonds?

That question is a great place to start our discussion of leverage. I'll get into the details of how you actually do the borrowing later in the lecture, but for now let's simply talk about why any investor would want to take on a leveraged investment in a financial asset.

The main reason is that leverage is a return multiplier—you can greatly increase your returns on investments by using leverage. Let me illustrate this by thinking about a leveraged investment in a $100 per share stock. Suppose the expected return on the stock is 8%, so this is not the world's most exciting stock. Maybe it has a really good dividend yield, though, or you've seen that its price doesn't tend to fluctuate all that much. You want to buy 100 shares of this stock but only want to spend $5000, so you borrow the other half of the money you need. For now, don't worry about how much interest you'll have to pay and who'll lend you the money. I'll get to that in a bit.

Just suppose for the sake of argument that you are able to borrow the $5000 and combine it with your own money to buy the 100 shares of stock for $10,000. You're now leveraged two-to-one, because you've bought assets worth twice as much as what you've paid for out of your own pocket.

Let's say a year goes by and, true to expectations, the stock returns exactly 8%. Just to make this concrete, let's assume the stock paid a dividend of $3 per share, which is a 3% dividend yield, and the price rose to $105 per share, which is a 5% capital gain. So when you sell the shares, you get $10,500 for the shares and you've been paid $300 in dividends, so you've received $10,800 in total value. Since $800 is 8% of $10,000, then the stock has indeed met its expected return of 8%.

But what's the actual return on your investment? Remember, you've only contributed $5000 out of pocket. During this one year, you invest $5000 but earn a profit of $800. Well, 800 is 16% of 5000. So your actual return here is 16%, not 8%. Your 2-to-1 leverage means that your return is multiplied by a factor of two. In other words, your leverage ratio tells you how many times the gross returns on the investment are multiplied when you use this amount of leverage. If your leverage ratio is four to one, for instance, your gross returns will be quadrupled, and gross returns don't include the interest or any fees associated with the loan.

Your actual return will be less when you also factor in the interest and any fees you have to pay on the $5000 loan. I really just want to highlight the return multiplier effect first, which is very transparent if we ignore that interest or fees on the loan for just a moment.

Of course, leverage's multiplier effect on returns cuts both ways. Now suppose that instead of increasing in price, that stock actually falls in price to $95 a share. That's not a disaster, because the stock still pays the 3% dividend, so when you sell the shares a year later, you end up with $9800. So your total money return is a −$200. That's negative 2% of $10,000, but you've invested $5000. So your actual return is −200/5000, which is −0.04 or −4%. So the 2-to-1 leverage ratio doubled your rate of loss; it turned a 2% loss into a 4% loss.

The real danger of leverage is that a change in price can more than wipe out your investment. You could actually end up losing more than what you've paid out of pocket. Again, let's stick with our simple example of 2-to-1 leverage, so you pay $5000 and borrow $5000 in order to buy $10,000 worth of shares.

Now let's suppose there's a terrible stock market crash and the price of this stock falls from $100 per share to $40 per share. Ouch! Also, let's assume that the company cuts the dividend to 0 in this case. So when you sell the shares, you only get $4000 a year later. You've not only lost all of your $5000, but you owe an additional $1000 on the loan, which you'll have to come up with somehow. So you've lost $6000 on a $5000 investment. Wow! Incidentally, the leverage multiplier still works in this case. You have a −$6000 payoff, which is −60% of $10,000. But the −$6000 is −120% of 5000, so your actual return is −120%.

This possibility of losing more than you actually invest is the really scary part of using leverage. Indeed, one of the most devastating effects of the financial crisis was that millions of homeowners ended up under water on their mortgages—that is, they owed more on the mortgage than the house was actually worth. When this happens, one of the likely outcomes is that the borrower will default on the loan, which is bad news for both the borrower and the lender. So most of the ways that investors are allowed to use leverage are set up so that it's very unlikely that the investor will lose more than the value of their investment. That protects both the investor and the institution that loaned the money to the investor.

Well, let's actually get into the details now of the ways that investors use leverage. There are basically two ways that investors can use leverage directly. One of them is by buying assets on margin, and we'll start there. I'll give the precise definition of what margin is in a few minutes, but for now, all we need to know is that buying assets on margin is nothing more than borrowing part of the money that you use to buy the assets.

In order to buy shares on margin, you generally have to go through a broker. The broker will actually be lending you the money that you use to buy assets, and since the broker is also handling the asset purchase transaction, they can handle the leverage in a pretty seamless way so that it looks like a normal asset purchase to you. In some countries, banks and other lenders will actually lend money to you in order to buy stocks. In the United States most lenders won't lend you money if you tell them that you're going to use the money to buy shares.

When you buy assets on margin, each broker will have a list of assets that they are willing to allow you to buy on margin. Brokers refuse to make margin loans on some types of highly risky assets, so not every asset out there is available for leveraged investing. The broker will also tell you the minimum stake that they will require you to hold in the asset, expressed as a percentage of the value of the asset. The minimum stake implies a maximum degree of leverage that they allow you to use on a particular investment. So, for example, if the minimum stake on an investment is 50%, the maximum leverage they allow you to use is two-to-one.

Now, I bring this up because the government establishes limits for margin buying that also specify the minimum ownership stake that an investor must take in the assets that they buy on margin. Do you know what branch of the government actually sets these limits? You'd think it would be the SEC, but for somewhat complicated reasons we don't have time to go into, it's actually the Fed.

Anyway, there are actually two types of minimum required ownership stakes, which are referred to as margin requirements. The word margin refers to the share of the asset owned by the leveraged investor. For example, a 40% margin requirement means that the investor must own 40% of the asset that they're using leverage to invest in.

The first margin requirement is called initial margin, and as its name suggests, it's the minimum ownership stake that you have to take in order to start a leveraged investment. For stocks, the Fed has currently set the minimum initial margin requirement at 50%. So when you buy stocks on margin, the most you will be able to borrow is half the value of the shares. As I mentioned a minute ago, brokers are also free to impose higher margin requirements on riskier shares and to refuse to lend on margin on risky investments entirely.

If you borrow from a broker and buy assets on margin, then the margin will fluctuate with the market price of the asset. If the asset price rises, then your margin increases, and if the market price falls, your margin decreases. I want to show you how this works, and in order to do that, I'll need to define margin more carefully.

Your margin in an investment at any time is given by the value of your equity stake in the asset divided by the total value of the asset. The value of your equity stake is the net value of what you own, and we calculate it by taking the current value of the asset and subtracting off the amount of the loan you took out to buy the asset.

Let's stick with our simple example of using margin to buy 100 shares of stock selling at $100 per share. The initial margin requirement is 50%, so you invest $5000 out of pocket and borrow the other $5000.

Now let's see what happens to your margin as the price of the asset changes. If the stock price rises to $105 per share, then the total value of the shares rises to $10,500. But you still only owe $5000, so your equity in the shares rises to $5500. That means that your margin is given by the following formula: $(10,500 - 5000)/10,500 = 52.38\%$. So margin does rise as the price of the asset rises.

That should mean that margin falls as the price of the asset falls. So let's see what happens when the price of the shares falls to $90 a share. The total value of the shares falls to $9000 (remember, we have 100 shares), but you still owe $5000 on the margin loan. So your equity, the difference, falls to $4000. And now your margin is $4000/$9000 = 44.44\%. So margin did fall when the price of the asset fell.

Thinking about what happens to margin when the price of the asset falls brings us to the second type of margin requirement, which is maintenance margin. Maintenance margin is the minimum level of equity that you have to maintain at all times after you make the initial leveraged purchase. Maintenance margin is usually set below the level of initial margin. Setting the maintenance margin limit below the initial margin requirement allows the price of the asset to fall a little ways without requiring the borrower to take any action. But it also protects the lender if the price falls too much. Here's how it works.

Generally, brokers will require maintenance margin of 30% on leveraged purchases of stocks. So if the price of the stock falls so much that your equity in the shares—your margin—goes below 30%, you get a margin call.

A margin call is a request from your broker to deposit cash or securities into your brokerage account in order to bring your equity in the shares at least back up to the maintenance margin level. Basically, the broker is requiring you to pay down your loan so that your equity in the shares goes back up to the minimum level specified by the maintenance margin. If you don't make your margin call, what happens? Well, the broker has the right to liquidate your position in that case—that is, sell off your shares—in order to pay off the loan.

Of course, that proposition raises two important questions. First, when will I get a margin call? This is a good calculation for anyone to make if they are going to engage in buying on margin. If you calculate the price of the asset that triggers a margin call, then you can watch the markets and be ready to act if the price of the asset falls to the trigger price.

Again, let's use our stock example. Let's let P stand for the price of the shares that will trigger a margin call. According to our definition of margin, this is going to happen when $P \times 100$ (that would be the market value of the shares) minus 5000 (the amount that you owe) divided by the market value of the shares ($P \times 100$) is less than 0.3, or 30% [$(P \times 100 - 5000)/(P \times 100) < 0.3$]. This isn't too hard to solve—just a couple of steps of algebra— and when you do solve it, you find that P equals $71.43, rounding up to the nearest penny. I've calculated it this way so that you know as soon as P drops to $71.42 or below, you'll get that margin call.

Now for the second question: if I can't make the margin call and the broker liquidates my position, will I still owe money? Well, that depends on how quickly the price of the asset continues to fall, once you get your margin call. Just for the sake of argument, suppose that you get a margin call on this stock investment and just don't have the cash or securities you need to bring the account back up to at least the maintenance margin. Let's say also that the broker liquidates your position, and by the time the broker is able to sell the shares, they've fallen to $70 per share in value. Well, the broker sells your 100 shares at $70 each, raising $7000. So there is enough to pay back the $5000 loan principal, and probably enough to pay back the interest and any fees on the loan as well.

I think this example clarifies why brokers want you to keep a fairly high level of maintenance margin on many of the assets that you can use leverage to buy. The maintenance margin gives the broker a cushion to protect their interests in case you can't meet your margin call, and it also protects you from having to come up with even more cash to repay the broker.

Less risky assets like government and municipal bonds will generally have much lower levels of initial and maintenance margin. The initial margin on U.S. Treasuries, for example, is about 10%. And the maintenance margin can be as little as only 2% for very short-term bonds. But even long-term bonds have maintenance margins of only about 6 or 7%. The reason for this, as you can probably guess, is that there's usually a lot less variation in the prices of government bonds than there is in the prices of stocks and other assets.

Before I move on to the next use of leverage, I want to point out again that when you use leverage to buy on margin, you are borrowing from the brokerage. And the broker is going to charge interest on that loan. Since this is fairly risky lending, you should expect to pay a higher rate than you would on other types of borrowing that you do, say for mortgage loans, home equity lines of credit, or car loans. Oh, and don't forget all the trading fees on top of that, too! So when you calculate your net or all-in return from a leveraged purchase of any asset, you need to remember to take account of the margin interest, trading fees, and any other fees from the transaction you paid.

Does all that sound too complicated? If it does, then one simpler way to make leveraged investments is to buy the shares of leveraged companies. A lot of high-achieving companies use fair amounts of leverage to maintain their high returns. For example, McDonalds, Merck, and Coca-Cola all leverage about two to one. General Mills, another high achiever, is levered at three to one, and even General Electric is leveraged at six to one.

Up to now, I've been talking about using leverage by borrowing money and investing the borrowed money into assets. But you can also borrow securities themselves. The main reason why you'd want to borrow securities is to engage in what's called a short sale.

In a short sale, an investor borrows securities, sells the borrowed securities immediately, and then hopes to buy them back later at a lower price. So you borrow securities when you believe that their value is going to fall. Keep in mind that when you borrow securities, the lender doesn't want to be repaid in money—the lender wants the securities back. That makes borrowing securities and short selling especially interesting and risky.

To make this concrete, I'll explain borrowing securities and short selling in terms of stocks, though of course you can sell just about any security short—at least in theory. Now, the first step in borrowing stocks and selling them short is actually locating someone who is willing to lend you the stocks in the first place. Because of the extra risk involved in short sales, securities lenders are extra particular about whom they lend to. So even if you identify a stock that you'd like to borrow and sell short, it could take your broker days to find another broker willing to lend the shares.

By the way, short selling any security without having borrowed it first is illegal. That transaction is called a naked short sale, and in most markets around the world, it's prohibited. But in the United States as well as in Europe during 2011, there were complaints in the markets that professional traders were being allowed to engage in naked short selling—at least to the extent that they sold the shares first and then worried about finding someplace to borrow them later.

Once you borrow the shares, you still may not be allowed to sell them. Why? Many markets have special rules called uptick rules. An uptick rule is a regulation aimed directly at limiting the practice of short selling. It says that a short sale cannot take place while the price of the asset is falling. In other words, the last tick, or price movement, must be in the upward direction, before a short sale can take place.

The SEC had uptick rules in place in the stock markets for years and years, but removed most of them right before the financial crisis. But once the crisis occurred, it actually banned short selling of certain types of stocks, like bank stocks. As you can guess, uptick rules make it that much harder to profit from short selling, because they put you at a bit of a disadvantage right off the bat.

If you manage to sell the shares that you borrow, then you have to keep in mind that if the shares pay a dividend, you have to pay any dividends earned on the shares to the person you borrowed the shares from. That person is the true owner of the shares, but you borrowed the shares and sold them to someone else. So there are two people expecting dividends from those shares. You have to pay those dividends to the lender out of your own pocket, and that further adds to the cost of short selling.

The lender of the shares has the right to ask for them back at any time. So you can sell them short one day and the lender may change her mind and ask for them back the next day. If that happens, you either have to quickly arrange another loan of securities, or you have to go back out into the market and buy the shares back. That transaction is known as covering your short position. The danger is that you'll have to cover your short position well before you're ready to, and in particular, before you've made any money.

And don't forget that you're using leverage, so you'll need to post margin to your broker. First, your broker will hold on to all the cash generated by the short sale. And on top of that, you'll have to deposit more cash or government securities in order to put your own skin into the game. Just like the case of buying on margin, when you sell something short, you have to establish an equity position in the trade. The margin requirements for short-selling stocks are usually the same for short sales as they are for leveraged purchases—50% initial margin and 30% maintenance margin. But you calculate the equity in your account differently for a short sale than you do for a leveraged purchase, and I'll show you that now.

For a short sale, your equity in the trade at any time, as a percent of the value of the shares, is the ratio of the net value of what you own divided by the current value of the shares. The net value of what you own is the total cash held by the broker, minus the current value of the shares that you sold short. Remember that the total cash held by the broker is equal to the proceeds from the short sale, plus the cash that you deposit for your initial margin.

So let's use our stock example again to make this concrete. If you borrow 100 shares of a stock currently selling at $100 per share and then sell them short, this generates $10,000 of cash that your broker will hold. Then you have to deposit another $5000 with the broker to give yourself an initial margin of 50%. Remember that the margin in a short sale is (cash held with broker − current value of shares)/current value of shares. So the cash held by the broker is $15,000 in total, and the market value of the shares at the moment you sell them short is $10,000, so when we put these numbers in the margin formula for a short sale, we get $(15,000 − 10,000)/10,000$ and that is exactly 50%.

Now, just as in the case of buying on margin, your margin will go up and down as the price of the shares does. But in this case, your margin goes up when the price of the shares falls, and it falls when the price of the shares rises. And again, your big fear is that the price of the shares rises after you sell them short, which will lead to losses.

Also, you'll want to know the price of the shares that will trigger a margin call from your broker. Using a 30% maintenance margin and P for the price of the shares that triggers the margin call, we know that you'll get a margin call when the value of your equity in the trade falls below 30%. So this happens when $(15,000 − 100P)/100P < 0.3$. Again, this only takes a couple of steps of algebra to solve, and when you do, you find that you'll get that dreaded call, e-mail, or text message (probably all three) when the price of the shares rises above $115.38.

Again, if you get that call and don't have the resources to bring the equity in your account back up above 30%, then the broker will cover the short position and end the transaction. If the broker is forced to do that at, say, $120 a share, then this will cost $12,000 to buy back the 100 shares. Since there's $15,000 of cash in your account, at least you won't owe the broker any more money. But you'll sustain a hefty loss on the money that you did put in already.

If I make short selling sound like a highly scary and dicey proposition, that's because it is. Our financial markets are skewed toward buying and holding, not short selling. So unless you really, really know what you're doing, you should stay away from short selling.

That isn't to say that people don't make money doing it. But those who do are willing to take risks, and they do their homework. In my opinion, you have to do even more research on the companies you want to short than on the companies you want to buy. That's because the deck is seriously stacked against you when you sell short, as we've learned.

In this lecture, we've looked into using leverage, and learned both the tempting rewards of using it as well as the potentially harsh punishments. As I mentioned at the beginning of the lecture, I'm not against using leverage as an investor—I'm completely in favor of using it wisely. Individual investors, and companies, can always use a little bit of leverage to turn otherwise boring and predictable investments into more exciting ones. But perhaps the best way for individuals to use leverage is to invest in the companies that use it wisely.

Choosing Bonds

Lecture 13

There are a few major issues that can help you narrow down your selection of bonds as part of a buy-and-hold investment strategy. The decision you make about default risk is the first big decision you need to make as a bond investor. Then, you should consider how you want to handle inflation. Finally, if you're in one of the top income tax brackets, you may also want to think about investing in tax-exempt bonds. Your attitude toward these major issues will help narrow down your choices to a manageable set.

Investing in Bonds

- The first big issue that you need to think about as a bond investor is **default risk**—the risk that the borrower won't be able to pay back all the promised principal and interest payments. Most people assume that a default implies that the borrower won't make any more payments and that the bonds become worthless—but this is rarely the case. Sometimes, a default event is simply a missed bond payment that the borrower makes up after a while.

- In many cases, defaults lead to rescheduled payments—not a permanent stop in payments. Nonetheless, a default dramatically reduces the value of your bonds, and it can make it difficult to sell them because only specialized investors are interested in defaulted bonds.

- Companies called **rating agencies** specialize in evaluating bonds and give out ratings based on the likelihood of full and on-time repayment of interest and principal. There are many rating agencies in the markets, but there are only 10 that have been recognized by the SEC as nationally recognized statistical rating organizations (NRSROs). Out of these 10, there are 3 dominant players: Moody's Investors Service, Inc.; Standard and Poor's Ratings Services (S&P); and Fitch, Inc.

- The rating agencies use a system of letters, along with pluses and minuses, to distinguish among the different qualities of borrowers. Moody's uses a system of capital and lowercase letters while S&P uses all capital letters.

- It's important to realize that the ratings system is not intended to correspond to any specific probabilities of default; rather, these are overall indications of the likelihood of full and timely repayment of promised interest and principal. The rating agencies have verbal interpretations of what the ratings mean.

Figure 13-1

Rating Scales	
S&P	**Moody's**
AAA	Aaa
AA	Aa
A	A
BBB	Baa
BB	Ba
B	B
CCC	Caa
CC	Ca
C	C

- At the top of the rating scale is the triple-A rating, which is denoted as AAA for S&P and Aaa for Moody's. S&P defines the triple-A rating as "extremely strong capacity to meet financial commitments." As you go down S&P's scale, the characterization of ratings goes to "very strong capacity" at double-A, "strong capacity" at single-A, and then "adequate capacity to meet financial commitments" at triple-B rating, which corresponds to a rating of Baa from Moody's.

- Because the triple-B rating is the lowest rating with at least adequate financial capacity, the triple-B bonds are regarded as the lowest so-called investment-grade rating. That means that institutional investors like pension funds, who are charged with investing in the best interests of their clients, are often prohibited from investing in any bonds with lower ratings than BBB or Baa.

- S&P refers to lower-rated bonds as speculative grade. This implies that anything rated double-B or lower needs at least a little luck in order to meet all of their financial obligations. Bonds rated double-B or single-B look OK for the short term but are vulnerable to a downturn in general economic conditions or in their own specific business. Bonds rated in the C range are dependent on favorable economic conditions in order to be able to make their promised payments, and below the C ratings is D, which stands for default.

- The **cumulative default rate** for corporate bonds is simply the fraction of all bonds in each rating category that have ever defaulted. As an investor, you will have to balance these default probabilities against the higher returns that lower-rated bonds promise, but building a bond ladder out of corporate bonds certainly isn't for everyone.

Commercial Paper
- **Commercial paper** is a special kind of corporate bond. It's unsecured, which means that it isn't backed by collateral, and it has very short maturity. However, commercial paper is a quite safe corporate bond. Only the largest and financially strongest firms are able to issue commercial paper, and defaults on the highest-rated commercial paper are extremely rare.

- However, because commercial paper is a very short-term instrument, it usually pays a very low rate of interest. In addition, the typical minimum size of a commercial paper lot is $1 million, so this effectively puts direct investment in commercial paper out of the reach of most individual investors.

- There are 2 ways for you to get access to investments that are similar to commercial paper. One way is to look for the longer-term version of commercial paper, medium-term notes (MTNs), which can be found at most bond brokers' websites. MTNs are rated like bonds and will probably have the same default track record as bonds.

- The other way to get access to commercial paper is by investing in a money market mutual fund, which is a type of mutual fund that invests the shareholders' deposits in short-term, high-quality bonds such as Treasury bills and commercial paper. These mutual funds earn interest rates that are usually significantly better than short-term bank deposit rates. Money market funds also offer the same types of conveniences as bank deposit accounts, such as access to ATM withdrawals and bill paying.

- The way that money market funds work is that investors buy shares in the mutual fund, where each share costs $1. The money market fund's managers take the cash from investors and buy short-term bonds. As these bonds pay interest, the money market fund passes along this interest to the investors in terms of new shares in the mutual fund.

- Because money market mutual funds are not bank accounts, they're not federally insured like bank deposits are, but their safety is supported by 2 mechanisms. First, there are some clear and strict SEC rules about the types of assets that money market mutual funds are allowed to invest in.

- The second mechanism is an informal bailout commitment on the part of the managers of the money market funds. Because money market funds are what initially attract customers, managers of these funds need to make sure that the fund fulfills its obligations, even if they have to pay out of their own pockets to keep the fund on its feet.

- When you invest in a money market mutual fund, you need to be very careful about what the fund tells you about the types of commercial paper that it will invest in. If you are tempted by a money market mutual fund that is returning more than other funds, you need to investigate whether this is because the fund is investing in lower-rated commercial paper, which carries a high risk.

- The low returns on most money market mutual funds also mean that they are really a substitute for holding cash. This means that they are not really great long-term investments, but there are circumstances where you might find yourself storing your cash in a money market fund for a longer period of time.

- For longer-term, fixed-income investments, however, you'll eventually want to find longer-maturity bonds that have the risk-return profile most attractive to you. Corporate bonds aren't going to be attractive to everyone, so you should consider the alternative: government bonds.

Government Bonds
- There is a surprisingly large and diverse set of government bond issuers. These days, even governments are rated by the major rating agencies, so you can use these ratings as a guide. The spirit of the ratings on government debt is about the same as corporate ratings, so it's OK to interpret them in about the same way.

- With high-quality government debt, like U. S. Treasuries, the risk of default is virtually zero, but you do have to consider inflation. The general term for a bond whose interest rate rises with inflation is an **indexed bond**, in the sense that the return is somehow indexed to inflation. In the United States, there are government bonds called Treasury inflation-protected securities (TIPS) as well as a series of inflation-indexed U.S. savings bonds.

- With TIPS, the principal of the bond is adjusted for inflation. The quoted interest rate on TIPS is the inflation-adjusted, or real, interest rate that the bond pays. Your total increase in value will depend on both the inflation rate as well as the inflation-adjusted rate the bond pays.

- In addition, the inflation is measured monthly with TIPS, and the interest adjustment happens twice per year. Even though deflation may decrease the interest payments you receive, the principal that you receive is protected against deflation. TIPS are actually quite affordable; unlike other government bonds, TIPS can be purchased in increments of only $100.

- The potential downside to TIPS is that they are longer-term bonds—they are only available in maturities of 5, 10, and 30 years—so when the TIPS are issued in the market, the promised rate of interest is largely driven by fears about how high inflation will be over the next 5, 10, and 30 years.

- When a regular Treasury bond is issued, its interest rate is influenced by the amount of inflation that is expected to occur over the life of the bond. In fact, the **Fisher effect** captures this relationship by stating that the interest rate on any bond is the sum of the real rate of interest plus the expected annual inflation over the life of the bond.

- When you buy a regular bond that isn't adjusted for inflation, you're hoping that inflation will be less than or equal to what the market expects it to be—but if inflation rises unexpectedly, you'll lose value.

- With TIPS, on the other hand, you know that you'll get compensated for whatever inflation occurs during the life of the bond, but the price you pay for that certainty may be that the inflation-adjusted return is lower than the inflation-adjusted return on a regular Treasury bond. The problem is that you won't know for sure until the bonds mature, so you must decide the amount of risk that you are willing to take.

- Bonds are one of the few types of investments that receive potential tax exemption, and for some investors, this is an attractive feature. For example, interest on Treasury bonds is exempt from state and local income taxes; however, the interest is taxed by the federal government, and capital gains are taxable as well.

- Municipal bonds carry the biggest potential tax advantage because the interest payments on many issues are exempt from federal income taxes. Because of this tax advantage, the interest rates paid on municipal bonds are always lower than the rates paid on fully taxable bonds.

- To find out whether any bond that pays tax-exempt interest is worth investing in, take the interest rate promised on the tax-exempt bond and divide that rate by 1 minus the tax rate you would otherwise have to pay on the interest if it were taxable. The answer tells you the equivalent taxable interest rate that you're earning on the bond.

- Municipal bonds are most relevant to investors who are in the top income tax brackets. In addition, municipal bonds carry default risk even though most are highly rated, so you should pay attention to those ratings and do your homework on the borrower—just like you would for a corporate bond.

Important Terms

commercial paper: A special kind of corporate bond that is unsecured and has very short maturity but that is quite safe.

cumulative default rate: The fraction of all corporate bonds in each rating category that have ever defaulted.

default risk: The risk that a borrower won't be able to pay back all the promised principal and interest payments.

Fisher effect: A theory that states that the interest rate on any bond is the sum of the real rate of interest plus the expected annual inflation over the life of the bond.

indexed bond: The general term for a bond whose interest rate rises with inflation.

rating agency: A company that specializes in evaluating bonds and that gives out ratings based on the likelihood of full and on-time repayment of interest and principal.

Suggested Reading

Bogle, *Common Sense on Mutual Funds*, chap. 7.

Brealey, Myers, and Allen, *Principles of Corporate Finance*, chap. 24.

Questions to Consider

1. Suppose you purchased a Treasury inflation-protected security (TIPS) with a principal of $1000 and held it for 2 years. During the first year, the total inflation was 4%. During the second year, the total inflation was 3%. What should the principal value be at the end of the second year?

2. Suppose that you know you will have to pay income taxes of 28% on any taxable interest income. A fully taxable bond is paying an interest rate of 6%. Suppose that a municipal bond that has the same characteristics as the fully taxable bond is offering an interest rate of 4.2%. The only difference between the 2 bonds is that interest payments from the municipal bond are tax-free. Which bond should you choose for your portfolio?

Choosing Bonds
Lecture 13—Transcript

In the previous lecture, we learned about the roller-coaster ride that leverage can take you on. In this lecture, let's come back to the hopefully safer world of bond investing.

In the lecture where I introduced bonds, we learned about the huge variety of bonds that are available for investors. Although it's great to have a choice, we all know that too much choice can be bewildering. Given that you'll want to add some bonds to your portfolio either now, or sometime in the future, how do you pick out the ones that are best for you from among the literally thousands of different ones on the market?

That's what this lecture is all about. There are a few big issues you should think about when it comes to bond selection, including default risk, inflation, and taxes. Your attitude toward these issues will help narrow down your choices to a manageable set. When you see some specific details about how these risks affect your bond investments, and what types of bonds can effectively mitigate these risks, I think that it becomes a lot easier to make up your mind about the kinds of bonds you'll want to hold.

In this lecture, I'm still thinking about bond investing from the standpoint of a buy-and-hold investor. In the introductory lecture on bonds, we learned about the strategy of building a bond ladder, so this lecture is partly about picking the bonds that you'll want to include in your bond ladder. We'll learn about some other ways to invest in bonds, too, in a future lecture.

The first big issue that you need to think about as a bond investor is default risk—the risk that the borrower won't be able to pay back all the promised principal and interest payments. When we think of default, most of us immediately assume that the borrower won't make any more payments, and the bond become worthless. But this is rarely the case. Sometimes, a default event is simply a missed bond payment that the borrower makes up after a while. And in many cases, defaults lead to rescheduled payments, not a permanent stop in payments. Nonetheless, as I've mentioned before, a default is going to dramatically reduce the value of your bonds. And it can make it difficult to sell them, because only specialized investors are interested in buying defaulted bonds.

So the big question is, how do you evaluate the probability of default on a bond? Companies called rating agencies specialize in evaluating bonds and they give out ratings based on the likelihood of full and on-time repayment of interest and principal. There are actually lots of rating agencies in the markets, but there are only 10 that have been recognized by the SEC and are called nationally recognized statistical rating organizations. And out of these 10, there are three really dominant players: Moody's; Standard and Poor's, known simply as S&P; and Fitch. Most bonds are rated by at least one of these firms, and in most cases, they carry ratings from two or more firms. I'll talk mostly about Moody's and S&P, since these two firms tend to rate most of the bonds that you'll be interested in.

The rating agencies use a system of letters, along with pluses and minuses, to distinguish between the different qualities of borrowers. Moody's uses a system of capital and lowercase letters, while S&P uses all capital letters. I tell my students that you can always remember who gave the rating, because Moody's has both capital and lowercase letters in its name, and uses a mix of capital and lowercase letters in its ratings. S&P, like its nickname, only uses capital letters in its ratings.

It's important to realize that the ratings system is not intended to correspond to any specific probabilities of default. Rather, these are just overall indications of the likelihood of full and timely repayment of promised interest and principal. The rating agencies have verbal interpretations of what the ratings mean, and I'll mention a few of them as I talk about the rating scale.

Here's a table that compares the bond ratings that Moody's and S&P use. At the top of the rating scale is the so-called triple-A rating, which is three capital A's for S&P and one capital A and two lowercase a's for Moody's. S&P defines the triple-A rating as "extremely strong capacity to meet financial commitments." Note again that there's no promise of probabilities here, just a verbal characterization. As we go down the scale, the characterization of ratings goes to very strong capacity at double-A, strong capacity at single-A, and then finally adequate capacity to meet financial commitments at S&P's triple-B rating, which corresponds in this case to a rating of Baa from Moody's.

Note that the triple-B rating is only associated with adequate financial capacity. Because this is the lowest rating with at least adequate financial capacity, the triple-B bonds are regarded as the lowest so-called investment-grade rating. This means that institutional investors like pension funds, who are charged with investing in the best interests of their clients, are often prohibited from investing in any bonds with lower ratings than BBB or Baa.

S&P refers to lower-rated bonds as speculative grade. This implies that anything rated double-B or lower needs at least a little luck in order to meet all of their financial obligations. Bonds rated double-B or single-B basically look okay for the short term, but are vulnerable to a downturn in general economic conditions, or in their own specific business. Bonds rated in the C range are actually dependent on favorable economic conditions in order to be able to make their promised payments. And below the C ratings is only D, which stands for—you guessed it—default.

All this information about the bond ratings does give a pretty good indication of the likelihood of default, but wouldn't it be nice to have some hard numbers to compare? Well, the rating agencies do collect statistics on the actual default rates that bonds in various ratings categories experience, and we'll look at some of those now.

The first set of statistics I'll show you is what is called the cumulative default rates in each ratings category, for corporate bonds. This is simply the fraction of all bonds in each rating category that have ever defaulted. Notice that the default rate runs from only 1/2 of 1% to just under 3% in the A categories, then jumps to between 10 and 50% in the B categories, to just under 70% in the C categories. Now, this isn't a default probability because it's showing you the fraction of all bonds over a very long period of time that have ever defaulted; but, it does give you an indication of the amount of risk you'll take on if you maintain a ladder of bonds in a certain rating category for a long period, say 30 years or more.

If you still want to see numbers that look more like real default probabilities—and if you're anything like me, you do—then I can show you these statistics as well. These are the average annual default rates between 1981 and 2008 of all corporate bonds around the world that were rated by S&P. So these numbers can be interpreted much more like the probability that a bond of a certain rating will default in a given year. Notice that the annual probability of default runs from virtually 0 to only a quarter of a percent for the investment grade bonds over this period. But the annual default rate jumps up to between 1 and 10% per year for bonds in the double-B and single-B range, and then it jumps up to over 20% per year for bonds in the C-range.

I hope that this gives you a good understanding of what you're getting yourself into when you invest in corporate bonds of various ratings. Basically, if you buy and hold a bond rated below investment grade, you're looking at a chance of at least 1% per year that this bond will default. And if you hold a series of below-investment grade bonds for a long period, then your chance of experiencing defaults on these bonds goes way up. The triple-B bonds don't do too badly in terms of annual probability of default, but it seems like the defaults manage to catch up over longer periods, as we see in that cumulative default rate of about 10%. But the A range features not only low annual default probabilities, generally lower than 1/10 of 1%, but also a very low rate of defaults over longer time horizons as well.

Now, you as an investor will have to balance these default probabilities against the higher returns that lower-rated bonds promise. It may be worth it to you to invest in a ladder of triple-B corporate bonds, because the increase in yield over, say, double-A bonds is too high to pass up, even when you consider the default risk. On the other hand, if you think about the amount of money that you will have locked up in your bonds, you may find that even a long-run default rate of 1% is too high. You may think that if you're the unlucky one, the damage to your portfolio will be too much to recover from. And that's a perfectly legitimate concern. I certainly think that building a bond ladder out of corporate bonds isn't for everyone.

Of course, you may think that those triple-A bonds don't seem too bad, and why not build a ladder out of those. Well, that's a great idea—until you realize how few triple-A corporations there are. As I speak, there are only

4 triple-A rated corporations in the United States. So a triple-A bond ladder may not be very diversified, which is also a concern. There does seem to be a much greater supply of double-A rated bonds, however, which are certainly worth thinking about as a source of a corporate bond ladder.

So, if you were hoping to find a safe and attractive corporate bond to invest in, you may be pretty disappointed. Or maybe you're skeptical. Surely, you think, huge and successful corporations like McDonalds and Intel must offer bonds that are quite safe?

The answer is that they do, but the bonds are special ones—called commercial paper. Commercial paper is a special kind of corporate bond. It's unsecured, which means that it isn't backed by collateral. And it has very short maturity—most of the commercial paper out there has a maturity of less than 270 days, and the vast majority of it has maturity of less than 3 months. But commercial paper is a quite safe corporate bond—only the largest and financially strongest firms are able to issue commercial paper, and defaults on the highest-rated commercial paper are extremely rare.

Of course, there's always a catch, and with commercial paper there are two. One of them you've probably already guessed. Since commercial paper is a very short-term instrument, it usually pays a very low rate of interest. And second, there's a little matter of minimum investment. The typical minimum size of a commercial paper lot is $1 million. So this effectively puts direct investment in commercial paper out of the reach of most individual investors.

But there are two ways for you to get access to investments that are similar to commercial paper. One way is to look for the longer-term version of commercial paper, which is called medium-term notes, or MTNs for short. You can find MTNs on most bond brokers' websites. You just need to keep in mind that MTNs are rated like bonds, and will probably have the same default track record as bonds.

The other way to get access to commercial paper is by investing in a money-market mutual fund. A money-market mutual fund is a type of mutual fund that invests the shareholders' deposits in short-term, high-quality bonds such as Treasury bills and commercial paper. These mutual funds were actually started in the 1970s to evade restrictions on bank deposit rates known as deposit-rate ceilings. They flourished then, and continue to do so now, because they can invest in commercial paper and earn interest rates that are usually significantly better than short-term bank deposit rates. Money market funds, as they're called, also offer the same types of conveniences as bank deposit accounts, such as access to ATM withdrawals and automatic bill paying.

It's important to realize that money market funds are not bank deposit accounts, though. The way that they work is that investors buy shares in the mutual fund, where each share costs one dollar. The money market fund's managers take the cash from investors and buy short-term bonds like t-bills and commercial paper. As these bonds pay interest, the money market fund passes along this interest to the investors in terms of new shares in the mutual fund. So if I invest $1000 into a money market fund, I'll own 1000 shares of the fund. If the interest rate earned on the fund is 2% per year, then at the end of the year I'll own 1020 shares in the fund, where each share is still worth one dollar each.

Since money market mutual funds are not bank accounts, they're not insured like bank deposits are. But their safety is supported by two mechanisms. First, there are some clear and strict SEC rules about the types of assets that money market mutual funds are allowed to invest in. Rule 2-a-7, for example, lays out that money market mutual funds must hold high-quality bonds of no more than 13 months of maturity and the average maturity of the entire fund can't be longer than 60 days. In addition, the main priority of the fund must be preservation of asset value at $1 per share rather than capital appreciation.

The second mechanism is an informal bailout commitment on the part of the managers of the money market mutual funds. The companies that offer money market mutual funds usually offer many other mutual funds as well, which earn far more management fees than the money market mutual funds. These fund management companies initially attract investors to their products through the money market mutual fund. So money market funds bring customers in the door.

The idea is that if the shareholders can't trust the money market fund, then they surely won't trust this company with their other investments. So the money market fund managers have a big incentive to make sure that the money market fund fulfills its obligations, even if the managers have to pay out of their own pockets to keep the fund on its feet. For example, in 1997 a small finance company named Mercury finance defaulted on its lower-rated commercial paper. This commercial paper promptly lost 25% of its market value. A money market fund operated by Strong Capital Management was a big holder of the Mercury Finance commercial paper, and the managers of the fund bought all the commercial paper from the fund with their own money, at its pre-default value of $180 million.! This example shows that even though money market mutual funds aren't federally insured, there are good reasons to believe that they're very safe investments.

Of course, when you invest in a money market mutual fund, you need to be very careful about what the fund tells you about the types of commercial paper that it will invest in. Some money market funds only invest in t-bills, and of course this is very safe. The downside is that the returns on these funds are fairly low. Money market funds increase the returns they offer their investors by buying higher-yielding commercial paper—which is fine, if the paper carries a high rating, known as A1 or P1 by the respective rating agencies.

Some money market funds try to further juice their returns by allowing themselves to invest in lower-rated commercial paper, and this is really where the risk lies. So if you are tempted by a money market mutual fund that is returning a bit more than all the other funds, then you really need to investigate what the fund is holding. And you need to ask yourself, whether the few extra hundredths of a percent are really worth the extra risk that the managers won't be able to bail out the fund in case a lot of their holdings default.

The low returns on most money market mutual funds also mean that they are really a substitute for holding cash, not really a great long-term investment. But there are circumstances where you might find yourself storing your cash in a money market fund for a longer period of time. For example, you may liquidate an investment and not know right away where to reinvest the money. Or returns on long-term bonds may be so low that they don't justify locking up the money for that long, and you want to wait and see whether interest rates will start to rise in the future. And of course, most experts remind us that we do need to have an emergency fund of cash, in case of some financial disaster in our lives like a layoff. In all these cases, money market mutual funds can be very attractive vehicles for storing cash for extended periods.

For longer-term fixed income investments, though, you'll eventually want to find longer-maturity bonds that have the risk-return profile most attractive to you. And the fact is that corporate bonds just aren't going to be attractive to everyone. So we should consider the alternative, government bonds.

As we learned in the introductory lecture on bonds, there is a surprisingly large and diverse set of government bond issuers out there. These days, even governments are rated by the major rating agencies, so you can use these ratings as a guide. But although the lettering system is the same, the letters don't quite carry the same meaning, because a government's willingness and ability to pay its debts is influenced by a different set of economic and political factors than corporate debt is. Nonetheless, the spirit of the ratings on government debt is about the same as corporate ratings, so I think it's okay to interpret them in about the same way.

With high-quality government debt, like U.S. Treasuries, the risk of default virtually goes to 0. So you have other considerations to think about. And the main one in my mind is inflation. I've discussed inflation a couple of other times in previous lectures, so I won't repeat any information about the damage that inflation can do. Instead, I want to consider the choice you have to invest in government debt that carries at least some explicit inflation protection.

The basic idea of a bond whose interest rate rises with inflation is actually a pretty old one, though these bonds haven't been around all that long in the United States. The general term for such a bond is an indexed bond, in the sense that the return is somehow indexed to inflation. In the United States, we have government bonds called Treasury Inflation-Protected Securities, or TIPS, as well as a series of inflation-indexed U.S. savings bonds. Other countries such as the United Kingdom also offer inflation-indexed government bonds.

How do TIPS Work? Basically, the principal of the bond is adjusted for inflation. For example, if the bond has a $10,000 principal or par value at the start of the year and inflation is 3% annually, then at the end of the year the bond principal will rise to $10,300. The reason the inflation adjustment is done this way is so that the interest rate on the bond can stay constant. This seems to be mostly a matter of clarity and convenience for investors. The quoted interest rate on TIPS is the inflation-adjusted or real interest rate that the bond pays. Your total increase in value will depend on both the inflation rate as well as the inflation-adjusted rate the bond pays.

Let me give you an example to show you how this works. Suppose you buy a Treasury Inflation-Protected Security with an initial principal value of $10,000, and the interest rate on the bond is fixed at 2% per year. If inflation is 3% over the course of the first year, then the Treasury marks up the principal on the bond to $10,300 at the end of the year. Then, during the next year, the Treasury pays you 2% interest based on the new principal of $10,300. So during the second year, you'll get 2% of $10,300, which is $206 in interest. Note that we have to find out what the inflation rate is before the Treasury marks up the principle of the bond—that can't be avoided. Any inflation-indexed security is going to face some kind of delay, based on the fact that we have to wait to measure the actual inflation.

Here are a few more details about TIPS that you ought to know. First, in my example I pretended that the inflation adjustment occurs only once per year, to keep it simple. But the inflation is measured monthly, and the interest adjustment actually happens twice per year, which is better for you. Second, TIPS will decrease the principal if there is deflation, so that the interest payment will fall if the CPI actually falls; but at maturity, the Treasury will repay either the adjusted principal, or the original principal, whichever is higher. That means that even though deflation may decrease the interest payments you receive, the principal that you actually receive is protected against deflation.

Finally, TIPS are actually quite affordable—unlike other government bonds, TIPS can be purchased in increments of only $100. Now, there is an alternative to TIPS offered by the U.S. Treasury, called I-Bonds. I-Bonds are inflation-indexed savings bonds, and they can be purchased directly through

Treasury Direct as well as through banks. I-bonds are even more affordable than TIPS, since the minimum purchase is only $25. But they don't adjust as rapidly to inflation, and they have other restrictions as well. For example, individuals are only allowed to purchase $5000 of I-Bonds per year, whereas they can purchase up to $5 million in TIPS.

Of course, TIPS do have a couple of potential downsides that you should also be aware of. First, there's the amount of the real return on TIPS. TIPS are longer-term bonds. They are only available in maturities of 5, 10, and 30 years. So when the TIPS are issued in the market, the promised rate of interest is largely driven by fears about how high inflation will be over the next 5, 10, and 30 years. When people get more worried about inflation, they flock into TIPS, which drives the price up and the promised interest rate down. And when inflation fears calm down, investors buy other bonds instead, so the promised rate on TIPS rises and the price of TIPS falls.

This leads to two potential problems. First, if you buy TIPS during a time when there's a lot of fear for future inflation, then the promised returns on TIPS will be very low. And second, if you have to sell your TIPS before they reach maturity, then you can suffer a capital loss on your TIPS, just like you can on any other bond.

How does the inflation protection in TIPS stack up against the inflation protection in normal government bonds? When a regular Treasury bond is issued, its interest rate is influenced by the amount of inflation that is expected to occur over the life of the bond. In fact, there's a well-known rule of thumb in economics called the Fisher Effect that captures this relationship. The Fisher Effect says that the interest rate on any bond is the sum of the real rate of interest, plus the expected annual inflation over the life of the bond. So when you buy a regular bond that isn't adjusted for inflation, you're hoping—or betting—that inflation will be less than or equal to what the market expects it to be. But if inflation rises unexpectedly, you'll lose value.

With TIPS, on the other hand, you know that you'll get compensated for whatever inflation occurs during the life of the bond—there won't be any nasty inflation surprises. But the price you pay for that certainty may be that the inflation-adjusted return is lower than the inflation-adjusted return on a regular

Treasury bond. And the problem is, you won't know for sure until the bonds mature. So the choice is really about risk. Do you want to take the risk that inflation will be higher than expected, or do you want to get rid of that risk? That depends on your own feelings about risk, as well as how you personally expect the markets and the economy to perform well into the future.

So far we've talked about default risk and inflation risk. The final aspect of bonds that may help you narrow down your choice is tax treatment. Bonds are one of the few types of investments that receive potential tax exemption, and for some investors, this is an attractive feature. For example, interest on Treasury bonds is exempt from state and local income taxes, though the interest is taxed by the federal government and capital gains are taxable as well.

But it's municipal bonds that carry the biggest potential tax advantage, since the interest payments on many issues are exempt from federal income taxes. Because of this tax advantage, the interest rates paid on municipal bonds are always lower than the rates paid on fully taxable bonds. The question, of course, is how much lower. Depending on your tax rate, you could still end up better off, on an after-tax basis, by investing in a municipal bond with a lower interest rate than in a fully taxable bond that pays a higher interest rate.

To find out whether any bond that pays tax-exempt interest is worth investing in, there's an easy way to compare the interest rate on a tax-exempt bond with the rate on a taxable bond. Simply take the interest rate promised on tax-exempt bond, and divide that rate by 1 minus the tax rate you would otherwise have to pay on the interest, if it were taxable. The answer tells you the equivalent taxable interest rate that you're earning on the bond. For example, if the municipal bond is paying a 5% interest rate, and your income tax rate is 35% of any taxable interest earned, then the equivalent taxable interest rate is $5/(1 - 0.35) = 7.69\%$. This is the rate that you should compare to other taxable bonds that you are also considering.

Now, as my example suggests, this is most relevant to investors who are in the top income tax brackets. In fact, the market interest rates on municipal bonds are usually driven by the investors in the top tax brackets—the rates get driven just to the point where high-tax investors are indifferent between tax-exempt and taxable bonds—so investors in lower income tax brackets probably won't find these bonds worthwhile.

In addition, you should remember that municipal bonds also carry default risk, even though most are highly rated. Although there has not been a default by a U.S. state in the postwar era, there have been a number of localities that have defaulted on their municipal bonds. So pay attention to those ratings and do your homework on the borrower, just like you would for a corporate bond.

In this lecture, we learned that there are 3 big issues that can really help you narrow down your bond selection. You'll notice that I started with default risk, because I think that this is really the big decision you need to make as a bond investor. I think it's wise to use ratings as an initial guide, just like we use financial ratios to identify good stocks. But you need to do your own homework on any risky borrower whose bonds you are thinking of buying.

Then consider how you want to handle inflation. There are good alternatives out there to fixed rate bonds, though the certainty they offer does come at the cost of a lower promised yield. But there's no need to expose yourself to inflation risk if you don't want to. And finally, if you're in one of the top income tax brackets, you may also want to think about investing in tax-exempt bonds, especially munis.

Hopefully this lecture gives you a compass for navigating that ocean of bonds out there. Given how important it is to move your riskier investments into bonds at some point in your investing lifetime, you will have to sail across this sea eventually. But now I think you have the tools to make it a safe and pleasant voyage.

Bond School
Lecture 14

O ne of the things that discourages people from bond investing is the potentially confusing terminology associated with bonds, including how bond rates and prices are quoted. If you know these things, you'll be a much more confident bond investor—even if you never actually trade bonds. You also have to understand bond pricing and the relationship between price and yield. In addition, you'll need to know about riding the yield curve, a bond trading strategy that is so simple that you can pursue it even if you are primarily a buy-and-hold bond investor.

Bond Payments and Rates of Return

- There are many different rates of return associated with bonds, and all of the various rates of return on bonds are quoted using a special form of a return called a **stated annual rate of return**, which always contains 2 pieces of information if quoted properly: It tells you an annual rate of return and the number of times per year the rate is compounded. The convention in the bond market is to quote every rate of return that has to do with a bond as an annual rate compounded semiannually, which means that the interest on a straight bond is paid twice per year.

- The whole point of quoting rates of return as stated annual rates is to give you a shortcut to finding a semiannual rate of return, which is an interest rate for a 6-month period. To find a semiannual rate of return given a quoted bond rate, simply divide the quoted rate by 2. You should assume that every interest rate associated with a bond is an annual rate compounded semiannually—unless you're told otherwise.

- The coupon size is determined by the **coupon yield**, which is the value of the annual coupon amount divided by par. The standard practice is to set the coupon rate equal to the market rate of return for the bond at the time the bond is issued. The bond market decides on an appropriate rate of return for the bond, based on the issuer's risk and market conditions, and this market rate is used for the coupon yield. Once the coupon yield is determined, it won't change over the life of the bond, so the size of the coupon remains fixed. After the bond is issued, however, the market rate of return will fluctuate according to market conditions and the financial strength of the borrower.

- The changes in the market rate of return on the bond will change the price of the bond. The price of a bond at any time is the present value of all its payments, and it depends on the relative sizes of the coupon yield and the market rate of return on the bond.

- The **current yield** is the annual coupon divided by the market price of the bond. The current yield expresses the rate of interest that the coupons represent if you buy the bond at the current market price.

- A **yield to maturity** is the average yield earned by a bond investor who buys the bond at the current market price and holds the bond to maturity. The market return on a bond is usually expressed as a yield to maturity.

- Even though we use the yield to maturity as if it's the return that you'll actually earn on the bond, there are 2 hidden catches in the yield to maturity: The yield to maturity is only exactly accurate if you actually hold the bond to maturity, and it assumes that when you receive the coupon payments from the bond, you are able to reinvest those coupon payments in a way that earns the exact same return as the market rate of return on the bond.

Bond Price and Bond Yield
- The amounts of the coupon payments on bonds are fixed when the bond is issued, and they don't change after that. Once the bond is issued, the market rate of return on the bond can and does change as market conditions and the financial condition of the borrower change.

- Dealers quote bond prices in percent of par, so to find the price of any bond, you take the quoted price and multiply it by the principal amount to get the actual dollar price you'd have to pay to buy the bond. The bond price is less than par when the market rate of return is higher than the coupon yield on the bond.

- When the market rate of return on a bond falls below the coupon yield, the price rises above its par value. Therefore, when the market rate is above the coupon yield, the price is below par. When the market rate is below the coupon yield, the market price is above par. When the market rate of return is exactly equal to the coupon yield, the price is exactly equal to par.

- This explains why most bonds set their coupons so that the coupon yield is exactly equal to the market rate of return when the bonds are issued; this makes it so the price of the bond is equal to its par value, which is really just done for the convenience of the borrowers and lenders by giving round dollar amounts.

- The relationship between yield and price is not linear, which means that there can be some very attractive opportunities for people who want to trade bonds actively. A small change in the market rate on the bond can translate into a relatively large change in price. Therefore, if you think you can predict changes in the market rate of return on a bond, you could make some very attractive returns as a bond trader.

- If you want to take advantage of the relationship between price and yield by trading, you may want to know that the longer the maturity of the bond, the steeper the yield-price relationship becomes. In other words, the price of a 30-year bond rises much more than the price of a 10-year note when the market interest rate falls by 0.5%. Therefore, people who are bond traders like to trade straight bonds that are 10 years or longer in maturity.

- However, if the market for a 10-year bond is much larger than the market for a 30-year bond from the same issuer, then trading the

Figure 14-1

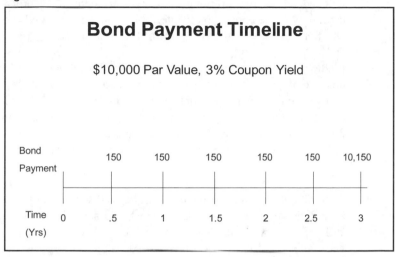

Bond Payment Timeline

$10,000 Par Value, 3% Coupon Yield

Bond Payment: 150 | 150 | 150 | 150 | 150 | 10,150

Time (Yrs): 0 | .5 | 1 | 1.5 | 2 | 2.5 | 3

10-year bond would probably make more sense because any loss in price sensitivity would be compensated by the improved ability to trade quickly.

- The chance to take advantage of large changes in bond prices as bond interest rates change is the big attraction of active bond investing. In order to be a successful bond trader, you need to predict correctly when bond interest rates will change, and you need to become very skilled at predicting when interest rates will fall, making any bonds you hold become more valuable.

- There are 2 basic reasons that a bond interest rate will fall. First, general economic conditions can change in a way that makes interest rates fall, or there can also be basic supply-and-demand reasons that bond interest rates fall.

- Interest rates are notoriously difficult to forecast, which explains why many bond traders prefer to make bets based on the second reason that bond rates might fall: A government or a company might have their bonds upgraded by a bond rating agency. This upgrade will reduce the risk premium that investors demand in order for them to hold the bonds, so the interest rate on the company's bonds will fall, which will make the price of the bonds rise.

- Predicting that a company or government will experience a ratings upgrade depends on the same type of financial analysis that you learned about in the context of stocks. As with the efficient markets hypothesis, if you wait too long to make up your mind, other investors will buy the borrower's bonds in anticipation of the ratings upgrade, so the price of the bonds will rise even before the upgrade happens.

- Even though this type of bond trading is well within the ability of an individual investor who is willing to do some homework, it's still made risky by the fact that, in order to make good profits, you have to act early—in other words, when an upgrade is still highly uncertain.

- Nevertheless, some investors pursue this strategy. One of the most lucrative—and risky—areas of the bond market to try this is in the area of high-yield, or non-investment-grade, debt. This part of the bond market is also known as **junk bonds**.

- In the past, bonds became junk bonds because the companies or governments that issued them fell on hard times. The only bonds that could be issued to the markets were investment-grade bonds, but over time, some borrowers would weaken and their bonds would be downgraded. Bonds that start out highly rated but then get downgraded to junk status are often called **fallen angels**, and there are plenty of fallen angels in current bond markets.

- Starting in the 1980s, it became possible for companies and even governments to issue brand-new, non-investment-grade bonds to the markets, which were willing to take a chance on these borrowers because they were young firms or developing economies that could tell convincing stories to the markets about their future growth. In addition, the interest rates on these bonds were very attractive.

- This is a very risky investing strategy. Many of these young firms fell back instead of rising up, and the default rates on non-investment-grade debt are quite high. In many cases, it may be difficult for investors to get adequate information to judge the financial strength of the company, so although this market does have a lot of potential, it's best left to the professionals.

Riding the Yield Curve

- The idea of earning a high interest rate and a capital gain sounds like the ideal bond-trading situation. You can take advantage of relatively safe opportunities like this even while pursuing a buy-and-hold bond investing strategy through a trade called riding the yield curve.

- The yield curve is a graph that shows the relationship between yield and maturity for a certain type of bond—most often for government bonds, and especially for Treasuries. The yields are the current market rates of return, so the yield curve changes every day as market returns change.

Figure 14-2

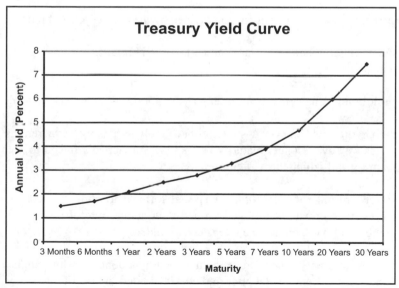

- Most of the time, as the maturity of a bond increases, its yield increases. Therefore, a 10-year note pays a higher interest rate than a 5-year note. When we see this relationship in the market, we say that the yield curve slopes up—just like in the chart.

- You can make extra returns on bonds by buying longer maturity bonds than you actually intend to hold to maturity and selling them after a few years. This strategy is called **riding the yield curve**.

- Riding the yield curve generates the highest returns when interest rates are fairly high. There seems to be a set of long-run average interest rates that the economy tends to return to, so if interest rates are too high today, they will probably fall to normal levels in a few years. If they do, you not only get the benefit of big capital gains, but you also earn high coupon payments while you wait.

Important Terms

coupon yield: The value of the annual coupon amount divided by par.

current yield: The annual coupon divided by the market price of the bond.

fallen angel: A bond that starts out highly rated but then gets downgraded to junk status.

junk bond: A bond that involves high-yield, or non-investment-grade, debt.

riding the yield curve: A strategy that involves making extra returns on bonds by buying longer maturity bonds than you actually intend to hold to maturity and selling them after a few years.

stated annual rate of return: A special form of a return that contains 2 pieces of information if quoted properly: an annual rate of return and the number of times per year the rate is compounded.

yield to maturity: The average yield earned by a bond investor who buys a bond at the current market price and holds the bond to maturity.

Suggested Reading

Bodie, Kane, and Marcus, *Essentials of Investments*, chap. 10.

Brealey, Myers, and Allen, *Principles of Corporate Finance*, chap. 3.

Questions to Consider

1. Suppose a bond has a par value of $100,000 and it pays a coupon of $2750 every 6 months. The market price of the bond is $98,624.15. What is the coupon yield of the bond? What is the current yield of the bond?

2. How would a bond dealer quote the price of the bond described in the previous question?

Bond School
Lecture 14—Transcript

In the last lecture, we learned about picking bonds as part of a buy-and-hold investment strategy, such as building a bond ladder. But this isn't the only way to invest in bonds. You can also trade bonds if you like—and this can be just as exciting, and risky, as trading stocks.

For example, one of the most daring and successful bond trades in recent memory happened in the year 2000. Back then, the U.S. government was running a huge budget surplus because of the booming economy, and in February of that year it decided to start repurchasing Treasury bonds on the open market. PIMCO, or the Pacific Investment Management Company, anticipated the government's move by buying large quantities of Treasury bonds starting in late January. The government's purchases of bonds drove bond prices much higher, so the values of PIMCO's bonds rose tremendously. It was reported that in just one week, PIMCO earned over $200 million in trading profits on long-term Treasury bonds. Try matching those profits by trading stocks!

If you want to trade bonds, though, you'll need to know a lot of details about bonds that I've been saving up for this lecture. There are many descriptive terms and even some bond jargon that you absolutely must understand if you're going to trade bonds. There are also many standard practices regarding how bond rates and prices are quoted that generally aren't explained well to new bond investors—everyone assumes that you already know them. In fact, there are so many of these terms and practices that bonds almost seem to have their own language—which I like to call Bondspeak. You also have to understand a little bit about bond pricing, and really understand the relationship between price and yield.

Even if you don't think you're going to trade bonds, you'll still want to learn these important terms and ideas. I think that one of the things that puts people off of bond investing is the potentially confusing terminology associated with bonds, including how bond rates and prices are quoted. If you know these things, you'll be a much more confident bond investor, even if you never actually trade bonds. In addition, we'll also learn about a bond trading strategy later in this lecture that is so simple that you can pursue it even if you are primarily a buy-and-hold bond investor.

Did that pique your curiosity? Good! Then let's get started. I'm calling this lecture "Bond School," because it's a really a language lesson in Bondspeak.

In the previous lectures on bonds, we've already learned a few terms that describe the parts of a bond. For example, I've mentioned that the interest payments on bonds are usually called coupon payments or coupons. This is because, back in the days of physical bonds, a bond contract would actually include a sheet of coupons that the bond holder would have to clip off with a pair of scissors every 6 months and mail to the issuer of the bond in order to receive the interest payment.

In addition, we've learned that the principal on a bond is called the par value, and for most bonds, the principal amount has been standardized to some round number. In the United States, for example, most corporate bonds have par or principal value of $10,000.

We've also learned one standard practice in the bond markets, which is that bonds generally make semiannual interest payments, that is, twice a year.

If we put these 3 pieces together, we can visualize the payments on a standard or straight bond by drawing a simple diagram. We'll let the par value be $10,000 and we'll let capital C stand for the coupon payment. Let's assume that the bond has maturity of 3 years, just to keep it simple. Since the payments on the bond are semiannual—every 6 months—this means that there will be 3 years times 2 payments per year, or 6 payments in total.

Now that we've visualized the bond payments, we can start to think about the rate of return on the bond and the size of the coupon payments. In order to do this, though, I need to tell you a little bit about the way that rates of return are quoted in Bondspeak.

As we'll see shortly, there are many different rates of return associated with bonds. And all of the various rates of return on bonds are quoted using a special form of a return called a stated annual rate of return.

A stated annual rate of return that is quoted properly always contains two pieces of information. First, it tells you an annual rate of return. And second, it tells you the number of times per year the rate is compounded. This is important because the convention in the bond market is to quote every rate of return that has to do with a bond as an annual rate compounded semiannually. The "compounded semiannually" part has to do with the fact that the interest on a straight bond is actually paid twice per year. Great, but what do I do with this information?

Well, the whole point of quoting rates of return as stated annual rates is to give you a shortcut to finding a semiannual rate of return, which is basically an interest rate for a 6-month period. To find a semiannual rate of return, given a quoted bond rate, simply divide the quoted rate by two. Again, every single rate that people quote for a bond is in terms of the annual rate compounded semiannually, so you need to get used to dividing those rates by two.

Now, most of the time bond yields are quoted improperly—that is, the person or the website who is telling you about the bond assumes that you know that the quotation convention in the bond market is that all rates are annual rates compounded semiannually. So they leave off the compounded semiannually part, because it's a hassle to say all the time. But you should assume that every interest rate associated with a bond is actually an annual rate compounded semiannually, unless you're told otherwise.

With that tidbit in mind, we can finally start to think about coupon size and the price of the bond. The coupon size is determined by the coupon yield, which is basically the value of the annual coupon amount, divided by par. So let's assume that the coupon rate of the bond is 3%, compounded semiannually. This means that the annual coupon amount of the bond is 3% of $10,000, or $300. So I take my coupon yield and divide by two to get 1.5%. This tells me the semiannual coupon yield for the bond, which means that the bond is paying a coupon of 1.5% of par every 6 months. Since par is $10,000, 1.5% of 10,000 is 150. So the bond is paying $150 every 6 months. This happens 6 times for my 3-year bond. And then at the end of 3 years, the bond also pays me back the $10,000. So the final payment is the final coupon, plus the par value, for a total of $10,150.

How is the coupon rate usually set? Well, the standard practice is to set the coupon rate equal to the market rate of return for the bond at the time the bond is issued. The bond market decides on an appropriate rate of return for the bond, based on the issuer's risk and market conditions, and this market rate is used for the coupon yield. Once the coupon yield is determined, it's set—it won't change over the life of the bond, so the size of the coupons stays fixed.

After the bond is issued, however, the market rate of return will go up and down according to market conditions and the financial strength of the borrower. The changes in the market rate of return on the bond will change the price of the bond. How?

Oh, I'm so glad you asked. The price of a bond at any time is the present value of all its payments. The market rate of return on the bond is used as the rate of return in the discounting formulas that we use to calculate the present value of the bond payments. Bond pricing is a fairly straightforward discounting calculation, and we'll learn about how to do these discounting calculations in a future lecture. The main point I'll make about bond pricing for now is that the bond price depends on the relative sizes of the coupon yield and the market rate of return on the bond. I'll have more to say about this in a few minutes.

Talking about the market rate of return on a bond makes me think of yet another bond term that I should mention—I told you there were a lot of them. This bond term is the current yield. The current yield is the annual coupon divided by the market price of the bond. The current yield expresses the rate of interest that the coupons represent if you buy the bond at the current market price. For example, if our 3-year bond with a 3% coupon yield had a market price of $9375.00 exactly, then the current yield would be 300/9375 = 0.032, or 3.2%. All this is really saying is that the annual coupons represent 3.2% of the market price. This isn't actually quite the market return, because the total market return would include both the income from the coupons and the capital gain or loss from holding the bond.

To get an idea of the total market return, we have to use a different concept of yield, and this is a yield to maturity. A yield to maturity is the average yield earned by a bond investor who buys the bond at the current market price and holds the bond to maturity. The market return on a bond is usually expressed as a yield to maturity. We know from the introductory lecture on bonds that bond markets are dealer markets. So when you go to buy a bond on the secondary market, you'll pay the dealer's ask price for the bond. Therefore, you'll often see the term "ask yield" for a bond, which is basically the yield to maturity, using the dealer's ask price as the market price.

Even though we use the yield to maturity as if it's the return that you'll actually earn on the bond, there are two hidden catches in the yield to maturity. First, the yield to maturity is only exactly accurate if you actually hold the bond to maturity. If you sell it before maturity, your actual return will be different, depending on the actual market price of the bond when you sell it. Second, the yield to maturity also assumes that when you receive the coupon payments from the bond you are able to reinvest those coupon payments in a way that earns the exact same return as the market rate of return on the bond.

For example, if the bond is quoted as having a 5% yield to maturity, we assume that when you get your coupons, you are able to reinvest them somewhere that will give you a 5% return. So a yield to maturity is a projected average return, assuming that you hold the bond to maturity and that you reinvest the coupons at a rate equal to the market rate of return on the bond. But in reality, your average return on the bond will probably be different from the yield to maturity, because you probably won't be able to reinvest your coupons at exactly the same market rate. And you might have to sell the bond before maturity as well. So your actual average yield could be higher or lower than the yield to maturity.

Now that we've learned about all the ways that we see the market rate of return on a bond quoted, we can get back to thinking about bond pricing. What I'm going to do next is talk about an extremely important aspect of bond investing—the relationship between price and yield. The first thing we'll do is see how the relationship between the coupon yield and the market return like the ask yield influences the price of a bond.

As I mentioned a few minutes ago, the amounts of the coupon payments on bonds are fixed when the bond is issued, and they don't change after that. This is why, by the way, many people refer to bonds as "fixed income" instruments. But once the bond is issued, the market rate of return on the bond can and does change as market conditions and the financial condition of the borrower change.

Remember that the bond we've been using as our example is a 3-year bond with a par value of $10,000 and a coupon of 3%, which is an annual rate compounded semiannually. And to begin with, let's suppose that the market rate of return on the bond is 4.5%. Just as a reminder, remember that I'm quoting all bond rates as annual rates compounded semiannually.

With an ask yield of 4.5%, the price of the bond is $9583.41. Remember, this is for a bond with a $10,000 par value. But bonds can come in virtually any principal amount. Even bonds from the same issue, with the same coupon yield and market rate of return, may have different principal amounts. For example, GM may issue bonds with a total principal value of $10 million, but the issue could be divided up into, say, 5 bonds of $1 million principal each and 500 bonds of $10,000 principal each. It would be tedious to have to re-calculate and quote all the different prices for different amounts of principal, so the bond market has adopted a special pricing convention.

Dealers quote bond prices in percent of par. So to find the price of any bond, you take the quoted price, in percent of par, and multiply it by the principal amount to get the actual dollar price you'd have to pay to buy the bond. In our example of the 3-year straight bond, the dealer would price the bond at 95.8341. So one thing we can say for sure, and this is true of all bonds, is that the bond price is less than par when the market rate of return is higher than the coupon yield on the bond.

Okay, now let's see the price of the bond when the market rate is less than the coupon yield. Now suppose that the market rate of return on the bond is 2.5%. That market rate of return is indeed less than the coupon yield on our bond, which we assumed was 3%. So when we calculate the price of the bond, we get $10,143.65. A dealer would quote this price as 101.4365. Hey, that's higher than the par value! What's going on?

Well, this is what happens when the market rate of return on a bond falls below the coupon yield—the price rises above its par value. So when the market rate is above the coupon yield, the price is below par. When the market rate is below the coupon yield, the market price is above par. And when the market rate of return is exactly equal to the coupon yield, the price is exactly equal to par. That explains why most bonds set their coupons so that the coupon yield is exactly equal to the market rate of return when the bonds are issued. This makes it so the price of the bond is equal to its par value, which is really just done for the convenience of the borrowers and lenders by giving nice round dollar amounts, like $10,000. These facts about the relationship between coupon yield, market rate of return, and market price hold true at every time between issuance and maturity, by the way.

The other important fact that you need to know about the relationship between price and yield is what it actually looks like. Let me show you a graph I made that pictures the relationship. I used a 10-year bond with a 6% coupon yield, because this helps emphasize the features of the yield-price relationship, but this basic picture is similar for all bonds. The graph has the market rate of return on the bond on the horizontal axis, and the price of the bond on the vertical axis. So the graph shows what happens to the price of the bond as interest rates go from 1/10 of 1% per year to 25% per year.

As you expect, the graph slopes down because as the market rate of return on the bond rises, the price falls. But notice how the line bends—it's not a linear relationship between yield and price. This means that there can be some very attractive opportunities for people who want to trade bonds actively. A small change in the market rate of return on the bond can translate into a relatively large change in price. That means that if you think you can predict changes in the market rate of return on a bond, you could make some very attractive returns as a bond trader. Suddenly, bonds sound a lot more exciting, right?

If you want to take advantage of the relationship between price and yield by trading, you may want to know that the longer the maturity of the bond, the steeper the yield-price relationship becomes; the steeper that graph becomes. In other words, the price of a 30-year bond rises much more than the price of a 10-year note when the market interest rate falls by 0.5%. So people who are bond traders like to trade straight bonds that are 10 years or longer in maturity.

Of course, a consideration here is the size of the market. If the market for a 10-year bond is much larger than the market for a 30-year bond from the same issuer, then trading the 10-year bond would probably make more sense—any loss in price sensitivity would be compensated by the improved ability to trade quickly.

The chance to take advantage of large changes in bond prices as bond interest rates change is the big attraction of active bond investing. In order to be a successful bond trader, you need to predict correctly when bond interest rates will change. And you need to become very skilled at predicting when interest rates will fall. Remember that bond prices rise as interest rates fall, so falling interest rates mean that any bonds you hold become more valuable now.

There are two basic reasons why a bond interest rate will fall. One reason is that general economic conditions change in a way that makes interest rates fall. For example, it's well known that in recessions and other economic slowdowns, bond rates fall. In addition, if inflation falls, then bond rates will also fall. There can be basic supply and demand reasons why bond interest rates fall as well. The supply of new bonds can simply decline if governments and companies don't need to borrow as much as before.

Even though there are many reasons why bond interest rates may fall—or rise—interest rates are notoriously hard to forecast. Even the big trading companies find it hard to consistently earn profits on bond trading that is based on these broader economic trends. If you really want to trade bonds, you should ask yourself why you think you have more insight into changes in economic conditions and their impacts on interest rates than all the other professional traders—and the economists who work full time for them.

The difficulty of predicting generalized increases and decreases in bond rates explains why many bond traders prefer to make bets based on the second reason why bond rates might fall. This reason is specific to individual issuers of bonds, and it is simply that a government or a company might have their bonds upgraded by a bond rating agency. For example, a company can have its bonds upgraded from triple-B to single-A as its financial condition strengthens. This upgrade will reduce the risk premium that investors demand in order for them to hold the bonds, so the interest rate on the company's bonds will fall. This in turn will make the price of the bonds rise.

Predicting that a company or a government will experience a ratings upgrade depends on the same sort of financial analysis that we've learned about in the context of stocks. You'll also need to do some research into the average financial characteristics of firms in each ratings category, so you can have some ideas about when a ratings upgrade might be likely. Again, though, keep in mind that you're competing with thousands of other investors who are thinking about whether a particular borrower will be upgraded. If you wait too long to make up your mind, other investors will buy the borrower's bonds in anticipation of the ratings upgrade, so the price of the bonds will rise even before the upgrade happens. Does that remind you of the arguments we learned about in connection with the efficient markets hypothesis? It should.

So, even though this type of bond trading is well within the ability of an individual investor who is willing to do some homework, it's still made risky by the fact that, in order to make good profits doing this, you have to act early—in other words, when any upgrade is still highly uncertain.

But some investors, nonetheless, like to pursue this strategy. And one of the most lucrative—and risky—areas of the bond market to try it is in the area of high-yield (or non-investment-grade) debt. You may also know this part of the bond market by its less-flattering name: junk bonds.

Now, in the old days, bonds became junk bonds because the companies or governments that issued them fell on hard times. The only bonds that could be issued to the markets were investment-grade bonds, but over time some borrowers would weaken and their bonds would be downgraded. Bonds that start out highly rated but then get downgraded to junk status are often called fallen angels, and there are plenty of fallen angels in the bond markets today.

But starting in the 1980s, it became possible for companies and even governments to issue brand-new, non-investment-grade bonds to the markets. The markets were willing to take a chance on these borrowers, because they were young firms or developing economies that could tell convincing stories to the markets about their future growth. In addition, the interest rates on these bonds were very attractive. So investors not only enjoyed the high interest rates on these bonds, they also bet that these firms would prove their financial strength to the markets and eventually experience upgrades on the bonds. This reasoning behind investing in high-yield debt is still valid today.

Of course, this is a very risky investing strategy. Many of these young firms didn't make it—they fell back instead of rising up. The default rates on non-investment-grade debt, as we learned in the previous lecture, are quite high. And in many cases, it may be difficult for investors to get adequate information to judge the financial strength of the company, especially if the company is small. So although this market does have a lot of potential, it's best left to the professionals. If you think this is a good opportunity, try to find a mutual fund or other pooled investment vehicle that invests in high-yield bonds.

This idea of earning a high interest rate and then a juicy capital gain on top of that sounds like the ideal bond trading situation. Wouldn't it be great if relatively safe opportunities like this actually existed? Well, the answer is that they do come along, once in a while. And you can take advantage of them even while pursuing a buy-and-hold bond investing strategy. This trade is called "Riding the Yield Curve," and here's how it works.

To understand this strategy, you have to understand what the yield curve is. The yield curve is a graph that shows the relationship between yield and maturity for a certain type of bond, most often for government bonds. In fact, when people talk about *the* yield curve, they usually mean the yield-maturity relationship on Treasuries. The yields are the current market rates of return, so the yield curve changes every day as these market returns change.

Here's a chart I made of a pretend yield curve. The annual yields on the bonds are on the vertical axis. The horizontal axis shows the standard maturities that we measure the market yields at. Notice though that the horizontal axis isn't drawn to scale.

Most of the time, as the maturity of a bond increases, its yield increases. So a 10-year note pays a higher interest rate than a 5-year note. When we see this relationship in the market, we say that the yield curve slopes up—just like in the chart.

If the yield curve slopes up, then as time passes and a 10-year note becomes a 9-year note, the yield on the note has to fall to bring it into line with the market rate of return on all the other 9-year notes in the market. But as we just saw, when the market rate of return on a bond falls, the price of the bond rises. So the price of the bond should rise, as its remaining time to maturity falls, again assuming an upward-sloping yield curve. What this means is that if you buy a long-term bond, you will experience capital gains on the bond as time passes.

This realization suggests that you can make extra returns on bonds by buying longer maturity bonds than you actually intend to hold to maturity, and selling them after a few years. This is the strategy called riding the yield curve. For example, you want to hold a bond for 5 years, but instead of buying a 5-year note and holding to maturity, you buy a 10-year note and hold it for 5 years, and then sell it. If the yield curve slopes up, then you'll earn some capital gains in addition to the coupon payments you receive.

Riding the yield curve generates the highest returns when interest rates are fairly high. If we look at the history of interest rates over the past 50 years, we can see that interest rates have been high and low but they generally haven't gone much above 20%, and they can't really go any lower than 0%. And on average, even long-term Treasury rates are in the high single digits. What this suggests is that there does seem to be a set of long-run average interest rates that the economy tends to return to. So if interest rates are too high today, they will probably fall to normal levels in a few years.

That in turn gives an opportunity to make significant profits from riding the yield curve. The strategy is to buy long-term Treasury bonds, like 20- or 30-year bonds, and hold them until yields fall back to normal levels. You not only get the benefit of big capital gains if interest rates fall back to their normal levels, but you also earn high coupon payments while you wait for that to happen.

So if you are a buy-and-hold bond investor with a ladder of Treasuries, all this requires that you do is to buy Treasuries that have longer maturity than the ones you usually buy. If you don't think you'll be put in a position where you have to sell these bonds, then you can do a little yield-curve riding and not really bear much risk at all. In fact, in early 2008, when the Federal Reserve started to raise interest rates every 6 weeks, I started making plans to do my own yield-curve riding, once rates rose enough. But before I could get started on that strategy, the economy went into a big recession, and you probably know the rest of that story, in terms of where interest rates went.

Hopefully, you have a good understanding now of what it takes to be successful if you want to trade bonds actively. Maybe you have a better understanding of why most individuals prefer to be buy-and-hold bond investors. I really hope, though, that you consider this strategy of riding the yield curve. I realize that this may not be the time in your investing life when you want to be holding a big portion of your investments in bonds, but if interest rates ever do start to look unusually high, think about whether this strategy might make sense. Also, when it does come time to move your more aggressive investments into bonds, consider buying some longer-maturity bonds than you need for your ladder and riding the yield curve with part of your bond ladder.

I think I hear the bell—class dismissed!

Picking Mutual Funds
Lecture 15

Unless you are going to put your savings in a balanced fund and leave the decisions to someone else, you need to do the same kind of homework on mutual funds that you would do on stocks, bonds, and other investments. In this lecture, you will learn that neither passively nor actively managed mutual funds are perfect and that you'll probably be happy with a well-chosen mix of both. Whichever funds you choose, treat them like long-term investments; don't chase last year's high returns. Think carefully about what you want in your investments, and make the most of this opportunity.

Categorizing Mutual Funds

- One of the reasons for the large and increasing diversity of mutual funds and ETFs is that the markets are responding to investor demands for more choices in their investments. This is a positive development, but it means that you need to be very selective and careful when choosing the funds you want to invest in.

- Generally, we categorize mutual funds by the assets they hold and what goal they're trying to achieve. The vast majority of mutual funds focus on stocks and bonds as their main investments, but there are funds that include other securities in their portfolios as well, including derivatives. **Equity funds** hold only stocks while **bond funds** hold only bonds. **Balanced funds** are mutual funds that hold both stocks and bonds in their portfolios.

- Equity funds can be further broken down according to the specific types of equity and the investment goals of the fund. Many mutual funds invest in a certain size of firm, where firm size is measured by its market value, which is also known as market capitalization.

- In addition to the focus on large-cap, mid-cap, or small-cap firms, there is a distinction between 2 investment goals: growth and value.

- One of the most popular pairings of size and growth is large-cap growth funds, which invest in the Coca-Colas of the world. Other funds might be bargain hunters, looking for value investments that seem to be underappreciated.

- Another type of equity fund is called an **income fund** because its focus is on earning high-dividend income. This focus is different from growth or value, which are both more focused on earning high capital gains.

- You don't necessarily have to settle on just income, growth, or value. There are also many **blend funds**, which try to select equities based on 2 different investment objectives.

- A final type of equity fund that appeals to many investors is **sector funds**, which invest in the shares of companies that are in the same type of sector or industry. Sector funds are for investors who intentionally want to take on concentrated risk in a particular industry because they believe that the industry as a whole will earn high returns relative to other industries or to the rest of the market.

- There's also a lot of diversity in bond funds, but the distinctions between the types of bond funds usually follow bond characteristics such as maturity, the type of issuer, and credit rating of the issuer.

- What all bond funds have in common is that the prices of shares fluctuate a lot due to changes in interest rates, which makes holding bond funds different than buying and holding bonds to maturity. If you hold bonds to maturity, then you're insulated from the price changes—but because the bond mutual fund has to report its net asset value daily, and because it also has to continually replace bonds that mature with other bonds, you never escape this price risk with bond funds.

- Don't forget that a unit investment trust can make long-term, buy-and-hold investments in portfolios of bonds. This option is worth considering if you want to buy and hold a piece of a well-diversified portfolio of bonds.

- Balanced funds put both stocks and bonds into the portfolio, and in many cases, this combination increases diversification and smooths out the return on the fund. Also, if you move your investments from equity funds into balanced funds, this effectively places more of your portfolio into bonds and helps protect the value of your portfolio from sudden market drops as you get closer to your financial goal.

- There is a fairly aggressive investment that's related to the balanced fund called an **asset allocation fund**, which is switched by managers between bonds and stocks whenever the markets seem to favor one investment over the other. These large swings are fairly risky, and they generate a lot of portfolio turnover, which can increase the tax bill from your mutual fund. Therefore, it's important to investigate these funds carefully before investing.

- In order to protect American investors, the SEC is very strict about allowing foreign mutual funds to offer their shares in the United States. Consequently, most foreign mutual funds won't allow Americans to invest in them. Therefore, if you want to diversify your portfolio geographically, you'll either have to buy foreign securities yourself or invest in American mutual funds that do it for you.

- There is a small but important distinction between types of mutual funds that invest in foreign assets. Funds that invest only in assets from outside the United States are called **international funds**, but many funds will invest in American and foreign assets, and these are called **global funds**.

Locating Information about Mutual Funds
- In addition to a mutual fund's summary prospectus, there is more information, in a more detailed form, in other documents that investment companies are required to disclose to the public. When

you start getting serious about a mutual fund, you need to find these documents and read the following information.

- First, you should look at the full prospectus. This document contains much of the same information as the summary prospectus but at a much higher level of detail that can give you better insights about how the fund managers will make their investment choices.

Many funds are equity funds, which hold only stocks, while bond funds hold only bonds.

- In fact, if you want a full listing of exactly what a fund's bylaws allow it to invest in, you can go to another document that a fund will publish called the statement of additional information, which is usually distributed with the fund's annual report.

- Each fund will tell you both the hard, or fundamental, rules that govern its investments and the nonfundamental rules that describe the fund managers' intentions. Fundamental rules can only be changed by shareholder vote, but nonfundamental rules can be changed by the fund managers at any time.

- Finally, there's no substitute for looking over the actual holdings of a mutual fund or ETF if you want to know what the fund is really doing with your money. The annual report of the mutual fund will give a complete list of the holdings of the mutual fund.

Actively versus Passively Managed Mutual Funds
- Thus far, it has been assumed that all mutual funds hire a team of professional stock and bond analysts and set off to beat the market,

but there are thousands of mutual funds that are passively managed. A passively managed mutual fund simply tries to mimic the return on some kind of benchmark asset. Usually, this benchmark asset is an index, such as the Dow Jones Industrial Average or the S&P 500. Generally, the managers of the fund simply buy and hold the assets that make up the fund, or they invest in futures contracts or other simple derivatives that directly substitute for holding the assets in the index.

- There are 2 big advantages of passively managed mutual funds. First, you pretty much know exactly what you're getting—as long as you understand what the benchmark asset is. In addition, generally, their expenses are much lower than those of actively managed mutual funds because the managers don't do nearly as much trading as active managers do.

- When deciding whether you should hold actively managed mutual funds, passively managed mutual funds, or both—and if both, how much of each—there are a few things you should consider. First, there's the issue of whether you should invest in all passively managed funds or all actively managed funds. This depends in part on how efficient you think the markets are. If you're a big believer in market efficiency, then you know that the best you can do as an investor is to buy a slice of the entire market, and passively managed mutual funds and ETFs give you a great opportunity to do that.

- On the other hand, if you think that the market isn't completely efficient, then there's room for skilled fund managers to earn market-beating returns over long periods of time. If that is the case, then you're passing up a great opportunity if you only stick to passively managed mutual funds. The problem with this view is that most actively managed mutual funds don't beat the market, but some do. The trick is to find those really gifted—or lucky— managers who produce long strings of market-beating returns.

- One potential downside to passively managed mutual funds is the explosion in the number and types of indexes that exist. On one hand, this gives us benchmarks to compare performance to, but on the other hand, the proliferation of indexes has introduced some of the problems of actively managed mutual funds to passively managed mutual funds. For example, it's easy to lull yourself into a false sense of security that you have a well-diversified portfolio when you really don't.

- However, the increase in the number of indexes means that actively managed mutual funds can generally find some index to compare their returns to that makes them look good. Therefore, you need to be skeptical of claims that actively managed mutual funds make about beating benchmarks. There's no substitute for looking at their actual returns, and risk, over time.

- There are a few popular but controversial active management strategies that might appeal to you when you're evaluating your preferences regarding mutual funds. Two of these are growth and value investing, and there's been a long-running debate over which one is the better long-term strategy. Both the growth and value strategies make sense and can be winners, but the question is whether the managers have both the skill to pick investments that really deliver and the discipline to stick to their investing program.

- Another mutual fund strategy that is becoming popular is the **socially responsible fund**, which is a mutual fund that pursues high returns but avoids investing in companies that engage in activities that some people find objectionable. The idea behind these funds is that investors may be willing to accept somewhat lower investment returns for the satisfaction of knowing that their savings don't support commercial activities that they object to.

- Beyond these ideas, there aren't any magic secrets to picking winning mutual funds. As with any other investment, you need to do your homework. Additionally, think about buying into a mutual fund as the start of a long-term, buy-and-hold investment. If you keep moving your investments from one hot mutual fund to the next, you'll probably end up with a string of disappointing returns.

Important Terms

asset allocation fund: A type of mutual fund that is switched by managers between bonds and stocks whenever the markets seem to favor one investment over the other.

balanced fund: A mutual fund that holds both stocks and bonds in its portfolio.

blend fund: A type of equity fund that tries to select equities based on 2 different investment objectives.

bond fund: A mutual fund that holds only bonds in its portfolio.

equity fund: A mutual fund that holds only stocks in its portfolio.

global fund: A type of mutual fund that invests in American and foreign assets.

income fund: A type of equity fund whose focus is on earning high-dividend income.

international fund: A type of mutual fund that invests only in assets from outside the United States.

sector fund: A type of equity fund that invests in the shares of companies that are in the same type of sector or industry.

socially responsible fund: A type of mutual fund that pursues high returns but avoids investing in companies that engage in activities that some people find objectionable.

Suggested Reading

Bodie, Kane, and Marcus, *Essentials of Investments*, chap. 4.

Bogle, *Common Sense on Mutual Funds*, chaps. 6 and 9.

Questions to Consider

1. Select the year you are most likely to retire and search for a target-date mutual fund—which is a mutual fund that automatically reshuffles the mixture of assets in its portfolio according to some future date—that most closely corresponds to your retirement year. Examine how the managers of this fund are allocating the fund's investments among different types of stocks, bonds, and perhaps other instruments. Does the mixture of investments seem attractive to you? Would you invest in the fund? If not, what don't you like about its holdings or management? How would you invest your retirement funds differently?

2. Go to a mutual fund company's website and find a global mutual fund and an international mutual fund. Find the annual report for each mutual fund and compare the stocks held by each. Which fund, in your opinion, is more geographically diversified?

Picking Mutual Funds
Lecture 15—Transcript

For the past few lectures, we've been learning about how to pick stocks and bonds. Now, it's finally time to turn to mutual funds and ETFs. I've saved the discussion of picking mutual funds for now, even though you probably have more money invested in them than you do in stocks and bonds put together. The main reason I did this is so that you have a better understanding of the types of decisions that mutual fund managers may be making on your behalf, if you invest in actively managed mutual funds or ETFs. Hopefully, you'll also be in a better position now to think critically about the stories that fund managers will tell about their investment strategies. And you'll also be able to make a better decision about whether you want to invest in actively managed funds at all.

As we learned in the introductory lectures on mutual funds and ETFs, there's an amazing variety of funds out there to choose from these days. So it's worth spending some time learning how to tell them apart. Your friends might choose mutual funds based on their names, but there are better ways to tell what a mutual fund's goals are. Not surprisingly, they have to do with reading the prospectus. Where I have I heard that before?

One of the reasons for the large and increasing diversity of mutual funds and ETFs is that the markets are responding to investor demands for more choices in their investments. This is basically a positive development, but it means that you need to be more selective and careful than ever, when you choose the funds that you want to invest in.

One of the potential sources of trouble for investors is that financial markets are just as fad- and fashion-driven as the markets for clothing and music. A lot of people devote too much time in financial markets chasing after the highest-returning mutual funds or the investment that is the flavor of the day. I'm going to show you why this strategy mostly leads to disappointment. A far better strategy is to think about what you want as an investor first, and then find the funds that best meet your needs.

I think the best place to start is to spend a few minutes trying to assign some broad categories to the incredible diversity of mutual funds out there. This is actually fairly difficult, because there are already over 10,000 different mutual funds available on the market and another 1500 or so ETFs, and this number keeps growing. There's a lot of experimentation going on all the time in terms of the mixture of assets offered in mutual funds.

But let's see if we can find some useful categories. Generally, we categorize mutual funds by the assets they hold and what goal they're trying to achieve. The vast majority of mutual funds focus on stocks and bonds as their main investments, though there are funds that include other securities in their portfolios as well, including derivatives. Many funds are equity funds that hold only stocks, while bond funds hold only bonds. *Balanced fund* is the term we give to mutual funds that hold both stocks and bonds in their portfolios.

Equity funds can be further broken down according to the specific types of equity and the investment goals of the fund. Many mutual funds invest in a certain size of firm, where firm size is measured by its market value, also known as market capitalization or market cap for short. So a fund manager can focus on large-cap or small-cap firms, and there are mid-cap funds out there as well.

At the same time, there is a distinction between two investment goals. On one hand, you have growth as an investment goal, which is a shorthand way of saying that the manager is looking for firms that are likely to grow rapidly— like Starbucks or Facebook did. On the other hand, you can have value as an investment goal—which means that the manager is looking for firms that are underappreciated, so that their current price doesn't reflect their true value.

So if I take this large cap versus small cap size distinction, and pair it with the growth-value difference in objective, this gives me a nice set of 4 boxes that I can use to characterize a lot of equity mutual funds. One of the most popular pairings is large-cap growth funds; these funds invest in the Coca-Colas of the world. Other funds might be bargain hunters, looking for so-called value investments. For example, a large-cap value fund might invest in large companies that have temporarily fallen on hard times. Right after the financial crisis of 2008, for instance, you could argue that a lot of the big banks, like Citibank, were candidates for value investors.

One of the nice things about this 4-box view of mutual funds is that it gives you a different dimension to diversification. You may be attracted to several good funds, but discover that they're all small-cap growth funds, for example. You could arguably do a better job of diversifying if you spread your investments around to all 4 boxes.

Another type of equity fund is called an income fund, because its focus is on earning high dividend income. This focus is different from growth or value, which are both more focused on earning high capital gains. But of course, you don't necessarily have to settle on just income, or just growth, or just value. There are also so-called blend funds, which try to select equities based on two different investment objectives. For example, a popular type of blend fund is the growth-and-income fund, which tries to invest in the stocks of companies that are growing quickly but still pay high dividends. You may remember from a previous lecture that some companies, like 3M, mange to do both of those things quite well.

A final type of equity fund that appeals to many investors is the sector fund. Sector funds invest in the shares of companies in the same type of sector or industry, like telecommunications, entertainment, consumer products, and so on. Sector funds are for investors who intentionally want to undiversify— they want to take on concentrated risk in a particular industry, because they believe that the industry as a whole will earn high returns relative to other industries or the rest of the market.

There's also a lot of diversity in bond funds, though the distinctions between the types of bond funds usually follow bond characteristics like maturity, the type of issuer, and credit rating of the issue. For example, different bond funds may hold long-term bonds, with maturities over 10 years; intermediate bonds, with maturities closer to 5 to 8 years; and short-term bonds, with maturities of 2 to 3 years. There are even so-called ultrashort bond funds that invest in bonds with less than one year left to maturity.

What bond funds all have in common is that the prices of shares fluctuate a lot, due to changes in interest rates. That makes holding bond funds a bit different than buying and holding bonds to maturity. If you hold bonds to maturity, then you're insulated from the price changes—but since the bond mutual fund has to report its net asset value daily, and since it also has to continually replace bonds that mature with other bonds, you never escape this price risk with bond funds.

Don't forget, though, that the investment known as a unit investment trust can make long-term, buy-and-hold investments in portfolios of bonds. This option is worth considering, if you want to buy and hold a piece of a well-diversified portfolio of bonds.

Balanced funds put both stocks and bonds into the portfolio, so you'd think that this combination would increase diversification and smooth out the return on the fund. And indeed this is the case for many balanced funds. Also, if you move your investments from equity funds into balanced funds, this effectively places more of your portfolio into bonds, and helps protect the value of your portfolio from sudden market drops as you get closer to your financial goal.

In fact, some balanced funds now call themselves "target date" funds and try to adjust the portfolio over time just as a financial planner would suggest. So, if I buy a 2050 target date fund, then I'm basically telling the manager of the fund that my target retirement year is 2050. When I first buy into the fund, most of the investment will be in stocks, but as my retirement date gets closer, the fund manager takes care of shifting an increasing proportion of the fund into fixed income instruments.

Many defined-contribution retirement plans are now using target-date type balanced funds as the default mutual fund for the employees. These funds are a great innovation for people who don't know much about investing, or just don't want to be bothered with all the details of managing their own portfolio. On the other hand, when you invest in a target date fund, you're handing over all the important financial decisions about what to buy, and when to shift your portfolio into bonds, to the mangers of the fund.

There's a cousin of the balanced fund that's actually a fairly aggressive investment. These mutual funds go by the name of asset allocation funds, and their strategy is to switch between bonds and stocks whenever the markets seem to favor one investment over the other. So in other words, when the fund managers believe the stock market will outperform the bond market, they'll shift the portfolio heavily into stocks in order to benefit from this opinion. And when the bond market looks like it will turn in better returns, the portfolio swings back into bonds. Needless to say, these big swings back and forth are fairly risky. And they generate a lot of portfolio turnover, which as we've seen can increase the tax bill from your mutual fund. So it's important to investigate these funds carefully before you take the plunge.

A final element of mutual fund diversity that I should mention is the international angle. In order to protect American investors, the SEC is very strict about allowing foreign mutual funds to offer their shares in the United States. Consequently, most foreign mutual funds won't allow Americans to invest in them. Therefore, if you want to diversify your portfolio geographically, you'll either have to buy foreign securities yourself, or invest in American mutual funds that do it for you. I'll have a lot more to say about this in a future lecture.

There is a small but important distinction between types of mutual funds that invest in foreign assets. On one hand, funds that invest only in assets from outside the United States are called international funds. But many funds will invest in American and foreign assets, and these are called global funds. So it's important to know which one your fund is.

Speaking of knowing what your fund is holding, there are additional sources of information about a mutual fund's investment strategy and actual investments that you should investigate before you buy into any mutual fund or ETF. In the introductory lectures on mutual funds and ETFs, we learned about the summary prospectus. But there's plenty more information, in a more detailed form, in the other documents that investment companies are required to disclose to the public. When you start getting serious about a mutual fund, you really need to go to these documents and read over the following information.

First, you should go and have a look at the full prospectus. This document contains much of the same information as the summary prospectus, but at a much higher level of detail that can give you better insights about how the fund managers will make their investment choices. For example, I compared the summary prospectus and the full prospectus for Fidelity's Equity Income Fund, a very standard large-cap blend fund. The discussion of investment strategies in the full prospectus informed me that the fund was allowed to buy and sell futures contracts and ETFs, which the summary prospectus didn't mention.

In fact, if you want a full listing of exactly what a fund's bylaws allow it to invest in, you can go to another document that a fund will publish called the statement of additional information, which is usually distributed with the fund's annual report. There is a section in the statement of additional information that details exactly what the fund is allowed to invest in, as well as any restrictions on the amount of each security it is allowed to invest in. Each fund will tell you both the hard or fundamental rules that govern its investments, and the non-fundamental rules that really describe the fund managers' intentions. Fundamental rules can only be changed by shareholder vote, but fund managers can change non-fundamental rules at any time.

Finally, there's no substitute for looking over the actual holdings of a mutual fund or ETF if you want to know what the fund is really doing with your money. The annual report of the mutual fund will give a complete list of the holdings of the mutual fund, usually as of the date of the annual report.

So far, I've been talking about mutual funds as if every one of them hires a team of professional stock and bond analysts and sets off to beat the market. But there are thousands of mutual funds that are passively managed. A passively managed mutual fund simply tries to mimic the return on some kind of benchmark asset. Usually, this benchmark asset is an index, like the Dow Jones Industrial Average, the S&P 500, or the Eurostoxx 50 index. Generally, the managers of the fund simply buy and hold the assets that make up the index, or they invest in futures contracts or other simple derivatives that directly substitute for holding the assets in the index.

There are two big advantages of passively managed mutual funds. First, you pretty much know exactly what you're getting—as long as you understand what the benchmark asset is. The other advantage of passively managed mutual funds is that generally, their expenses are much lower than those of actively managed mutual funds, because the managers don't do nearly as much trading as active managers do.

So what's best for you? Should you hold actively managed funds, passively managed funds, or both—and if both, how much of each? Let's see what you need to consider.

First, there's the issue of whether you should invest in all passively managed funds, or all actively managed funds. This depends in part on how efficient you think the markets are. If you're a big believer in market efficiency, then you know that the best you can do as an investor is to buy a slice of the entire market and hold that. Passively managed mutual funds and ETFs give you a great opportunity to do that.

These days, there are indexes that cover just about every stock market in the world, as well as regional indexes. And there are major bond indexes as well, that cover just about all the main bond markets and types of bonds in the world. So if you want to own a slice of the entire world market for stocks and bonds, it's possible to do that.

On the other hand, if you think that the market isn't completely efficient, then there's room for skilled fund managers to earn market-beating returns over long periods of time. And if that is the case, then you're passing up a great opportunity if you only stick to passively managed mutual funds. The problem with this view, as we learned in the lecture on the efficient markets hypothesis, is that most of the actively managed mutual funds out there don't beat the market. But the truth is that some do, and some managers do turn in market-beating returns for years on end. The trick is to find those really gifted—or lucky—managers who do produce long strings of market-beating returns. This is a big question, and I'll come back to that in a few minutes.

In my opinion, there should be room in your portfolio for both kinds of mutual funds and ETFs. I think it's a good idea to hold a fair amount of your portfolio as a slice of the entire market, which includes not only global diversification but diversification across asset classes, like bonds and real estate and even other things in addition to stocks. Personally, I like to weight my portfolio more toward the passive, broad indexes, and make a couple of carefully researched bets on what I consider exceptional actively managed funds. But it's your choice—my main point is for you to be intentional about this choice.

Now, one potential downside about passively managed mutual funds is the explosion in the number and types of indexes out there. Just as the number of country indices has exploded, so have indexes for sectors, company size, bond maturity, bond issuer, and so on. For just about any kind of niche investment you can think of, there's an index now, and usually there are several. On the one hand, that's a good thing—this gives us benchmarks to compare performance to. But on the other hand, the proliferation of indexes has introduced some of the problems of actively managed mutual funds to passively managed mutual funds.

What I mean by this is that it's now easy to lull yourself into a false sense of security that you have a well-diversified portfolio when you really don't. If you hold a bunch of index funds, but the indexes are the small-cap growth index, the high-yield bond index, and the emerging markets stock index, then you really aren't that well diversified in your holdings. In fact, you're really just making the sorts of bets that actively managed mutual funds make.

On the other hand, the increase in the number of indexes means that actively managed mutual funds can generally find some index to compare their returns to that makes them look good. You may notice, for example, that hardly any actively managed mutual fund compares itself to a broad market index any more. They all compare themselves to some niche index that describes their investment objective. And, surprise—this fund beats its tailor-made benchmark. I'm not suggesting that all mutual funds play this game, or that none of the specialized indexes are reasonable benchmarks. But I do think that you need to be skeptical of claims that actively managed mutual funds make about beating this or that benchmark. There's no substitute for looking at their actual returns, and risk, over time.

Speaking of actual returns and risk, we know that mutual fund prospectuses are required to show the average returns of the fund over the past 1-, 5-, and 10-year periods, as well as the year-by-year returns for the past 10 years. This is good information that helps you see both the level of returns, and the consistency of returns over time. If you want to, you can even go to one of the many free websites and download price data on just about any mutual fund out there.

Even though they're not traded, mutual funds do have stock ticker symbols and most online sites will give you free access do their daily and monthly historical prices. You can use these historical prices to construct your own measures of returns, and risk, for the mutual fund. I'll be more specific about how to do both of those things in a couple of future lectures. But the point that I want to emphasize is that this plain information about year-by-year returns and their consistency is better information than index comparisons made by most actively managed funds.

Well, if you buy into my argument that there's room in your portfolio for at least one actively managed mutual fund, which one should you pick? Here's your chance to think carefully about both your preferences, as well as your beliefs about the market, and choose funds that you think will be great investments. As I keep mentioning, there are funds that cater to just about every investment interest out there.

For example, you may want to make a big bet that Brazil's markets will continue to grow and add lots of value. Or you may think that the next big thing is solar energy, and you want to invest in that industry. Or you may think that this strategy of finding high-dividend-paying firms is the right way to pick stocks, so you want to find a fund manager who pursues that strategy. Chances are, if somebody thinks something is a good investing idea, there's probably a fund for it by now. Keep in mind, though, that many of the specialized funds are likely to be ETFs these days, especially if the investing idea you have in mind involves an alternative asset.

A few popular but controversial active management strategies that might appeal to you are also worth mentioning specifically. Two of these are growth and value investing, because there's been a long-running debate over which one is the better long-term strategy. There have been a number of successful growth-oriented mutual funds out there, and some growth-oriented managers like Peter Lynch have deservedly become the stuff of investing legend. What's interesting to me, though, is that the most successful growth investors seem to have a tempered approach to growth. That is, they still want to get good value, so they always think in terms of the growth for the price.

On the other hand, there have also been some very successful value investors. Two that come to mind are Warren Buffett and Bill Miller, who is one of the co-managers of a mutual fund called the Legg Mason Capital Management Value Trust. Value investors usually have a lot of patience, since they are betting that the market will eventually recognize that a company is worth a lot more than previously thought.

One thing that you should keep in mind is that both the growth and value strategies make sense, and can be winners. The question is whether the managers have both the skill to pick investments that really deliver, and the discipline to stick to their investing program.

Yet another mutual fund strategy that is getting more and more attention is the so-called socially responsible fund. These mutual funds pursue high returns but avoid investing in companies that engage in activities that some people find objectionable. Firms that these funds avoid may make particular products like tobacco, or engage in particular production or employment practices, or do business in countries that do not abide by international standards of human rights, for example. The idea behind these funds is that investors may be willing to accept somewhat lower investment returns for the satisfaction of knowing that their savings don't support commercial activities that they object to. Only time will tell if this idea has staying power in the market, but there seem to be plenty of investors who think so.

Beyond these ideas, I should note that there aren't any magic secrets to picking winning mutual funds. As with any other investment, you need to do your homework. Suppose an investing idea really does resonate with you. Then find the group of funds that seem to pursue this idea. Look at their summary prospectuses to find the funds that claim to do what you're interested in. Then examine the performance information in terms of their average returns and the consistency of these returns over the past 10 years or more. Those two steps should help you narrow down your list of mutual funds.

Then, once you get the field narrowed down to just a handful of funds, go into the details in the full prospectus, the annual report, and the statement of additional information. You should be able to see the similarities and differences between the funds fairly clearly. And if the funds are actively managed, find out who the managers are and look them up on the Internet.

Mutual fund managers like to get media exposure for their funds, so they will often appear in the media discussing their investment philosophies and what investments they are considering now. This can be a great source of information that can help convince you either way about investing in a particular mutual fund.

Think about buying into a mutual fund as the start of a long-term, buy-and-hold investment. I realize that most of us will be investing in mutual funds through a 401-K or similar plan that calls on us to make monthly contributions. And I also know that it's relatively easy, and almost costless, to switch between the various mutual funds offered in your company's savings plan. But please, please, please don't become one of those investors who chases after the latest fad or the mutual fund with the hottest returns this quarter. This is a terrible investing strategy that too many people fall into.

Let me explain why I'm so down on this investing strategy. Suppose I'm a bright investment manager who actually has some good insights about how to value companies and their financial assets, and I'm pretty good at picking stocks or bonds. For a while, my mutual fund hums along, racking up very nice returns, but I stay under the radar because my fund is fairly small. But at some point, my mutual fund gets noticed by some personal-finance website or magazine or money-management guru. Suddenly, my name is in lights and my mutual fund is the flavor of the day.

What happens then? The money comes flooding in! Suddenly, I now have to find places to invest tens of millions of dollars at once, when a few months ago I was making investments on the order of a few hundred thousand dollars. First off, it's likely that I can't keep investing in the same companies as before. When I start spending $1 million at a time on a smaller company's stocks or bonds, this will start to push the company's price around and make the investment much less attractive. So now I have to find bigger companies to invest in, and maybe I'm not that great at investing in bigger companies.

In addition, I've got to come up with a bigger number of investing ideas. I have so much money coming in that I need to spread it around to 50 new investments. But what if I only have 30 good ideas? Then I have to start investing in the ideas that I know aren't as good. Or I have to hire a bunch more managers to help me out, but they don't necessarily share my investment philosophies or insights. But if I take the investors' money, I have to do something with it. Sure, I could close the fund to new investments, but that's hard to do because my salary is based on the size of my fund.

So after the money comes rushing in, my returns fall back toward the average. That helps explain, by the way, why many fund managers have a great year once in a while, followed by disappointing years. Part of the reason is that they can't invest the flood of new money very well.

Hopefully, this story will help convince you that if you keep moving your investments from one hot mutual fund to the next, you'll probably end up with a string of disappointing returns. You'll be part of the flood of money that swamps many mutual funds and drives their returns back to the average. So my advice is to seek out long-term commitments with mutual funds that have demonstrated that they haven't been ruined by success. That's one more criterion you can add to your list when it comes time to decide on an actively managed mutual fund.

Well, it's time to wrap up. I hope I've convinced you that unless you are going to put your savings in a target-date mutual fund and leave the driving to someone else, you need to do the same kind of homework on mutual funds that you would do on stocks, bonds, and other investments.

Remember that neither passively indexed nor actively managed mutual funds are perfect, and you'll probably be happier with a well-chosen mix of both. But whatever funds you do choose, treat them like long-term investments.

Don't chase last year's high returns. With so many different mutual funds and ETFs available, this is one of those rare chances in life where you can make the world conform to your wishes, rather than the other way around. Think carefully about what you want in your investments, and make the most of this opportunity.

Investing in Foreign Assets
Lecture 16

In the next few lectures, you're going to be introduced to assets other than stocks, bonds, mutual funds, and ETFs that you may want to consider. In this lecture, you'll learn more about foreign assets. There are plenty of amazing opportunities outside the United States, and they are all rooted in real assets. However, be sure not to overweight foreign markets because many of them have a lot of progress to make, but make enough room in your portfolio that you can benefit from their growth and development—as well as from the diversification protection that they offer.

Foreign Assets
- If you're holding well diversified mutual funds, or if you're covered by a pension, you probably already have some foreign assets in your portfolio. Bonds from foreign companies or foreign governments can offer safe and attractive returns.

- There are 2 main reasons that make the extra work of investing in foreign assets pay off. The first of these is diversification. One of your goals as an investor is to make sure that your portfolio is well diversified, and if you're an investor who believes markets are pretty efficient, then you'll want to own a slice of the entire market—and that means the global financial market.

- More countries are reaching the same level of economic development and sophistication as the United States and Europe. Many countries' financial markets are starting to have the same types of companies as the rest of the world, which is not good for diversification because diversification depends on different assets acting in different ways.

- Additionally, financial markets around the world have become a lot more tightly connected than they were even a few years ago. If the prices in globalized financial markets become more synchronized over time, then there's much less diversification benefit. The whole point of being diversified is that when the U.S. market falls, another market somewhere else in the world is likely to be going up.

- Therefore, many people think foreign diversification is losing its benefit. Markets do seem to move together more today than they used to, but on average, there still seems to be plenty of room for a diversification benefit. There's also evidence that the synchronization of the global economy goes through cycles.

- The idea that many countries are still at an earlier stage of economic development leads to the second main reason to invest in foreign assets: to take advantage of higher economic growth in other countries. On a very large scale, someone who invests in the assets of rapidly industrializing nations—or even in the assets of countries that are already developed—is taking part in a global IPO for the entire country. Not every company in these economies is going to be a winner, but the overall growth of these economies means that many companies will be.

Allocating Foreign Assets

- The Bank for International Settlements (BIS) is an international organization that facilitates cooperation between central banks and bank regulators around the world. They collect data on the size of the global bond markets. As of the end of 2010, the world bond market had about $67 trillion of bonds outstanding, and the United States had $25 trillion of that total—or about 38%.

- That total includes both government bonds and private bonds. However, when you break it down, the total size of the global government bond market was $39 trillion at the end of 2010 while the private bond market was $28 trillion.

- According to the World Bank, which has data on the value of world stock markets, the global stock market was worth about $55 trillion at the end of 2010, and the U.S. market was worth about $17 trillion. When the stock market values are broken down by region of the world, the U.S. stock market is just under 1/3 of the entire world market by value. In addition, Europe and Asia each have almost an identical share of the world stock market.

- The United States makes up 1/4 of the global government bond market, 1/3 of the global stock market, and about 1/2 of the private debt market. Europe and Asia both have large government bond markets and large private bond markets, but the rest of the world really doesn't yet. If you were to truly make your portfolio reflect the global market, you could use these weights as a starting point for shaping your portfolio.

- However, even though the rest of the world does account for a huge part of the financial market, foreign markets just don't adhere to the same standards of transparency, rules of law, and basic fairness that characterize the U.S. financial markets. This means that investor protections that we take for granted in the United States simply don't exist—or only exist on paper in many other countries.

Figure 16-1

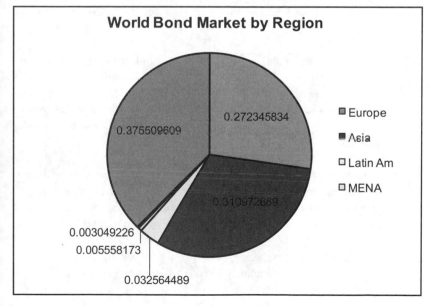

- Additionally, the level of government involvement in the economies of many countries is far higher than in the United States, which means that companies may behave very differently in how they conduct business and how they treat their shareholders. It also may mean that governments will restrict foreign ownership of their domestic companies so that foreigners may end up paying inflated prices for shares of successful firms.

- Another thing to keep in mind is that the huge size of the rest of the world's markets also disguises a wide range of sizes. The size of many equity markets around the world is small enough so that they can be easily manipulated by local investors, so you have to be wary of plunging into these markets without doing a good amount of research on them first.

Investing in Foreign Assets
- In general, buying and holding foreign assets directly is expensive and inconvenient—and may even be dangerous. Many U.S. brokers will help you buy foreign assets directly through business partners in overseas markets, but this adds significantly to the trading costs you'll pay.

- On the other hand, it's possible to hold a foreign brokerage account, but this is not usually a good idea unless you have a truly compelling reason to do so. Holding foreign bank accounts or brokerage accounts can make the IRS wonder whether you're trying to hide income or assets overseas, so it usually attracts their attention.

- The biggest concern for holding foreign assets directly is the danger of losses from **foreign exchange risk**, which is the risk that any capital gains or other returns on an investment in foreign assets will be offset by unfavorable changes in the exchange rate.

- Changes in the exchange rate can also work in your favor, but adding the foreign exchange risk to the extra expense and hassle of investing directly in foreign assets makes this option even less attractive.

- There are many good ways to invest in foreign assets—they're just less direct. A stock instrument called American depository receipts (ADRs) claim checks on foreign stocks that have been deposited in American banks. Similarly, some foreign governments and companies will issue bonds in the United States that are payable in U.S. dollars.

- By far, the best way to buy foreign assets is through mutual funds or ETFs. Mutual funds can hire experts who can navigate foreign markets, and they also have resources to manage the foreign exchange risk associated with foreign investing. They originated as a better way to invest in foreign assets.

- However, you should check the annual reports of the mutual funds and the ETFs you are interested in to see exactly what foreign assets are being held in these funds. You want to make sure that your global fund isn't just holding many U.S. companies and only a smattering of foreign assets. In addition, you can and should blend a mix of passive funds and active funds in your foreign portfolio.

Foreign Exchange

- The foreign asset that you should probably avoid investing in is **foreign exchange**, which is also known as foreign currency trading or forex trading. Foreign exchange can seem really attractive; it is one of the largest and most active asset markets on the planet.

- When you trade forex, you're betting on the direction of exchange rates. For example, since its introduction as a currency in the early 2000s, the price of 1 euro has fluctuated between roughly $0.80 and $1.70. If you think that the price of the euro in terms of U.S. dollars will go up, then you can buy euros in the hopes that the price of a euro will go up, and you can sell the euros later for more dollars than you paid to buy them.

- There are 2 major complaints with trading currencies as an investment strategy: Trading currencies is a very short-term investing strategy that requires a lot of active trading—which gets very expensive and can take up a lot of time—and exchange rates are some of the hardest financial prices to predict.

- Generally, forex trading is done with huge amounts of leverage, and that's the big danger. High leverage plus lots of price fluctuations lead to investors losing lots of money in short periods of time.

- There are 2 main ways that individuals usually trade foreign currencies. The first way is by using a **futures contract**, which is simply a standardized agreement in which an investor pays a price now, called the futures price, to be entitled to receive an asset on a later date specified in the contract.

- Buying a futures contract on an asset is really just a substitute for buying and holding the actual asset. The main reason that an individual investor would want to buy a futures contract is that it could be much cheaper than buying the asset outright.

- One of the main reasons that investors are interested in futures contracts is to take advantage of the low margin requirements—but low margins also mean high leverage. Therefore, unless you are an experienced investor who has studied the futures markets and really knows what you're getting into, you might want to leave the leveraged investing in futures to the professionals.

- The second way that individuals generally invest in foreign currency is through a broker using margin, and in the case of foreign exchange, the leverage that brokers will let investors take on is even higher than the leverage that is allowed in the futures contracts.

- If you really want to invest in foreign currencies, try ETFs. There are ETFs that directly hold foreign currencies, such as the euro. However, if you do this, make sure that the ETF isn't using leverage.

- Another way that people are investing in foreign exchange that is nearly as dangerous as these leveraged purchases of currency is a strategy called the carry trade, which is a way to take advantage of differences in interest rates between countries—but it relies on stable exchange rates to make it work.

- With the carry trade, an investor borrows a sum of money in a currency that has a very low interest rate. Then, the investor finds a country with relatively high interest rates, exchanges the currency for the high-interest-rate country's currency, and invests in the country's bonds.

- The part of this trade that makes it the carry trade is that the investors doing it are carrying, or holding on to, the risk that the foreign exchange rates will change—and they probably will—between the time that they buy the foreign asset and the time they sell the foreign asset and change the currency back to dollars.

Important Terms

foreign exchange: One of the largest and most active asset markets on the planet that involves betting on the direction of exchange rates.

foreign exchange risk: The risk that any capital gains or other returns on an investment in foreign assets will be offset by unfavorable changes in the exchange rate.

futures contract: A standardized agreement in which an investor pays a price now, called the futures price, to be entitled to receive an asset on a later date specified in the contract.

Suggested Reading

Bodie, Kane, and Marcus, *Essentials of Investments*, chap. 19.

Bogle, *Common Sense on Mutual Funds*, chap. 8.

Prior, "Costly Currency."

1. Websites such as Stock-Encyclopedia.com maintain extensive lists of ETFs (http://etf.stock-encyclopedia.com/category/) that you can browse to find opportunities for investing in single countries or in regions. Browse a list of international stock or bond ETFs and find one that interests you. Why did you pick this country or region? How has this ETF performed this year? Would you consider adding this ETF to your portfolio?

2. Select a major currency that trades actively against the U.S. dollar—such as the euro, pound, or yen—and search for a graph of the exchange rate that covers at least the past 2 years. (Most free financial websites will have such graphs.) Note the variation in the exchange rate during the past 2 years and how many times the rate bounces up and down. What do you think is the most likely direction for this exchange rate over the next year? Given the past exchange rates, are you confident enough in your prediction to buy or sell the foreign currency as an investment? Why or why not?

Investing in Foreign Assets
Lecture 16—Transcript

So far we've been learning all about the ways to pick stocks, bonds, mutual funds and ETFs for your investment portfolio. In the next few lectures, I'm going to branch out into some other assets that you may also want to consider. Some of the assets we'll learn about are ones I consider must-haves for your portfolio. Others are optional, and I'll even toss in a few assets that you hear about a lot, but I think you're best off if you avoid.

In this lecture, I'll actually include both a must-have investment and one to avoid—and they're both different types of foreign assets. I've mentioned foreign assets here and there during the previous 9 lectures, but it's time that I got into some more details about what they can do for you. Chances are, if you're holding well-diversified mutual funds, or if you're covered by a pension, you already have some foreign assets in your portfolio. After all, there are plenty of global blue-chip firms that aren't headquartered in the U.S.—like Toyota, or Adidas, or Petrobras. And bonds from foreign companies or foreign governments can also offer safe and attractive returns.

But most of us, when it comes right down to it, would rather invest in companies that are closer to home. Actually, this is a well-known finding in behavioral economics, called home bias. And it makes sense that we're more likely to invest in companies and assets that we're more familiar with. The question, then, is this: Is there anything about foreign assets that justifies the extra effort required to learn about foreign companies and markets?

I'm glad you asked. There are two main reasons I can think of that make the extra work of investing in foreign assets pay off. The first of these is diversification. One of your goals as an investor is to make sure that your portfolio is well diversified. In fact, I recently heard John Bogle, the founder of Vanguard Investments and a longtime advocate of passive mutual fund investing, say that diversification was the first, second, and third most important goal for your portfolio. And if you're an investor who believes markets are pretty efficient, then you'll want to own a slice of the entire market—and that means the global financial market.

There's a lot more to this idea of geographic diversification, though, including some controversy.

A couple of decades ago, most people who looked into the diversification benefits of investing in foreign assets found that the typical American investor only needed a little bit of foreign diversification—say, 10–15% of the portfolio—to get a large benefit from geographic diversification. But as time went by, more and more investors and academics started to question this rule of thumb. That's because the world has been changing pretty rapidly over the past 20 years.

First, more countries are reaching the same level of economic development and sophistication as the U.S. and Europe. For example, you may remember the Asian Tiger economies of the 1990s. A few of these countries, like South Korea and Taiwan, have basically achieved the same level of development of the United States and Europe. Or look at many of the so-called Transition Economies from the former Soviet Union, especially the Eastern European countries like Poland, Estonia, and the Czech Republic.

These countries have joined the European Union and their economies have the same level of development as the rest of the European Union. This means that these countries' financial markets will have the same types of companies as the rest of the world, issuing stocks and bonds that basically behave like the stocks and bonds issued everywhere else. That's not good for diversification, because diversification depends on different assets acting in different ways. Why go to the trouble of finding, say, a chemical company in the Czech Republic whose stock behaves just like the stock of Dow Chemical?

The other reason why foreign diversification has been under suspicion lately is because of the globalization of all markets. Financial markets around the world have become a lot more tightly connected than they were, even a few years ago. That means that investors' money is flowing more freely between the global markets, pushing prices up together across markets, and then pushing them down together as well. If the prices in globalized financial markets become more synchronized over time, then again there's much less diversification benefit. The whole point of being diversified was that when the U.S. market falls, another market somewhere else in the world is likely to be going up.

Therefore, many people think foreign diversification is losing its benefit. Are they right? As an economist, I always try to let the data decide, and here's what I can tell from the work that's been done by researchers. Markets do seem to move together more today than they used to, though on average there still seems to be plenty of room for diversification benefits. You just might not get it from the same countries that you used to! On top of this, there's also evidence that the synchronization of the global economy goes through cycles as well. In other words, we go through periods when the markets seem to move together, and other stretches of time when they just don't.

At the end of the day, I'm still a believer in the power of geographic diversification in my portfolio. I think that there are still many countries that are going through very different stages of economic development. And these different stages of development will lead the financial markets in those countries to behave in ways that are very different from the behavior in the United States and Europe.

The idea that many countries are still at an earlier stage of economic development leads to the second main reason to invest in foreign assets. And that's to take advantage of higher economic growth in other countries. On a very large scale, someone who invests in the assets of developing countries like Vietnam, South Africa, and other rapidly industrializing nations is really taking part in a global IPO for the entire country. Not every company in these economies is going to be a winner, but the overall growth of these economies means that a lot of the companies will be.

And even countries that are already developed can experience high growth. For example, Ireland became one of Europe's fastest-growing economies in the late 1990s. To the extent that turnaround stories like these depend on factors internal to the country, and not on the international economy, investing internationally can give you both high returns and diversification benefits.

So, if you're convinced that holding foreign assets can both increase your average returns and diversify your portfolio, the question of foreign investing becomes first a matter of allocation. That is, how much of your overall portfolio should you invest in foreign assets?

I thought than an interesting way to take a look at this question would be to show you some numbers on the sheer sizes of the global bond and equity markets, to see just how large they are and what fraction of them is made up of the U.S. market. Let's start with the bond markets.

I found data from the Bank for International Settlements, or BIS, which is an international organization that facilitates cooperation between central banks and bank regulators around the world. They collect data on the size of the global bond markets. As of the end of 2010, the world bond market had about $67 trillion of bonds outstanding. And the United States had $25 trillion of that total, or about 38%.

That total includes both government bonds and private bonds. The numbers are even more interesting when you break it down between the two. The total size of the global government bond market was $39 trillion at the end of 2010, while the private bond market was $28 trillion.

The U.S. makes up a quarter of the global government bond market, and about half of the global private bond market. Second, Europe and Asia both have large government bond markets and large private bond markets, but the rest of the world really doesn't yet.

Now let me turn to stocks. For this information, I went to the World Bank, which has data on the value of world stock markets as of the end of 2010. The global stock market was worth about $55 trillion at the end of 2010, and the U.S. market was worth about $17 trillion. Again, I broke down the stock market values by the region of the world and made a pie chart out of that information. Here's that pie chart. In this one, we can see that the U.S. stock market is just under one-third of the entire world market, by value. Also, notice that Europe and Asia each have almost an identical share of the world stock market.

So the United States makes up a quarter of the global government bond market, a third of the global stock market, and about half of the private debt market. So if you were to truly make your portfolio reflect the global market, you could use the weights from the pie charts as a starting point for shaping your portfolio.

But let me actually caution you against doing that—at least right now. Even though the rest of the world does account for a huge part of the financial market, foreign markets just don't adhere to the same standards of transparency, rule of law, and basic fairness that characterize the U.S. financial markets. This means that investor protections that we take for granted in the United States simply don't exist, or only exist on paper in many other countries. Even well developed markets in Europe have different practices and different standards of professional conduct from the United States. For example, for many years, insider trading was not illegal in many countries, and in other countries is only weakly regulated today.

Also, the level of government involvement in the economies of many countries is far higher than in the United States. This means that companies may behave very differently in how they conduct business and how they treat their shareholders. It also may mean that governments will restrict foreign ownership of their domestic companies, so that foreigners may end up paying inflated prices for shares of successful firms.

Another thing to keep in mind is that the huge size of the rest of the world's markets also disguises a wide range of sizes. For example, the Asian markets are really dominated by Japan and Hong Kong. If you want to invest in Vietnam's stock market, you certainly can—but as a friend of mine who does this for a living warned me, a stock investment in Vietnam is much more like a venture capital investment, in terms of the time needed as well as the risk involved. The size of many equity markets around the world is small enough so that they can be easily manipulated by local investors, so you have to be wary of plunging into these markets without doing a good amount of research on them first.

So, do invest in foreign assets—but don't try to overweight your portfolio toward them, at least not yet. I think that the day is coming when it will be wise to devote a majority of your investments to companies and governments outside the United States, but we're not there yet.

The other warning that I want to pass on about investing in foreign securities regards how to do it. In general, buying and holding foreign assets directly is expensive and inconvenient, and may even be dangerous. Many U.S. brokers will help you buy foreign assets directly, through business partners in overseas markets, but this adds significantly to the trading costs you'll pay. On the other hand, it's possible to hold a foreign brokerage account, but this is not usually a good idea unless you have a truly compelling reason to do so. Holding foreign bank accounts or brokerage accounts can make the IRS wonder whether you're trying to hide income or assets overseas—so it usually attracts their attention. And who needs that?

But the biggest concern for holding foreign assets directly is the danger of losses from foreign exchange risk. This is simply the risk that any capital gains or other returns on an investment in foreign assets will be offset by unfavorable changes in the exchange rate. For example, if you want to buy the stock of the French petrochemical company Total, you would have to first exchange U.S. dollars for euros, and then purchase the shares with euros. By the way, you'll pay a commission fee right off the bat for buying the foreign currency. Suppose you buy 100 shares of Total for 20 euros each, or 2000 euros. With the commission, the price of the euro was $1.35 each, so you pay a total of $100 \times 20 \times 1.35 = \$2700$ for the shares.

Suppose the price of Total rises to 21 Euros per share, but the value of the euro falls so that the price of 1 euro goes from $1.35 to $1.26 after the commission on the currency. So you sell your shares for 2100 euro and then buy dollars with the 2100 euro at $1.26 per euro. Then you end up with $2100 \times 1.26 = \$2646$. So even though the share prices went up, you've incurred a tidy loss of 54 bucks!

Now, changes in the exchange rate could also work in your favor, and sometimes will. But the point I'm trying to make is that adding the foreign exchange risk on to the extra expense and hassle of investing directly in foreign assets makes this option even less attractive.

However, there are many good ways to invest in foreign assets—they're just less direct. For example, in my lecture on ETFs I mentioned a stock instrument called an American Depository Receipt, or ADR. ADRs are basically claim checks on foreign stocks that have been deposited in American banks. They trade like regular American stocks and are priced in dollars.

There are over 250 different ADRs listed on the New York Stock Exchange alone, representing companies from all over the world. As you might expect, though, it's mainly the blue-chip companies that go to the trouble of becoming listed on the U.S. stock markets. And some observers claim that because of the increase in stock market regulations such as the Sarbanes-Oxley Act, many foreign companies have abandoned their ADR listings in the United States. So these American-listed foreign company shares may be getting harder to find.

Similarly, some foreign governments and companies will issue bonds in the United States, payable in U.S. dollars. I mentioned these so-called Yankee bonds in my introductory lecture on bonds. You will have to check the inventory of various dealers and brokers to find them, and the supply of these bonds depends on U.S. interest rates relative to the interest rates available in other countries. Also, to the extent that U.S. investors have not been very big buyers of foreign bonds, many foreign issuers tend to try other markets rather than the United States. For example, Japanese investors have long been known to buy lots of foreign bonds, since the domestic interest rates in Japan have been extremely low for decades.

By far, the best way to buy foreign assets is through mutual funds or ETFs. Mutual funds can hire experts who can navigate foreign markets, and they also have resources to manage the foreign exchange risk associated with foreign investing. And as we learned in connection with the previous lecture on picking mutual funds and ETFs, the increasing specialization of these instruments means that you can probably find a fund that invests in the countries and in the assets that you are most interested in adding to your portfolio.

ETFs are the champions of passive investing in country indexes or regional indexes of stocks and bonds, which reflects the fact that they originated as a better way to invest in foreign assets. The only caution here, of course, is to check the annual reports of the mutual funds and the ETFs to see exactly what foreign assets are being held in these funds. Remember that distinction between global and international mutual funds that I mentioned in the lecture on picking mutual funds, for example. You want to make sure that your global fund isn't just holding a lot of U.S. companies and only a smattering of foreign assets.

Just as we learned in the lecture about picking mutual funds, there's no reason why you can't, or shouldn't, blend a mix of passive funds and active funds in your foreign portfolio. You should aim to hold part of your foreign investments in a set of broad indices that capture at least the European and Asian markets, and hopefully the up-and-comers in Latin America, Africa, and the Middle East as well. But there's also room to invest in individual countries that seem poised for high growth, as well as choosing actively managed international funds with good track records.

As promised, I'm going to turn to the foreign asset that you should probably avoid investing in—foreign exchange. Foreign exchange, also known as foreign currency trading or simply forex trading, can seem really attractive. This is one of the largest and most active asset markets on the planet. Each day, about $4 trillion in currencies gets traded—that is, $2 trillion of various currencies are traded for $2 trillion of other various currencies. And the rates always seem to be moving up and down, so it seems like there are plenty of opportunities for traders to make money.

And some of the most legendary trades involve large bets on the direction of exchange rates. You may have heard, for example, about how the famous investor George Soros made $1 billion betting that the value of the British pound would fall in late 1992. Investment websites and even newspapers now are full of advertisements for foreign exchange trading and the testimonials of traders who make hundreds of thousands of dollars a year trading currencies—or so they claim.

Before I get too far into this, I should tell you what it is that you're actually trading when you trade forex. Basically, you're betting on the direction of exchange rates. Let's take the euro as an example. The price of one euro, since its introduction as a currency in the early 2000s, has fluctuated between roughly $.80 and $1.70. If you think that the price of the euro in terms of U.S. dollars will go up, say from $1.30 to $1.40, then you can buy euro in the hopes that the price of a euro will go up, and you can sell the euro later for more dollars than you paid to buy them.

Fundamentally, I have no problem with trading currencies, if that's what you really want to do. But I have two major complaints with this as an investment strategy. First, trading currencies is basically a very short-term investing strategy, and it requires a lot of active trading—which gets very expensive. And it takes up a lot of time, which most of us don't have to devote to sitting in front of a computer screen watching forex quotes.

My second major problem with trading currencies as an investing strategy is that exchange rates are some of the hardest financial prices to predict. Sure, academic economists have theories, but none of them have proven to be much good for actually predicting the value of exchange rates or the changes in exchange rates. When we invest in stocks and bonds, we can't predict the future exactly, but we do have some models that do a decent job of explaining why some firms become more valuable over time. But if you don't really have an idea of how to predict exchange rates successfully, or even explain why they change, then it's hard to tell trading from gambling. And the last time I checked, gambling wasn't that great of an investing strategy.

But my real problem with trading foreign currency is the way in which most foreign currency trading is done. Generally, forex trading is done with huge amounts of leverage, and that's the big danger. High leverage plus lots of price fluctuations leads to investors losing lots of money in short periods of time.

Let me show you the two main ways that individuals usually trade foreign currencies. The first way is by using futures contracts. A futures contract is simply a standardized agreement in which an investor pays a price now, called the futures price, to be entitled to receive an asset on a later date specified in the contract. So buying a futures contract on an asset is really just a substitute for buying and holding the actual asset. You buy futures contracts for the same reason you'd buy and hold the asset itself—you think the price of the asset is going to go up. The main reason why an individual investor would want to buy a futures contract, then, is that it could be a lot cheaper than buying the asset outright.

For example, one of the most popular foreign exchange futures contracts is the euro futures contract, priced in U.S. dollars, which is traded on the Chicago Mercantile Exchange, or CME. When you buy a euro futures contract, you are committing to buy 125,000 euro and pay the futures price, which is expressed in U.S. dollars. Now, if the euro is priced at $1.40, then the value of this contract in dollars is $175,000. But the initial margin on this contract is about $5400, and the maintenance margin is about $4000. That means that the initial margin is only about 3%. This low level of initial margin makes it very cheap to invest in euros, which helps explain why this contract is so popular. On the other hand, the low level of margin also means that it's easier to get a margin call, since the price of the euro does bounce around quite a bit. And you'll have to meet that margin call very quickly—generally the same day—or your position will be liquidated.

So one of the main reasons why investors are interested in futures contracts of any kind is to take advantage of the low margin requirements. But always remember that low margin means high leverage—think of that leverage multiplier that we learned about in the lecture on using leverage. So unless you are an experienced investor who has studied the futures markets and really knows what you're getting into, I'd leave the leveraged investing in futures to the pros.

The second way that individuals generally invest in foreign currency is through a broker, using margin. And in the case of foreign exchange, the leverage that brokers will let investors take on is even higher than the leverage that is allowed in the futures contracts. For example, the typical foreign exchange broker will let an individual investor use margin to achieve leverage of 50 to 1. And some brokers will allow leverage of 200 to 1 or even higher. A leverage ratio of 50 to 1 means that an investor will deposit $1000 with the broker and control $50,000 worth of foreign currency.

Assume that you use 50 to 1 leverage to buy euro, where the price is initially $1.40 per euro. So you deposit $1000 with your broker and buy $50,000 worth of euro, which is 35,714.29 euro. If the price of the euro rises to $1.42, then your euro are now worth $50,714.29. You've made a profit, before trading commissions and interest, of $714.29. Of course, if the price of the euro falls to $1.38 instead, your 35,714.29 euro will only be worth $49,285.71, which results in a loss of $714.29. So a movement of $0.02 in the price of the euro almost wipes you out! This is precisely the reason I'm so down on investing in foreign currency.

If you really, really want to invest in foreign currencies, try the ETF route. There are actually ETFs out there that directly hold foreign currency like the euro—no leverage, just a cheap way to make a bet on the exchange rate. But if you do this, make sure that the ETF isn't using leverage. There are lots of leveraged foreign currency ETFs out there, too.

Now, there's a second way that people are investing in foreign exchange that is nearly as dangerous as these leveraged purchases of currency. This is a strategy called the carry trade. The carry trade is actually a way to take advantage of differences in interest rates between countries, but it relies on stable exchange rates to make it work. Professional investors have made billions of dollars of profits on the carry trade in the past two decades, and this trade is increasingly being offered to individual investors as well.

The carry trade works like this. First, an investor borrows a sum of money in a currency that has a very low interest rate. For many years, this currency was the Japanese yen, but after the financial crisis, European countries and even the United States had such low interest rates that traders started to borrow in euros and dollars as well.

The next step is to find a country with relatively high interest rates, exchange your currency for the high-interest-rate country's currency, and invest in the country's bonds. For example, Australia and Brazil have had much higher interest rates than other countries for long periods of time, so investors have been buying high-yielding assets in these countries as part of the carry trade.

So, imagine that you borrow $10,000 in the United States at 2% interest, and then buy the equivalent amount of Brazilian reais, and then buy a Brazilian government bond yielding, say, 12%. Wow! The 10% difference in interest rates makes it look like you've earned $1000 a year for free!

Well, it's not for free, and that's the big problem. The part of this trade that makes it the carry trade is that the investors doing it are carrying, or holding on to, the risk that the foreign exchange rates will change between the time that they buy the foreign asset and the time they sell the foreign asset and change the currency back to dollars.

Again, an example will show you best what I mean. Suppose you're able to borrow $10,000 at a 2% rate of interest, and you don't have to pay anything back for one year. So, in one year you'll need to pay your lender $10,200. You take the $10,000 and buy Brazilian reais with it. The real costs $0.60 each, so you are able to buy 16,666.67 reais. You put this in a one-year government bond yielding 12%. So, one year from now, your Brazilian bond pays you 18,666.67 reais, and then you go to buy U.S. dollars with this amount. But wait—now the Brazilian real is only worth $0.55, not $0.60! So you can only buy $10,266.67 with your reais.

On the positive side, you can still afford to pay back your loan in full—but you only have $66.67 left over. And that isn't even counting the transactions costs that you'll have to pay in the real world. So again, it's easy to lose money if exchange rates change—and they tend to bounce around quite a bit.

Judging by the surge in ads during the past few years, it seems like there's been an explosion of interest in the carry trade among retail investors. And even I used to dream about being able to do this trade—in the abstract. But again, this strategy boils down to buying currency and using a lot of leverage—so it's just as easy to lose a lot of money as it is to make it. The upshot, of course, is don't try this at home!

In the end, remember the idea of investing in real assets. There are plenty of amazing opportunities outside the United States—about $80 trillion worth, according to the statistics we saw earlier—and they are all rooted in real assets. So do invest abroad, but don't invest in money, invest in the companies and the projects that make money, no matter what color the money is or what kinds of funny pictures they put on it.

Don't overweight foreign markets, since many of them have a lot of growing up to do, but do make enough room in your portfolio that you can benefit from their growth and development, as well as from the diversification protection that they offer. So tell your 401-K to pack its bags and get ready to search the 4 corners of the globe for the great investments out there waiting to be discovered.

Options Are for Everyone
Lecture 17

Derivatives are specialized tools for advanced investors. They're usually bit players in an investment portfolio that are used for hedging certain kinds of risk. In this lecture, you're going to be introduced to one of the most interesting derivatives—options—and by the end of the lecture, you might be convinced that they have a place in your portfolio. You will learn that options are not just for hedging; they play a long-term, return-enhancing role that can help your money work harder for you. Best of all, the options strategies that you'll learn about have extremely low risk.

Financial Options

- An **option**, one of the most fascinating derivatives, is a contract that gives its buyer the right, but not the obligation, to take some action. Usually, the action involves buying or selling something. If you hold an option to do something, you'll only do it if it's in your best interest. If it's not, then you walk away, and all you've lost is the cost of the option.

- **Financial options** are the right to buy or sell a particular asset at a preagreed price on or before a certain date. The right to buy an asset is a **call option** on the asset while the right to sell is called a **put option** on the asset. If you exercise your right to buy or sell, you're exercising the option. The preagreed price is called the strike price of the option, and the last day that you're able to exercise this right is called the expiration date of the option.

- **Stock options** are rights to buy or sell shares of a particular company, and **index options** are options on futures contracts on stock indexes. Call options are the right to buy stocks or futures contracts on stock indexes while put options are the right to sell these assets.

- The main reason you'd want to invest in put options is to protect your portfolio from a fall in stock prices. However, using put options to protect your portfolio is so expensive that you probably shouldn't use them, especially in a long-term investing context.

Call Options

- Options are traded on exchanges—just like stocks—and the price of an option is also called the premium. Strike prices of option contracts cluster around the current market price of the stock, and there can be multiple contracts at the same strike price because the contracts can have different expiration dates. Most exchanges offer a rolling set of contracts that expire every 3 months.

- For example, if you pay the option premium of $2.80 for Nike, then you own the right—but not the obligation—to buy 1 share of Nike at a price of $100 on or before the expiration date in January. If you buy this call option, then you are hoping that the price of Nike shares rises above $100 per share between September, for example, and the contract expiration in January.

Figure 17-1

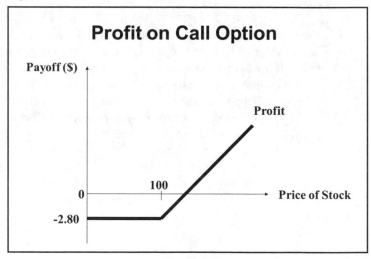

- If the market price of the stock goes above the strike price on the call option, then your call options have gone into the money. This simply means that you can make a positive profit by exercising them. Of course, the higher the price of Nike shares goes before you exercise the call option, the higher your profit will be.

- What if the price of the stock stays below $100 per share between September and the contract expiration in January? If you exercised the option, you'd have to pay $100 per Nike share, but the market value of the Nike shares is below $100 per share. In this case, instead of exercising the option, you'd let it expire. You've lost $2.80 per option that you bought plus the commission and any other trading costs, but that's all you've lost—a fraction of the value of the stock.

- If the price of Nike shares rises above the strike price, your profit rises at a dollar-for-dollar rate. If the price of Nike stays below the strike price of the call option, you lose the price of the option—no matter whether the price of the shares rises to $99.99 or falls to a penny per share. The existence of limited losses and the potential to enjoy gains leads to an asymmetry in your profits, which is the big attraction of options.

- Financial economists represent this asymmetrical behavior in your profits with a payoff, or profit, diagram, which has the price of the stock on the horizontal axis and the amount of profit from the option on the vertical axis.

- The prices of options are determined by supply and demand—just like in any other financial market—but many of the suppliers and demanders of options also know the theory of option pricing, and these theories lead to some easy-to-use option pricing formulas that give a ballpark estimate of the value of an option.

- A call option will give you a profit if the price of the stock goes above the strike price of the option, so option pricing is about the likelihood that this will happen. There are 5 things that affect this probability in general, but the most important 3 are the strike price of the option, the time to expiration, and the amount of variation in the price of the shares.

- In general, the higher you set the strike price of a call option, the less likely it is that the stock price will rise above the strike price, so call option premiums fall as the strike price rises. Additionally, the more time you have until expiration, the better the chance that the stock price will wander above the strike price. Finally, the more price of the stock bounces around, the higher the chance that it will bounce up above the strike price of the call option, so stocks with more variation in their prices will have more expensive call options.

Options Investments

- A **covered call** is a type of options investment that is a combination of a stock and a call option that you can use to enhance your returns on stocks that you own. People generally use this strategy on stocks that they intend to own for a long time but want to squeeze some income out of.

- The covered call strategy involves writing, which is another word for selling, call options on shares of stock that you currently own. The covered call strategy requires you to sell call options—and anyone can buy or sell call options.

- When you sell, or write, call options, you are selling to someone else the right to buy shares from you at a preagreed strike price. Therefore, when you write call options, you are creating an obligation for yourself to sell your shares—or to pay the buyer of the call options the difference between the market price of the shares and the strike price, if the price of the shares rises above the strike price.

- The covered call strategy is dangerous if you don't already own the shares, but what's so fascinating about the covered call is that owning the shares converts a risky transaction—selling call options—into an extremely safe investment.

- When writing call options, the trick is to pick a strike price for the options that is high enough that it seems pretty unlikely that the share price will rise that high before expiration. On the other hand, you need to set the strike price low enough so that the option premium makes it worth your while to do this trade. Therefore, there is a tradeoff at work, and you may not think that the tradeoff is worth it for all your shares all the time. This strategy tends to work well for popular stocks that also have active options trading surrounding them.

- Regardless of whether you exercise your call option or let it expire, there really isn't the possibility of losing money. In fact, you really only lose out on part of some really high returns—if the options do go into the money and get exercised. In that case, you'll have to settle for a smaller return—but never a negative one. Therefore, this strategy is an important one to consider: It's very safe and easy, and it can improve the return on any stock that has options traded on it.

- If you like the idea of using covered calls but are still hesitant to try this on your own—or if you don't think that you'll have the time to do this—then you can try the alternative: actively managed mutual funds that pursue covered call investment strategies.

- In addition to covered calls, there's another investment strategy that uses the power of options to offer a great opportunity to investors. The general name for these investments is structured products, and they often go by the name of bull CDs, as in bull-market CDs, or option-embedded CDs.

- There are hundreds of different types of **structured products**, which combine different financial instruments into a new one or slice the payments from a financial instrument in new ways.

- There is a type of structured product that is aimed at prudent individual investors and is available through many banks, brokerages, and other dealers that is commonly referred to as a CD—but it's a CD with a couple of special features.

- The first feature of these CDs is that instead of paying a flat rate of interest, they will pay you the return on some index—usually a stock index like the S&P 500. This is already quite different from an average CD, but it gets better. If the S&P 500 falls during the time that you own the CD, the CD will give you your initial deposit back, so you won't suffer any losses—except, of course, for the fact that you earned a zero return.

- Not only is this legal, but it's also pretty safe—for the buyer of the CD as well as for the company that offers it. The payoff of this special CD is a lot like an option payoff: You get to enjoy any gains in the S&P 500 index, but you don't have to suffer any of the losses between now and the maturity of the CD.

- Thanks to the power of options, banks and brokerages can offer investors a product that looks too good to be true: You get the appreciation of a stock index with very minimal risk of losing any of your principal. These CDs can be great products for investors who are highly risk averse or who want to try to improve the returns on their portfolio but simply can't afford capital losses.

- There are some bull CD products that promise twice the return on the index if the index rises—or possibly even more. These products work the same way as normal bull CDs, but they multiply returns by purchasing more call options. They can afford to buy more call options because they invest your deposit in much riskier loans. Therefore, you should stick with the plain products that simply offer the gain on the index with no multiplier, and never buy a bull CD that doesn't promise to return your full deposit if the index goes down.

Important Terms

call option: The right to buy an asset.

covered call: A type of options investment that is a combination of a stock and a call option that you can use to enhance your returns on stocks that you own.

financial option: The right to buy or sell a particular asset at a preagreed price on or before a certain date.

index option: Options on futures contracts on stock indexes.

option: A contract that gives its buyer the right, but not the obligation, to take some action—which usually involves buying or selling something.

put option: The right to sell an asset.

stock option: The right to buy or sell shares of a particular company.

structured product: A product that combines different financial instruments into a new one or that slices the payments from a financial instrument in new ways.

Suggested Reading

Bodie, Kane, and Marcus, *Essentials of Investments*, chap. 15.

Hull, *Fundamentals of Futures and Options Markets*, chap. 10.

Wooley, "Squeeze Your Portfolio Harder."

Questions to Consider

1. On a free financial website, find the price of a call option that expires in 2 or 3 months from now on a company that interests you. Compare the strike price of the call option to the current market price of the stock. Then, find a chart that shows how the price of the stock has behaved recently. (Most free financial websites will show such charts.) Given the behavior of the stock price, how likely do you think it is that the stock price will rise (further) above the strike price of the option?

2. Suppose you are currently holding 100 shares of a stock that has a current market price of $50. Suppose you look up the options prices and find that there are call options trading on your stock that expire 3 months from now with a strike price of $55. How large of an option

premium would it take for you to be interested in selling 100 covered call options on your stock if the stock has been trading between $48 and $53 for the past year? What if the stock price was $40 a year ago but has been steadily rising during the past year?

Options Are for Everyone
Lecture 17—Transcript

In this lecture, I'm going to finally address the D-word: derivatives. You may have noticed that I haven't mentioned derivatives all that much so far, and when I have, I haven't had many good things to say about them. And that's mainly because derivatives are specialized tools for advanced investors. They're usually bit players in an investment portfolio, used for hedging certain kinds of risk. Or, if they're the main focus of your investing, then you're probably doing a lot of short-term speculating that really isn't the sort of investing that I think most people have either the time or the stomach for.

But in this lecture, I'm going to introduce you to one of the most fascinating derivatives—options—and try to convince you that options have a place in your portfolio. And it's not just for hedging, either—it's a long-term, return-enhancing role that can help your money work harder for you. And best of all, the options strategies that we'll learn about in this lecture have extremely low risk. I know, it sounds like crazy talk, but when you see exactly how these investing strategies work, I think you'll become an options believer.

So let's get right down to thinking about what options are and how they work. As we've learned repeatedly in this course, all financial instruments are nothing but contracts. And an option is just a specialized type of contract. An option is a contract that gives its buyer the right, but not the obligation, to take some action. Usually the action involves buying or selling something.

If you have the right to do something but you're not required to do it, you'll only do it if it makes you better off, right? That's the beauty of options. If you hold an option to do something, you'll only do it if it's in your best interest. If it's not, then you'll walk away, and all you've lost is the cost of the option. Options give you a choice. And having more choices is always a good thing!

Financial options are usually the right to buy or sell a particular asset, at a pre-agreed price, on or before a certain date. The right to buy an asset is called a call option on the asset, while the right to sell is called a put option on the asset. If you exercise your right to buy or sell, we say that you're exercising the option. The pre-agreed price is called the strike price of the option. And the last day that you're able to exercise this right is called the expiration date of the option.

The options that I'll be talking about in this lecture are stock options and index options. Stock options are rights to buy or sell shares of a particular company. Index options are actually options on futures contracts on stock indexes. I realize that I'll have to explain those index options more carefully when I get to them later in the lecture, so don't worry about them just yet.

In addition, the only options we'll be learning about are call options—the right to buy stocks or futures contracts on stock indexes. Put options, the right to sell these assets, are also interesting. But the main reason you'd want to invest in put options is to protect your portfolio from a fall in stock prices. Put options do provide insurance against a drop in stock prices, but this insurance is definitely not cheap! Using put options to protect your portfolio against a drop in market prices is so expensive that I recommend against using them, especially in a long-term investing context.

Instead, we're going to learn about the return-enhancing opportunities presented by call options. But before we can do that, we need to know something more about call options.

As I said earlier, a call option on a share of stock is the right to buy the share at a pre-agreed price called the strike price. To make this concrete, let me introduce an actual stock option. How about options on Nike? Now, options are traded on exchanges, just like stocks. So I look up the prices of exchange-traded options, search for Nike, and this will take me to a big table of option price quotes, and all of them are for options on Nike shares.

There are so many contracts because they vary in 3 main ways. First, there's the basic distinction between call options and put options. Since I'm only interested in call options, which again give the holder the rights to buy shares in Nike, I'll ignore the put options.

Now we can look at strike prices and expiration dates. Strike prices of option contracts cluster around the current market price of the stock, for reasons that

I'll get into in a minute. Suppose the price of Nike stock today is about $88 per share. Then there will be strike prices at $90, $92.50, $95.00, $100, and so on. The strike prices go up in minimum increments of $2.50. So there are contracts with a $90 strike price, some with a $95 strike price, and so on. There are also strike prices below the current market price, because the contracts go out for up to two years ahead. So, two years ago, the price of Nike was lower and people set the strike prices at lower values, like $80 and $85.

We can have multiple contracts at the same strike price because the contracts can have different expiration dates. Most exchanges offer a rolling set of contracts that expire every 3 months. Some contracts have expiration dates in March, June, September, and December, and others have a different cycle. For Nike, the expiration months are January, April, July, and October. So we can have several contracts with a $95 strike price. We can have one contract with a $95 strike price that expires in October, another one with a $95 strike price that expires in January, and so on. I'm going to assume that it's currently late September, and I'm going to work with the call option on Nike that has a $100 strike price and expires in January. Option contracts expire mid-month, actually on the 18th of the month, usually.

The price quote on the January call options with a $100 strike price says 2.80, which means that each call option would cost $2.80. The price of an option is also called the premium. The connection to insurance premium, by the way, is actually intentional. If I pay that option premium of $2.80, I then own the right but not the obligation to buy one share of Nike at a price of $100 on or before the expiration date in January. So if I do buy this call option, then I'm hoping that the price of Nike shares rises above $100 per share between now, late September, and mid-January.

If that happens—if the market price of the stock goes above the strike price on the call option—then I say that my call options have gone into the money. This simply means that I can make a positive profit by exercising them. So suppose the price of Nike shares goes up to, say, $108 per share. Then what I can do is exercise my call options, and buy 1 share of Nike at $100 per share for each of these call options I own. Since the market price of each share is $108, then I can turn around and sell these shares for $108 per share and make an immediate $8 per share profit on each share I've bought.

This profit of $8 per share is the gross profit from the trading—remember that I paid $2.80 for the call option, and I'll have to pay trading commissions for the options trade as well as the stock trade. So my net, or all-in profit, will be smaller than $8 per share. Of course, the higher the price of Nike shares goes before you exercise the call option, the higher your profit will be. Your profit rises by one dollar for each dollar the price of Nike rises above $100 per share before expiration, and before you exercise the call options. So if I wait a little bit, and the price rises from $108 to $111 per share, then my profit rises from $8 to $11 per share.

What happens if the price of the stock stays below $100 per share? For example, what if the price of the stock rises from $88 now to $98 or even to $99.99 between now and the contract expiration in January? Well, sorry! If you exercised the option, you'd have to pay $100 per Nike share. But the market value of the Nike shares is below $100 per share. Why buy something for more than the market price if you don't have to? So in this case, instead of exercising the option, you'd let it expire. You'd just walk away. You've lost $2.80 per option that you bought, plus the commission and any other trading costs. But that's all you've lost. I know that it's a bummer to lose any money, but really you've only lost a fraction of the value of the stock.

So notice that there is an asymmetry in your profits. If the price of Nike shares rises above the strike price, your profit rises at a dollar-for-dollar rate. If the price of Nike stays below the strike price of the call option, you lose the price of the option, no matter whether the price of the shares rises to $99.99 or falls to a penny per share.

Financial economists represent this behavior with what they call a payoff or a profit diagram. Here's the diagram, which has the price of the stock on the horizontal axis and the amount of profit from the option on the vertical axis.

What I'm going to do with this diagram is to show you the graph of what your profit looks like for each possible price that the share of Nike stock can be at the expiration date of the option. I'll be assuming that the price of the option is $2.80, and the strike price of the option is $100. I'm going to ignore the trading commissions in this diagram, but keep in mind that most brokers will charge a flat rate per trade, and so you'd have to figure out the commission per option from that flat rate.

We just learned that if the price of the share stays below the strike price of $100, the option will have 0 value at expiration. If that happens, then the option pays you 0 and you've paid the price or the premium, so you've lost that amount. And you lose this amount no matter whether the price of the share is $1 or $99. That means that we can represent the profit on this option as a flat line at −$2.80 running between 0 and $100.

If the price of the share goes above $100, though, the option goes into the money and starts to profit. For each dollar the price of the share goes above $100, the profit on the option rises by $1. This means that the profit line changes when we pass $100 on the horizontal axis. The profit goes from being a flat line to a line with a slope of 1.

This is the classic diagram of the profit from buying a call option. This clearly shows the asymmetry in the profit that I mentioned. And this asymmetry is the big attraction of options. This diagram says that when I buy this call option, I have the potential to earn a lot of profit, but my losses are going to be limited. Limited losses and the potential to enjoy gains are the distinctive characteristics of insurance.

One thing you're probably wondering is how we determine the prices of options. Why does this call option on Nike cost $2.80, and not $0.13, or $50? There really are two answers, but they're related. The first answer is that it's supply and demand, just like in any other financial market. But the second answer is that many of the suppliers and demanders of options also know the theory of option pricing, and these theories lead to some easy-to-use option pricing formulas that give a ballpark estimate of the value of an option.

I won't go into those theories, but I can tell you the general idea behind them. As we've seen in the profit diagram, a call option will give you a profit if the price of the stock goes above the strike price of the option. So option pricing is really about the likelihood that this will happen. In other words, the more likely someone thinks it is that the price of Nike will rise above $100 before January, the more they will be willing to pay for the call option.

There are basically 5 things that affect this probability in general, but the big 3 things are the strike price of the option, the time to expiration, and the amount of variation in the price of the shares.

In general, the higher you set the strike price of a call option, the less likely it is that the stock price will rise above the strike price. So call option premiums fall as the strike price rises. Second, the more time you have until expiration, the better the chance that the stock price will wander above the strike price. So the option premium on a call option with 6 months until expiration will be higher than the premium on the identical call option with only 3 months left until maturity. We can see that in the options price table we looked at earlier, too. There's an April call option with a strike price of 100, which is selling for $5.60—which is double the price of the same call option that expires in January.

And finally, the more the price of the stock bounces around, the higher the chance that it will bounce up above the strike price of the call option. So stocks with more variation in their prices will have more expensive call options.

If we keep this up, you'll be an options trader before we know it. But my purpose isn't to turn you into an options trader. It's to make you comfortable enough with the options contract to think about making a couple of investments that I'll turn to next.

The first options investment that I'll talk about is called a covered call. The covered call is a combination of a stock and a call option that you can use to enhance your returns on stocks that you own. People generally use this strategy on stocks that they intend to own for a long time, but want to squeeze some income out of them. For example, I had a teaching assistant about 10 years ago who funded his skydiving hobby by writing covered calls on some Microsoft shares that he owned.

The covered call strategy involves writing, which is another word for selling, call options on shares of stock that you currently own. For example, if you currently own 100 shares of Nike, then you could write 100 call options on Nike as part of your covered call strategy. I'll show you exactly how in just a minute.

The covered call strategy requires you to sell call options. As I hinted at a couple of minutes ago, anyone can buy or sell call options. When you sell, or *write*, call options, you are selling to someone else the right to buy shares from you at a pre-agreed strike price. So when you write call options, you are creating an obligation for yourself. You are obligated to sell your shares, or actually to pay the buyer of the call options the difference between the market price of the shares and the strike price, if the price of the shares rises above the strike price.

Wait a minute, you might be saying—that sounds dangerous! Well, it is, if you don't already own the shares. But the whole point of this strategy is that you are going to be writing call options on shares you already own. If you write call options on these shares and the options go into the money, you simply sell your shares, use the proceeds to pay the holder of the call options, and then figure out what to do with the leftover cash. In other words, when you write call options on shares you already own, you're covered—hence the name, covered calls. If you sell call options without already owning the shares, you're doing some pretty risky speculation. One of the things that's so fascinating about the covered call is that owning the shares converts this risky transaction—selling call options—into an extremely safe investment.

Let me give you an example to show you what I mean. Suppose it's late September and you notice that the January call options on Nike shares, with a strike price of $100, are selling for $2.80 per option. You already own 100 Nike shares, and the current market price is $88 per share, so you decide to write 100 of these call options. So you collect $280, less trading commissions, and you wait to see what happens between now and January.

One of two things can happen. The first thing is that Nike stock doesn't go above $100 per share. Nike shares would have to go up $12 per share in a little over 3 months in order for these options to go into the money. That's a rate of increase of about 67%, on an annualized basis. Talk about swoosh! So it's probably not that likely to occur. If it doesn't actually happen, you keep your $280, minus trading costs. So it's like an extra dividend that you've earned on the shares. Using $88 as the price, this is a dividend yield of just over 3% in 3 months, or an annual rate of over 13%. Not too shabby. Of course, that is ignoring trading costs, so the actual return would be a little bit lower. Still, given that Nike's actual dividend yield is only about 1.4%, it's a vast improvement.

And of course, you could repeat this transaction again in January, once the options expire. The trick is to pick a strike price for the options that is high enough that it seems pretty unlikely that the share price will rise that high before expiration. But on the other hand, you need to set the strike price low enough so that the option premium makes it worth your while to do this trade. So there is a tradeoff at work, and you may not think that the tradeoff is worth it for all your shares, all the time. This strategy tends to work well for popular stocks that also have active options trading surrounding them.

Now, the other possibility is that the options actually do go into the money. Suppose, for example, that Nike's price rises to $110 per share and the holder of the options exercises them. In most cases, options are cash settled, which means that you would have to simply pay the difference between the market price of the shares and the strike price of the options. So in this case, what you'd do is sell your 100 shares at the current market price of $110 per share, for a total of $11,000. Then you'd owe $10 per share times 100 shares to the option holder for a total of $1000. Of course, you also have to figure in trading costs.

But let's think about your return in this case. You sold your shares for $11,000, paid $1000 to the holder of the call options, and you earned $280 on the calls. So you have $10,280 from this transaction, before trading costs. Now, if we again treat $88 as the starting price, then you've made a 16% return in 3 months. Whoa! That's pretty good. And you have this cash in hand now, so you can reinvest it into whatever you want. For example, you could actually reinvest it in those Nike shares, if you think that the stock still has the potential to appreciate even more. Or you could find another company's stock to invest in, and play the covered calls game with a new stock.

Notice that with either outcome, I haven't even mentioned the possibility of losing money. In fact, the only thing you've really lost in any sense is that you've lost out of part of some really high returns, if the options do go into the money and get exercised. So you'll have to settle for a smaller return in that case, but never a negative one. And that's why I think this strategy is an important one to consider—it's very safe, easy to do, and it can improve the return on any stock that has options traded on it.

If you like the idea of using covered calls, but are still hesitant to try this on your own, or if you don't think that you'll have the time to do this, then you can try the alternative. There are actually actively managed mutual funds that pursue covered call investment strategies. The fund managers invest in stocks that they think will deliver high returns through following a covered call investment strategy. So look for those funds if you like covered calls but don't want to do it by yourself.

In addition to covered calls, there's another investment strategy that uses the power of options to offer a great opportunity to investors. The general name for these investments is structured products, and they often go by the name of bull CDs, as in bull market CDs, but I like to call them option-embedded CDs. Now, if you're familiar with the causes of the global financial crisis of 2008, then you know that some types of structured products were heavily implicated as causes of the problems in the markets.

But there are literally hundreds of different types of structured products out there. The name structured product means that some clever financier has figured out a way to combine different financial instruments into a new one, or that the payments from a financial instrument are being sliced and diced in different ways. Some structured products are clearly aimed at the professionals and risk lovers out there, while other ones are clearly aimed at prudent individual investors who know a good deal when they see one.

Of course, I'll be talking about a structured product that goes in the latter category. This type of structured product is available through many banks, brokerages, and other dealers, and it is commonly referred to as a CD. But it's a CD with a couple of special features.

The first feature of these CDs is that instead of paying just a flat rate of interest, they will pay you the return on some index, usually a stock index like the S&P 500. That's already quite different from your average CD. But it gets better. If the S&P 500 falls during the time that you own the CD, the CD will actually give you your initial deposit back. So you won't suffer any losses, except of course for the fact that you earned a 0 return. But compared to an actual investment in the stock index, this is fantastic!

Of course, the question is, how can they do that? You may also ask, is that legal? Well, I'm happy to say that not only is this legal, but it's also pretty safe—for the buyer of the CD as well as for the company that offers it. Notice that the payoff of this special CD is a lot like an option payoff—you get to enjoy any gains in the S&P 500 index, but you don't have to suffer any of the losses between now and the maturity of the CD. Limited losses, but lots of upside potential—that's an option, for sure.

And that explains, by the way, how a bank or other company can offer such a product. Here's how they work. First, the bank takes your deposit and invests it in some kind of asset. For example, a bank may simply make loans with your deposit. The loans are going to earn some kind of interest, and the bank takes the interest from those loans and buys call options on the S&P 500 index.

TAh, there are those stock index options I mentioned earlier. Stock index options are actually options on the stock index futures contracts. For example, there is a very actively traded futures contract on the S&P 500. The futures contract on the index is a great substitute for holding the index directly, because it's cheaper to buy, and its price movements are strongly tied to the movements of the actual index. So an option on the futures contract is a great substitute for an option directly on the S&P 500 index. And the options are fairly cheap, too.

In fact, the interest earned on the loans that the bank makes using your deposit is enough to pay for options on the stock index futures contract. And there'll still be enough money left over to compensate the bank for arranging the CD. Hey, the bank's got to eat, too.

Then, if the stock index goes up in value, the options go into the money, and bank will give you the profit on the stock options. The profit on the options will yield the same rate of return as on the stock index. If the stock index goes down, the options expire worthless. But the money you deposited at the bank isn't in the stock market, so the value of your deposit isn't at risk from a stock market decline. The money you deposited has been loaned out to the bank's customers. So the money is at risk—but this is the same risk you take with any deposit offered by any bank.

So, thanks to the power of options, banks and brokerages can offer investors a product that looks too good to be true—you get the appreciation of a stock index, with very minimal risk of losing any of your principal. These CDs can be great products for investors who are highly risk averse, or who want to try to improve the returns on their portfolio but simply can't afford capital losses.

A word of caution is in order here. There are some bull CD products that promise twice the return on the index if the index rises, or possibly even more. These products work the same way as normal bull CDs, but they multiply returns by purchasing more call options. They can afford to buy more call options because they invest your deposit in much riskier loans. So they are much riskier than normal bull CDs, and I don't recommend any bull CD that promises to multiply the returns on an index. Stick with the plain products that simply offer the gain on the index with no multiplier. And never buy a bull CD that doesn't promise to return your full deposit if the index goes down.

In this lecture, we've learned a couple of things. First, certain types of options really can enhance the return on your investments, with minimal risk involved. And second, financial engineering doesn't just produce financial Frankensteins, it can also create products that are useful and safer than the ingredients that go into them. Covered calls, for example, take one of the riskiest derivatives positions out there and turn it into a no-lose way to juice the returns on your favorite stock. And option-enhanced CDs deliver the upside return potential of a stock index with none of the stocks' downside risk and only a minimal risk that you lose anything at all. You should definitely consider adding these option-enhanced investments to your short list of investment options.

Real Estate and Commodities
Lecture 18

In this lecture, you're going to learn about investing in 2 of the most popular tangible assets: real estate and commodities. As a result of this lecture, you might decide to look into using REITs, or mutual funds that invest in REITs, as a way to invest in real estate. The income-producing potential of real estate combined with its diversification benefits make it a great choice for everyone's portfolio. On the other hand, you should be prepared for a wild ride if you decide to add any commodities to your portfolio.

Mortgage-Backed Securities

- In the case of regular bonds, the payments on the bond come from the borrower's income. For example, companies pay their bond payments out of the money that they earn from operations, and governments pay their bond payments out of the tax revenues they raise. Corporations that issue mortgage-backed securities pay their bond payments out of mortgage payments that are made by homeowners.

- A **mortgage-backed security (MBS)** is a special type of bond that is issued by a special corporation that buys and holds hundreds or thousands of mortgages. Each month, the borrowers on these mortgages send in their mortgage payments, and these payments ultimately get sent to the corporation that holds the mortgages. This company then pays out almost all of the cash to the holders of the mortgage-backed securities—but at 6-month intervals, like the payments on a regular bond. The company organizing the mortgage-backed security keeps a small portion of the incoming mortgage payments to cover its expenses, which are small, and to compensate the owners of the company for their efforts.

- Therefore, holders of mortgage-backed securities are entitled to receive some slice of the mortgage payments of hundreds or thousands of homeowners, and there are a couple of different ways that mortgage-backed securities transmit the cash to the holders of the securities. The simple way is called a pass-through security, in which the special corporation organizing the MBS simply passes the mortgage payments on to the bondholders—after taking out a small cut, of course.

- The other way to organize an MBS is to use the collateralized debt obligation (CDO) structure. The CDO divides its payments into several different sets, called tranches, which differ according to the priority of the claim that each one has on the mortgage payments and the share of the total promised mortgage payments that each tranche is entitled to.

- If you have the highest priority claim on the mortgage payments, which is called the AAA or supersenior tranche, then you get paid off first—and whatever is left after you've been paid is then paid to the next people in line.

- In the CDO, different investors receive different sets of payments while in a pass-through security, every investor gets the same thing. Additionally, in a CDO, the first people in line have an excellent chance of getting everything they're entitled to while the people at the end of the line are virtually guaranteed to suffer some losses.

- Beginning in 2007, mortgage-backed securities got a terrible reputation because many MBSs organized in CDO form were stuffed full of subprime mortgages that defaulted in record numbers.

- Not only is there a big difference between pass-through securities and CDOs, but there's also an equally big difference between so-called private-label MBSs and the MBSs that carry a guarantee from a government agency or government-sponsored enterprise.

- Pass-through mortgage-backed securities really can't hold subprime mortgages because the default rate on subprime mortgages is too high for most investors' comfort. Only CDOs, which concentrate the default risk in the lower tranches, which are the last in line to receive payments, can work for subprime mortgages.

- Furthermore, there are plenty of mortgage-backed securities that carry a government guarantee. If you're looking for safety, the MBS that is arranged by Ginnie Mae, the Government National Mortgage Association, carries a double government guarantee. This means that the interest paid on Ginnie Mae's MBS is almost the same as the rate on government bonds of the same maturity.

- The safety of investing in government-guaranteed MBSs can take away some of the benefits of investing in real estate. The returns on these safe mortgage-backed securities are not going to rise and fall much with the property markets. This means that you'll not only miss out on higher returns, but you could also miss out on some potential diversification benefits.

Real Estate
- An investment that is more closely connected to real estate markets than government-guaranteed MBSs is the **real estate investment trust (REIT)**, which is similar in its organization to a closed-end mutual fund. It's a company that sells shares to investors once, at the beginning of the fund, and then uses the proceeds to invest in a portfolio of real estate assets. The shares of the REIT trade on stock exchanges—just as shares of closed-end mutual funds do.

- The main difference between REITs and closed-end mutual funds is that REITs are required to pay out at least 90% of their income as dividends to the shareholders. This means that REITs can be attractive for their dividends as well as for the possibility of capital gains. The capital gains on REITs have tended to be modest, so the returns on them have primarily been delivered through the dividends they pay.

- There are 2 main types of REITs that you should be aware of. The main type of REIT is the **equity REIT**, which invests directly in real estate—buildings and land. Equity REITs buy buildings and manage them, or even develop real estate projects and manage them.

- **Mortgage REITs**, on the other hand, invest in mortgages and mortgage-backed securities. Either type of REIT investment is fine in principle, but mortgage REITs tend to be highly leveraged, and because of this, they also have to devote a lot of attention to hedging the interest rate risk that comes with being highly leveraged. Therefore, mortgage REITs are not recommended investments— unless you feel comfortable evaluating and monitoring highly leveraged investments.

- Usually, equity REITs use leverage as well, but they do so at much lower rates. One of the things that you need to check before you invest in an equity REIT is its leverage ratio: If a REIT has debt of more than 2/3 of the value of its assets, then you should pass it up in favor of another REIT with a lower debt-to-assets ratio.

© Digital Vision/Thinkstock.

Many people invest in real estate by buying and renting out residential properties.

- The other thing that you'll want to pay attention to is the type of property that the REIT intends to invest in. The type of property, and of course its location, will determine a lot about the returns on the REIT, so you need to do your homework by investigating what the REIT actually holds.

- In addition, you should keep in mind that the REIT is going to manage properties, and it will make money by collecting rent, which will change as economic conditions change. Additionally, if a REIT owns buildings that have longer-term leases, then its income will be less sensitive to changes in the local economy where the buildings are located.

- If you're not excited about the prospect of researching a large set of REITs and trying to choose one or more, then you can invest in a mutual fund or ETF that buys REIT shares. In fact, this is not only a good way to go for U.S. REITs, but it's also probably the best way to go if you want to try some foreign real estate investments.

- Another interesting real estate investment is timberland. The attraction of timberland is very similar to REITs; it can offer an attractive dividend and diversification opportunity. Companies called timber investment management organizations (TIMOs) are big players in this business. Unfortunately, the minimum investments in many TIMOs are quite large—typically at least $1 million. However, you can buy into a timber ETF that holds shares in many TIMOs.

Commodities

- Real estate isn't the only tangible investment. One category of physical investments that used to be only the realm of specialists is commodities. It's now easier than ever to invest in commodities, but ease of investing doesn't automatically make commodities a great investment.

- Stocks, bonds, and real estate all either promise explicit income to the investor, or they promise growth that leads to increased value in the future. However, commodities don't do either one of these things. For example, if you buy a million gallons of unleaded gasoline, it won't pay you any dividends or grow into more gasoline. Therefore, commodities shouldn't be a standard part of anyone's portfolio—unless there is a compelling reason to include them.

- There are 2 possibly compelling reasons that you'd want to invest in commodities. The first reason is that commodities could be an inflation hedge. When the general price level rises, this means that most prices rise—but not necessarily all of them. Therefore, if you're looking for an inflation-hedge investment, you need to find commodities that tend to rise right along with the price level.

- This tends to be the main problem with investing in commodities as an inflation hedge. The total picture seems to indicate that most commodities just don't have a close enough link to the price level to be considered great inflation hedges—outside of the times when inflation is already a problem.

- The second reason that you might want to invest in commodities is because you believe that there's a long-term trend toward higher commodity prices. This involves global economic growth, especially in emerging market economies such as Brazil, India, China, and many others. As these economies develop, they'll demand more energy and raw materials that go into producing goods and services, and as the people in these countries move up the income ladder, they'll demand more luxury goods that consume more commodities.

- Most international organizations that deal with economic development, such as the International Monetary Fund, predict that economic growth in emerging markets will be much higher than in the industrialized world for some time to come. This means that these economies will continue to increase their demand for commodities, which will push prices of energy, minerals, and other commodities higher and higher.

- If you think that long-term economic development will lead to increased demand for commodities, then you need to consider which commodities are especially likely to be in high demand and short supply over the coming decade or longer. This is tricky because when the price of a commodity rises significantly, everyone suddenly scrambles to figure out how to make more of it, and supply will increase over time. Sometimes the increases in supply will overtake the increases in demand, and the commodity price will fall rather than rise.

- On the other hand, there may be tremendous opportunities for people who can anticipate how the tastes of people in emerging markets will change as they move up the income ladder.

- No matter which motivation you have for investing in commodities, if you want to invest in them, you're going to have to do a lot of research. If you think that commodities will give you good inflation protection, then you'll have to find the commodities that currently do the best job of keeping up with prices, and if you're going to invest in commodities as a bet on growth, then you'll have to keep up with the developments in the global markets for the commodities you'd like to invest in.

Important Terms

equity REIT: A type of REIT that invests directly in real estate—buildings and land.

mortgage-backed security (MBS): A special type of bond that is issued by a special corporation that buys and holds hundreds or thousands of mortgages.

mortgage REIT: A type of REIT that invests in mortgages and mortgage-backed securities.

real estate investment trust (REIT): A company that sells shares to investors once, at the beginning of a fund, and then uses the proceeds to invest in a portfolio of real estate assets.

Suggested Reading

Hough, "REITs, Don't Fail Me Now."

National Association of Real Estate Investment Trusts, "All about REITs."

Pleven, "The Case against Commodities."

Questions to Consider

1. The National Association of Real Estate Investment Trusts (NAREIT) maintains a directory of publicly traded REITs at http://www.reit.com/IndividualInvestors/PubliclyTradedREITDirectory.aspx. Go to this site, find one of the listed REITs, and find its real estate investment strategy as well as its current dividend information, including its dividend yield. Would you consider investing in this REIT based on this information?

2. Using a free financial website, find the ETF for a common investment commodity like oil, gold, gasoline, or natural gas. What exactly does this ETF invest in?

Real Estate and Commodities
Lecture 18—Transcript

We've been learning about all kinds of investments in this course, but everything we've learned about so far are financial assets—or what we used to call paper investments, back when we still had paper bonds and stock certificates. It's time that we learned about investing in real, tangible assets you can really sink your teeth into, or, at least reach out and touch. In this lecture, we're going to learn about investing in two of the most popular tangible assets: real estate and commodities.

Investing in tangible physical assets like real estate is certainly very popular among many individual investors. Many people invest in real estate by buying and renting out residential properties, ranging from one small home to entire apartment buildings. Since I live in a college town, several of my friends and neighbors—and even some professors I know—have all purchased rental properties and become landlords.

I can understand why they do this. The cash returns to being a landlord, especially in an area with several colleges and universities, can be substantial. But of course, becoming a landlord isn't for everyone. It has its own set of challenges and problems that can make it more of a hassle than it's worth. So, are there good ways to invest in real estate without needing to become a landlord?

By now you should know that I don't ask questions like that unless the answer is yes. There are several ways that individual investors can make real estate investments without having to get dragged into the chore of day-to-day property management. We'll learn about 3 of these ways in this lecture, beginning with mortgage-backed securities.

Oops! Did I just say something wrong? Well, you might think so, since mortgage-backed securities developed a terrible reputation during the financial crisis of 2008. Before I address that issue, let me just define what a mortgage-backed security is, and tell you a little about how it works. A mortgage-backed security is simply a specialized type of bond. In the case of regular bonds, the payments on the bond come from the borrower's income. For example, companies pay their bond payments out of the money that they earn from operations, and governments pay their bond payments out of the tax revenues they raise. Corporations that issue mortgage-backed securities pay their bond payments out of mortgage payments that are made by homeowners.

A mortgage-backed security, or MBS for short, is issued by a special corporation that buys and holds hundreds or thousands of mortgages. Each month, the borrowers of these mortgages send in their mortgage payments, and these payments ultimately get sent to the corporation that holds the mortgages. This company turns around and pays out almost all of this cash to the holders of the mortgage-backed securities, but at 6-month intervals, like the payments on a regular bond. The company organizing the mortgage-backed security keeps a small portion of the incoming mortgage payments to cover its expenses, which are small, and to compensate the owners of the company for their efforts.

So holders of mortgage-backed securities are entitled to receive some slice of the mortgage payments of hundreds or thousands of homeowners. I say "some slice of the mortgage payments" because there are a couple of different ways that mortgage-backed securities transmit the cash to the holders of the securities. The simple way is called a pass-through security, in which the special corporation organizing the MBS simply passes the mortgage payments on to the bondholders—after taking out a small cut, of course.

The other way to organize an MBS is to use the so-called CDO structure, where CDO stands for collateralized debt obligation. The CDO divides its payments up into several different sets, called tranches. The word tranche comes from the French word for slice. The tranches differ according to the priority of the claim that each one has on the mortgage payments, and the share of the total promised mortgage payments that each tranche is entitled to.

If you have the highest priority claim on the mortgage payments, which is called the triple-A or supersenior tranche, then you get paid off first—and whatever is left after you've been paid is then paid to the next people in line. So in the CDO, different investors receive different sets of payments, while in a pass-through, every investor gets the same thing. And in a CDO, the first people in line have an excellent chance of getting everything they're entitled to, while the people at the end of the line are virtually guaranteed to suffer some losses.

Mortgage-backed securities got such a terrible reputation because many mortgage-backed securities, organized in CDO form, were stuffed full of subprime mortgages that defaulted in record numbers, beginning in 2007. The losses on the defaults of the subprime mortgages were so large that even the first investors in line to be paid off from the mortgage payments suffered losses. And since these tranches were rated triple-A, this came as a huge shock to these investors.

After that fiasco, why should anyone invest in mortgage-backed securities? Well, because not all MBS are the same. Not only is there a big difference between pass-through securities and CDOs, but there's also an equally big difference between so-called private-label MBS and the MBS that carries a guarantee from a government agency or government-sponsored enterprise.

First, pass-through MBSs really can't hold subprime mortgages, because the default rate on subprime mortgages is too high for most investors' comfort. If all the investors have to share equally in the default risk, as they do in a pass-through MBS, then the organizers won't be able to find enough investors who are willing to share the risk. Only CDOs, which concentrate the default risk in the so-called lower tranches, which are the last in line to receive payments, can work for subprime mortgages.

The second reason why you should still be interested in investing in MBS is that there are plenty of MBSs that carry a government guarantee. For example, the MBSs organized by Fannie Mae and Freddie Mac have a guarantee on all payments of interest and principal. Fannie and Freddie were taken over by the U.S. government in 2008, and so this guarantee remains in place now and will remain so until all the MBSs arranged by these companies mature.

But there's actually an even better source of MBSs, if you're looking for safety. This is the MBS that is arranged by Ginnie Mae, the Government National Mortgage Association. Ginnie Mae is a federal agency that was created in the late 1960s. Ginnie actually invented the mortgage backed security in 1970 and has been successfully issuing them ever since.

What Ginnie Mae does is to organize pools of mortgages issued under the Federal Housing Administration and Veterans Administration mortgage programs. You may know that the FHA and VA programs are federal mortgage insurance programs for low-income families and for veterans, respectively. So Ginnie Mae organizes MBSs out of pools of mortgages whose payments are already guaranteed by the U.S. government.

And on top of that, Ginnie Mae adds her own guarantee to the payments on the bonds themselves. So MBSs organized by Ginnie Mae carry a double government guarantee. It's hard to get safer than that. Of course, this means that the interest paid on Ginnie Mae's MBSs is almost the same as the rate on government bonds of the same maturity. But if you're looking for a safe way to invest in real estate, it's almost impossible to find something safer than that.

But the safety of investing in government-guaranteed mortgage-backed securities can take away some of the benefits of investing in real estate. The returns on these safe mortgage-backed securities are not going to rise and fall all that much with the property markets. This means that you'll not only miss out on higher returns, but you could also miss out on some potential diversification benefits.

Generally, real estate markets don't move in lockstep with the stock and bond markets, and this means that they can provide good diversification. But you have to find an investment that is more closely connected to real estate markets than government-guaranteed MBSs.

One of these investments is the real estate investment trust, or REIT for short. A REIT is very similar in its organization to a closed-end mutual fund. It's a company that sells shares to investors once, at the beginning of the fund, and then uses the proceeds to invest in a portfolio of real estate assets. The shares of the REIT trade on stock exchanges, just like shares of closed-end mutual funds do.

The big difference between REITs and closed-end mutual funds, though, is that REITs are required to pay out at least 90% of their income as dividends to the shareholders. This means that REITs can be attractive for their dividends as well as for the possibility of capital gains. The capital gains on REITs have tended to be modest, so the returns on them have primarily been delivered through the dividends they pay.

There are two main types of REITs you should be aware of, and you'll probably only be interested in one of them. The main type of REIT, judging by the fact that 90% of REITs are organized this way, is the equity REIT. Equity REITs invest directly in real estate—buildings and land. They buy buildings and manage them, or even develop real estate projects and manage them. Mortgage REITs, on the other hand, invest in mortgages and mortgage-backed securities. Either type of REIT investment is fine in principle, but mortgage REITs tend to be highly leveraged, and because of this they also have to devote a lot of attention to hedging the interest rate risk that comes with being highly leveraged. So I don't recommend them unless you really feel comfortable evaluating and monitoring highly leveraged investments.

That isn't to say that equity REITs don't use leverage themselves. Actually, they usually do—but they do so at much lower rates. Still, one of the things that you need to check before you invest in an equity REIT is its leverage ratio. If a REIT has debt of more than two thirds of the value of its assets, then you should pass it up in favor of another REIT with a lower ratio of debt to assets.

The other thing that you'll want to pay attention to is the type of property that the REIT intends to invest in. A lot of REITs invest in retail space, like shopping malls and strip malls. Office REITs invest in office buildings, which can be in the hearts of big cities but can just as easily be in the suburbs. Healthcare REITs invest in hospitals, clinics, nursing homes, and even retirement communities. And of course there are also residential REITs, which mainly invest in multifamily homes and apartment buildings. There are even hotel REITs.

The type of property, and of course its location, will determine a lot about the returns on the REIT, so as always, you need to do your homework by investigating what the REIT actually holds. For example, there's a huge difference in office REITs that invest in buildings inside the Chicago Loop, versus office REITs that invest in office parks in the suburbs of Phoenix.

In addition, keep in mind that the REIT is going to manage properties, and it will make money by collecting rent. Rents change as economic conditions change—so a great-returning REIT today can become a low-returning REIT next year if the economy where the buildings are goes into a recession. That also depends, of course, on how long the leases are. If a REIT owns buildings that have longer-term leases, then its income will be less sensitive to changes in the local economy where the buildings are located. Residential leases, for example, run only about one year into the future. Most office leases last a few years, shopping mall leases run between 7 and 10 years, and healthcare facility leases can go out to 15 years.

Wow—that's a lot to consider, in terms of how to choose a REIT. Now, if you're not excited about the prospect of researching a large set of REITs and trying to choose one or more, then you can always invest in a mutual fund that buys REIT shares, or an ETF that does the same. In fact, this is not only a good way to go for U.S. REITs, it's probably the best way to go if you also want to try some foreign real estate investment.

If you've traveled to any large city in a developing economy, like Mumbai or Shanghai, you know that foreign real estate markets also present tremendous growth opportunities. Unfortunately, investing in foreign real estate presents the same problems to investors as any other foreign assets: they're a hassle to buy and own, and they can generate tax problems for you. Therefore, the best way to access this opportunity is through U.S.-based mutual funds or ETFs that invest in the shares of foreign REITs.

One other very interesting real estate investment is timberland. The world's wood products increasingly come from managed forests, and many of these managed forests are owned by private companies that specialize in buying and managing timberland. The attraction of timberland is very similar to REITs. The land that the trees sits on can appreciate in value, and over time the trees on the land will be harvested and sold to the producers of various wood products. In fact, most pieces of timberland are divided up into trees of differing maturities, so that each year a different set is harvested and sold to generate income. Just like REITs, timberland can offer an attractive dividend and a diversification opportunity. Big institutional investors, like pension funds and university endowment funds, have taken advantage of timberland investments for decades.

Companies called timber investment management organizations, or TIMOs, are big players in this business. Unfortunately, the minimum investments in many TIMOs are quite large—typically at least $1 million. But as always these days, ETFs come riding to the rescue—you can buy into a timber ETF that holds shares in many TIMOs. In fact, the first timber ETF adopted the ticker symbol CUT. Is it just me, or are these ETF managers having just a little more fun than everyone else in the investing business?

Real estate isn't the only tangible investment out there. One category of physical investments that used to be only the realm of specialists and, let's just say, eccentric people, is commodities. These days, though, commodity investing has gone mainstream. The amazing increases in commodities prices that we saw both before and after the financial crisis of 2008 grabbed headlines as well as the attention of millions of investors. And, as I've mentioned in my introductory lecture on ETFs, it's now easier than ever to invest in commodities.

But ease of investing doesn't automatically make commodities a great investment. Let's step back and think carefully about why you'd want to invest in commodities. Then we can think about the types of commodities to invest in, and the different ways you can do it.

Commodities are different from the other investments we've been discussing so far in this course. Stocks, bonds, and real estate all either promise explicit income to the investor or they promise growth that leads to increased value in the future. Commodities don't do either one of these things. For example, if you buy a million gallons of unleaded gasoline, it won't pay you any dividends and it won't grow into more gasoline, or anything else for that matter. So we have to be careful about including commodities in our investment portfolios. They shouldn't be a standard part of anyone's portfolio unless you have a compelling reason to include them.

In my opinion, there are two possibly compelling reasons why you'd want to invest in commodities. The first reason is that commodities could be inflation hedges. You may remember from my very first lecture that inflation is one of your worst enemies as an investor. So we should take any investment that is a potential inflation hedge seriously. Now, when the general price level rises, this means that most prices rise, but not necessarily all of them. So if we're looking for an inflation hedge investment, we'd need to find commodities that tend to rise right along with the price level.

And that tends to be the main problem with investing in commodities as an inflation hedge. There are several regularities that we tend to see in the relationship between commodity prices and some index of the general price level, like the CPI, and they indicate that commodities are a so-so hedge against inflation. First, over short periods when inflation is high and increasing, commodity prices generally rise very strongly. Sounds good, right? But on the other hand, commodity prices tend to rise very strongly, and then decline very strongly—that is, they tend to overreact to fears about inflation and then they correct themselves. So, in other words, commodity prices tend to overshoot the target, if the target is the general price level.

During the times when inflation isn't as strong, commodity prices tend to be driven by events specific to the commodity, like weather for agricultural commodities. So the price of soybeans can soar if there is an extended drought in the U.S. Midwest, or crop failures in China, but this will have a limited impact on the price level. What the total picture seems to indicate is that most commodities just don't have a close enough link to the price level to be considered all that great of inflation hedges outside of the times when inflation is already a problem.

Of course, some commodities have a closer connection to the price level than others. For example, for many years oil was considered a good inflation hedge because of the dependency of the entire economy on oil. Also, gold has traditionally been known as an inflation hedge. This is because of its potential role as a substitute for money. Let's see how well they do as inflation hedges.

If we look at the price of a barrel of oil over the last few decades, and the price of an ounce of gold, and compare both of these to the consumer price index, we can see some of the problems I've been mentioning. During times of inflation fears, the prices of oil and gold tend to overshoot, and during times of low inflation, the prices of the commodities respond to supply and demand conditions in their own markets without much regard for the general price level. Notice, for example, how the prices of both gold and oil fell or stagnated during much of the past 3 decades, while the price level continued to rise. Neither commodity looks all that great as an inflation hedge, in my opinion.

The real question, in my mind, is whether commodities make a better hedge against inflation than inflation-indexed bonds, which we've learned about in some detail in an earlier lecture. Personally, I think inflation-indexed bonds do a much better and more consistent job of hedging against inflation than commodities do. So I'm not a big believer in commodities as a good inflation hedge for a long-run investor.

But there's still a second reason why you might want to invest in commodities. And this is because you believe that there's a long-term trend toward higher commodity prices. This is basically a story about global economic growth, especially in the emerging market economies like Brazil, India, China, and many others. As these economies develop, they'll demand more energy and raw materials that go into producing goods and services. Also, as the people in these countries move up the income ladder, they'll demand more luxury goods that consume more commodities. For example, one of the things that people consume a lot more of as they get richer is meat. So more grain is needed to feed the animals that produce meat, because it takes more grain to produce a pound of meat than a pound of bread. That means that grain prices will rise.

Most international organizations that deal with economic development, like the International Monetary Fund, predict that economic growth in emerging markets will be much higher than in the industrialized world for some time to come. This means that these economies will continue to increase their demand for commodities, which will push prices of energy, minerals, foodstuffs, and other commodities higher and higher.

If you believe this story of long-term economic development leading to increased demand for commodities, then you need to think about what commodities are especially likely to be in high demand and short supply over the coming decade or longer. This is tricky, because as the example of oil shows, when the price of a commodity rises significantly, suddenly everyone scrambles to figure out how to make more of it, and supply will increase over time. Sometimes the increases in supply will actually overtake the increases in demand, and the commodity price will fall rather than rise. The recent discovery of ways to exploit the huge, untapped reserves of natural gas trapped in shale formations throughout the world is a case in point.

On the other hand, there may be tremendous opportunities for people who can anticipate how the tastes of people in emerging markets will change as they move up the income ladder. For example, think what would happen if the populations of India and China all suddenly switched to coffee from their traditional tea.

No matter which motivation you have for investing in commodities, if you want to invest in them, you're going to have to do a lot of research. If you think that commodities will give you good inflation protection, you'll have to find the commodities that currently do the best job of keeping up with prices. You may have to download data on commodity prices and, as I've done, graph the price level and the commodity prices on the same graph and use your judgment. And if you're going to invest in commodities as a bet on growth, then you'll have to keep up with the developments in the global markets for the commodities you'd like to invest in. You'll have to anticipate where the innovations in supply and demand for the commodities are likely to be, and guess how much these will affect the values of the commodities you're interested in.

Now that we have some idea of why we'd want to invest in commodities, let's consider how to do it. I want to start by going over an old argument about investing in commodities and see whether this rule of thumb still works today. Up to about 20 years ago, the old-school advice for investing in commodities boiled down to the following rule: don't invest in gold, invest in the mining company. The general form for this rule is don't invest in the commodity, invest in the commodity producer—or perhaps the commodity distributor.

Why was this rule part of the conventional wisdom of investing back then? It's mainly because to invest directly in commodities, you had to do one of two things. First, you could buy the commodity yourself, and that's just plain expensive when you factor in the dealer markups on both buying and selling and the storage costs. The other way was to deal in the futures markets for the commodity, but that required a lot of expertise in using these contracts— in fact, it still does. And the transaction costs of buying and selling contracts do add up over time, pushing down your overall return.

On the other hand, if you buy into a commodity producing company, you get the same exposure to the underlying commodity. Again, think about a gold mining company. If the value of gold goes up, then the value of the mining company's proven gold reserves also goes up, and the price of the mining company's stock should increase. In addition, the managers of the mining company are also working to smooth the earnings of the company, so the stock won't bounce up and down nearly as much as the price of the commodity. So buying the mining stock was actually seen as superior to investing in the commodity directly, since you avoid the transaction costs and get the chance for the managers to smooth the value of the company out.

These days, of course, we have ETFs that offer us the chance to invest in commodity indexes as well as in individual commodities. And ETFs can invest in both the commodity and the producers. Did you know, for example, that in addition to gold and platinum, you can also invest in ETFs that hold metals like lithium and uranium? So, if I can buy an ETF that invests directly in one of these commodities, or a commodity index, I don't have to bear all the transaction and storage costs that people had to pay to own the stuff directly.

In addition, when I buy the stock of a commodity producer, I do get the exposure to the commodity, but I might also get a lot of exposure to stuff I don't want in my portfolio. For example, let's think about oil companies. When I buy the stock of a diversified oil company, I don't just get oil, but I also get refining and distribution. I could also get exposure to low-margin, low-profit gas stations. And no matter what company I buy, I get exposure to all the problems of modern corporate management, like bad investment decisions, overuse of the corporate jet, tax problems, labor disputes, and all sorts of other value-destroying headaches. And all I wanted was an investment in a few barrels of oil!

So on the surface, it seems like this old-school argument isn't valid any more. We can find cheap ways to make investments directly into commodities, so who needs the companies to do it for us? Well, if the companies are cheap relative to the value of the commodity, even after factoring in all the potential problems I just mentioned, then it could be a much better deal to buy the stock of the producer than the commodity itself. If you think that the commodity price will continue to rise, and the producer's shares are undervalued now, relative to the current price of the commodity, won't they be even more undervalued if the commodity price continues to rise?

That seems like an even better opportunity to earn a high return than investing directly in the commodity. Of course, this may turn out to be a riskier investment than you want to undertake. But it's important to realize that there are still occasions in which buying the commodity producer seems like a better investment than buying the commodity itself.

That about does it for my brief look at investing in tangible assets. From this discussion, I hope you come away with the desire to look into using REITs or mutual funds that invest in REITs as a way to invest in real estate. The income-producing potential of real estate, combined with its diversification benefits, make it a great choice for everyone's portfolio. On the other hand, I don't think that investing in commodities automatically qualifies for inclusion in your investment plans. But, if you think that commodities do a great job of hedging your exposure to inflation risk, or if you think that commodity prices are destined to rise as the emerging markets grow, then you have sufficient reason to look into adding commodities to your list of investments. But you should be prepared for a wild ride in any commodity that you add to your portfolio. And you may be better off investing in great companies that are also commodity producers.

Cycles and Market Timing
Lecture 19

I n this lecture, you'll learn about the role of economic cycles in financial markets and what they mean to you as an investor. You'll learn about 3 important cycles that affect the financial markets, and you'll learn whether the existence of these cycles means that you can—or should—try to time your investments according to these cycles. In fact, the markets will cycle, but the long-run trend moves steadily upward. In order to take full advantage of market cycles, the best strategy is to use dollar-cost averaging and to remain invested in the market over the long term.

Price Cycles
- Most financial markets seem to go through periods of generally rising prices and optimistic sentiment about future prices that are followed by periods of widespread decline in prices and investor pessimism. A **bull market** is a market in which bonds and other securities are rising in value; a **bear market** is a market in which bonds and other securities are declining in value.

- The existence of bull and bear markets leads investors to try to time their buying and selling of stocks and other securities. According to market timers, the best times to buy are at the ends of the bear markets and the beginnings of bull markets because at those times, the market prices are relatively low and are on their way up. The time to sell is at the end of the bull market when prices are peaking.

- The problem is knowing when a bull market is ending or a bear market is beginning. Prices don't rise smoothly during bull markets or fall smoothly during bear markets; they bounce up and down from day to day. While it's true that in a bull market the increases in price outweigh the decreases, even in the middle of a bull market, there can be some pretty big market losses.

- However, there is an investment strategy that tries to figure out whether price trends will continue or reverse called **technical analysis**, which uses information in prices as well as in the volume of trading to make predictions about future price movements. This strategy relies heavily on examining charts and graphs of stock prices.

- There are many different technical analysis tools, but there are 3 that are the most common. One of the hallmarks of technical analysis is the charts and graphs that analysts make. These charts and graphs often track moving averages of prices over time. Moving averages are tools that help reveal the trends in a set of data because they smooth out the short-term bumps. If the actual daily price rises above sets of moving averages, this is a bullish sign that the price will continue to rise; if the price falls below moving averages, it's a bearish sign.

- In addition to charts of moving averages, technical analysis uses data on breadth and trading volume. The breadth of the market is the number of companies that gain in value during some period of time minus the number of companies that lose value during that period. The stronger the breadth on the side of the gainers, the stronger the bullish signal is, and the stronger the breadth on the side of the losers, the stronger the bearish signal is.

- Finally, the traders' index (TRIN) is a ratio formed by taking the average number of shares traded of the companies whose prices fell and dividing this by the average number of shares traded of the companies whose prices rose. If the TRIN is greater than 1, it's a bearish signal to investors; if the TRIN is less than 1, it's a bullish signal.

- These technical analysis tools are intended to identify existing trends in prices and also to predict when the trends are about to reverse. The studies that find some benefit of technical analysis tend to find that the benefits are so small that they are more than offset by the increase in trading costs that you would incur if you let technical analysis tell you when to buy and sell.

- One of the big problems with technical analysis is that its predictions always look better in hindsight. That is, once you see how the market actually performed, it's easy to find patterns in the prices. It's much harder to make a successful bet before you know whether there really is a trend or just a false signal of a trend.

- Another type of price cycle that would be beneficial to be able to detect is a price bubble. When an economist wants to test whether an asset price has a bubble in it, the economist first has to assume some fundamentals-based model of the asset's value.

- If an economist finds a bubble in the price of an asset, he or she can't be sure whether there actually is a bubble or whether his or her fundamentals-based model of the price of the asset is wrong. Because there aren't any reliable tests for bubbles, investors tend to use other measures of value as well as their own intuition about what's happening in the markets.

- If you really think there's a price bubble in some market, you should try to stay out of it until you're sure the bubble has burst or until you're sure you were wrong about the bubble. In the meantime, find other good investments for your savings.

Business Cycles

- The **business cycle** is the cycle of expansion and recession that characterizes our overall economy. The typical business cycle tends to last about 4 years, and we spend a little over 1/2 the time in expansion and the rest in recession.

- Regardless of the length of the business cycle, it has definite impacts on the markets for various investments. Stocks are especially sensitive to the business cycle because corporate earnings react strongly to the state of the overall economy. However, the flow of credit to business and the risk of default also depend on the state of the business cycle, so bond returns also vary significantly over the business cycle.

- Many companies' fortunes are so strongly tied to the business cycle that they're referred to as **cyclical companies**. These are the manufacturers and distributors of big-ticket consumer items like cars, appliances, and furniture. Some investors try to move investments into these industries when the business cycle turns up and move investments out when the recession comes.

- A similar strategy involves luxury goods and lower-priced goods. During expansions, incomes are rising and people tend to buy more luxury goods or higher-priced name-brand versions of the products they buy every day—and this is reversed when the economy goes into a recession.

- During a recession, the rule of thumb is to sell off your investments in companies that make or market luxury goods or name brands and buy investments in companies that make middle-range or discount goods, store brands, and even generic products. When pursuing this strategy, make sure that your impression of a company and its products matches the reality of what people actually buy.

- It's also crucial to remember that stocks are priced based on future earnings and dividends, so stocks predict the turning points of the business cycle. Therefore, investors need to act ahead of time because stock prices recover and start to rise again before economic growth actually picks back up.

- Many investors who want to time the business cycle search for all kinds of interesting macroeconomic data that are hopefully the earliest leading indicators. The idea is that these special indicators can reveal business cycle turning points even before most companies experience them. If you can rearrange your portfolio before the rest of the market realizes what's going on, then you could generate good returns.

- Of the many indicators that exist, there are 3 that are especially interesting. First, there's the price of copper, which is still a staple good in most manufactured products because everything runs on electricity. Because of this, the price of copper rises and falls as businesses expand and contract their production. Additionally, because copper is an input, its price will start to rise well in advance of an upturn in the economy—and fall in advance of a downturn.

- A second indicator is the Job Openings and Labor Turnover Survey (JOLTS), which is published each month by the Bureau of Labor Statistics and gives a much more in-depth picture of the labor market than the unemployment rate does. Because of the unique data it gathers—including whether people are quitting or being laid off from work—the JOLTS can help people spot emerging trends in the labor market whose impacts won't be felt in the overall economy for a while.

- Finally, an indicator that shows just how arcane these indicators can be is the sales of corrugated cardboard boxes. The idea is that big-ticket

The invasion of the real estate market by inexperienced investors might be a signal that a bubble has formed.

merchandise is all shipped in large cardboard boxes and that the demand for cardboard boxes increases when companies anticipate that they'll be selling more of these items.

Interest Rate Cycles

- Interest rates tend to vary over the business cycle, but they march to a slightly different beat because of the large influence that our central bank, the Federal Reserve, has on interest rates and credit. The Fed is responsible for 2 things: to fight inflation and to help the economy maintain high employment and robust growth. As a result, sometimes the Fed's actions are motivated by fears of inflation, and at other times, its actions are intended to stimulate the economy.

- When the Fed takes action in the financial markets, it does so in ways that raise and lower the cost of borrowing. This, in turn, affects the returns on other assets like stocks. Therefore, whenever the Fed takes strong action against inflation, borrowing costs go up rapidly and credit shrinks. On the other hand, when the Fed tries to stimulate the economy, interest rates fall and credit becomes easier to get.

- The influence of the Fed on the economy is always debated, but it's impact on the financial markets is strong: When the Fed makes interest rates go up, prices of financial assets tend to fall, and when the Fed makes interest rates fall, asset prices tend to rise.

- The problem is that are thousands of professional investors who are already watching the Fed—and all the other economic indicators. Most importantly, these other investors are already adjusting their portfolios to reflect their beliefs about the future of interest rates and of the business cycle.

- Even though that there are some strong cycles in the financial markets, trying to use them to time the market isn't worth your trouble. The signals that these cycles give on a day-to-day basis aren't clear enough to be reliable.

- The best strategy to use, therefore, is **dollar-cost averaging**, which involves investing a certain amount of money each month and staying fully invested in the market at all times. If you do that, your investing will naturally tend to smooth out many short-term—and even long-term—bumps and dips in prices. The average cost of your investments will end up on the lower side of the range, which gives you a good chance to earn solid returns over the long term.

Important Terms

bear market: A market in which bonds and other securities are declining in value.

bull market: A market in which bonds and other securities are rising in value.

business cycle: The cycle of expansion and recession that characterizes our overall economy.

cyclical company: A company that is strongly tied to the business cycle because it is a manufacturer or distributor of big-ticket consumer items like cars, appliances, and furniture.

dollar-cost averaging: A strategy that involves investing a certain amount of money each month and staying fully invested in the market at all times.

technical analysis: A type of analysis that uses information in prices as well as in the volume of trading to make predictions about future price movements.

Suggested Reading

Bodie, Kane, and Marcus, *Essentials of Investments*, chaps. 9 and 12.

Zweig, "Why Buying on the Dips Isn't All It's Cracked Up to Be."

Questions to Consider

1. One of the things that technical analysis is known for is finding meaningful patterns in price charts that supposedly predict price increases or decreases. One of the best known of these patterns is the head and shoulders formation. Do an Internet search for the term "head and shoulders formation" and read a few articles on this famous pattern. What is it supposed to predict? Do you believe that it works? If so, do you think you could identify such a pattern in time to benefit from it?

2. The National Bureau of Economic Research (NBER) is responsible for designating the start and end of business cycles. Its complete list of American business cycles can be found at http://www.nber.org/cycles/cyclesmain.html. Go to this website and look at the information about the most recent business cycle. Are we currently in an expansion or a contraction? Given that the average cycle is between 5.5 and 6 years long, are we due for a change from expansion to contraction or vice versa? How does the current phase of the business cycle affect your investment plans?

Cycles and Market Timing
Lecture 19—Transcript

So far we've spent a lot of time in this course learning about all different types of investments, but I think it's time to move on to some other very important issues that all investors should understand.

The issue we'll learn about in this lecture is the role of economic cycles in financial markets, and what they mean to you as an investor. If you pay even a little bit of attention to the financial press, you've probably seen many different articles claiming that "now is the time to buy consumer stocks" or "now is the time to dump your bonds" or any number of similar claims. Each one urges you to buy or sell some broad category of investment, and some even advise people to get out of the market completely. All of these articles claim that some economic cycle that predicts the market or even drives the market has reached a critical turning point. And this means that investors need to rearrange their portfolios right now in order to benefit from this opportunity, or avoid disaster.

These claims are virtually guaranteed to raise your anxiety level as an investor, so in this lecture, we'll try to ease that anxiety. We'll learn about 3 important cycles that affect the financial markets. And we'll also learn whether the existence of these cycles means that you can, or should, try to time your investments according to these cycles.

Let's start by looking at price cycles in financial markets, exemplified by the bull and bear market cycles in the stock market. It's hard to deny that most financial markets seem to go through periods of generally rising prices and optimistic sentiment about future prices, followed by periods of widespread decline in prices and investor pessimism.

The existence of bull and bear markets leads investors to try to time their buying and selling of stocks and other securities. According to market timers, the best times to buy are actually at the ends of bear markets and the beginnings of bull markets, because at those times the market prices are relatively low and are on their way up. And of course, the time to sell is at the end of the bull market, when prices are peaking.

Sounds great, right? There's only one little problem—how can you tell when a bull market is ending or a bear market is beginning? Prices don't rise smoothly during bull markets or fall smoothly during bear markets—they tend to bounce up and down from day to day. And while it's true that in a bull market the increases in price outweigh the decreases, even in the middle of a bull market there can be some pretty big market losses. For example, consider what people call the greatest bull market in U.S. history, which ran from 1982 until late in the year 2000. In October 1987, there was the Black Monday crash, when the market lost a quarter of its value in just a few days.

Put yourself in the shoes of an investor who just experienced that loss. You'd have to ask yourself, is this the end of the bull market, which has already lasted almost 5 years? How could anyone have predicted that this would turn out to be just a hiccup—albeit a pretty big one—in a bull market that would run for another 13 years? I certainly don't recall anyone making that kind of an argument at the time.

Figuring out when bull and bear markets are coming to an end is, to say the least, pretty difficult. But there is an investment strategy that actually does try to figure out whether price trends will continue on or reverse themselves. It's called technical analysis, but because it relies heavily on examining charts and graphs of stock prices, the practitioners of technical analysis are often called "Chartists." Technical analysis uses information in prices, as well as in the volume of trading, to make predictions about future price movements.

Judging by the abundance of technical analysis tools on investing websites, most investors seem to believe that technical analysis is useful. Just about any free financial website that provides price quotes will also enable you to use some technical analysis on past prices, so I take this as a sign that this method of technical analysis must be in high demand from investors. I think the appeal of technical analysis comes from the fact that when we look at prices we can see obvious trends in past prices. Technical analysis tries to identify current price trends, so that we can take advantage of them.

There are many different technical analysis tools, but I'll talk about 3 of the most common. As I mentioned a minute ago, one of the hallmarks of technical analysis is the charts and graphs that the analysts make. These charts and graphs often track moving averages of prices over time. Let me explain what a moving average is by giving you an example.

Suppose I have data on the daily closing prices of a stock or a stock index over the past 10 years. Then I have roughly 2500 daily prices. Instead of looking at only the graph of these prices, I'm going to do the following mathematical operation on these prices and then add this to the chart.

I'm going to take the first 50 days of data, call them days 1 through 50, and calculate their average price. And then I'll take days 2 through 51 and calculate their average price. And then I'll take the average of day 3 through day 52, and so on until I reach the end of the data set. The resulting set of numbers is called a 50-day moving average.

Moving averages are tools that help reveal the trends in a set of data because they smooth out the short-term bumps. And technical analysis is all about looking for trends in prices. What technical analysis usually does is to calculate not one set but two sets of moving averages. One set of moving averages will typically be this 50-day moving average. The other set of moving averages will use the same data, but take a 200-day moving average. Then the chartist will put both moving averages, along with the actual prices, on the same graph.

The chartist looks over the graph to see whether the actual daily price line rises above, or falls below, both sets of moving averages. If the price line rises above both sets of moving averages, this is a bullish sign that the price will continue to rise. And if the price falls below both moving averages, it's a bearish sign. Of course, there are also specific formations in these moving averages that some technical analysts will look for, but these are highly subjective and much less simple to see.

In addition to these charts of moving averages, technical analysis uses data on breadth and trading volume. The breadth of the market is simply the number of companies that gain in value during some period of time, minus the number of companies that lose value during that period. People who talk about breadth usually convert the numbers to ratios, so they use phrases like "gainers outnumber losers two to one" or similar language. The stronger the breadth on the side of the gainers, the stronger the bullish signal is; the stronger the breadth on the side of the losers, the stronger the bearish signal is.

The final technical analysis statistic that's worth understanding is the so-called TRIN, which is short for Traders' Index. The TRIN is a ratio formed by taking the average number of shares traded of the companies whose prices fell, and dividing this by to the average number of shares traded of the companies whose prices rose. So this is related to breadth, but factors in the volume—that is, the number of shares traded—as well. If the TRIN is greater than one, it's a bearish signal to investors. It means that there are a lot of sellers pushing the losing shares down, but not as many buyers pushing the gaining shares up, so on net there is negative pressure on prices. If the TRIN is less than one, though, it's a bullish signal.

These technical analysis tools are intended to identify existing trends in prices and also to predict when the trends are about to reverse themselves. Those things would be really good to know, especially if the information is reliable. So, is it?

Economists have studied this question extensively, and generally, the answer is mixed. Some studies find that technical analysis works, at least a little bit, while other studies conclude that it doesn't work at all. But even the studies that find some benefit from technical analysis tend to find that the benefits are so small that they are more than offset by the increase in trading costs that you would incur if you let technical analysis tell you when to buy and sell.

One of the big problems with technical analysis is that its predictions always look better in hindsight. That is, once you see how the market actually performed, it's easy to go and find patterns in the prices. It's much harder to make a successful bet before you know whether there really is a trend, or just a false signal of a trend.

Another type of price cycle that would be good to be able to detect, especially given the experiences in various financial markets during the past two decades, is a price bubble. If an asset's price has a bubble in it, then we could get out of that market and wait until the bubble bursts, right?

Well, that depends on whether we can actually tell when stock prices, or the prices of any other assets, have bubbles in them. The challenge of identifying price bubbles captured the attention of economics researchers back in the late 1980s, when the question of a stock price bubble came up in connection with the great bull market. What the economists found was that they couldn't come up with a reliable test for the existence of bubbles in any asset's price. The reason why is pretty simple, and it has an important lesson for investors.

When an economist wants to test whether an asset price has a bubble in it, the economist first has to assume some fundamentals-based model of the asset's value. Well, there are several different fundamentals-based models, and lots of variations on each one. If an economist finds a bubble in the price of an asset, she can't be sure whether there actually is a bubble, or whether her fundamentals-based model of the price of the asset is wrong. So we really can't know, at least in a statistical sense, if a bubble is present.

Hopefully this brings to mind what we learned in the lecture about fundamentals-based stock pricing. Small changes in the parameters of the DDM led to really large changes in the implied values of the companies. So it's entirely plausible that a fundamentals-based model that seems okay actually leads to a false conclusion about the existence of a bubble.

Since there aren't any reliable tests for bubbles, investors tend to use other measures of value, as well as their own intuition about what's happening in the markets. For example, P/E ratios or other comparables-based measures are commonly used to make arguments about bubbles. In fact, after the company LinkedIn went public in 2011, people pointed out that its P/E ratio was a whopping 666, and used this evidence to argue that we were witnessing the start of a second dotcom bubble.

In addition, investors also use anecdotal evidence of herd behavior and other forms of so-called irrational exuberance to argue that bubbles have formed. For example, one rule of thumb that has existed at least since the 1920s takes the form of, "if your cab driver is giving you stock tips, it's time to get out of the market."

Bubble markets seem to be taken over by a gold-rush type atmosphere in which people who never cared about investing before are suddenly drawn to a particular market. Do you remember the day trading craze of the dotcom boom? How about all the house flippers who invaded the real estate market in 2005 and 2006? The invasion of a market by inexperienced investors who don't even believe they need to learn the ropes is, in my mind, one of those hard to measure but easy to see signals that a bubble has formed in a particular market.

Knowing or suspecting that there's a price bubble, and staying out of the market are two different things. As we've seen before in the dotcom boom as well as in the real estate bubble of the mid-2000s, these episodes can go on for years. It's hard to watch lots of other investors get rich, at least on paper, and it's tempting to think that you can join in the fun, for just a little while, and then get out of the market before the party ends.

On the other hand, some people become convinced that the bubble has to burst very soon, and they try to take short positions. Either way, bubbles are so unpredictable that neither strategy is really advisable. If you really do think there's a price bubble in some market, you should try to stay out of it until you're sure the bubble has burst, or you're sure you were wrong about the bubble. In the meantime, find other good investments for your savings.

So it's really tough to call the turning points of asset price cycles, even in markets that seem to have bubbles in them. Because of this difficulty, a popular rule of thumb has developed over the years that avoids trying to call the turning points, but still tries to time the market. This rule of thumb simply says, "buy on the dips." That is, wait to buy into the market until there is a significant fall in prices, say 5% or so.

This advice seems pretty attractive, but how does it work as an investment strategy? Unfortunately, it doesn't seem to do that great either. Some dips are just interruptions in a longer upward trend, but other dips occur right before the market falls. In other words, there's nothing really special about small dips in the market that would lead you to believe that the dips are better times to invest than any other time. And if you try to increase the size of the dip, say to 10%, then your strategy just starts to look like plain old market timing.

So far, we've been learning about price cycles in financial markets. Let's move on to the second major type of cycle that investors pay attention to—the business cycle. The business cycle is the cycle of expansion and recession that characterizes our overall economy. The typical business cycle tends to last about 4 years, and we spend a little over half the time in expansion and the rest in recession. During the past couple of decades, though, economists noticed that the business cycle was getting longer, and the amount of time spent in recession was getting shorter. Economists referred to this as "the great moderation." Whether the great moderation is a permanent development or just a temporary phenomenon remains to be seen.

But regardless of the length of the business cycle, it has definite impacts on the markets for various investments. Stocks are especially sensitive to the business cycle, because corporate earnings react strongly to the state of the overall economy. But the flow of credit to business, and the risk of default, also depend on the state of the business cycle, so bond returns also vary significantly over the business cycle.

Many companies' fortunes are so strongly tied to the business cycle that they're referred to as cyclical companies or cyclical stocks. These are the manufacturers and distributors of big-ticket consumer items like cars, appliances, and furniture. When the economy is expanding healthily, families are more willing and able to purchase a new car or appliances, generally on credit. But when the economy turns down and families worry about layoffs, they postpone any big or non-necessary expense—so these products are among the first expenses that families cut in a recession.

The companies that make these products have high profits during the boom times and low profits or even big losses during the recessions. Their stocks vary over the business cycle, which means that some investors try to move investments into these industries when the business cycle turns up, and move investments out when the recession comes.

A similar strategy involves luxury goods and lower-priced goods. During expansions, incomes are rising and people tend to buy more luxury goods, or higher-priced name brand versions of the products they buy every day. For example, they'll buy Tide detergent instead of the store brand. And of course, this is reversed when the economy goes into a recession. This leads to an old rule of thumb that says, in a recession, sell whiskey and buy beer. In other words, sell off your investments in companies that make or market luxury goods or name brands, and buy investments in companies that make middle-range or discount goods, store brands, and even generic products. This trading down and trading up behavior of consumers gets more pronounced, the stronger the expansion or contraction, and the longer it lasts.

Of course, you need to be careful when you pursue this strategy to make sure that your impression of a company and its products matches the reality of what people actually buy. For example, some manufacturers of name brand products also have a thriving business in producing store brands, so they will do well in either an expansion or a recession. If you don't know that, though, you could mistakenly sell their shares at the start of a recession.

It's also crucial to remember that stocks are priced based on future earnings and dividends, so that the market is always pricing stocks based on their future performance. This means that stocks actually predict the turning points of the business cycle, and not the other way around. In fact, the S&P 500 stock index has been one of the components of the Index of Leading Economic Indicators for a long time. What that means for investors is that they can't wait until the recession comes, or the recovery for that matter, to make adjustments to their portfolios. They need to act ahead of time, because stock prices recover and start to rise again before economic growth actually picks back up. This makes the job of the investor who times the market based on the business cycle that much more difficult.

Many investors who want to time the business cycle search for all kinds of interesting macroeconomic data that are hopefully the earliest leading indicators. The idea is that these special indicators can reveal business cycle turning points even before most companies experience them. If you're the first one to know about the change in the business cycle, and can rearrange your portfolio before the rest of the market realizes what's going on, then you could generate good returns. Everyone who follows this strategy has their own favorite set of indicators, but I'll mention 3 interesting ones here.

First, there's the price of copper. Copper is still a staple good in most manufactured products, since everything runs on electricity these days. Nothing seems to work for electric connections quite as well as copper. Because of its nearly universal presence, the price of copper rises and falls as businesses expand and contract their production. This relationship has performed so well over the decades that some people call copper "Dr. Copper" because it diagnoses the state of the economy. And since copper is an input, its price will start to rise well in advance of an upturn in the economy, and fall in advance of a downturn.

A second indicator, which also has a great name, is the JOLTS survey, published the second Tuesday of each month by the Bureau of Labor Statistics. The name JOLTS stands for Job Openings and Labor Turnover Survey, and it gives a much more in-depth picture of the labor market than the unemployment rate does. The JOLTS survey shows how many job openings there are, it breaks down whether people are quitting or being laid off of work, and it shows what industries are doing all the hiring.

As with Dr. Copper, the JOLTS survey can help people spot emerging trends in the labor market whose impacts won't be felt in the overall economy for a while. For example, one key part of the JOLTS survey is the number of people who have quit their jobs. If the quit rate rises, this is a sign that more people are finding better jobs, which is a positive sign.

Finally, one indicator that shows just how arcane these indicators can be is the sales of corrugated cardboard boxes. The idea there is that big-ticket merchandise, like electronics, furniture, and appliances, is all shipped in big cardboard boxes. When companies order more of these products, their suppliers need to order more boxes to ship them in. So the demand for cardboard boxes goes up when companies anticipate that they'll be selling more of these big-ticket items. Incidentally, this one was supposed to be one of Alan Greenspan's favorite indicators when he was the chairman of the Federal Reserve.

Mentioning the Federal Reserve brings me to the third important cycle you should know about—the interest rate cycle, or the credit cycle. As I mentioned a few minutes ago, interest rates tend to vary over the business cycle. But they march to a slightly different beat. That's because of the large influence of our central bank, the Federal Reserve (Fed), on interest rates and credit.

The Fed is responsible for two things—on the one hand, it's an inflation fighter. But on the other, it's also responsible for helping the economy maintain high employment and robust growth. So sometimes the Fed's actions are motivated by fears of inflation, while at other times, its actions are intended to stimulate the economy.

This dual mandate, as it's called, means that the Fed isn't always reacting to the state of the business cycle. In fact, most of the time the Fed is trying to act before inflation, or recession, get to be real problems. For example, one former Chairman of the Fed, William McChesney Martin, famously said that the job of the Fed was to take the punch bowl away just when the party was getting interesting.

When the Fed takes action in the financial markets, it does so in ways that raise and lower the cost of borrowing. And this, in turn, affects the returns on other assets like stocks, since stocks are substitutes for bonds. So whenever the Fed takes strong action against inflation, borrowing costs go up rapidly and credit shrinks. On the other hand, when the Fed tries to stimulate the economy, interest rates fall and credit becomes easier to get.

The influence of the Fed on the economy is always debated, but its impact on the financial markets is pretty clear. When the Fed makes interest rates go up, prices of financial assets tend to fall, and when the Fed makes interest rates fall, asset prices tend to rise. In fact, the influence of the Fed on the financial markets is so strong that just about every bank and financial company has at least one economist who is in charge of what we call "Fed-Watching."

A Fed-watcher sorts through all the public statements of the Federal Reserve's Board of Governors and other economists, looking for clues about what the Fed will do to interest rates and credit at its next Open-Market Committee meeting. These meetings take place about every 6 weeks. If you anticipate that the Fed will decide to cut interest rates or otherwise push more money into the economy at its next meeting, then you can try to boost your holdings of stocks and bonds to benefit from the increases in stock and bond prices that should result from this decision.

Now, here's the problem—and it's the same problem with trying to time your investments over the business cycle, too. There are thousands of professional investors out there who are already watching the Fed and all these economic indicators. They're actually calculating the probabilities of changes in interest rates and other indicators, based on what has been happening in the markets. And most importantly, these other investors are already adjusting their portfolios to reflect their beliefs about the future of interest rates and the future of the business cycle.

So if you're going to try to time the market, you're automatically putting yourself into competition with thousands of investors who are more informed and have more resources at their disposal to make predictions and strategies. And they're already pushing market prices around. Again, this should sound a lot like the efficient markets hypothesis to you—because that's what's going on. The professional investors are making market prices reflect what they know and believe about the future. So in order for you to be a successful market timer, you have to somehow do a better job than these professionals at predicting when the business cycle will turn a corner, or when the Fed will decide to raise and lower the interest rates. Because if you don't, then you can't expect to earn anything more than the average return for all your efforts.

Hopefully, I've convinced you that even though there are some strong cycles in the financial markets, trying to use them to time the market just isn't worth your trouble. The signals that these cycles give on a day-to-day basis just aren't clear enough to be reliable. So you could end up buying or selling at terrible times, all the while thinking that you're doing the right thing.

So where does that leave you? Well, I almost hate to have to say it, because it's one of those things that you've probably already heard 100 times, but your best bet is to use dollar-cost averaging. This is also known as investing a certain amount each month, and staying fully invested in the market at all times. If you do that, your investing will naturally tend to smooth out a lot of the short-term bumps and dips in prices. This happens because some months your investments will be cheaper, and you can buy more units, and other months they'll be more expensive, and you'll buy fewer units. The average cost of your investments will end up on the lower side of the range, which gives you a good chance to earn solid returns over the long haul.

In addition, if you stay in the market long enough, then dollar-cost averaging also helps to smooth out the much larger dips and bumps as well. For example, suppose you invest a certain amount each month in stocks, and a price bubble forms for a year and then bursts. If you stay in the market for several years after that, the effect of the bubble on your investments will fade because you have only invested a small portion of your wealth into overpriced shares, and even those shares will have time to recover.

The thing to remember about investing is, to steal a phrase from the technical analysts, the trend is your friend. Not the short-term trends that many investors chase, but the long-term trends that drive economic growth. Economic theory says that in the long run, the size of our economy and our financial markets is driven by the size of the population and the level of technology. As long as both of these keep growing, there will be solid growth in the economy, as well as in the prices of the assets that form the foundation of the economy, over the long haul. The longer you can stay invested in the market, the more your wealth will benefit from, and come to mimic, these long-run growth patterns.

So, when you see the articles urging you to buy now or sell now, relax. Yes, the markets will cycle, spin, gyrate, and make all kinds of other moves as well, but they're all wobbles around the long-run trend, which is moving steadily upwards. Use dollar-cost averaging, and stay invested in the market, so you can take full advantage of that.

Deciding When to Sell
Lecture 20

In all the previous lectures, you've been learning about buying. However, once you buy various types of investments, you're eventually going to have to sell them—if for no other reason than needing to convert them to cash one day. Knowing when to sell an investment is just as important as knowing what to buy. It turns out, though, that making the decision to sell an investment can be difficult. In this lecture, you'll learn about the different reasons you'd want to sell your investments so that you can formulate a selling plan that includes setting targets and annual rebalancing.

Selling Assets: Falling Prices

- Behavioral economists have developed a special term for the main problem that people have when they should be selling an investment called the **disposition effect**, which states that people hate to sell losing investments—they'll hold on to them for years, hoping that some miracle will push the price back up to what they paid.

- Behavioral economists also say that people tend to sell winning investments too quickly, but it also seems likely that people are reluctant to cash out a big winner because it may still go up in value.

- Either way, it seems that our emotions can get the better of us when it comes to selling our investments, and the only effective way to mitigate this emotional influence is to have a plan in place that tells you when you're going to sell.

- The key to selling individual assets—as opposed to index mutual funds and ETFs—is to have a plan in place that provides discipline that you can live with. The guidelines that you should follow are based on the following principle: If you're going to buy and hold an individual asset, you should have a pretty compelling reason to hold it, and if you don't, you should sell the investment. The way that you should implement this principle is to translate it into concrete numbers.

- There's a similar principle for actively managed mutual funds you may invest in. Presumably, you invest in an actively managed mutual fund because you expect it to deliver some kind of solid return over the long term—for example, 8% per year. As long as the mutual fund delivers this average return, you should keep holding on to it. If it doesn't, then you should sell your shares and move your money into a different investment.

- In general, however, don't rush to sell shares in a mutual fund just because of 1 year of bad performance. If the fund has 2 really lackluster years in a row or delivers inconsistent returns over several years, start your investigation. Sometimes the entire market isn't doing well, and your fund is actually doing better than others at holding on to its value; if that's the case, there's not much reason for selling.

- If you buy a stock because you think the price will go up—that is, because you expect capital gains from it—then set some kind of a target that would cause you to reevaluate the stock. For example, set a target of a 25% increase in price.

- For most stocks, if they increase significantly in a relatively short period of time, then they probably won't continue increasing in that manner. However, sometimes you'll find stocks that have a really large potential for continued appreciation, and you'll want to keep hanging on to those shares.

- In addition, you should set a target for reevaluating if the price falls. However, in this case, you should set the target at a smaller loss—10%, for example. At this point, you'll want to sell some investments, but you might continue to hold others if you really think the price will rebound—but if the price drops more, then you'll sell it.

- Some successful investors set targets based on the gains or losses in the overall market, rather than on their individual investments. The good thing about this strategy is that it imposes discipline on your buying and selling, but relying on the overall market is a bit too much like trying to time the market.

- In order to have the flexibility to hang on to investments that go on impressive runs, you have to be honest with yourself. It even helps to have a spouse or friend to bounce ideas off of and to defend your decisions to hang on to them.

Asset Allocation

- **Portfolio allocation** refers to the way in which you divide your investments across different investment categories. There are 2 dimensions along which you'll want to think about portfolio allocation. One dimension is the type of investments you want to hold. The second dimension is geographic—how much you want to invest in the United States, or your home-country market, versus other markets around the world.

- However you decide to divide your allocation choices, it's helpful to represent the options in a table: For example, let the rows correspond to the different geographic options and the columns to the different instruments. The key is to make your table as simple as you can while still reflecting the allocation options that are important to you.

- Once you have a table, you should fill in the boxes you've created with numbers that represent the share of your portfolio

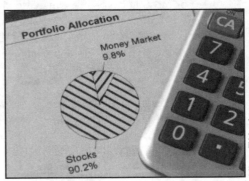

An ideal portfolio does not exist; you should adjust your allocation goals to suit your needs.

you want to hold in each of the various assets. How you decide to allocate your portfolio across these 2 dimensions depends on your preferences and beliefs.

- The most important preference is risk aversion. The safest asset you can invest in is cash held in the United States, but there are plenty of very safe investments available. In other words, you don't have to put all your money into government bonds; there are ways to get the benefits of higher returns and diversification while still having a pretty safe portfolio.

- The belief that makes the biggest difference in how you invest is how efficient you believe the markets are. The more efficient you believe they are, the more of your portfolio you should be investing into broad indexes that mimic the makeup of the entire financial market.

- The financial market is composed of many different assets, and much of the market is held outside the United States. If you take market efficiency seriously, then you technically want your portfolio allocation to mimic the actual allocation of the entire global market.

- However, there are some good reasons not to do that. Remember that just because a foreign market is large, it doesn't mean that it's efficient or even safe for investing. This is mainly true for emerging markets, but even established markets in Europe and Asia have different practices and different degrees of efficiency.

- Many people miss out on great opportunities by allocating too little of their savings to foreign assets. There is tremendous growth potential in many emerging economies, which translates into great growth opportunities in their financial markets as well. Therefore, it might be a good idea to put up to about 1/3 of your portfolio in foreign assets.

- If you're not such a strong believer in efficient markets, then you can put more of your savings into individual assets and actively managed mutual funds that you think will beat the market return. However, the more of these assets that you put in your portfolio, the more frequently you'll want to check them—and the more time you'll need to spend looking for the next round of investment candidates. This can be fun to a certain extent, but it can also become a huge chore.

- All investors should include at least some investments that they think will beat the market and at least some that track the market.

- The last asset allocation issue to keep in mind is the relative return. Although it's tempting to keep all of your savings in extremely safe investments, these investments tend to have very low average returns. Most investment advisors, therefore, recommend that everyone invest a significant portion of their savings into stocks because their average returns have tended to be much higher than the returns on bonds over the long run.

- Stocks deserve a large allocation in your portfolio—even if you're close to retirement—for 2 reasons. First, if you have enough time, then stocks will deliver significantly higher returns than bonds over the long run.

- In addition, there are many safer options for stock investments. There are ways to stay invested in stocks so that you can keep the chance for good capital gains but at the same time earn steady income, such as using covered calls to improve the return on stocks.

Selling Assets: Portfolio Rebalancing

- The first reason to sell assets is because your investment falls in price or otherwise fails to perform as you expect it to, and rebalancing is the second reason that you'll want to sell.

- As time goes by, some of your investments will have great returns and really grow in value; other investments will grow only a little, and some will even lose value. This means that, after as little time as a year, the asset allocations that you spent time agonizing over are completely unbalanced.

- If you don't occasionally readjust your portfolio, then the differences in returns that you will receive over time will gradually reshape your portfolio into something you don't recognize. Your portfolio could increase its sensitivity to assets you don't want much exposure to, and it could become concentrated in a few assets. Both of those situations could lead to nasty surprises.

- Therefore, you should recheck your allocations at least once a year and rebalance your portfolio. This includes selling off parts of the investments that now take up a larger share of your portfolio than you like and using the money to buy more of the investments that have become underrepresented.

- When you rebalance your portfolio, you'll end up selling portions of the assets that have gained the most and buying more of the assets that have had the lowest returns. Therefore, if you're disciplined about rebalancing, then you don't have to feel as bad about giving up market timing.

- Economists have found that portfolio rebalancing can add a few tenths of a percent of return to your investing if you stick to it, and this small percentage can make a significant difference over the long run.

- Of course, your target allocation for your portfolio won't necessarily stay the same over time. In fact, most experts recommend that you change your allocation significantly as you get older and closer to your investing goals.

- In particular, everyone should increase the share of their savings in low-risk assets like government bonds as they get closer to needing the money they've saved. You don't want to be in a position where you need to spend cash tomorrow, but a market crash wipes out your savings today. However, as always, what looks good on paper is much harder to do in real life.

- Each year, when it comes time to rebalance your portfolio, this is your chance to cash out some of the gains you've made from your investments and put that cash into bonds.

Important Terms

disposition effect: An effect that describes the notion that people hate to sell losing investments—they'll hold on to them for years, hoping that some miracle will push the price back up to what they paid.

portfolio allocation: The way in which you divide your investments across different investment categories.

Suggested Reading

Bogle, *Common Sense on Mutual Funds*, chap. 3.

Stewart, "Breaking Up Is Hard to Do."

Swensen, *Unconventional Success*, chap. 6.

Questions to Consider

1. Without looking at your actual investment portfolio, guess what its allocations are across asset classes and across geographic regions. To keep things simple, use only 3 or 4 asset classes such as bank deposits (and money market mutual funds), stocks (and stock mutual funds), bonds (and bond mutual funds), and other investments. Then, divide the geographic regions into the United States, other developed markets, and emerging markets. Draw a table or create a table on a spreadsheet and fill in the boxes to the best of your memory. Then, compare your table to your actual portfolio's allocations. How did you do? Does your memory reflect the ancient past of your portfolio, the current reality, or wishful thinking about the future of your portfolio?

2. Similarly, look through the recent performance of your investments for big gainers and for big losers. Is it time to sell one or more of your big gainers? If not, what is your compelling reason for continuing to hold each investment? Is it time to sell one or more of your big losers? If not, what is your compelling reason for holding on?

Deciding When to Sell
Lecture 20—Transcript

In all the lectures up to now, I've been talking about buying—buying stocks, buying bonds, buying mutual funds, ETFs, and even options. But once you buy all these investments, you're eventually going to have to sell them—if for no other reason, because some day you'll need to convert them to cash. And as you might imagine, knowing when to sell an investment is as important as knowing what to buy.

It turns out, though, that selling an investment can be really hard to do. The transaction itself isn't hard at all, unless the market for the investment is small and illiquid, and we've learned to steer clear of those kinds of investments. What's hard is actually making the decision to sell. You may recall that we learned all the way back in the first lecture that we're often our own worst enemies when it comes to investing. Well, selling is one of those times.

Selling is so hard that behavioral economists have developed a special term for the main problem that people have when they should be selling an investment. It's called the disposition effect. This effect says that people hate to sell losing investments—they'll hold on to them for years, hoping that some miracle will push the price back up to what they paid.

Behavioral economists also say that we tend to sell our winning investments too quickly. But I'm not as convinced by that effect. I think that people also are reluctant to cash out a big winner, because it may still go up in value. If you're holding a stock that's already doubled in value, but you think it's the next Google, you'd be a fool to sell it, right?

Either way, it seems that our emotions can get the better of us when it comes to selling our investments. And the only effective way to mitigate this emotional influence is to have a plan in place that tells you when you're going to sell. In this lecture, we'll learn about the different reasons why you'd want to sell your investments, so that you can formulate your own selling plan.

I'm going to start by tackling the disposition effect head on. So I'm mainly thinking about an investing context in which you've bought a particular asset, like a stock, or maybe an actively managed mutual fund. This discussion really isn't aimed that much at passive investments like index mutual funds and ETFs. We'll talk about when to sell those investments in a few minutes.

The whole key to selling individual assets is to have a plan in place that provides discipline you can actually live with. So what I'm going to recommend are not so much hard and fast rules, but guidelines—reality checks, really. And these reality checks are based on the following principle. If I'm going to buy and hold an individual asset, I should have a pretty compelling reason to hold it. And if I don't, I should just sell the investment.

The way that you should implement this principle is to translate it into some concrete numbers. If you buy an individual stock, it must be because you expect it to deliver some solid return. If you buy a stock because of its high dividend yield, then presumably you can hold it as long as it keeps delivering that high dividend for you. If it stops doing that, you should reevaluate the stock with the presumption that you'll sell it unless you find some other compelling reason to hold it.

There's a similar reality check for actively managed mutual funds you may invest in. Presumably, you invest in an actively managed mutual fund because you expect it to deliver some kind of solid return over the long haul—like 8% per year. And you're confident about this, because you've done your homework and checked the mutual fund's long-term performance, as well as its actual investments. As long as the mutual fund delivers this average return, you should keep holding on to it. But if it really starts look like it can't deliver any more, then you should sell your shares in it and move your money into a different investment.

This is a little trickier than selling off a stock that doesn't pay good dividends anymore, because the mutual fund manager may simply be having a bad year, and that happens. So in general, don't rush out to sell shares in a mutual fund just because of one year of bad performance. But if the fund has two really lackluster years in a row, or delivers inconsistent returns over several years, start your investigation. Of course, sometimes the entire market isn't doing well, and your fund is actually doing better than others at holding on to its value. If you think that's the case, there's not much reason for selling. But if you look into the fund and find that the managers have changed, or the fund's investments have changed significantly, it may be time to look for other investments to switch into.

Now let's consider when to sell stocks that you're holding because you expect capital gains from them. The capital gains are your compelling reason to hold them. If you buy a stock because you think the price will go up, then set some kind of a target that would cause you to reevaluate the stock. For example, set a target of a 25% increase in price. If your stock's price rises by 25%, then take the time to reevaluate whether you think it still has significant appreciation potential. For most stocks, my guess is that if they go up that much in a relatively short period, then it's hard to think that they'll keep going up significantly. But once in a while you'll find stocks that have a really large potential for continued appreciation, and you'll want to keep hanging on to those shares.

Also, you should set a target for reevaluating if the price falls. But here, you have to be careful with the target. Remember the danger of that disposition effect—the more the price falls, the harder it's actually going to be to make yourself sell the investment. So my suggestion is to set the target at a smaller loss, say 10%. Again, you're not committing to sell if the price falls 10%—you're just going to reevaluate the investment at that point. Some you'll actually want to sell, but others, you'll end up putting on probation, or if you're a fan of the old movie *Animal House*, double-secret probation. The idea with probation is that you continue to hold an investment if you really think the price will rebound—but if the price drops some more, so that the total decrease in price is, say, 15% below what you paid, then you'll sell it.

I know that some successful investors set targets based on the gains or losses in the overall market, rather than on their individual investments. For example, some investors recommend that you sell off some of your winners when the overall market rises by 25%, and buy the investments you've had your eye on whenever the market declines by 10%. The good thing about this strategy is that it imposes discipline on your buying and selling, and for the most part that's a good thing. But relying on the overall market strikes me as a bit too much like trying to time the market, which as you know, I'm not a fan of. I'd much rather consider investments on their own merits, but still use this idea of targets to impose some discipline on my selling.

I'd also like to have the flexibility to hang on to investments that go on impressive runs. Again, the idea is that I want to be able to hold on to an Amazon or a Google during their heydays, as long as I think their increase in value is coming from some legitimate source, and not just speculation. But in order to make this work, you have to be honest. Do I really think this stock is a great company, or is this just wishful thinking? Here's where it helps to have a spouse or friend to bounce ideas off of, and to defend your decisions to. Having to explain your decisions to someone with a skeptical ear is the best reality check I know of.

Now let's move on to the next big reason why you will want to sell—portfolio rebalancing. In order to learn about portfolio rebalancing, we should first learn more about portfolio allocation—that is, how you have your investments divided up across different investment categories. So let's talk about portfolio allocation now, and then later we'll turn to rebalancing.

Given what we've been learning about in this course, you can probably guess that there are two dimensions along which you'll want to think about portfolio allocation. One dimension, of course, is the type of investments you want to hold. In this course, we've learned about several big categories of investments, such as bonds, stocks, real estate, and commodities. We've also learned about mutual funds and ETFs, but these actually represent different ways to invest in each of these main categories of investments. For example, you could hold 20% of your portfolio in bonds, and this could be a mixture of bonds you hold directly and shares in bond mutual funds.

The second dimension to your allocation decision is geographic—how much you want to invest in the United States, or your home-country market, versus other markets around the world. You could see this as a simple decision between the United States and the rest of the world, or you can break down the geography in different ways. For example, you could simply divide up the world regionally: Europe, Latin America, Asia-Pacific, Middle East, and

Africa, for example. Or you could divide up the rest of the world between foreign developed markets and emerging markets.

However you decide to divide up your allocation choices, it's helpful to represent the options in a table. We'll let the rows of the table correspond to the different geographic options, and the columns of the table represent the different instruments. I'd put these columns in it that stand for the main categories of investments: cash, bonds, stocks, real estate, commodities, and other investments. Note that I've added two categories to the ones I mentioned a minute ago. One is cash, and this could be in the form of a short-term bank deposit, a money market mutual fund, or money held in your brokerage account. The other category is other investments, and that is simply a catchall category. For example, you may still want to invest in foreign currency or in derivatives, even after learning about their risks.

As far as geography goes, I'll keep it simple and put in rows for the United States, developed foreign markets, and emerging markets. But you should build your table to represent the main options that are important to you. If you want to be more precise about how you allocate your portfolio geographically, go ahead and add the relevant rows. Similarly, you may want to further break down the types of investments you want to represent in your allocation. For example, you could break down the bonds category into government bonds and private bonds. Or you could break down the stocks category into large-cap and small-cap categories. The key is to make your table as simple as you can, but still reflect the allocation options that are important to you.

Once you have a table, now comes the hard part—filling in those boxes with numbers that represent the share of your portfolio you want to hold in each of these different assets. How you decide to allocate your portfolio across these two dimensions depends on your preferences and beliefs—things that we've been talking about throughout this course. What I'll do now is discuss how some key preferences and beliefs affect how you want to divide up your investments across instruments and across countries.

Let's start with the most important preference—risk aversion. Notice that I've set up the table so that the safer assets are on the upper left-hand side of the table. So the safest asset you can invest in is cash, held in the United States. The more risk-averse you are, the larger the numbers you'll put in the upper-left-hand corner of the table and the smaller the numbers will be as you move toward the lower right-hand side of the table. Just keep in mind that there are plenty of very safe investments available so that you don't have to put all your money into government bonds. You can get the benefits of higher returns, and diversification, while still having a pretty safe portfolio.

Similarly, if you're risk averse, this may change your understanding of the broad categories of investments we have listed in the table. Bonds to you may then only mean government bonds, and stocks may only mean broad index mutual funds, or high-dividend, large company stocks. That's fine— the idea isn't to force yourself to hold things you aren't comfortable with, but simply to help you see where your savings are and help you manage that.

Now let me turn to your beliefs about the markets. The one belief that makes the biggest difference in how you invest, of course, is how efficient you believe the markets are. The more efficient you believe they are, the more of your portfolio you should be investing into broad indexes that mimic the makeup of the entire financial market. It's hard to find a single index that covers the entire market. For example, a popular stock index is the S&P 500 index, but that only covers the largest 500 companies. If you hold only that, then you'll be missing all the mid-cap and small-cap companies, so you'll need to also buy into indexes that hold those stocks.

When it comes to holding the market, another consideration is whether you want to include assets beyond stocks and bonds. For example, in the United States the real estate market is about the same size as the bond market. And each of these markets is actually larger, in total value, than the stock market. So if you really want to mimic the breakdown of the U.S. market, you'd need to spread a little over one-third of your savings into the bond and real estate markets, and a little over a quarter into the U.S. stock market. And that doesn't even include other assets, like commodities.

Don't forget that the U.S. market is only a part of the global market. You may remember that the U.S. bond market makes up about a third of the value of the global bond market and about a quarter of the value of the global equity market. Good information on the value of the real estate market globally is hard to find, but it's difficult to imagine that the U.S. market makes up much more than 10 to 20% of the value of the world's real estate.

All this information about the actual makeup of the U.S. and global financial markets may make your head start to spin. But the point I want you to remember is that the financial market is composed of a lot of different assets, and a lot of it is held outside the United States. If you take market efficiency really seriously, then technically, you want your portfolio allocation to mimic the actual allocation of the entire global market.

Now, there are some good reasons, though, why you might not want to do that. As we learned in the lecture on foreign assets, just because a foreign market is large, that doesn't mean it's efficient or even safe for investing. This is mainly true for emerging markets, though even established markets in Europe and Asia have different practices and different degrees of efficiency. So my best advice is not to try to mimic the actual allocations of assets in the world markets.

But as I look across the advice that's commonly given to savers, I think that people are missing out on great opportunities by allocating too little of their savings to foreign assets. There is tremendous growth potential in many emerging economies, which translates into great growth opportunities in their financial markets also. In addition, as these economies grow, it's inevitable that their markets will become better regulated, more transparent, more representative of their economies, and more efficient. So I think that it's a good idea to put up to about a third of your portfolio in foreign assets. Of course, that's my opinion—if this makes you uncomfortable, then decrease this share. Maybe you don't want any foreign assets in your savings. As long as it's your own decision, that's fine.

If you're not such a strong believer in efficient markets, then you can put more of your savings into individual assets and actively managed mutual funds that you think will beat the market return. My only caution is not to bite off more than you can chew. The more of these assets that you put in your portfolio, the more frequently you'll want to check them, and the more of your time you'll need to spend looking for the next round of investment candidates. This can be fun, to a certain extent, but it can also become a huge chore. And just like professional fund managers, you probably have a limited supply of really great investment ideas.

My advice to all investors is to include at least some investments that you think will beat the market, and at least some investments that track the market. For example, even if you think the markets are very efficient, you can still put 5 to 10% of your savings, if you wish, into a couple of attractive investments. Or, if you're on the other end of the spectrum, you may find that putting, say, 15% of your portfolio in index funds that you don't have to worry about will help you find the time to manage the other 85% of your portfolio that you're actively investing.

Finally, the last asset allocation issue to keep in mind is the relative return. Although it's tempting to keep all of your savings in ultra-safe investments, and you can certainly do that, these investments tend to have very low average returns. You may remember an earlier lecture when I mentioned that short-term government bonds, for example, barely even keep up with inflation. Most investment advisors, therefore, recommend that everyone invest a significant portion of their savings into stocks, since their average returns have tended to be much higher than the returns on bonds over the long run. For people who've just started their careers, I've seen recommended allocations of up to 85% stocks, and even for people who are close to retirement many experts still recommend allocations of up to 40% in stocks.

I tend to agree that stocks deserve a big allocation in your portfolio, even if you're close to retirement, for two reasons. First, if you have enough time, then I think stocks will indeed deliver significantly higher returns than bonds over the long run. And even if you're on the verge of retirement, chances are that you'll go on to live for quite a few years. So you still have more time than you think.

The second reason that I think it's good to have a high allocation of stocks is that, as we've learned, there are lots of safer options for stock investments. For example, we've learned about high-dividend stocks and preferred shares. And we've learned about using covered calls to improve the return on stocks. So there are ways to stay invested in stocks so that you can keep the chance for good capital gains, but at the same time, earn steady income.

Well, that's a long discussion about asset allocation, but I hope that it helps you think through the choices that you need to make. Now that we've learned about the allocation step, we can move on to learn about portfolio rebalancing. Rebalancing is the second big reason why you'll want to sell assets. Remember that the first reason to sell is because your investment falls in price or otherwise fails to perform as you expect it to.

The rationale for rebalancing goes like this. As time goes by, some of your investments will have great returns and really grow in value. Other investments will grow only a little, and some will even lose value. This means that, after as little time as a year, the asset allocations that you spent all this time agonizing over are totally out of whack. Let me show you what I mean. Just for the sake of an example, let's suppose that you have $100,000 invested and your preferred allocation is 50% U.S. stocks, 30% foreign stocks, and 20% U.S. government bonds. So you have $50,000 in U.S. stocks, $30,000 in foreign stocks, and $20,000 in U.S. government bonds.

Let's say a year goes by, and you look at the current values of your investments. Let's suppose that U.S. stocks had a poor year, and only returned 4%. This means that your U.S. stocks increased in value to $52,000. But foreign stocks had a great year, gaining a total of 20%. So they increased in value to $36,000. And government bonds gained 5%, so they went up in value to $21,000.

If you add up all the new values, your portfolio has increased in value to $109,000. So your total return was 9%, which is actually pretty good. But now, notice that the shares of each investment in your portfolio have changed. Now your U.S. stocks account for 52,000/109,000 = 47.7% of your portfolio, the foreign stocks account for 36,000/109,000 = 33.0% of the portfolio, and the bonds make up the remaining 21,000/109,000 = 19.3%. So the higher return on the foreign stocks means that now they make up a larger share of your portfolio, and the shares in your other investments have fallen.

You might look at this and say, so what? That's not a very big change. That's true for one year, but what if this goes on for several years? After 3 years of these same returns, and assuming no new investing into any of these assets, the share of your portfolio in foreign stocks has grown to 39.5%, and the share in U.S. stocks has shrunk to 42.8%. Now it's starting to look like a much different portfolio than the one you started with.

And that's the problem. If you don't go back occasionally and adjust your portfolio, then the differences in returns will gradually re-shape your portfolio into something you don't recognize. Your portfolio could increase its sensitivity to assets you don't want much exposure to, and it could become concentrated in a few assets. Both of those situations could lead to nasty surprises. For example, if you let your portfolio run wild, so to speak, and you end up with a much larger share in foreign bonds, then a foreign market crash can do much more damage to your portfolio than you expect.

The answer, of course, is to re-check your allocations at least once a year, and re-balance your portfolio. That means that you sell off parts of the investments that now take up a larger share of your portfolio than you like, and use the money to buy more of the investments that have become under-represented. For example, after one year, if we wanted to preserve our original allocation of 50% in U.S. stocks, 30% in foreign stocks, and 20% in U.S. government bonds, then we would sell $3300 of the foreign stocks, invest $2500 of it into U.S. stocks, and the other $800 of it into U.S. government bonds.

Notice that portfolio rebalancing actually has a little bit of market timing to it. When you rebalance your portfolio, you'll end up selling portions of the assets that have gained the most and buying more of the assets that have had the lowest returns. So if you're disciplined about rebalancing, then you don't have to feel as bad about giving up market timing. Economists have found that portfolio rebalancing can add a few tenths of a percent of return to your investing, if you stick to it. And a few tenths of a percent can make a significant difference over the long run.

Of course, your target allocation for your portfolio won't necessarily stay the same over time. In fact, most experts recommend that you change your allocation significantly as you get older and closer to your investing goals. In particular, everyone should increase the share of their savings in low-risk assets like government bonds as they get closer to needing the money they've saved.

Experts disagree over exactly how much you should have allocated to bonds as you get older, but most recommendations I've seen actually have people increase their bond holdings twice in their lives—first, when their kids get to college, and then again for retirement. For example, the share of bonds goes up to 40% when college expenses start, then it falls back to around 25% or even less until people get close to retirement. When you get close to retirement, the share goes back up above 40% to between 50 and 75%.

The rationale for doing this is quite sound, and I discussed it all the way back in my very first lecture. You don't want to be in a position where you need to spend cash tomorrow, but a market crash wipes out your savings today. But as always, what looks good on paper is much harder to do in real life.

I think that most people who take charge of their investing do so because they want to earn high returns and squeeze as much value as they can, for as long as they can, out of their investments. So for many of us, myself included, it's really hard to think about investing over half of my portfolio in bonds. I don't want to give up my exciting, high-yielding stocks for boring old government bonds!

Fortunately, though, I think there's a fairly painless way to do this, and it works through what we've just learned about—portfolio rebalancing. Each year, when it comes time to rebalance your portfolio, this is your chance to cash out some of the gains you've made from your investments and put that cash into bonds. You can think of it as a way to make sure that you hang on to the gains that your high-yielding investments have earned. And you need to remind yourself that you're still invested in these high-yielding instruments, so if they continue to do well, you'll get those gains, too. In fact, if it makes you feel better, you can tell yourself that professional gamblers often use the strategy of taking some of their gains off the table as they win them.

Do you see what I'm doing? I'm appealing to my own emotions, my sense of self-esteem, to make it easier to do something that I know is good for me, but I find hard to do. So the bonds I buy from this strategy are more than just the responsible thing I have to do to be grown up and prudent. As the pile of bonds that I buy from this rebalancing grows, I'm building a financial monument to my own clever investing. Doesn't that sound great?

In this lecture, we've really gotten into the financial planning issues that I mentioned all the way back in my first lecture. If you're an active investor trying to beat the market, you need to set realistic targets for gains and losses, and be sure to reevaluate your investments when you hit those targets.

You also need to draw out an allocation table, like I did, and fill it in. And you can't just do it once, either. You need to map out your broad allocation between riskier investments and safe investments over time, so that you keep sheltering more and more of your portfolio from sudden market drops. And once you write down an allocation, don't treat it like it's written in stone. As you learn more about how the markets work, and about your own skills and preferences as an investor, you can adjust your allocation goals. Remember that there's no ideal portfolio out there—build one that suits your needs.

Finally, also remember that selling is always going to be tough—so you need to set rules and follow them. Setting targets and sticking with annual rebalancing will help. And once in a while, you may even need to do a sales job on yourself, to make sure that you sell assets when you need to.

Risk, Return, and Diversification
Lecture 21

E veryone seems to think that as you bear more risk, you'll earn a higher return, but this really isn't true. In fact, it's an oversimplification of the true relationship between risk and return. The truth is that some risks, called systematic risks, are highly rewarded while others, called idiosyncratic risks, are worth nothing. In this lecture, you're going to learn how the risk-return relationship frames your investment choices. Additionally, you'll learn that diversification is the best way to ensure that you earn the expected returns you are entitled to, given the systematic risk you take on.

The Risk-Return Relationship

- Investments are risky because their returns are random—they're determined at least partially by chance. However, returns are one of the most important factors in our investment decision. We have to find some way of guessing what the return on an investment will be so that we can make a good decision about whether to buy it.

- Our best guess of an investment's future return is called the **expected return** because if it's really our best guess, it represents the return we truly expect the investment to deliver. There are several possible ways to calculate the expected return on an investment, but the most practical way is to use the average of past returns. The difficult part is deciding how much of the past you want to use in your average.

- The problem is that there are 2 opposing forces at work. Statistically, if everything else were equal, then you'd get the most accurate guess of future returns by using as many years of past returns as you can. However, everything else isn't equal. In particular, companies—and the entire economy—can change dramatically over time.

- We need to limit how far back we go in time when we calculate average returns. It's good to try to go back further than 10 years into the past—perhaps even out to 20 years, over several different horizons—because using more returns in the average should allow the short-term ups and downs to cancel each other out, leaving a clear picture of the long-term average return over the full range of market and economic conditions.

- Once you've estimated an expected return, it's essential to realize that you can't think of the expected return like it's the actual return that you automatically earn every year. The expected return is an average return that you should expect to earn if you hold the investment over a long period of time.

Measuring Risk

- One way to sharpen our definition of risk is to say that it is the possibility of earning a negative return on our investment; it is the chance that our actual return will fall short of what we expect it to be.

- The actual return on an investment is the sum of the expected return and the unexpected return: $R_i = E_i + U_i$, where R is the actual return, E is the expected return, U is the unexpected return, and the subscript i references the type of asset that this is. The unexpected return could be positive or negative.

- We now have a better picture of what risk is—

Financial economists have found that some risks are highly rewarded, but others are worth nothing.

getting a negative value for the unexpected return, U. However, we need to refine our measure of risk by adding in something specific about the size of the unexpected return, and we can do this in several different ways. An easy way is to use the range between the highest and lowest returns within the set of annual returns to get a feel for the size of the unexpected return.

- By examining a list of annual returns, we can develop an idea of risk in terms of how bad things could get, but hopefully the really big losses are fairly rare. We'd also like to know what the average level of risk is in our investments—how big the unexpected return is when we have a bad year, but not a disastrous year, for one of our investments. This average level of risk, known as the **standard deviation of returns**, is how most professionals view risk.

- The standard deviation of returns is a useful concept that tries to measure the average size of the unexpected return, or in other words, how much the actual return could differ from the expected return on average. Most spreadsheets have a built-in function to calculate standard deviation, so if you have a list of annual returns, it's easy to calculate the standard deviation of the returns using this function.

- We can use the standard deviation of returns to form a range of average returns. To construct this range, we take the expected return and add the standard deviation of returns to it to get the top end of the range. Then, we subtract the standard deviation of returns from the expected return to get the bottom end of the range. Basically, 2/3 of all returns will fall within this range.

Diversification

- **Diversification** is the practice of investing in several or many different assets rather than only one or a few assets. One way that investors diversify is by investing in different kinds of assets— stocks, bonds, and real estate, for example. Additionally, there are great reasons to diversify geographically by investing in foreign stocks and bonds as well as domestic stocks and bonds.

- Diversification is fairly simple to implement in practice. You don't actually need to hold that many different assets to become fairly well diversified. Additionally, there are many assets that already come prediversified—especially mutual funds and ETFs.

- Diversification isn't just about making sure that you limit your total loss by spreading out the risk; it actually reduces risk. For example, if the actual return is $R_i = E_i + U_i$ and you only have one asset— asset 1—then the actual return is going to fully reflect both the expected return and the unexpected return on asset 1.

- However, what if you added another asset, asset 2, to your investment portfolio? If you assume that 1/2 of your savings are invested in each asset, then you can calculate the total return to your portfolio by adding the returns on both assets and dividing by 2. Then, your total return is given by this equation: portfolio return = $1/2 \times (R_1 + R_2) = 1/2 \times (E_1 + E_2) + 1/2 \times (U_1 + U_2)$, where U_1 and U_2 are the unexpected returns from each asset.

- Each unexpected return may be positive or negative, or one may be positive and the other may be negative. When one is positive and the other is negative, then they tend to cancel each other out—at least a little. With only 2 assets, they will only cancel out part of their unexpected returns part of the time.

- The more assets you add, the more offsetting of unexpected returns you'll get. In other words, if you're holding many different types of assets, chances are that several of them have positive unexpected returns, but several others have negative unexpected returns. As a result, more unexpected returns will cancel each other out as you add more assets of different kinds to your portfolio, leading to actual risk reduction.

- However, there is a limit to diversification. Even if you have the most well-diversified portfolio, you will still experience unexpected returns because diversification reduces risk but can't eliminate it.

- There will also be problems if your assets really aren't as different as you thought. For example, if 2 companies seem different but both companies' profits are heavily dependent on demand in China, then their returns could move together much more than you expect, including their unexpected returns.

- **Correlation** is the statistical term that describes this comovement. Diversification works better as the correlation between the assets' returns declines. This idea helps to explain the fact that even after you fully diversify, there will still be unexpected returns in your portfolio, driving the actual return away from the expected return. This is because there are 2 different types of risk in unexpected returns, and diversification only gets rid of one of them.

- The type of risk that diversification reduces, through this cancellation process, is called **idiosyncratic risk**, which is a risk that is specific to each particular asset and doesn't share anything in common with any other assets—it's not correlated across assets. When we increase the number of assets in a portfolio, we expect that, on average, the idiosyncratic risks will cancel each other out— that the actual return will get closer to the expected return.

- The other type of risk in the unexpected return is called **systematic risk**, which is a risk that is common across assets—meaning that when this risk creates a positive unexpected return in one asset, it's doing the same thing to all other risky assets. Systematic risk is risk that you can't get rid of through diversification.

- Economists still can't quite agree on what causes systematic risk. There are many ideas, but they all seem to be similar. Most theories about the sources of systematic risk involve risks to the overall economy, to the financial markets, or to both.

- Economists know that people are risk averse, but if you compensate them, they'll bear it. Additionally, if there's a risk that they have to pay to get rid of, they'll probably put up with at least some of it. However, if there is a risk that we can get rid of for free, no risk-averse person would pass up the chance to eliminate that risk.

- Diversification gets rid of idiosyncratic risk, and you don't have to pay extra to diversify your portfolio, especially if you choose a prediversified asset like a mutual fund. Therefore, there's no reason to expect compensation for bearing idiosyncratic risk.

- Systematic risk is the risk that you can't get rid of, so in order to induce a risk-averse person to hold an asset with systematic risk, they have to be compensated for that. The compensation comes in the form of a higher expected return from holding that asset—relative to an asset with no systematic risk.

- The relationship between risk and return is that higher systematic risk leads to higher expected return. You only get paid to hold systematic risk, not all risk, and you can only expect to get paid—you won't necessarily get all the compensation you demand. Of course, if you hold the asset long enough, then your actual compensation should come close to the expected return.

- There are many different theories about what determines investment returns, but they all agree that idiosyncratic risk is worthless while systematic risk is compensated. Furthermore, they all agree that any asset that has no systematic risk should earn the risk-free rate of return—the return on a government bond. Even an asset with a highly risky return should only earn the risk-free rate on average, if all the risk is idiosyncratic risk.

- Each different theory of returns is essentially a different story about systematic risk that explains what the sources of systematic risk are and how the risk is compensated. None of these theories has proven to do a much better job at estimating expected returns than using averages of past returns.

- Even though we don't know how much systematic risk is in any given asset, there's probably a fair amount of idiosyncratic risk in most investments. Therefore, it's imperative that investors take advantage of diversification. You'll earn nothing from holding idiosyncratic risk in your investments, so try to get rid of as much as you can through diversification.

Important Terms

correlation: The statistical term that describes the comovement of 2 different companies' returns, including unexpected returns.

diversification: The practice of investing in several or many different assets rather than only one or a few assets.

expected return: The best guess of an investment's future return; represents the return that is truly expected to be delivered by the investment.

idiosyncratic risk: The type of risk in an unexpected return that is specific to each particular asset and doesn't share anything in common with any other assets; risk that you can reduce through diversification.

standard deviation of returns: A useful concept that tries to measure the average size of an unexpected return, or in other words, how much the actual return could differ from the expected return on average.

systematic risk: The type of risk in an unexpected return that is common across assets; risk that you can't get rid of through diversification.

Suggested Reading

Bodie, Kane, and Marcus, *Essentials of Investments*, chap. 5.

Bogle, *Common Sense on Mutual Funds*, chap. 1.

1. Past returns may not give a good idea of the expected returns of a company if the company's business has changed dramatically. What companies can you think of whose businesses have changed dramatically in recent years? What are the sources of the changes? Do you think these companies' expected returns have increased or decreased as a result of the changes in their businesses? Why?

2. Diversification only works if the values of different investments move in different directions—that is, if the returns on different assets have low correlations. Do you think that correlations between different investments' returns change over time? Why or why not?

Risk, Return, and Diversification
Lecture 21—Transcript

Up to this point in the course, we've been focusing on how to choose investments that earn good returns. Very early in the course, for example, we learned whether it's possible to earn returns that are better than the market return. And then, in just about every lecture covering the various instruments, we've learned something about their returns. For example, we learned about dividends as a source of good returns as well as a signal of good returns to come. And we learned about bonds that offer returns that keep up with inflation. All this talk about returns, though, should make you start to wonder where the risk is. After all, if somebody's earning a return, they must be taking on some kind of risk, right?

The relationship between risk and return is something we hear so much about that we actually tend to take it for granted. Everyone seems to know that as you bear more risk, you'll earn a higher return.

But let's take a step back from the cliché for a second and ask a couple of questions. First, do we even know what we mean by risk? And second, what if our belief that higher risk leads to higher returns isn't actually true?

I hope that second question got your attention because it really isn't true that higher risk leads to higher returns. This catchy statement is a big oversimplification of the true relationship between risk and return. Financial economists have spent decades thinking about risk and return, and what they've basically found is that not all risks are created equal. Some risks are highly rewarded, while others are literally worth nothing. Wouldn't you like to know which ones are which?

In this lecture, we're going to take a deeper look at the relationship between risk and return in investing. We'll learn a more accurate way to think about this relationship, including what kinds of risk are rewarded. And I'll explain how the risk–return relationship frames your investment choices.

To get started on this, let me go back to the first question I mentioned a minute ago. Do we really know what risk is? Well, sort of. Investments are risky because their returns are random—they're determined at least partially by chance.

To illustrate this, I gathered data on a single stock—the Kellogg Company—from one of the free financial websites. I downloaded the monthly adjusted closing price from Kellogg for the past 20 years. I'd like to have the annual prices, but most websites only give you daily and monthly data. So I calculated the annual return on Kellogg myself, where the annual return is simply the percent change from the January first adjusted closing price in one year to the January first adjusted closing price the following year. Here's what a bar graph of these annual returns looks like.

Wow! There are some really high returns in there—two of them are over 40%. But there are also some big negative returns in there, too—3 of them were losses of more than 10%, and one of them was almost a 40% loss. Plus, there doesn't seem to be any real pattern there. The returns bounce up and down unpredictably.

Notice how this randomness, or risk, changes our understanding of returns. So far, we've mostly been talking about investment returns as if we know what they're going to be. But it's hard to look at this graph and conclude that the return on Kellogg will be, say, 5% next year. Actually, based only on looking at the graph, I can't make a sensible guess at all. Next year's return may be great, but it may be awful.

And yet, we need to try to say something about next year's return, because returns are one of the most important factors in our investment decision. We have to find some way of guessing what the return on an investment will be, so that we can make a good decision about whether to buy it.

We call our best guess of an investment's future return the expected return, because if it's really our best guess, it represents the return we truly expect the investment to deliver. There are several possible ways to calculate the expected return on an investment. But the most practical way is to use the average of past returns.

That seems sensible, but it's actually a lot harder to put into practice than you might think. It's not because the calculations are hard—I think you'll agree that finding an average return is easy to do. No, the hard part is simply deciding how much of the past you want to use in your average. Do you use the past 10 years of returns, like mutual funds are required to do? Would 20 years be better? Or why not only the past 5 years?

The problem here is that there are two opposing forces at work. Statistically, if everything else was equal, then you'd get the most accurate guess of future returns by using as many years of past returns as you can. But the problem is, everything else isn't equal! In particular, companies—and the entire economy—can change dramatically over time.

For example, think about a company like IBM. Twenty years ago, IBM was one of the big producers of desktop and laptop computers, as well as a producer of hardware and software for large mainframe computers. But today, IBM doesn't produce personal computers at all—and most of its revenue comes from consulting services. It's hard to think that the returns that IBM earned in the 1990s, when it still relied heavily on PCs for revenue, do a good job of representing its returns today, or into the future.

So we need to limit how far back we go in time when we calculate average returns. I think it's good to try to go back further than 10 years into the past, perhaps even out to 20 years. That's because using more returns in the average should allow the short-term ups and downs to cancel each other out, leaving a clear picture of the long-term average return. And, as we've seen during the last half century, it's possible to have both bull and bear markets that last for 10 years, which also tend to distort the average levels of returns. If we can include up to two decades of returns in our averages, then we can be more confident that we're seeing the average return over the full range of market and economic conditions.

If the company and the economy don't change too dramatically, then looking at the average returns over several different horizons up to 20 years could be helpful. For example, I collected some numbers on the returns on Kellogg's stock over the past 20 years. Kellogg's business has certainly changed during this time, but its main business still seems to be one of selling cereals and other breakfast foods. When I calculated the average returns to Kellogg's stock over longer and longer periods, here's what I found.

Each of these averages represents the compound average return over the most recent 5-, 10-, 15-, and 20-year period. As you can see, the average return changes as you include more of the past—but not in a predictable way. Notice that the most recent 10-year period seems to be much higher than all the other averages, so if I simply used that, I'd probably overestimate the return. Based on all the averages, especially that 20-year average, I'd say that the expected return to Kellogg is somewhere in the high single digits—maybe 7% would be a good guess. I'm not using any formula to get that 7%. I'm just eyeballing the numbers and hoping that the 20-year number actually lets the true average come through, as I mentioned a minute ago.

Once we've estimated an expected return, it's essential to realize that we can't think of the expected return like it's the actual return that we automatically earn every year. Again, think about how much the actual return bounces around from year to year! The expected return is an average return that we should expect to earn, if we hold the investment over a long period of time. This is an extremely important point, because I think that many people hear the term *expected return*, or *average return*, and automatically believe that the investment delivers this return, just like clockwork.

When people believe this, they tend to panic when the investment has a really bad year and shows a big loss. A lot of people will then sell their investment at this point, locking in that loss. But if you understand what's going on, then you know that big positive returns are also possible from year to year, so that if you hang on to your investment and resist the urge to sell, you'll probably experience positive returns in future years that will pull your total return up to the expected return.

This discussion of the expected return already gives us one correction to the catchphrase "higher risk, higher return." The return we're talking about is not the actual return, but the expected return. If there is any relationship between risk and return, it will be between risk and expected return. Now let's move on to think more carefully about exactly what risk is, and how we measure it. That'll help us find the relationship between risk and expected return.

When people use the word risk, they really mean the possibility that something bad will happen. In the context of investing, the bad thing we worry about is losing money. In other words, we worry that the value of our investments may fall, so that we suffer a loss, which is a negative return. So to put this together, one way to sharpen our definition of risk is to say that it is the possibility of earning a negative return on our investment. But even that definition of risk is still not quite right.

We've just learned about how investors come to expect a particular return from each of their investments. So a bad outcome occurs when an investment's return doesn't live up to its expectations. An investment could return 5% in a year—but if we expected the return to be 9%, this is still a bad outcome.

So risk is the chance that our actual return will fall short of what we expect it to be. Let's try to visualize this idea of risk by writing down the actual return on an investment as the sum of two parts—the expected return on this investment, and the unexpected return.

We write $R_i = E_i + U_i$. The unexpected return could be positive, or it could be negative. Again, I write this as $R_i = E_i + U_i$, where R is the actual return, E is the expected return, U is the unexpected return, and the subscript i references the type of asset that this is. So each different subscript refers to a different asset.

Now we have a better picture of what risk really is—it's simply getting a negative value for this unexpected return, U. This is a step in the right direction, but we need to refine our measure of risk by adding in something specific about the size of the unexpected return. And we can do this in several different ways.

One easy way is to go back to our set of annual returns and use the range between the highest and lowest returns to get a feel for the size of the unexpected return. Here's a table in which I've already ranked the annual returns over the past 20 years on Kellogg stock:

One thing that really jumps out when you look at this ranked list of returns is that the overall range of returns is really large. It runs from −39% to positive

49%. Looking over the actual returns like this gives you a better feel for how bad things could get, because it shows you how bad they've actually been.

On the other hand, the list of returns also shows that positive returns outnumber negative ones, and this is generally true for stocks and other investments. So the picture we get is that returns can be all over the place, but if you hang in there, eventually you'll experience a greater number of positive returns that will eventually outweigh even really large negative returns. You may remember all the way back in my very first lecture, I said that time can be your greatest ally when you invest. That's another way to see why this is true.

So far, we have an idea of risk in terms of how bad things could get, and that is useful. But hopefully these really big losses are fairly rare. What we'd also like to know is what the average level of risk is in our investments—how big the unexpected return U is when we have a bad year but not a disastrous year for one of our investments. This average level of risk is really how most professionals view risk, and there's a term they use for this average level of risk that you may have heard or seen before.

The term is the *standard deviation of returns*, and it has a fairly precise statistical definition. Since this isn't a statistics course, I won't get into the details of how it's defined or calculated. But as I just mentioned, it's a useful concept that tries to measure the average size of the unexpected return, or in other words how much the actual return could differ from the expected return on average.

Most spreadsheets have a built-in function to calculate standard deviation for you, so if you have a list of annual returns, like the returns I showed you for the Kellogg stock, it's easy to calculate the standard deviation of the returns using this function.

We can use the standard deviation of returns to form a range of average returns. To construct this range, we take the expected return and add the standard deviation of returns to it to get the top end of the range. Then we subtract the standard deviation of returns from the expected return to get the bottom end of the range. There's a well-known rule of thumb which says that about two-thirds of all returns will fall within this range. So we should expect to see lots of returns throughout this range.

For example, returning to the Kellogg returns, I used a spreadsheet to find that the standard deviation of returns over the past 20 years was 20.8%. So the average size of an unexpected return on Kellogg stock is 20.8%. Remember that I also said that my expected return for the stock was about 7%. Therefore, the lower end of the normal range of risk on Kellogg stock would be $7 - 20.8$ or -13.8%. That's still a pretty big loss, but it's much lower than the 39% loss that could happen! Besides, the flip side of this calculation says that gains of up to 27.8%—that's the upper end of the range—should also be fairly common.

Hopefully, this discussion has given you a more concrete understanding of what return and risk really mean for investors, as well as how we measure return and risk in practice. Now that I've introduced the concepts of expected returns and unexpected returns, I'm going to use them to discuss diversification. Diversification is a useful risk-management tool, for sure, but it also reshapes our entire understanding of risk and leads us to refine our understanding of the relationship between risk and return.

We've all probably heard about diversification, perhaps in the context of investing, or maybe in some other life situation. Diversification is often defined as not putting all your eggs in one basket, and this phrase is a decent description. Diversification is simply the practice of investing in several or many different assets, rather than only one or a few assets. One way that investors diversify is by investing in different kinds of assets—stocks, bonds, and real estate, for example. Also, we've discussed reasons to diversify geographically, by investing in foreign stocks and bonds as well as domestic investments. Diversification is simple to envision, and even fairly simple to implement in practice. You don't actually need to hold that many different assets to become fairly well diversified. And these days, there are many assets that already come pre-diversified—especially mutual funds and ETFs.

I think diversification has become so widely accepted and practiced because it's fairly easy to understand how it protects you—at least on a very basic level. As the phrase "don't put all your eggs in one basket" suggests, if you divide your eggs between a lot of baskets, then if you drop one basket, you still have eggs in all the others. But diversification isn't just about making sure that you limit your total loss by spreading out the risk. Diversification actually reduces risk, in a particular way. We can see how this works using expected returns and unexpected returns.

Remember that we can write the actual return as $R_i = E_i + U_i$, where R is the actual return, E is the expected return, U is the unexpected return, and the subscript that references the type of asset is i.

Suppose I hold only one asset, asset 1. Then the actual return is going to fully reflect both the expected return and the unexpected return on asset 1, and I have to live with whatever unexpected returns I receive. But now think about adding another asset—asset 2—to my investment portfolio. If I assume I invest half my savings in each asset, then I can calculate the total return to my portfolio by simply adding up the returns on both assets and dividing by two. Then my total return is given by this equation:

Total Portfolio Return = $1/2 \times (R_1 + R_2) = 1/2 \times (E_1 + E_2) + 1/2 \times (U_1 + U_2)$.

But notice that U_1 and U_2 are unexpected returns. They may each be positive or negative, or one may be positive and the other may be negative. When one is positive and the other is negative, then they tend to cancel each other out, at least a little. Of course, with only two assets, they will only cancel out part of their unexpected returns, part of the time.

But what if I added several more different kinds of assets, maybe a dozen or more? The more assets I add, the more offsetting of unexpected returns I'll get. In other words, if I'm holding lots of different types of assets, chances are that several of them have positive unexpected returns, and several others have negative unexpected returns. So I'll get more unexpected returns cancelling each other out, as I add more assets of different kinds to my portfolio. That's actual risk reduction.

And that's how diversification works. By holding more assets of different kinds, the influence of unexpected returns on your portfolio declines. The actual return isn't pushed as far away from the expected return as before, because the unexpected returns are cancelling each other out somewhat. In other words, the range of variation in the returns on your portfolio falls, which means that your actual returns are closer to what you expect to receive.

Does this mean that if we continue to diversify, we'll completely get rid of unexpected returns and all risk goes away? I wish the answer were yes, but unfortunately that's not the case. There's a limit to diversification. Even if you have the most well diversified portfolio out there, you will still experience unexpected returns. So diversification reduces risk, but can't eliminate it.

There will also be problems if your assets really aren't as different as you thought. For example, suppose you invest in the shares of Coca Cola and also of Caterpillar. These are pretty different industries, you think, so this seems like a good step toward diversification. But what if it turns out that both companies' profits are heavily dependent on demand in China? Then their returns could move together a lot more than you expect, including their unexpected returns. It's important to make sure when you diversify that the returns of the assets you're buying really don't move together very much.

Correlation is the statistical term that describes co-movement. Two investments whose returns both go up and down together are said to have highly correlated returns. So what this means is that diversification works better as the correlation between the assets' returns declines.

This idea about correlation and diversification actually helps to explain my previous point, which you are hopefully still wondering about. Even after you fully diversify, there will still be unexpected returns in your portfolio, driving the actual return away from the expected return. How can that be? The answer is that there are two different types of risk in unexpected returns, and diversification only gets rid of one of them.

The type of risk that diversification reduces, through this cancellation process, is called idiosyncratic risk. It's called idiosyncratic because it's specific to each particular asset and doesn't share anything in common with any other assets. This means that idiosyncratic risk is not correlated across assets. When we increase the number of assets in a portfolio, we expect that, on average, the idiosyncratic risks will cancel each other out. The actual return will get closer to the expected return, the more assets we include in the portfolio.

The other type of risk in the unexpected return is called systematic risk. This is a risk that is common across assets, meaning that when this risk creates a positive unexpected return in one asset, it's doing the same thing to all other risky assets as well. By saying that risk is common across assets, we're saying that diversification won't reduce it. So in a very real sense, systematic risk is risk that you can't get rid of through diversification.

What causes systematic risk? Well, this is an issue that economists still can't quite agree on. There are lots of ideas, but they all seem to be similar. Because investment in financial assets is ultimately tied to real assets, as I've mentioned in previous lectures, just about all investments are exposed to fluctuations in the overall economy, such as the business cycle, and perhaps also to fluctuations in the financial markets that connect businesses with households. So most theories about the sources of systematic risk involve risks to the overall economy, the financial markets, or both.

This distinction between different types of risk changes the way we perceive risk, but it also changes the way we value risk. Economists know that people are risk averse, meaning that we don't like to bear risk. But if you compensate us, we'll bear it. And if there's a risk that we have to pay to get rid of, we'll probably put up with at least some of it. But if there is a risk that we can get rid of, for free, there's no way that any risk-averse person would pass up the chance to eliminate that risk.

Diversification gets rid of idiosyncratic risk. And it's basically free—you don't have to pay extra to diversify your portfolio, especially if you choose a pre-diversified asset like a mutual fund. Therefore, there's no reason to expect compensation for bearing idiosyncratic risk; you can get rid of it for free.

Systematic risk is the risk that we can't get rid of. So in order to induce a risk-averse person to hold an asset with systematic risk, then they have to be compensated for that. And the compensation comes in the form of a higher expected return from holding that asset, relative to an asset with no systematic risk.

Now we can finally restate our catchphrase about risk and return correctly. Rather than higher risk, higher return, the truth about risk and return is higher systematic risk, higher expected return. First, you only get paid to hold systematic risk, not all risk. And second, you can only expect to get paid— you won't necessarily get all the compensation you demand. Of course, if you hold the asset long enough, then your actual compensation should come close to the expected return.

This still leaves an important question unresolved: what is the compensation rate for bearing systematic risk? The answer depends on what you believe is the source of systematic risk.

There are many different theories about what determines investment returns, but they all agree that idiosyncratic risk is worthless, while systematic risk is compensated.

And they all agree that any asset that has no systematic risk should earn the risk-free rate of return. That's a return on a government bond. Even an asset with a highly risky return should only earn the risk-free rate on average, if all the risk is idiosyncratic risk.

Each different theory of returns is essentially a different story about systematic risk that explains what the sources of systematic risk are, and how the risk is compensated. Unfortunately, we don't have a universally accepted theory of systematic risk. Some economists believe that there is a single source of systematic risk, but they can't agree on what it is. Other economists believe that there are several sources of systematic risk, and they can't agree on a common set of sources either. And none of these theories has proven to do a much better job at estimating expected returns than using averages of past returns.

The distinction between systematic and idiosyncratic risk is still useful, though. We can benefit from this insight even though we can't take full advantage of the idea. I think that even though we don't know for sure how much systematic risk is in any given asset, there's probably a fair amount of idiosyncratic risk in most investments. Therefore, it's absolutely imperative that investors take advantage of diversification, which reduces idiosyncratic risk regardless of whether we know what the sources of systematic risk are. Remember that you'll earn nothing from holding idiosyncratic risk in your investments—so try to get rid of as much as you can through diversification.

This practical advice brings us to the end of our discussion of risk, return, and diversification. It would have been nice to be able to give you some very specific advice about how to concentrate your portfolio in the risks that earn high returns. But as we've seen, once of the main effects of risk on investing is that it makes it extremely difficult to draw any precise conclusions about future returns, including expected returns. That's a permanent source of frustration for all investors.

But don't let this stop you from investing—we've learned a lot about how to deal with the presence of risk in our investments, and now your job is to put these lessons to work. First, try to use several historical averages of past returns to get a feel for the expected return on an investment.

Also, try not to think about expected returns as a single number. Instead, think about a range of returns that you should regard as ordinary or usual. To find this range of ordinary or usual returns, add and subtract the standard deviation of annual returns to the expected return. If the lower end of this range of returns makes you nervous, then find assets with lower risk! Also, if you're already holding an asset that experiences a large negative return, hang in there and wait for the asset to experience the higher returns that should balance it out.

Next, try to choose investments that are risk–return bargains. These investments offer relatively high expected returns, and relatively low standard deviations of returns at the same time. But be aware that other investors are also looking for these bargains, so if you find one, you'll need to act fast to buy it before other investors drive its price up.

And finally, don't try to guess which investments have high levels of systematic risk, even though these assets should theoretically offer better returns. Instead, focus your investing on diversification, so that you get rid of unproductive idiosyncratic risk and leave only the systematic risk in your portfolio. If you take away nothing else from this lecture, you need to remember that diversification is the best way to ensure that you earn the expected returns you are entitled to, given the systematic risk you take on.

Unfortunately, the real relationship between risk and return is messy—it doesn't fit inside the neat little cliché that most people use. But having a better understanding of the true relationship between risk and return will help you stay motivated to keep investing over the long haul, no matter what unpleasant surprises the market may deliver in the short run.

Time Value of Money
Lecture 22

In the final 3 lectures of this course, you will be introduced to some essential skills that will help you turn your investing ideas into concrete actions. In this lecture, you'll learn 3 skills that are essential to making good decisions about investing: comparing returns across different investments, projecting the future value of an investment, and estimating a reasonable price for an investment. Additionally, you're going to learn to use time value of money tools—including the timeline, rate of return calculations, compounding, and discounting—that you'll need to take charge of your financial planning and investing.

Comparing Returns across Investments

- Suppose you buy a share of stock for $50 and hold it for a while. One day, you check the price and see that it's gone up to $59. In addition, the stock has also paid some dividends that you put in a bank account. The total value of the dividends is $3.25, including interest, on the same day that you checked the stock price. Therefore, the total value of your investment when you checked the price is $59 + $3.25 = $62.25.

- When you ask the question of what your return is so far, without caring much about how long you've been holding it, you're asking what the holding period return is on your investment. The holding period return, also called the **periodic return**, is the return you earn for holding an investment for 1 period, where the period can be any length of time. This is a very important way of calculating and quoting the rate of return on an investment.

- The first step in calculating the periodic return on your investment is simply to visualize what's going on. To help with this, we will apply a few of the most useful tools in investing that are called time value of money tools. The first tool we'll use is the timeline, which is simply a line you draw to show the amount and timing of income and expenditures. It can also show how much something is worth at a point in time.

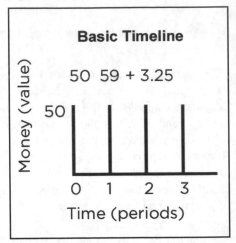

Figure 22-1

- Draw a line and divide it up into units of time—years, months, days, or whatever time period you want to use. We usually start the timeline at time 0, which we think of as now, or the start of some investment project that we're considering. Time 1 is 1 period from now, and time 2 is 2 periods from now, and so on. You can number the periods below the timeline and write in the amount of money coming in or going out above the timeline.

- Start by assuming that you buy the stock at time 0, and check the value of the stock and the dividends at time 1. The length of time between time 0 and time 1 is completely arbitrary for now. Continuing with this example, you should have the value of $50 at time 0, the stock price of $59, and the dividend of $3.25 all added together at time 1. The total value is the value of the stock plus any dividends.

- Because you want to be able to think about the general definition of the periodic rate of return, you can redraw this investment using P for the price of the share and D for the total value of the dividend, using subscripts to denote the time. For example, you buy the stock at price P_0, and when you check the price of the stock at time 1, the price is P_1. Also, the total value of the dividends that have been paid between time 0 and time 1 is D_1.

- To calculate the periodic return, take the total value of your investment at the end of the period, which is $62.25, and subtract what you paid for it: $50. This gives you the dollar value of your periodic return, which is $12.25.

- In general, the dollar value of the periodic return is $P_1 + D_1 - P_0$. Grouping the P's together, you get $P_1 - P_0 + D_1$ as your dollar return. This rearrangement shows that the periodic return on any investment is the sum of 2 parts: the change in the price of the investment—called the capital gain, which can be positive or negative (capital loss)—and the income paid by the investment, which is the dividend.

- On the example stock investment, the capital gain is $9, and the dividend is $3.25. Therefore, the periodic return in terms of money is $9 + $3.25 = $12.25. To express the return as a percentage of what you paid for the investment, first divide the dollar periodic return by your starting price to convert it to a decimal: $12.25/$50 = 0.245, or 24.5%.

- The fraction $(P_1 - P_0 + D_1)/P_0$ gives your return between now and time 1. This return is a periodic rate of return because it's the return over a single period of any arbitrary length. In general, you can measure the return between any 2 points in time, t and $t + 1$, by using the formula $r_{t+1} = (P_{t+1} - P_t + D_{t+1})/P_t$.

- If you plug the numbers from the example into the definition of the periodic return, the calculation is: $r_p = ($59 - $50 + $3.25)/$50 = 0.245$, or 24.5%—just as you found with the earlier equation.

- The advantage of the periodic rate of return is that it's the correct way to measure a return over any length of time. You can use periodic rates of return to calculate how much interest you've earned, or how much you owe, during any period. The drawback of periodic rates is that it's difficult to compare periodic rates of return to each other unless the periods are exactly the same length.

Projecting the Future Value of an Investment

- Suppose you want to know what this stock investment will be worth 5 periods from now, assuming that the periodic rate of return is 24.5%. To answer this question, we need to use another time value of money tool called **compounding**, which describes the fact that if you leave money in an investment, the interest earned during 1 period will start to earn its own interest in subsequent periods.

- To illustrate how compounding works, let's say that you put $1 in a bank account today. Then, after 1 period, the account will be worth $1 + r$ dollars, where r is the periodic rate of interest paid by the bank. Compounding works for any number of periods: If you put $1 in the bank today and leave it in there n periods, then the value of the account at time n—that is, n periods from now—is $(1 + r)^n$ dollars.

- **Future value** is the value of an investment, or a debt, at a future date n periods from the current time. If you know the periodic rate of return on an investment, you can forecast what its future value is by applying this compounding formula: $FV_n = (PV)(1 + r_p)^n$, where FV stands for future value at time n (that is, n periods from now) and PV stands for present value—which is what something is worth now, at time 0. The r_p is the periodic rate for whatever compounding period is used to calculate your returns.

- Using your original investment, you can apply the future value formula to calculate a future value, assuming that the investment keeps up the periodic rate of return of 24.5% for 5 more periods: $FV = \$62.25 \times 1.245^5 = \$186.20$.

- Using the same numbers you started with, you can also calculate return in terms of years. For example, what's your return per year if the stock price went up from $50 to $59 and you earned a total of $3.25 in dividends in 3 years?

- The present value of the investment is $50, and the future value of the investment is $62.25. You also know n, which is 3. You don't know r_p, but you want to find it by using the future value formula: $62.25 = 50 \times (1 + r_p)^3$, which leads to $r_p = 0.0758$, or 7.58%.

- Because we're assuming that the length of the periods are measured in years, that means that r_p is an annual rate—but it's actually the average annual rate, or the compound average annual rate. The average annual rate of return is the rate of return that you effectively earn on an investment each year, assuming that this return stays the same and is compounded each year. Many people also call this an effective annual rate of return or a compound average rate of return.

- The equation $(1 + r_p) = (1 + r_{AAR})^n$ allows you to convert back and forth between periodic rates of return and the equivalent average annual rates of return. In this equation, n is the length of the period—measured in years. In other words, if r_p is the periodic rate for 1 day—a daily rate—then n equals 1/365.

- This formula is important for being able to compare rates of return between different investments. Although some investments will tell you their average annual rate of return—mutual funds, for example—many times you can't find that information directly, so you'll have to use the formula to convert the periodic returns to average annual returns and then compare the average annual returns.

Estimating a Reasonable Price for an Investment
- Suppose someone wants to sell you a bond that promises to pay you $10,000 6 years from today. You know that the average annual rate of return on this bond is 4% per year. How much would you be willing to pay for the bond now?

- Because you know the future value and the rate of return but don't know the present value, you can use the future value formula, but you'll have to solve it for the present value: $PV = (FV)/(1 + r)^n$. To find the present value of an investment, divide by the compounded rate of return. This operation is called **discounting** because it shows that the present value is going to be less than the future value of the investment—for any positive rate of return.

- Discounting is one of the most powerful tools in finance; it gives you a way to find the value today of something that is promised to you in the future. In finance, the price of any investment today should be equal to the sum of the present values—the discounted values—of all its future payments.

- To find the price of the example bond, you can use the discounting formula: $PV = \$10,000/1.04^6 = \$7903.15$.

- If someone wants to sell you a bond that makes 2 different payments on 2 different future dates, you can find the present value of each payment separately and then add the 2 present values together. The sum will give you the total present value of the bond. The present value of a set of payments is always equal to the sum of the present values of each payment calculated separately.

Important Terms

compounding: A time value of money tool that describes the fact that if you leave money in an investment, the interest earned during 1 period will start to earn its own interest in subsequent periods.

discounting: A time value of money tool that is used to find the present value of an investment by dividing the future value by the compounded rate of return: $PV = (FV)/(1 + r)^n$.

future value: The value of an investment, or a debt, at a future date n periods from the current time: $FV_n = (PV)(1 + r_p)^n$, where FV stands for future value at time n (that is, n periods from now) and PV stands for present value—which is what something is worth now, at time 0. The r_p is the periodic rate for whatever compounding period is used to calculate your returns.

periodic return: The return you earn for holding an investment for 1 period, where the period can be any length of time.

Suggested Reading

Berk and DeMarzo, *Corporate Finance*, chap. 4.

Brealey, Myers, and Allen, *Principles of Corporate Finance*, chap. 2.

Questions to Consider

1. If you buy a share in a mutual fund for $42 and 6 years later it is worth $73.30, what is your average annual rate of return on this investment?

2. Suppose there is a 3-year bond that pays 6 $150 coupons every 6 months and a $10,000 principal payment at the maturity of the bond. If the market rate of return on the bond is 4.5%, then the price of the bond is $9583.41, rounding to the nearest penny. Can you show, by discounting the 6 payments that the bond makes ($150, $150, $150, $150, $150, and $10,150) at the periodic rate of 2.25%—remembering that for bonds, you divide the quoted rate by 2 to get the periodic rate—per period, that this is the correct price of the bond?

Time Value of Money
Lecture 22—Transcript

During this course, we've learned about some of the most fundamental and important ideas in investing, like the efficient markets hypothesis and the relationship between risk and return. I don't think you're really ready to invest until you understand these ideas and make up your own mind about where you stand on them.

In addition to understanding ideas, you also need to master some skills, if you really want to take charge of your own investing. So in the final 3 lectures of the course, I'm going to introduce some essential skills that will help you turn your investing ideas into concrete actions. These skills really complement the ideas we've been learning, and they seriously enhance your ability to evaluate investment choices and make financial plans.

In this lecture, we'll learn 3 skills that are essential to making good decisions about investing: comparing returns across different investments, projecting the future value of an investment, and estimating a reasonable price for an investment.

All 3 skills involve calculating and comparing numbers that describe your investments. I believe that it's extremely important for you to learn how these calculations and comparisons work. First, you may want to do some of these calculations yourself—or need to do them yourself—in order to make investing decisions. But even if you have somebody else generate these numbers for you, you'll still want to know where these numbers come from and what they mean. That's why, in this lecture, we're going to learn to use a few of the most useful tools in investing—the time value of money tools.

The time value of money tools I'm going to introduce in this lecture include the time line, rate of return calculations, compounding, and discounting. These 4 tools work together, first to help you picture—literally picture—an investment or investing decision. And then this picture, plus some handy formulas we'll learn, will help you find realistic numbers that you can use in your investing decisions.

And best of all, these tools are actually pretty easy to learn. They don't rely on complicated mathematics. In fact, you probably learned much of the math that I'll use in this lecture in grade school. Just imagine how different fifth grade would have been if your teacher would have said, "I'm going to teach you math that could make you rich some day!"

I'm going to introduce the time value of money tools by asking some simple questions related to the 3 essential investing skills that I introduced a minute ago. The first skill I mentioned was the ability to compare returns across investments.

In order to build up this skill, we have to start with a really basic question that every investor wants to know the answer to: what's the return on my investment? To make this concrete, suppose I buy a share of stock for $50 and hold it for a while. One day I check the price and see that its gone up to $59. In addition, the stock has also paid me some dividends that I put in a bank account. The total value of the dividends is $3.25, including interest, on the same day that I checked the stock price. So the total value of my investment when I checked the price is $59 + $3.25 = $62.25.

Notice that I haven't specified the length of time that I've been holding the share of stock. I'm not concerned yet with the return per year, I just want to know how to calculate the return I've earned so far.

When I ask this question—what's my return so far (without really caring that much about how long it's been)—I'm asking what the holding period return is on my investment. The holding period return, also simply called the periodic return, is the return that you earn for holding an investment for one period, where the period can be any length of time you want. As we'll see, this is a very important way of calculating, and quoting, the rate of return on an investment.

The first step in calculating the periodic return on my investment is simply to visualize what's going on. So the first time value of money tool I'll introduce is the time line. The time line is one of those simple but surprisingly powerful tools that can help you organize your thinking when you're faced with complex situations. As its name suggests, the time line is nothing more than a line that you draw to show you the amount and timing of income and expenditures. It can also show you how much something is worth at a point in time.

What we do is draw a line and divide it up into units of time—years, months, days, or whatever time period you want to use. We usually start the time line at time 0, which we think of as now, or the start of some investment project that we're considering. Time 1 is one period from now, time 2 is two periods from now, and so on. I usually number the periods below the time line and write in the amount of money coming in or going out above the time line.

Now let me use the time line to visualize this stock investment. I'm assuming that I buy the stock at time 0, and check the value of the stock and the dividends at time 1. Again, the length of time between time 0 and time 1 is completely arbitrary for now. So here is what the investment looks like so far. I have the value of 50 at time 0 and the stock price of 59, and the dividend of $3.25, added together at time 1. Note that the total value is the value of the stock, plus any dividends.

Since I want to be able to think about the general definition of the periodic rate of return, let me redraw this investment using P for the price of the share and D for the total value of the dividend. I'll use subscripts to denote the time when I measure these values. So I buy the stock at price P_0, and when I check the price of the stock at time 1, the price is P_1. Also, the total value of the dividends that have been paid between time 0 and time 1 is D_1.

Now I'll calculate the periodic return. I take the total value of my investment at the end of the period, which is $62.25, and subtract what I paid for it—$50. That gives me the dollar value of my periodic return, which is $12.25.

In general terms, using the Ps and Ds, the dollar value of the periodic return is $P_1 + D_1 - P_0$. If I group the Ps together, I get $P_1 - P_0 + D_1$ as my dollar return. I like to write it this way because it shows that the periodic return on any investment is the sum of two parts. One part is the change in the price of the investment, which is called the capital gain. The capital gain can be positive or negative, and a negative change in price is often called a capital loss. The second part of the return is the income paid by the investment, which I'm calling a dividend in this case.

On the example stock investment, the capital gain is $9, and the dividend is $3.25. So again, the periodic return in terms of money is 9 + 3.25, or $12.25. We usually express returns as percents, so I divide the dollar periodic return by my starting price to convert it to a decimal. The answer gives me my return as a percentage of what I paid for the investment. So 12.25/50 = 0.245 or 24.5%.

So the fraction $(P_1 - P_0 + D_1)/P_0$ gives me my return between now and time 1. This return is a periodic rate of return, since it's the return over a single period of any arbitrary length. The length of the period could be a year, a month, a decade, literally any length of time you want it to be. And in general, I can measure the return between any two points in time, t and $t + 1$, by using the formula $r_{t+1} = (P_{t+1} - P_t + D_{t+1})/P_t$. Notice that I use the $t + 1$ subscript on r, the periodic return, to remind me that the return is earned between time t and $t + 1$.

If I plug the numbers from my example into the definition of the periodic return, the calculation looks like this: r_p = (59 − 50 + 3.25)/50 = 0.245 or 24.5%, just like I found a minute ago.

The advantage of the periodic rate of return is that it's the correct way to measure a return over any length of time. All you need to know are the starting value and the ending value of the investment, including the dividends or income, if any.

It may seem like periodic rates of return aren't very useful, but in fact they're used all the time. You can use periodic rates of return to calculate how much interest you've earned, or how much you owe, during any period. You may have noticed, for example, when you read your credit card statements, that your credit card company calculates any interest you owe them by multiplying your balance by a periodic rate of return. For most credit cards, the company calculates your average daily balance and then multiplies that by a daily periodic rate to get the daily interest you owe. Then it multiplies this interest by the number of days in the billing cycle to get the total interest that you owe.

The drawback of periodic rates is that it's hard to compare periodic rates of return to each other, unless the periods are exactly the same length. For example, if I earn a periodic rate of return of 200%, it sounds great—if the period is 1 year. But what if the period is, say, 25 years? Then it doesn't sound so amazing.

We'll come back to this problem of comparing returns in a bit. First, though, I'll ask a simpler question related to my periodic rate of return. Remember that we found that the periodic rate of return was 24.5%. Wow! What will my investment be worth in the future if it keeps up this return? This is something that most investors want to know about their investments, especially when the investments are doing well. Note also that this is the second skill that I mentioned at the start of the lecture.

Keep in mind that we want to know the future value of the investment, but we haven't specified the length of each period, so we'll ask the question in terms of periods. Don't worry, we'll bring in days, months, and years in a little bit. For now, though, suppose we ask what will this stock investment be worth 5 periods from now, assuming that the periodic rate of return is 24.5%.

We need to use another time value of money tool to answer that, and this tool is called compounding. Compounding is one of the basic ideas behind the time value of money. You're probably a little familiar with it already, if you've ever left some money sitting in a bank account for a while. Compounding describes the fact that if you leave money in an investment, the interest earned during one period will start to earn its own interest in subsequent periods, and so on.

To illustrate how compounding works, let's say you put one dollar in a bank account today. Then, after one period, the account will be worth $1 + r$ dollars, where r is the periodic rate of interest paid by the bank.

If you leave the money in the account for another period, then the bank will pay you interest on the total amount in the account at the start of the period.

So at the end of the second period, your account contains the money you started the period with, which is $1 + r$ dollars. But the bank also pays you interest on that amount, which is $r(1 + r)$ dollars. You can of course simplify that to $(1 + r)^2$ dollars. This works for any number of periods, so that if you put $1 in the bank today and leave it in there n periods, then the value of the account at time n—that is, n periods from now—is $(1 + r)^n$ dollars. This is easy to visualize on the timeline. Here the timeline shows that a dollar deposited in a bank at time 0 will keep earning interest and growing for as long as you leave it in the bank. For example, if I put $100 in a bank deposit that earns a periodic return of 5%, then the value of my deposit at the end of period 3 will be $100 \times 1.05^3 = \$115.76$.

This compounding calculation is called the future value calculation. Future value is the value of an investment, or a debt, at a future date n periods from now. If I know the periodic rate of return on an investment, I can forecast what its future value is by applying this compounding formula: $FV_n = PV \times (1 + r_p)^n$. In this equation, the FV stands for future value at time n (that is, n periods from now) and PV stands for present value. Present value, of course, is what something is worth now, at time 0. The r_p is the periodic rate for whatever compounding period is used to calculate your returns. Notice that we use periodic rates of return whenever we do compounding. This is very important to remember.

Let's use the time line to visualize the future value equation. At time 0, we have some investment worth PV. After n periods, the investment is worth FV (future value), which is equal to $PV \times (1 + r)^n$.

Let's return to our original investment. We wanted to know what our investment would be worth after a certain amount of periods if it kept up a certain rate of return. We can answer our question by applying the future value formula. Remember that the present value of the stock investment is $62.25 and the periodic rate of return we're assuming is 24.5%. Let's calculate a future value, assuming that the investment keeps up this rate of return for 5 more periods.

Then the future value equation becomes $FV = 62.25 \times (1.245)^5 = 186.20$. So this is what the stock investment will be worth after 5 more periods, if it maintains the 24.5% return per period. Not too bad!

That's all very nice, but most of us like to think of returns in terms of years. So let's ask a question about our stock investment in these terms. We'll use the same numbers as we started with, but now let's say you have held the stock for 3 years. What's your return per year if the stock price went up from $50 to $59 and you earned a total of $3.25 in dividends in 3 years?

Now we can visualize the stock investment a bit differently than before. Instead of one period of unknown length, now we're assuming that you've held the stock for 3 one-year periods. So the picture on the time line looks like this.

But notice that it's the same basic picture as we used to visualize the future value equation. So we can use the future value equation to find our annual rate of return. We know the present value of the investment, which is $50. Remember that on the time line, now is time 0, so I put the $50 present value at time 0. We also know the future value of the investment, which is 62.25. We also know n, which is 3, for 3 years. The thing we don't know and want to find out is r_p. Here's the equation.

This equation isn't hard to solve. We have $62.25 = 50 \times (1 + r_p)^3$, and with a little algebra, we find that $r_p = 0.0758$ or 7.58%.

This method works for fractions of years, too. Suppose for example, that I bought the stock in our example on October 1, 2011, and sold it on July 31, 2013. The length of the period is 1 year and 9 months, or 1.75 years. We can solve for the r_p again using the future value formula as before, only instead of using 3 for the number of periods, I use 1.75 for the number of periods.

So we have $62.25 = 50 \times (1 + r_p)^{1.75}$. When I solve for r_p this time, I get $r_p = 0.1334$ or 13.34%.

Since we're assuming that the length of the periods are measured in years, that means that this r_p is an annual rate. But it's more than an annual rate—it's the average annual rate, or better yet, the compound average annual rate.

The idea behind the average annual rate of return is that it's the rate of return that you effectively earn on an investment each year, assuming that this return stays the same and is compounded each year. Many people also call this average annual rate of return an effective annual rate of return, or the compound average rate of return.

Before I move on to use the average annual rate of return, let me show you the connection between the periodic rate of return and the average annual rate. The periodic rate and the average annual rate are simply two different ways of expressing the same information about a return.

If the periodic rate and the average annual rate are really just different ways of looking at the same thing, then you should be able to go back and forth between them. To see that this is indeed true, let's take yet another look at the future value equation. All I'm going to do is write the same future value equation in two ways. First, let's pretend that the length of the periods in the future value equation is one year. That means that the periodic rate of return in the future value equation is an average annual rate, and in fact let's call it r_{AAR}. So we can write our future value equation as $FV = PV \times (1 + r_{AAR})^n$. This means that this is the future value equation for an n-year-long investment.

If we take that future value equation and divide both sides by PV, then we get $FV/PV = (1 + r_{AAR})^n$. So what, you ask?

Now let's write the same future value equation a second way. This time, we'll assume that the period length is just one period—but this one period is n years long, so it covers the same amount of time as our previous future value equation. The future value equation for a one-period investment is simply $FV = PV \times (1 + r_p)$, where r_p is the periodic rate of return for this one period. When we divide both sides by PV this time, we get $FV/PV = (1 + r_p)$.

Since the future value and the present value are the same in both equations, this means that I can set the right-hand sides of each equation equal to each other, so $(1 + r_p) = (1 + r_{AAR})^n$.

This shows you how to convert back and forth between periodic rates of return and the equivalent average annual rates of return. All you need to remember is that in this equation, n is the length of the period measured in years. In other words, if r_p is the periodic rate for a month, then n equals 1/12 (since one month is 1/12 of one year). And if r_p is the periodic rate for one day—a daily rate—then n equals 1/365. For example, we saw that the average annual rate on our stock was 7.58%. What kind of return would that be on a daily basis?

We can use the formula I just showed you.

The r_{AAR} equals 0.0758 and n equals 1/365. When we put these numbers into the formula and solve, we get $(1 + r_p) = (1.0758)^{1/365}$, or $r_p = 0.0002$, rounded to the nearest ten-thousandth.

I wanted to show you this formula because it's extremely important for being able to compare rates of return between different investments. Although some investments will tell you their average annual rate of return—mutual funds, for example—many times you can't find that information directly and you'll have to calculate it yourself.

Here's an example that shows you what I mean. Suppose you and a friend are comparing rates of return on your investments. You say that you made a 15% return over two years, and your friend brags that he earned 23% over 3 years. Who did better?

These are two periodic rates where the periods are of different lengths, so you can't tell just by comparing returns. And don't just divide the return by the number of years—that's a totally incorrect way of finding an average annual return, and it can lead to big mistakes. You have to use the formula I just showed you to convert the periodic returns to average annual returns, and then compare the average annual returns to each other. That's the only reliable way to compare returns on different investments.

So let's settle your argument over who's a better investor. For your investment, $r_p = 15\%$ and $n = 2$, so the equation is $(1.15) = (1 + r_{AAR})^2$, which means that your average annual return is 0.0724 or 7.24%. For your friend, his equation is $1.23 = (1 + r_{AAR})^3$, which means that his average annual rate of return is 0.0714 or 7.14%. So you did just a teeny bit better.

So far we've used this example of a stock investment to learn several time value of money tools. Now I'll shift gears to a different example, to introduce the final time value of money tool for this lecture.

Suppose someone wants to sell you a bond that promises to pay you $10,000 6 years from today. You know that the average annual rate of return on this bond is 4% per year. How much would you be willing to pay for the bond now?

This question stands the compounding question on its head. Instead of trying to project the future value of an investment, we're trying to find what something is worth today. That's the third essential investing skill that I mentioned at the start of this lecture—finding the right price for an investment.

To find this price, the first thing I can do is simply draw the payment schedule on the time line. We can visualize the bond as a single payment of $10,000 at time 6. So I know the future value, and the rate of return, but I don't know the present value. Well, I can still use the future value formula, but I'll have to solve it out for the present value. That's not too hard, though—I get $PV = FV/(1 + r)^n$.

All we do to find the present value of an investment is to divide by the compounded rate of return. We call this operation discounting, because it shows that the present value is going to be less than the future value of the investment, for any positive rate of return. As an important note, remember that the rate of return is the appropriate periodic rate; we always use periodic rates when compounding and discounting.

Discounting is one of the most powerful tools in finance. You may remember from my very first lecture that most financial assets are contracts that promise to give you payments in the future in exchange for lending money today. Discounting gives us a way to find the value today of something that is promised to you in the future. In other words, discounting the future payments from an investment is one of the standard ways that we use to find the right price for the investment today. So in finance, we often say that the price of any investment today should be equal to the sum of the present values—the discounted values—of all its future payments.

You may remember a statement like this from the lecture on fundamentals-based stock pricing. According to the fundamentals-based view of stock prices, the price of a stock should be equal to the present discounted value of all future dividends.

Let's return to the bond pricing example. To find its price, we can use the discounting formula. The future value is the bond payment of $10,000. The rate of return is 4%, and the number of annual periods is 6 since the bond pays you 6 years from now. Then the price you'd be willing to pay today is the present value of this $10,000 payment, which is given by $PV = 10,000/1.04^6 = \$7903.15$.

What if someone wants to sell you a bond that makes two different payments, on two different future dates? Well, you can use the same basic approach. Find the present value of each payment separately, and then add the two present values together. The sum will give you the total present value of the bond. Suppose, for example, that the bond we just examined makes a second payment of $10,000 in another 6 years after the first payment, or 12 years from now in other words. How much is this two-payment bond worth, if the average annual return on the bond is still 4%?

We can get out the timeline again and show those payments. There's a payment of 10,000 at time 6 and a second payment of 10,000 at time 12. We know that the present value of the first payment is $7903.15, and the present value of the second payment is $10,000/1.04^{12} = \$6245.97$. Then the sum of these payments is $14,149.12, which is the price you should be willing to pay.

This example highlights a very useful property of present values—they are additive. That is, the present value of a set of payments is always equal to the sum of the present values of each payment calculated separately. So if I have an investment that makes 6 payments, its present value is simply the sum of the present values of each individual payment.

In this lecture, we've learned just about all the time value of money tools you'll need to take charge of your financial planning and investing. More importantly, we've learned how to combine these tools in ways that give us real investing skills. For example, one of the main things we've learned is the right way to calculate returns and compare returns across investments. That's a key skill, because this information about returns isn't presented in a uniform way in the financial markets.

Also, we've learned how to calculate future values, and we've made a good start on present values as well. In the next lecture, we'll learn how to put these time value of money tools to work to help us make financial planning decisions.

Financial Planning
Lecture 23

In this lecture, you're going to use the time value of money tools you learned in the previous lecture to do some financial planning, which can help you answer some of the big financial questions you might have, such as how much money you should be investing now for retirement. The calculations you'll learn to apply in this lecture are the kinds of calculations that you'll want to do every so often to check on the progress of your investments—so that you can decide whether you need to make adjustments to your strategy.

Financial Planning for Retirement

- Financial planning is one of the key first steps that you need to take when you start investing. Good financial planning helps you see the full range of financial possibilities for your life.

- Financial planning comes down to one basic task: finding a balance between the amount of money you need to reach a particular financial goal and the value of your investments. There is an equation that is used to guide financial planning, which states that the amount of money needed at some point in time is equal to the value of the investments at that same point in time.

Basic Equation of Financial Planning

$$\text{Amount of Money Needed at Time } t = \text{Value of Investments at Time } t$$

- This equation expresses a condition for personal financial equilibrium that we're trying to satisfy. We know that we'll have a workable financial plan if we can find numbers that make this equation balance. Turning this basic equation into a tool that you can use to make decisions is the tricky part of financial planning.

- First, we're going to focus on financial planning for retirement because it's something that everyone needs to do, and it's one of the more complex financial planning problems. You'll be able to apply everything from this lecture to other financial planning problems.

- Suppose you plan to retire at a certain age—65 or 70, for example— and after that time, your income will either be close to zero or much less than it is today. During the years that you work, you invest some funds each year, and these investments will hopefully grow into a large sum that will be enough to provide for your needs during retirement. The retirement planning problem is to find the right numbers that turn this general idea into a workable plan that you are comfortable with.

- First, draw a timeline and fill in information that describes this financial planning problem. Start by making a mark somewhere toward the right end of the timeline that represents the number of years from now that you'll retire. For example, let's say that you think your retirement is 30 years away from now. Put a 30 under the mark you made, which means that your retirement date is time 30.

- To keep things simple, you expect that during your retirement, you won't have any income from working; you'll be living off of the value of your investments and Social Security.

- Then, you'll need to estimate how many years you'll live during your retirement. You don't want to run out of money after you retire, so think carefully about how long you expect to live. Suppose you conclude that you expect to retire 30 years from now and live for another 20 years after that.

- The more difficult calculation you need to make is how much money you'll need during each year of retirement. Retirement experts tend to think about this question in terms of the fraction of your preretirement salary that you'll need to maintain your lifestyle. There seems to be general agreement that you'll want to spend about 70% of your preretirement salary each year during retirement.

- However, you'll want to make 2 adjustments to this number. First, forecasts indicate that Social Security payments will be about 20% of your preretirement salary, so we can use that number to reduce the amount that you'll have to pay out of your own investments.

- Then, you should adjust this number for increased costs during retirement, especially medical care. Assume that you'll need an additional 10% of preretirement salary to pay for the increased cost of medical insurance and medical care that isn't covered by insurance.

- If you assume that you need 70% of your preretirement salary and then subtract 20% for Social Security, that leaves 50%. However, you then add 10% for higher medical expenses, which means that, during retirement, you'll need to pay 60% of your preretirement salary out of your investments.

- Suppose you make $80,000 per year currently. To estimate what you'll be earning 30 years from now, you need to take inflation into account. The simplest way to do this is to use inflation-adjusted numbers, which are adjusted for the average rate of inflation.

- You can use today's price as your guess of a future price, if you're willing to assume that this price goes up at the same rate as the general inflation rate. Using this strategy, you're also assuming that your raises, on average, will make your salary keep up with inflation. Remember to be consistent and only use inflation-adjusted prices and rates of return in all of your calculations.

- If you make the equivalent of $80,000 the year before you retire, then you're spending 60% of $80,000, or $48,000, per year for each of the 20 years of retirement. On your timeline, put in $48,000 starting at time 31 and ending at time 50. This set of expenditures represents your financial goal.

	A	B	C
1	Amount of Money Needed to Fund Financial Goal		
2	Number of Periods of Spending (n)	Amount Spent Per Period (C)	Return on Invested Funds (r)
3	20	48,000	.02
4	Amount Needed = $(C/r)(1 - (1/(1 + r))^n)$		
5	$784,868.80		

- Next, you can represent your investing on the timeline. Assuming that S is the amount of investing you do each year while you're working, put an S on top of your mark for each year, starting at time 1 and ending at time 30.

S = Investments while Working

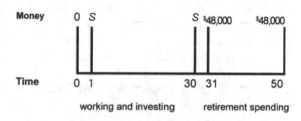

- To solve the planning problem, you need to put this information into the financial planning equation. Start by finding the amount of money you'll need to have at time 30 in order to be able to spend $48,000 per year for the next 20 years.

The Present Value of an Annuity

- Another time value of money formula is the present value of an **annuity**, which is a financial instrument that makes a fixed payment each period for a finite number of periods. Many financial instruments and investments are annuities—or are made up of annuities plus other payments.

- In an annuity, there are n payments of C each. To find the present value of the annuity, use this formula: $PV = C/(1 + r) + C/(1 + r)^2 + C/(1 + r)^3 + \ldots + C/(1 + r)^n$. Then, factor out the payment, C, and do some algebra to simplify this equation to: $(C/r)(1 - (1/(1 + r))^n)$.

- In the annuity formula, C is the amount of the cash flow, or payment, n is the number of periods the cash flow is paid or received, and r is the rate of return you are earning. Because the time periods we're using are years, the rate of return is an annual rate—it's the average annual rate you are earning on your investments.

- Next, insert the numbers that correspond to C, n, and r from your retirement planning problem. The value of this annuity represents the minimum amount of money that you need to have at time 30 in order to afford this retirement.

- Assume that on your retirement date, you move most of your riskier, higher-yielding, long-term investments into less risky, lower-yielding investments. You'll be spending some of your accumulated investments each year, but the rest will still be invested, and it will be earning some lower but still nontrivial return.

- Because we're using inflation-adjusted rates of return, the rate we choose represents the extra return on top of inflation that we think our investments will earn. A solid long-term investment will probably generate about 2% more than inflation without taking on very much risk, so 0.02 would be the interest rate.

- You now have all the numbers you need to calculate the value of the annuity. The cash payment C is 48,000, the number of payments is 20, and the rate of return on the annuity is 2%, or 0.02. You can put these numbers into the formula, and then you can use a calculator or spreadsheet to find out what this value is.

- If set up properly, the spreadsheet can take the values from your assumptions about C, n, and r and use them to calculate the value of the savings needed with the annuity formula. When all the

	A	B	C
1	Total Value of Investments		
2	Number of Periods of Spending (n)	Amount Spent Per Period (C)	Return on Invested Funds (r)
3	30	S	.035
4	Value of Investments		
5	#VALUE!		

appropriate information is entered, the spreadsheet calculates that the amount of money you need to have at time 30 is $784,868.80— so that you can spend $48,000 per year for the next 20 years without running out, as long as the money you haven't yet spent is earning an inflation-adjusted return of 2% per year.

- Next, use the financial planning equation, in which you are investing S per year for 30 years. You can find the value of this annuity by assuming some rate of return. You should use a higher rate of return than you did before because you have more time to invest, which means that you can afford to be more aggressive with your investments. Assume that you can earn 3.5% more than inflation on average.

- To figure out what these numbers will amount to when you retire, you have to do a 2-step time value of money calculation. First, your investments form another annuity—a 30-year annuity that makes payments of S per year, earning 3.5% per year. Using the annuity formula, you can calculate the value of this annuity. However, the answer is the value of the annuity at time 0; the second step involves calculating the value of your investments as of time 30.

- You can use compounding to calculate the future value of any amount of money that is invested at some fixed rate of return by using the future value equation: $FV_n = (PV)(1 + r)^n$.

- The trick is to use the total value of the annuity at time 0 as the present value in this equation, which means that you'll compound the time-0 value of the annuity by 30 years at 3.5% in order to find the future value of the annuity at time 30.

	E	F	G	H	I	J
1	Value of Future Investments			Value of Past Investments		
2	Number of Periods of Investing (n)	Amount Invested Per Period (C)	Return on Invested Funds (r)	Current Value	Number of Periods Held	Return on Invested Funds
3	30	15203.95	.035	50000	30	.025
4	Value of Investments $= (C/r)(1 - (1/(1+r))^n)(1+r)^n$			Value of Past Investments $= V(1+r)^n$		
5	$784,868.80			$104,878.38		
6	Total Value of Investments					
7	$889,746.98					

- Using the formula, you find that S equals $15,203.95 per year. This is the amount that you'll need to invest this year if you want to reach your retirement goal. This number is inflation-adjusted, so this amount really is the number you need to invest today—at today's prices. You'll have to increase that amount each year to keep up with inflation.

- The calculations you've done so far all assume that you haven't done any investing yet. To account for this, you need to modify your financial planning equation slightly. You need to include that the value of your investments at a point in time is the sum of the value of your previous investments—that is, all the investments you made before now—plus the value of your current and future investments.

- The next step is calculating what the value of those previous investments will be at some point in the future. Hopefully, you know the current value of your previous investments, or you can look them up by checking your account statements from banks, brokers, or mutual funds. Then, it's a straightforward matter of compounding at an appropriate rate of return for the correct number of years using the basic future value equation.

Important Term

annuity: A financial instrument that makes a fixed payment each period for a finite number of periods.

Suggested Reading

Bodie, Kane, and Marcus, *Essentials of Investments*, chap. 21.

Greene, "Don't Join the Ostrich Generation."

Questions to Consider

1. In addition to saving for retirement, people often have financial goals such as saving for their children's education or saving for the down payment for a vacation home. What is one of your other financial goals? Have you thought about how much money you will need to have saved and how far into the future you will need (or want) to have the money? Use a financial planning template to help you plan to meet this financial goal, especially the amount you will need to save each year in order to reach your goal.

2. The U.S. Social Security Administration sends periodic updates to everyone who has earned enough credits to qualify to receive social security benefits when they retire. These updates detail a person's social security earnings and make a projection of the payment that each contributor will receive upon retirement. You can also estimate your retirement benefits from social security at http://www.socialsecurity. gov/planners/calculators.htm. Find the current estimate of your monthly social security benefits from either source. Given the estimated size of your monthly benefits, do you believe that they will account for 20%

of your preretirement income? In other words, if you multiply this projected benefit by 5, do you think this is a good estimate of your preretirement income? If not, what fraction of your income do you think this benefit represents? How do you need to adjust your financial planning assumptions?

Financial Planning
Lecture 23—Transcript

In this lecture, we're going to use the time value of money tools we learned in the previous lecture to do some hands-on financial planning.

Financial planning is one of those key first steps that you need to do when you start investing. It helps you figure out some answers to your big questions, like "how much should I be investing?" Good financial planning also helps you see the full range of financial possibilities for your life. If you have a financial plan that works for you, it'll both help you sleep better at night, and it'll help motivate you to keep investing.

Financial planning comes down to one basic task—finding a balance between the amount of money you need to reach a particular financial goal, and the value of your investments. Since we're talking about balancing these two amounts, it suggests that we can set up an equation to guide our financial planning. And here it is—the amount of money needed at some point in time is equal to the value of the investments at that same point in time. What this equation expresses is a condition—specifically, a condition for personal financial equilibrium that we're trying to satisfy. We know that we'll have a workable financial plan if we can find numbers that make this equation balance.

Turning this basic equation into a tool that you can use to make decisions is the tricky part of financial planning. But I'll show you how to do it right.

First, we need to pick a financial planning problem to solve. I'm going to focus on financial planning for retirement, because it's something that everyone needs to do, and it's one of the more complex financial planning problems. You'll be able to apply everything we do in this lecture to other financial planning problems, and they'll seem easier to solve than this one.

Here's the basic retirement planning scenario. Suppose you plan to retire at a certain age, say 65 or 70, and after that time your income will either be close to 0, or it will be much less than it is today. During the years that you work, you invest some money each year, and these investments will hopefully grow into a large sum that will be enough to provide for your needs during retirement. The retirement planning problem is to find the right numbers that turn this general idea into a workable plan that you are comfortable with.

As I mentioned in the lecture on the time value of money, the best way to attack most financial problems is to draw a picture. So let's draw a time line, and start filling in information on the time line that describes our financial planning problem. Start by making a mark somewhere toward the right end of the time line.

This mark represents the number of years from now that you'll retire. That number depends on your age now, and the age at which you'd like to retire. Let's say that you think your retirement is 30 years away from now. So I put a 30 under this mark, which means that my retirement date is time 30.

To keep things simple, you expect that during your retirement, you won't have any income from working. You'll be living off of the value of your investments and Social Security.

You'll need to estimate how many years you'll live during your retirement. You really don't want to run out of money after you retire, so do think carefully about how long you can expect to live. For example, Americans who are 60 to 69 years old have a life expectancy of about 80 to 83 years. Suppose you conclude that the best number for you, given when you want to retire, is 20 years. So you expect to retire 30 years from now and live for another 20 years after that.

Now there's an even harder calculation you need to make—how much money you'll need during each year of retirement. Retirement experts tend to think about this question in terms of the fraction of your pre-retirement salary that you'll need to maintain your lifestyle. From my reading, there seems to be general agreement that the number is around 70%. That is, you'll want to spend about 70% of your preretirement salary each year during retirement.

But we'll want to make two adjustments to this number. First, we should account for Social Security. The forecasts I've seen indicate that Social Security payments will be about 20% of your preretirement salary. We can use that number to reduce the amount that we'll have to pay out of our own investments.

We also should adjust this number for increased costs during retirement, especially medical care. As I mentioned in my first lecture, the price of medical care is rising more quickly than the general price level. And in addition, retirees consume more healthcare services than younger people do. So to be on the safe side, let's assume that we'll need an additional 10% of preretirement salary to pay for the increased cost of medical insurance, and medical care that isn't covered by insurance.

Let's review these numbers before we go on. We assume that we'll need 70% of our pre-retirement salary. Then we subtract 20%, because we'll receive that much from Social Security. That leaves 50%. But then we add 10% for higher medical expenses. That means that, during retirement, we'll need to pay 60% of our pre-retirement salary out of our investments.

Okay. Now let's suppose you make $80,000 per year currently. Won't we need to estimate what you'll be earning 30 years from now?

This brings up the question of how to deal with inflation in these financial planning problems. One way to do this is to include inflation in every calculation you make. You can do this, but it gets cumbersome and messy. The other way to do this is to use inflation-adjusted numbers—in the sense that they're adjusted for the average rate of inflation.

The nice aspect of the inflation-adjusted approach is that it allows us to use the following neat little trick: I can use today's price as my guess of a future price, if I'm willing to assume that this price goes up at the same rate as the general inflation rate. So if I use today's salary as my best guess of my pre-retirement salary, I'm not assuming that I'm getting no raises for the next 30 years. Actually, I'm assuming that my raises, on average, will make my salary just keep up with inflation. Unless I have very good reason to believe that my raises are going up faster than the average inflation rate, this seems like an acceptable assumption.

I like the inflation-adjusted approach because it keeps the calculations simpler. The only thing I have to remember is to be consistent and only use inflation-adjusted prices and rates of return in all of my calculations. As long as I keep all my calculations in inflation-adjusted terms, the answers I'll get to my planning problems will be right. And I can still adjust prices that I believe will grow a lot faster—or a lot more slowly—than the general rate of inflation.

I'm going to use the inflation-adjusted approach and assume that your salary just keeps up with inflation, so that you make the equivalent of $80,000 the year before you retire. So we're talking about spending 60% of $80,000, or $48,000 per year, for each of the 20 years of retirement. On our time line, we put in $48,000 starting at time 31 and ending at time 50.

This set of expenditures represents your financial goal. Notice that we start your spending at time 31 because it's a convenient and more accurate way to represent the fact that the spending during your first year of retirement will take place between time 30 and time 31.

Now let's represent your investing on the timeline. I'm going to set the problem up assuming that I want to find out how much I should invest each year. Let's let S stand for the amount of investing you do each year while you're working. That means we put an S on top of the mark for each year, starting at time 1 and ending at time 30. Again, we put the first investment at time 1 to reflect the fact that even though you're going to start investing right now at time 0, you'll probably invest steadily during the year, setting aside part of each paycheck. So it's more accurate, and appropriate, to represent the fact that your investing during the first year takes place between time 0 and time 1.

That completes the timeline—we've visualized our retirement planning problem.

To solve the planning problem, we need to put this information into our financial planning equation. Let's start by finding the amount of money you'll need to have at time 30 in order to be able to spend $48,000 per year for the next 20 years.

This is the point where we need to bring out one more time value of money formula—the present value of an annuity. An annuity is a financial instrument that makes a fixed payment each period, for a finite number of periods.

In the picture, C is the payment that is made each period. N is the number of periods that the payments are made, so it's also the total number of payments.

Lots of financial instruments and investments are annuities, or are made up of annuities plus other payments. A set of mortgage payments or car payments is an annuity, and most bonds are a combination of an annuity and one or more additional payments. Note, though, that when I use the term annuity here, I'm not referring to the annuities that are sold to retirees. Those are a special type of annuity, and we'll learn about those in the next lecture.

The annuity formula isn't terribly complicated, but it's not that intuitive, either. But let me try a little anyway. In an annuity, we have n payments of C each. So when we find the present value of the annuity, it looks like $PV = C/(1 + r) + C/(1 + r)^2 + C/(1 + r)^3 + \ldots + C/(1 + r)^n$.

We can factor out the payment, C, and then do some algebra to simplify this down. When you do all that, you get this formula: $C/r(1 - 1/(1 + r)^n)$.

In the annuity formula, C is the amount of the cash flow, or payment, N is the number of periods the cash flow is paid or received, and r is the rate of return you are earning. Since the time periods we're using are years, the rate of return is an annual rate and really, it's the average annual rate you are earning on your investments.

If we put in the numbers that correspond to C, N, and r from our retirement planning problem, then the value of this annuity represents the minimum amount of money that we need to have at time 30 in order to afford this retirement.

But we're still missing the interest rate on this annuity. What should we use? Let's assume that on your retirement date, you move most of your riskier, higher-yielding, long-term investments into less risky, lower-yielding investments. I realize that you'll want to start this process sooner than that in reality, but again we're trying to keep the calculations simple. You'll be spending some of your accumulated investments each year, but the rest will still be invested, and it will be earning some lower but still nontrivial rate of return.

What's a reasonable r? Keep in mind that we're using inflation-adjusted rates of return, so the rate we pick represents the extra return on top of inflation that we think our investments will earn. As I mentioned in my first lecture, it's harder to beat inflation than you might think. So choosing a return of, say, 10% would be amazingly high. A solid long-term investment will probably generate about 2% more than inflation without taking on very much risk. So let's enter 0.02 for our interest rate.

Now we have all the numbers we need to calculate the value of the annuity. Our cash payment C is \$48,000, the number of payments is 20, and the rate of return on the annuity is 2%, or 0.02. We put these numbers into the formula, and then we can use a calculator or spreadsheet to find out what this value is.

Before I do that, though, I want to recommend that you take the time to put this information into a spreadsheet, and that you make some neatly organized tables to keep track of this information. If you do this, then as you follow along with this example, you'll be building up a financial calculator that you can always use to help you think about your financial planning problems.

Let me do just that. I'm going to build a table on a spreadsheet and I'll give it a special title. I'm calling it the Amount of Money Needed table—that's one half of the financial planning equation. Since the amount of money needed is going to be the value of an annuity, I'm going to put 3 columns in this table that will keep track of the variables I need to use to calculate the value of the annuity.

Instead of just calling the variables C, N, and r, as I did with the general version of the annuity formula, I'm going to put in labels that describe in words what these variables represent. That way, I can always open up the spreadsheet and remember what these numbers really mean.

The first column I label the Number of Periods of Spending, which of course is the same as the number of years spent retired. If you want to label it the number of years retired, that's fine—I'm trying to keep the labels fairly general, so I don't have to change them when I use this table to solve other financial planning problems. Right below the label, I'll enter the value I assumed for this number—20. The next column I'll label Amount Spent Per Period, and in the row below the label I'll enter the value I assumed for the amount spend each year during retirement, which is $48,000. The third column I label Return on Invested Funds, and enter my return of 2%.

Below these variables, I'm going to enter in the actual formula I need to use to calculate the annuity value. When I enter that formula, instead of entering numbers, I'm going to enter in the cell addresses on the spreadsheet that contain the numbers that I'm assuming for the values if C, N, and r. If I set up the table this way, then I can always go back and change my assumptions easily, and not have to keep entering the same formula into the spreadsheet over and over to see how numbers change. Hopefully you die-hard calculator users out there can see the benefit of doing these calculations on a spreadsheet instead of a calculator.

Before I enter in any formulas, though, I'll put in a label, so I know what it is I'm calculating. I'm going to call this the Amount Needed, and to remind myself of what formula I'm using, I'll write the formula in there as well. When I write the formula in there, I'll use the same special characters that the spreadsheet uses when I put in actual formulas into the cells. That will also help remind me what is going on in the table.

In the row below that label, I'll enter in the annuity formula, so that it will take the values from my assumptions about C, N, and r and use them to calculate the value of the savings needed.

When this is all entered in, the spreadsheet calculates that the amount of money we need to have at time 30 is $784,868.80. This is the amount of money we need to have at time 30, so that we can spend $48,000 per year for the next 20 years without running out, as long as the money we haven't yet spent is earning an inflation-adjusted return of 2% per year.

Now we'll turn to the other side of the financial planning equation. We are investing $\$S$ per year for 30 years. Again, this is an annuity, so we can find the value of this annuity by assuming some rate of return. What should we use for the rate of return here? Let's use a higher rate of return than we did before. We have more time to invest, so we can afford to be more aggressive with our investments. Let's assume that we can earn 3.5% more than inflation, on average. This is almost double the inflation-adjusted return we assumed above, so even though the absolute size of the increase in return doesn't seem all that impressive, it really is.

Okay, so we're going to invest $\$S$ per year for 30 years, and during these 30 years, every dollar invested is earning a 3.5% inflation-adjusted annual return. What's that going to amount to when we retire?

To figure this out, we have to do a two-step time value of money calculation. First, we recognize that our investments form another annuity—a 30-year annuity that makes payments of $\$S$ per year, earning 3.5% per year. We can calculate the value of this annuity, using the annuity formula. But notice that this answer tells us the value of the annuity at time 0. But in the first part of the financial planning problem, we calculated the amount of money needed at time 30, not time 0. So we have to also calculate the value of our investments as of time 30.

That's why we need to take a second step. We know that we can use compounding to calculate the future value of any amount of money that is invested at some fixed rate of return, and we learned the future value equation in the previous lecture. The formula is simply this: $FV_n = PV \times (1 + r)^n$.

The trick is to use the total value of the annuity at time 0 as the present value in this equation. That means that we'll compound the time-0 value of the annuity by 30 years at 3.5% in order to find the future value of the annuity at time 30. Here's what the calculation looks like.

I realize that we can simplify this expression, but I like to leave it in this form because it reminds us that what we're calculating is an annuity value that is then compounded forward in time.

Let's return to our spreadsheet to show this calculation. Just like we did when we calculated the amount of money needed, we neatly label the variables we need to use, so we can always understand what we did. I'm going to put this table right next to the one I made to calculate the amount of money needed. And I'm going to label this table the Total Value of Investments. The formula has 3 variables, so we can set up a table that looks exactly like the Amount of Money Needed table.

I'll label the first variable Number of Periods of Investing, and the value I'll put in the cell below the label is 30. I'll call the second variable I put in the table Amount Invested Per Period, and the value we'll have to use right now is just S. I'll label the third variable Return on Invested Funds, and below it I enter the return we're assuming for these invested funds, which is 3.5%.

In the next two rows of the table, I'll put in a label called Value of Investment and then below it I'll enter the formula that we need to use to calculate the future value of that annuity. Since we haven't entered any number for S, the spreadsheet can't calculate the value of your investments at time 30, so it gives an error in the cell after we entered the formula.

Don't worry about that error message, because our next step will be to find a number for S. We could enter numbers for S into the table, and use trial and error to find a value for S that balances our financial planning equation. But a much faster way is simply to set up a calculation that solves for S, given the other variables in the financial planning equation. This is easier than it sounds, since we already have a number for the amount of money needed.

If we set up the basic equation of financial planning, and enter in all the numbers we know, then we get this equation, which, if you look at it, is surprisingly simple to solve. Notice that on the right-hand side of the equation we have S times some number, so we can solve for S by dividing both sides of the equation by this number multiplying the S. But then we have to translate this solution into the correct cell references, so we can enter it on the spreadsheet.

The numerator of the solution is the Amount of Money Needed from Cell A5. The numbers in the denominator are the Rate of Return on Invested Funds, from Cell G3, and the Number of Periods of Investing, from Cell E3. We can rewrite the solution for S, substituting in the cell references containing these numbers, and this is the formula for the solution that we enter into another part of the spreadsheet.

Notice that I'm putting this solution all the way over in Column K, so that I have some room for a few other things that I'll put in columns H, I, and J later. When we enter the formula correctly, we get the answer that S equals $15,203.95 per year. This is the amount that you'll need to invest this year, if you want to reach your retirement goal. It's the actual amount you need to save this year.

I keep mentioning that all our numbers are inflation-adjusted, and this one is, too, but keep in mind that inflation-adjusted values means that they're measured in terms of current prices. So this amount really is the number you need to invest today, at today's prices. Does the amount you need to invest seem like a lot? It is—it's slightly more than a sixth of your salary. And you'll have to increase that amount each year to keep up with inflation.

Now that we've solved for S, the amount of money you need to invest each year, we can go back and enter this value into cell F3. Once you do this, you can use these tables as a template. Just copy and paste them to different areas of this spreadsheet, or to different spreadsheets entirely. After you copy them, you can change one or more of your assumptions and see how this change affects the balance of your financial plan. This is a great way to compare various "what if" scenarios to see whether different choices will make you better off.

There are lots of scenarios that you'll want to investigate using these templates. For example, what if you want to retire early? Then you'll have to shorten the time you invest, and lengthen the time you're retired. What if I want to invest more aggressively while I'm working? Then you can increase the return you earn. And so on.

One of the things you'll discover is that changing different assumptions about your investing, and your retirement, will have different sized impacts on your ability to reach your financial goals. Of course, you also need to reality check the assumptions you make. Can I really save that much every year? Will my investments really earn that much, year in and year out? These are the types of questions you'll need to keep in mind as you propose changes to your investment plan.

These are almost the full set of recipes that you'll need to remember and use as you do your financial planning. But the calculations I've shown you so far assume that you haven't done any investing at all yet. I realize, though, that you may have already set aside some investments. How do you factor these in?

The answer is fairly simple. First, we need to modify our financial planning equation just slightly. Remember that the financial planning equation sets the amount of money you need at a point in time equal to the value of your investments at a point in time. We need to spell out explicitly that the value of your investments at a point in time is the sum of the value of your previous investments—that is, all the investments you made before now—plus the value of your current and future investments.

The next step is calculating what the value of those previous investments will be at some point in the future. Hopefully you know the current value of your previous investments, or you can look them up easily by checking your account statements from banks, brokers, or mutual funds. Then it's a straightforward matter of compounding at an appropriate rate of return for the correct number of years, using the basic future value equation.

Remember, you want to find the value of everything as of the same point in time, and for this problem a convenient coordinating point is your retirement date.

As an example, let's assume that your previous investments are worth $50,000 right now and you anticipate that they'll earn an average rate of 2.5% more than inflation over the next 30 years.

We'll want to add this information to the spreadsheet we've been building, so that including the value of previous investments can be a normal part of our financial planning.

We can simply add a new section to our template, which we label Value of Past Investments, and set it up as in my diagram.

For clarity, I've changed the label of the other section from Total Value of Investments to Value of Future Investments. Then we can add one more column for the total value of all investments, which is the sum of the Value of Past Investments and Value of Future Investments.

Now we're set up to use this template for our financial planning. Copy, paste, modify, and compare.

It's been a pretty intensive lecture, but we accomplished a lot. We developed a simple financial planning template that you can build on a spreadsheet. You can copy and modify this template in order to compare all kinds of retirement scenarios you want to consider. And you can use it to solve other financial planning problems as well.

In addition, this template enables you to reassess your investment plan at any time. You can say, "Okay, here's what my investments are really worth right now," and then re-calculate what you'll need to invest from that point onward. This is the kind of calculation that you'll want to do every so often to check on the progress of your investments, so you can decide whether you need to make adjustments to your strategy. And if you do need to make adjustments, then this template will help you identify specific changes that will get you where you want to go.

Taking Charge of Your Investments
Lecture 24

In this lecture, you'll learn about some of the practical issues that you'll encounter as you turn your financial plan into financial reality. You'll learn how to allocate your investments across tax-advantaged savings plans, how important it is to consolidate your investment information, and how to invest after you reach retirement. The 2 main things to remember about investing are to not invest in anything that you're not comfortable with and to keep saving and investing—even if you haven't found your ideal investments yet. After taking this course, you should feel prepared to reach your financial goals.

Savings Plans
- Over the years, Congress has created a number of **tax-advantaged savings plans** to encourage saving, especially for retirement. The proliferation of different plans means that there are special plans for people in various economic situations, and depending on your employer and income, you may be able to take advantage of more than one plan. On the other hand, the confusion level has definitely risen over the years as new plans have been introduced.

- Most of the savings plans that you're probably familiar with have the feature that contributions to these plans are not taxed. These plans include traditional IRAs and employment-related savings plans such as 401(k)s, 403(b)s for employees of nonprofits, SIMPLEs for employees of small companies, and SEPs for the self-employed. These plans are commonly called tax-deferred savings plans, which refers to the fact that you are deferring the income taxes on the contributions you make. However, you still have to pay Social Security and Medicare taxes on these contributions.

- Tax-deferred savings plans provide an incentive for people to contribute more money to these plans as they are working, and the investments in these plans will grow without being subjected to

465

income or capital gains taxes each year. However, eventually, you'll owe taxes on these savings. The withdrawals you make, when you make them, will be taxed as ordinary income. This seems like a good idea because most people will face a lower tax rate after retirement than they do while they're working.

- The federal government has what it calls mandatory withdrawals, in which once you reach the age of about 70, the government assumes that you are starting to withdraw money from your tax-deferred accounts and will charge you a minimum amount of tax based on this assumption—even if you don't actually withdraw any money from it.

- The other big category of savings plans tax your contributions but don't tax the withdrawals. The main example of this type of plan is the Roth IRA, which was introduced in 1998. If you invest in a Roth IRA, you pay income taxes on the contributions but not on the withdrawals—as long as the withdrawals have been held in the account long enough and you are older than about 59.

- If you leave your investments in the accounts long enough, and your investments deliver at least an average positive return, then you'll end up paying less tax on each dollar invested in a Roth IRA than you would in a tax-deferred savings plan. How much, of course, depends on many assumptions, and it might not necessarily be that large of a savings. However, because of the tax savings, many financial advisors urge people to put as much money as they can into Roth IRAs.

- Since 2005, it's been possible for everyone with a traditional deferred savings plan to move their savings from that plan into a Roth IRA if they choose. In order to do that, however, you have to pay income taxes on the accumulated savings in these plans. Consult a financial planner or tax advisor to help with this decision.

Employer-Sponsored Savings Plans

- Suppose your choice between savings plans boils down to an employer-sponsored tax-deferred 401(k) plan versus saving money in a Roth IRA. If your employer matches part of your 401(k) contribution, this can easily tip the scales in favor of the tax-deferred savings plan.

- Most employers contract with a few investment providers and give their employees a limited set of choices for their tax-deferred investments. Most employers will offer a set of options that try to cover a range of risk preferences, but they won't necessarily offer a very broad range of assets beyond American stocks and bonds.

- If your company's choices really don't deliver what you want as an investor, then you have to be more strategic. The first step is to figure out how much you want to invest in total to meet your financial goals.

- You should always take full advantage of your company's matching program—if it has one. Even if the investment options aren't the best ones for you, think of the matching contribution as extra return that you earn on these funds. Then, if you still want to save more, you should open a traditional IRA or Roth IRA to fill in the gaps in your company's offerings.

- The total amount that you can contribute to your IRAs is $5000 annually. If you hit that limit, then you may want to go back to putting more money into your employer's 401(k) plan—just to take advantage of the tax break. Individuals can save up to $16,500 per year through 401(k) or 403(b) plans before the employer match, so you probably have more capacity for tax-advantaged saving than you have money to save.

- Additionally, there are income limits that you must satisfy in order to be able to contribute to any kind of IRA. If your income is higher than these limits, then your effective contribution limit is currently $16,500 per year—the maximum amount you can put in your

401(k)—and you may want to save more than that. In this case, take advantage of the employer match, if any, as well as any tax advantages you get through a 401(k)-type program, but you will want to be more strategic about what to keep in your 401(k) and what not to, keeping in mind that you need to be smart about taxes.

- Another factor that you should consider if you are choosing whether to do some of your saving through individual IRAs is behavioral economics. One seemingly trivial advantage of company-sponsored programs that turns out to be important is that they're automatic, and once you enroll in the program, chances are that you won't be quick to pull out of it. If you intend to do part of your saving through an individual savings plan, you need to make sure that you can commit to making contributions.

As you enter retirement, plan to stay invested in the market—in case you outlive the rest of your savings.

- A final issue with regard to your investment options within a 401(k) plan is what form the company's matching contributions take. In many companies, the matching contribution takes the form of stock in the company. The idea behind this is to improve employees' incentives to work hard as well as to keep the cost of the matching contributions low for the company. However, if you stay with an employer for a long time, then these matching contributions can really add up and your investments can become seriously overweighted toward your employers' stock.

- If your matching contributions do take the form of company stock, you need to look at the fine print of your company's savings program to see whether, and under what conditions, you're allowed to trade in some of your shares in the company for shares in the other investment options in the 401(k) plan. To the extent that you can, you need to periodically convert some of these shares and invest in other assets so that your portfolio stays as diversified as possible.

- If you don't like the investment alternatives that your company provides, then talk to someone in the human resources department about it. Companies do respond to employee concerns about the savings plans as well as to the government's mandates about the programs.

Routine Maintenance

- Once you get started investing, the next practical issue is to do routine maintenance on your investments. Start by gathering the information on all your investments so that you can see where you stand. If you consolidate your investing information, you'll be able to see your total progress toward your financial goals.

- Setting up a spreadsheet won't take very long, and once you have it, you can update it once a year. There are some great personal finance software packages that will assemble all your data automatically if you don't want to do it yourself. Rebalancing your portfolio is important, including gradually moving your winnings into safe bonds and locking in the gains you made.

Post-Retirement Investing

- Eventually, it will be time to start spending the savings that you've accumulated. When you reach retirement, you may not have to worry about saving, but you do still have to worry about investing. Once you retire, you might even face the most difficult and confusing investment decisions because you need to find a way to make your savings stretch out over the rest of your life—and you don't know how long that'll be.

- Plan to keep a significant share—about 1/4 of your portfolio— invested in stocks, mutual funds, and other long-term investments because if you live to retirement age, then you can generally look forward to a very long retirement. Think of the money that you leave invested in the market as your insurance policy against outliving the rest of your savings.

- As for the rest of your savings, you should move it into safe assets like government bonds and TIPS by the time you retire so that you don't have to worry about a sudden crash in the prices of your investments.

- There are fundamentally 2 options for converting your holdings of bonds to cash so that you have a steady income stream: You can either manage the conversion yourself, or you can buy an investment product that will dole out money to you. These products are called annuities, but they're generally very different from the annuities that you learned about in the financial planning lecture.

- The standard annuity product differs from a regular annuity in 2 ways: The annuities that most retirees buy don't have a set ending date—they go on until you die—and they are variable annuities, which means that the payment from the annuity will fluctuate depending on the returns on some investment portfolio that the company offering the annuity invests in. The company will guarantee you a minimum investment return, but it could also pay you a higher return if its investments do well.

- As a result of the risks that the annuity company takes on— including your mortality risk and general investing risks—the annual payments the annuity company offers you are going to be a fairly small percentage of the total cost of the annuity. You need to be careful to investigate the details of the annuity and make sure that you're not giving up excessive fees to the annuity company.

- Your alternative is to set up a ladder of TIPS so that you collect some fraction of the total amount set aside for your retirement income. Just as in the case of the choice between Roth IRAs and tax-deferred IRAs, the annuity decision is one where just about everyone could benefit from some professional advice.

tax-advantaged savings plan: A plan that is issued by the government that encourages saving, especially for retirement, because income taxes are deferred on the contributions that are made. This type of plan includes traditional IRAs and employment-related savings plans such as 401(k)s, 403(b)s for employees of nonprofits, SIMPLEs for employees of small companies, and SEPs for the self-employed.

Suggested Reading

Hough, "Getting the Most from a Lame 401(k) Retirement Plan."

Pearlman, "Annuities Provide Shelter in a Storm but Come With Their Own Risks."

Ruffenach, "Do-It-Yourself Annuities"

Questions to Consider

1. One reason to continue to invest in a 401(k) retirement plan through your employer is the existence of matching contributions that your employer makes because this automatically increases your effective return on your investment. These contributions are usually capped at some maximum amount, however. If your employer does match your 401(k) contributions, what is the maximum amount that you can receive from your employer? How much do you need to contribute in order to maximize your employer's matching contribution? Once you've maximized the matching contribution, what is your best retirement savings alternative: more investing in a 401(k), a Roth IRA, or some other plan?

2. If you are a homeowner, an additional source of postretirement income is your home. A product that enables retirees to use the value of their home to fund their retirement spending is the reverse mortgage. The U.S. Federal Housing Administration has a reverse mortgage product called the home equity conversion mortgage (HECM) that you can learn about at http://portal.hud.gov/hudportal/HUD?src=/program_offices/housing/sfh/hecm/hecmhome. Look at some of the information on this site regarding this product. Is this a product that you think you would be interested in?

Taking Charge of Your Investments
Lecture 24—Transcript

Well, it's hard to believe, but we've reached the final lecture in the course. By now I hope you feel ready to take control of your investments. We've already learned about most of the essential investment opportunities, and issues, that you should be aware of. But there are still a few important issues and products that we need to cover. And most importantly, we need to think about the big picture—or rather, your big picture.

In the past few lectures, we've been learning about financial planning, including when to sell your investments. I'm going to stick with this theme of financial planning, and get into some of the practical issues that you'll need to deal with as you turn your financial plan into financial reality.

The first practical issue I'll start with is tax-advantaged saving plans—IRAs, 401Ks, and the like. Although most people talk about their saving plans as if they are investments—I hear people talk about putting money into their 401Ks all the time—these saving plans simply are a package that holds your actual investments. But as we've seen before, the packaging is important, too, especially since in this case, the packaging has significant tax implications.

Over the years, Congress has created a number of tax-advantaged saving plans to encourage saving, especially for retirement. The proliferation of different plans means that there are special plans for people in various economic situations, and depending on your employer and income, you may be able to take advantage of more than one plan. On the other hand, the confusion level has definitely risen over the years as new plans have been introduced.

In an attempt to keep it simple, I'm going to draw one big distinction between the various saving plans out there and mostly lump the different saving plans into one of two categories. That distinction is whether the contributions to the plan are taxed.

Most of the savings plans that you're probably familiar with have the feature that contributions to these plans are not taxed. These plans include traditional IRAs and employment-related saving plans such as 401Ks, 403Bs for employees of nonprofits, SIMPLEs for employees of small companies, and SEPs for the self-employed. These plans are commonly called tax-deferred saving plans, which refers to the fact that you are deferring the income taxes on the contributions you make. You should keep in mind, however, that you still have to pay Social Security and Medicare taxes on these contributions.

The idea behind tax-deferred saving plans is that it gives an incentive for people to contribute more money to these plans as they are working. And the investments in these plans will grow without being subject to income or capital gains taxes each year. But eventually, you'll owe taxes on these savings. The withdrawals you make, when you make them, will be taxed as ordinary income. This seems like a good idea, because most people will face a lower tax rate after retirement than they do now, while they're working. Remember that in our financial planning lecture we learned that most people try to plan to live on 70% of their pre-retirement income after retirement. This drop in income is likely to mean that your withdrawals from the saving plan will be taxed at a lower rate.

And though it's tempting to think that you might not withdraw any of the savings, and leave a big pot of money for your kids, keep in mind that the federal government has what it terms "mandatory withdrawals." That is, once you reach the age of 70 and a half, the government assumes that you are starting to withdraw money from your tax-deferred accounts and it will charge you a minimum amount of tax based on this assumption, even if you don't actually withdraw any money from it.

Now, the other big category of saving plans tax your contributions but don't tax the withdrawals. The main example of this type of plan is the Roth IRA, which was introduced in 1998. Employers are also allowed to offer so-called Roth 401K plans that are employer-sponsored saving plans that carry the same tax treatment as the Roth IRA. If you invest in a Roth IRA, you pay income taxes on the contributions but not on the withdrawals, as long as the withdrawals have been held in the account long enough, and you are older than 59 and a half.

Many observers have correctly pointed out that, if you leave your investments in the accounts long enough, and your investments deliver at least an average positive return, then you'll end up paying less tax on each dollar invested in a Roth IRA than you would in a tax-deferred saving plan. How much, of course, depends on a lot of assumptions, and it might not necessarily be that large of a savings. But because of the tax savings, many financial advisors urge people to put as much money as they can into Roth IRAs. Of course, there are limits on the amount you can place in a Roth IRA each year, and this amount is currently $5000 per year, or $6000 if you are age 50 or older. In addition, if your income is too high, then you're not eligible to contribute to a Roth IRA.

But since 2005, it's been possible for everyone with a traditional deferred saving plan to move their savings from that plan into a Roth IRA if they choose. But in order to do that, you have to pay income taxes on the accumulated savings in these plans. So if you're serious about making the conversion then you need sit down with a financial planner or your tax advisor and crunch some numbers. This is definitely a decision that you'll want to get some outside help with!

The Roth-versus-tax deferred comparison that we just learned about ignores one key aspect of employee-sponsored saving plans, which is the possibility of matching contributions. Suppose your choice between saving plans boils down to an employer-sponsored tax-deferred 401K plan versus saving money in a Roth IRA. Now, if your employer matches part of your 401K contribution, this can easily tip the scales in favor of the tax-deferred saving plan.

The possibility of matching contributions leads me to the subject of your choices of investments within an employer-sponsored saving plan. Most employers contract with a few investment providers and give their employees a limited set of choices for their tax-deferred investments. It's generally not an awful choice—recently I saw that the average number of investments offered in 401K plans was about two dozen—but compared to the thousands of mutual funds and ETFs available, it's still fairly limited.

Most employers will offer a set of options that try to cover the range of risk preferences out there, from very conservative to fairly aggressive, but they won't necessarily offer a very broad range of assets beyond American stocks and bonds. In addition, as I've mentioned before, most employers will also have a set of target-date funds available for people who just don't want to worry about how to invest their savings.

Hopefully, your employer will offer a decently diversified set of investment options. By decently diversified, I'm hoping that it includes the following investments. First, there should be some ultra-safe options, like a money market mutual fund, super-safe private bonds called guaranteed investment contracts, and some kind of government bond fund. There should also be at least one riskier fixed-income investment available, such as a corporate bond fund or bond index fund.

The plan should also include a selection of U.S. stock mutual funds, including at least one broad market index fund like an S&P 500 index fund. In addition, the plan should offer some actively managed mutual funds that really differ from each other in terms of their investments. And finally, there should be at least one international or global mutual fund option available. And this is all in addition to the target-date funds that most companies have been making available. Hopefully, your 401K menu will be more diversified than that, and also give you some choices between passively managed funds and actively managed funds.

But what should you do if your company's choices don't really deliver what you want as an investor? In that case, you have to be more strategic. The first step is to figure out how much you want to invest in total to meet your financial goals. You may remember that we learned about this process in the lecture on financial planning.

In my opinion, you should always take full advantage of your company's matching program, if it has one. Even if the investment options aren't the best ones for you, think of the matching contribution as extra return that you earn on these funds. Then, if you still want to save more, you should open a traditional IRA or a Roth IRA, and fill in the gaps in your company's offerings by using one of these saving plans.

Please note, though, that the total amount that you can contribute to your IRAs is $5000 annually. If you hit that limit, then you may want to go back to putting more money into your employer's 401K plan, just to take advantage of the tax break. Individuals can save up to $16,500 per year through 401K or 403B plans, before the employer match. So you probably have more capacity for tax-advantaged saving than you have money to save.

Remember, though, that there are income limits that you must satisfy in order to be able to contribute to any kind of IRA. If your income is higher than these limits, then your effective contribution limit is $16,500 per year currently—the maximum amount you can put in your 401K—and you may well want to save more than that. In this case, my advice is still to take advantage of the employer match if any, as well as any tax advantages you get through a 401K-type program. But you will want to be more strategic about what to keep in your 401K and what not to. Once again, the name of the game is to be smart about taxes.

For example, if you want to hold bonds as part of your savings, then you can hold tax-advantaged bonds such as treasuries, TIPS, or municipal bonds in a taxable investment account. Since most of the interest on these bonds isn't subject to federal income tax, you can hold these bonds as part of your taxable savings without too much of a cost in terms of foregone return. Then you'll leave the riskier, higher-returning investments in your tax-deferred savings.

On the other hand, passively managed ETFs can also help in this situation. If you hold a passive ETF for longer than one year in a taxable account, then any gains are taxed as capital gains, rather than as income, when you sell the ETF. Again, keep in mind that this only applies to passive ETFs— if you hold mutual funds, you'll have to pay annual capital gains taxes as well as income tax on the dividends collected by the funds. And all your contributions to taxable accounts are themselves taxable, so this puts these funds at an automatic disadvantage to tax-deferred investments.

Another factor that you should consider if you are choosing whether to do some of your saving through individual IRAs is behavioral economics. One seemingly trivial advantage of company-sponsored programs that turns out to be important is that they're automatic. Even though IRAs and other individual investments that you make yourself can be more attractive than your employer's program, the one big thing that your employer can do is actually force you to save. Well, they can't force you to save, but once you enroll in the program, chances are that you won't be quick to pull out of it. So every pay period, money will be automatically put into your 401K investments. And that consistency is worth a lot—it's certainly worth a lot more than good intentions!

One problem that many people have with individual IRAs is that they intend to make an IRA contribution, but they want to invest the whole year's contribution in a lump sum right before the tax deadline for IRA contributions—which is usually April 15th. But when it comes to April 15th, the money isn't there to put into the IRA. So if you intend to do part of your saving through an individual saving plan, you really need to make sure that you can commit to making those contributions.

One final issue with regard to your investment options within a 401K plan is what form the company's matching contributions take. In many companies the matching contribution takes the form of stock in the company. The idea behind this is to improve employees' incentives to work hard, as well as to keep the cost of the matching contributions low for the company.

Since the company isn't obligated to match at all, it's hard to be too choosy about the form that these matching contributions take. But if you stay with an employer for a long time, then these matching contributions can really add up and your investments can become seriously overweighted toward your employers' stock. This isn't just a theoretical issue—when firms like Enron went bankrupt in the early 2000s, employees lost millions of dollars of savings that took the form of company stock.

If your matching contributions do take the form of company stock, then you need to look at the fine print of your company's saving program to see whether, and under what conditions, you're allowed to trade in some of your shares in the company for shares in the other investment options in the 401K plan. And to the extent that you can, you need to periodically convert some of these shares and invest in other assets, so that your portfolio stays as diversified as possible. This can be really hard to do if your company's stock is rising fast—but just remember the example of firms like Enron, and realize that you need the insurance that diversification provides. You're already relying on the company for your income, right?

Finally, if you don't like the investment alternatives that your company provides, then by all means, talk to someone in the Human Resources department about it. Companies do respond to employee concerns about the saving plans, as well as to the government's mandates about the programs. So it can't hurt to let the HR department know that you'd like to see more choices of mutual funds or more diverse investments offered.

The first set of practical decisions regards how to allocate your investments between all the different saving plans that are available to you. You'll need to take your list of desired investments, which hopefully you've been forming throughout this course as you've learned about different instruments, and compare your ideal list to the actual options that are available to you through your employer's 401K or other tax-advantaged saving program. Make your best choices, keeping in mind that the tax advantages and potential matching contributions of an employer-sponsored program can do a lot to offset a less-than-ideal set of investment options. And if you do find that you want to use individual IRAs or even taxable accounts to fill in the gaps left by your employer's program, make sure that you can commit to the contributions. You may want to look into whether you can arrange automatic withdrawals through your bank, or whether your employer offers supplemental saving programs that basically do the same thing.

Once you get started investing, the next practical issue is to do routine maintenance on your investments. Seriously—think about it as having the same importance as getting your car's oil changed on schedule. Sure, you can probably live without doing it for quite a while, but if you make the time and effort to do it regularly, you'll get much more performance and enjoyment out of your investment—and you'll dramatically cut the risk of an unexpected breakdown, which is always followed by an expensive overhaul.

The first step in this process is simply gathering together the information on all your investments so you can see where you stand. If you're like me, then you probably have multiple investments spread between 401Ks with current and former employers, your spouse's 401Ks, your other tax-advantaged accounts you manage yourself, your brokerage accounts, and of course let's not forget any bank accounts that you are also holding as investments, like long-term saving accounts or even possibly money market deposit accounts. Oh, and don't forget any real investments that you want to count, like your home or other property, and any other possessions that you count as investments.

You probably know, roughly speaking, where you keep all the statements and about what your investments are worth. But have you ever sat down and put all the information, in one place? I know, you're thinking, "What a great idea!" But at the same time you're thinking, "What a hassle!" Actually, setting up a spreadsheet won't take all that long, and once you have it, you can just update it once a year.

All I have in mind is a table that has a separate column for each investment you own, where each specific mutual fund or individual security gets its own column, even if it's held as part of your 401K or other plan. Each row of the table is a year. You can put a new row in the table every year, where you measure the value of all your investments at the end of the year. You can do the updating as often as you like—for example, most mutual funds will send you quarterly statements—but you only need to update this once a year, and it's best to do it as of the end of whatever tax year you're using. Since most of us use the calendar year for our tax year, you should put in the value of the investments as of December 31st.

If you're feeling really ambitious, you could also add a worksheet that describes exactly what each investment is, and why you started investing in it. You could also include information about what price you bought the investment at, or what your expected return is for the investment. And, for individual investments like stocks, you can put in the prices that will trigger your reevaluation exercise that we learned about in the lecture on when to sell investments.

If you have all this information in one place, then you don't have to hunt around for all this information when you really need it to make an investing decision. It will also serve as a reminder to actually exercise that selling discipline that's so important.

Of course, you don't need to go to all the effort of setting up a new spreadsheet if you don't want to. There are some great personal finance software packages out there that will do a lot of this stuff automatically, and that can be a great way to go. My point is that you really don't need all the bells and whistles and up-to-the-nanosecond updates on your investment values to be a successful investor. All you really need to do is to sit down at least once a year and look over how your portfolio is doing. You need to see the big picture and think about whether to make some adjustments. As we learned in the lecture on knowing when to sell, one of the most important tasks you should do is rebalance your portfolio, especially so you can gradually move your winnings into safe bonds and lock in those gains that you made.

You'll also have all the information in front of you so you can ask whether you want to make bigger changes to your portfolio. For example, maybe when you start investing, you decide to stick close to home and invest most of your savings into U.S. stocks and bonds. But as you get experience in the markets, you realize that you want to shift your portfolio more heavily into foreign assets. Having all the information in front of you about what you have now will make this decision much easier to visualize. You can make decisions about exactly how much money you want to invest in foreign assets, and how much of your existing holdings you'll want to sell to get the cash you'll need.

And best of all, if you consolidate your investing information in one place, you'll be able to see your total progress toward your financial goals. Now, I realize that when markets go down, we don't necessarily want to know how our investments did. But being able to see the progress, whatever it is, is crucial for you as an investor. If you're going to need to make adjustments to your financial plans, it's best to know about them sooner rather than later.

Okay—so as you invest, bring in your portfolio for an annual checkup and tune-up. Eventually, though, it will be time to start spending the savings that you've accumulated. And you may think then that the hard part of your job is over—and in some respects, it is. When you get to retirement, for example, you don't have to worry about saving.

But the truth is, you still have to worry about investing. In fact, many people think that once you retire, you face the most difficult and confusing investment decisions of all. That's because you need to find a way to make your savings stretch out over the rest of your life—and you don't know how long that'll be. And the investment products that are commonly offered to retirees tend to be extremely difficult to understand, so it's hard to know whether you're getting a good deal on them.

Let's spend a few minutes learning about your post-retirement investment strategy. Now, the first thing to keep in mind is to plan to stay invested in the market. By that, I mean that you should plan to keep a significant share, say one quarter of your portfolio, invested in stocks, mutual funds, and other long-term investments. That's because if you live to retirement age, then you can generally look forward to a very long retirement. Think of the money that you leave invested in the market as your insurance policy against outliving the rest of your savings.

As for the rest of your savings, you should have moved it into safe assets like government bonds and TIPS by the time you retire. So you shouldn't have to worry about a sudden crash in the prices of your investments. But the question here is how to convert your holdings of bonds to cash, so you have a steady income stream. There are fundamentally two options.

Option one is for you to manage that conversion yourself. If you're invested in government bonds and TIPS, for example, you can set up bond ladders that liquidate every month or every few months, providing a steady stream of cash. With a little assistance from a financial planner, you can calculate exactly how much you can liquidate each month depending on how many years you want your bonds to last after you retire.

The other option is to buy an investment product that will dole out money to you. These products are called annuities, but they're generally very different from the annuities that we learned about in the financial planning lecture. The standard annuity product differs from a regular annuity in two ways. First, the annuities that most retirees buy don't have a set ending date—they go on until you die.

The second way that the typical annuity sold to a retiree is different is that it is a variable annuity. That is, the payment from the annuity will fluctuate, depending on the returns on some investment portfolio that the company offering the annuity invests in. So, when you buy a variable annuity, the company offering the product takes your lump-sum payment and invests it in some assets that the company hopes will earn a high return. The company will guarantee you a minimum investment return, but it could also pay you a higher return, if its investments do well.

Sounds like a great idea, right? It can be, if the price is right. The company offering this product to you is taking on your mortality risk, just like an insurance company does. So it's little wonder that many of the firms offering these products are insurance companies. The company is going to charge you for bearing and managing this risk. In addition, the company is going to be investing the money you give them, just like a mutual fund does. And again, it'll build management fees into the price of this product. And, to the extent that it guarantees you a minimum payment on the annuity, the company is also bearing the risk that its investment returns will be less than the returns that it's promising you.

So the net result is that the annual payments the annuity company offers you are going to be a fairly small percentage of the total cost of the annuity. For example, the payment you receive each year may be something like 4 or 5% of the cost of the annuity. I'm not saying that this is necessarily a bad deal, because the annuity company is taking on several risks, but I'm also saying that it isn't automatically a good one. You need to be careful to investigate the details of the annuity, and make sure that you're not giving up excessive fees to the annuity company.

Remember that your alternative is to set up a ladder of TIPS or other government bonds so that you collect some fraction of the total amount set aside for your retirement income. You can compare how much you'd be able to collect from this do-it-yourself strategy to the amount that an annuity company is offering, to get some idea of whether it's really worth it to have the annuity company take on the risks of managing your retirement income. Again, just as in the case of the choice between Roth IRAs and tax-deferred IRAs, the annuity decision is one where just about everyone could benefit from some professional advice.

That about does it for the practical issues you need to consider for your investing. We've learned about allocating your investments across all the tax-advantaged savings plans, so that you find the right place to hold all the great investments you've been learning about in the course. And we learned how important it is to get all your investment information organized into one place, so that you can do an annual portfolio tune-up. And finally, we tackled the big question of how to invest after you reach retirement. We've demystified annuities, and we've learned a simple do-it-yourself alternative that you can use to manage your own retirement income, or to do comparison shopping for annuities.

Wow, we've come a very long way in this course. You may remember that my first lecture was about how to stop worrying and start investing. I hope that by now, you've stopped worrying and are excited to start looking for the right kinds of investment opportunities for you. In this course, we've learned about the full range of products that I think all investors should at least consider. I hope I've changed your mind about a few investments that you thought were too dangerous, or too boring, to consider before, and I've also shown you a couple of attractive investments that you weren't aware of.

More importantly, I hope I've convinced you that you can chart your own path to investing success. No matter what you believe about market efficiency, no matter how risk averse you are, and no matter how much or how little time you have to devote to investing, there are lots of good investment options to suit your particular needs. There's no need to ever just follow the crowd—do what's best for you.

In this course, we've learned a lot of do's and don'ts of investing. I hope you remember them all, but let me leave you with two of the most important ones. First, don't invest in anything that you're not comfortable with. Hopefully this course has raised your comfort level with many investments, but if you're ever offered an investment that you don't understand or that doesn't seem right, just remember that example of Warren Buffett, and say, "No, thanks."

Second, do keep saving, and do keep investing, even if you haven't found your ideal investments yet. It's okay to take your time to look for great investments—in fact, I encourage you to take your time—but in the meantime, put your money to work in one of the many safe and flexible investments, like money market funds or TIPS, that we've learned about in this course. It's essential that you put time on your side by investing sooner rather than later and making a long-term commitment to regular investing.

I hope that this course has made you eager to get your current investments organized and to make plans for your future investments. In other words, I hope that you really feel prepared now to find good investment opportunities and take advantage of them. And I hope you feel confident that you can use what you've learned in this course to reach your financial goals. I'm going to stop lecturing and get out of your way, so you can get out there and do just that. Good luck, and happy investing!

Glossary

accrual: One particular set of procedures for recognizing revenue and expenses.

annuity: A financial instrument that makes a fixed payment each period for a finite number of periods.

ask price: The price at which the dealer will sell a share of stock to you, or the asking price.

asset: Anything that holds onto its value over time.

asset allocation fund: A type of mutual fund that is switched by managers between bonds and stocks whenever the markets seem to favor one investment over the other.

balanced fund: A mutual fund that holds both stocks and bonds in its portfolio.

bear market: A market in which bonds and other securities are declining in value.

behavioral economics: Blends psychology and physiology with economics to gain a better understanding of how people's decision making goes wrong—especially in situations involving investing.

beta: A measure of the riskiness, or return variation, of a stock; the number of units of risk in a stock, where one unit of risk is equivalent to the amount of risk, or return variation, in the overall stock market.

bid-ask spread: The difference between the ask price and the bid price.

bid price: The price at which the dealer will buy the stock from you, or the offering price.

bill: A bond that matures in less than 1 year.

blend fund: A type of equity fund that tries to select equities based on 2 different investment objectives.

bond fund: A mutual fund that holds only bonds in its portfolio.

bond ladder: A set of bonds that has one bond maturing every year, every quarter, or maybe even every month. As one bond matures, you can use the cash from the bond if you need to, but you can also buy a new bond to replace it. If you always buy the same maturity of bond, then you end up with a self-replenishing set of bonds that generates a steady stream of cash.

book building: The process of building up a demand curve for a company's shares that is carried out by an investment bank.

broker: A type of intermediary in the financial markets who simply helps buyers locate sellers—and vice versa—and arranges the sale.

bull market: A market in which bonds and other securities are rising in value.

business cycle: The cycle of expansion and recession that characterizes our overall economy.

call option: The right to buy an asset.

capital asset pricing model (CAPM): A model that is used to estimate expected rates of return for stocks.

capital expenditure: A purchase of real assets, such as equipment and factories.

capital good: A type of real asset that is involved in the production of goods, such as machines, buildings, factories, and the land that they sit on.

closed-end mutual fund: A type of mutual fund that only issues shares once and doesn't redeem shares unless the entire fund is liquidated.

commercial paper: A special kind of corporate bond that is unsecured and has very short maturity but that is quite safe.

compounding: A time value of money tool that describes the fact that if you leave money in an investment, the interest earned during 1 period will start to earn its own interest in subsequent periods.

confirmation bias: Describes the tendency for people to only notice evidence that supports their beliefs and ignore evidence that contradicts it.

correlation: The statistical term that describes the comovement of 2 different companies' returns, including unexpected returns.

coupon: An interest payment.

coupon yield: The value of the annual coupon amount divided by par.

covered call: A type of options investment that is a combination of a stock and a call option that you can use to enhance your returns on stocks that you own.

cumulative default rate: The fraction of all corporate bonds in each rating category that have ever defaulted.

current yield: The annual coupon divided by the market price of the bond.

cyclical company: A company that is strongly tied to the business cycle because it is a manufacturer or distributor of big-ticket consumer items like cars, appliances, and furniture.

dealer: A type of intermediary in the financial markets who connects buyers and sellers indirectly.

default risk: The risk that a borrower won't be able to pay back all the promised principal and interest payments.

depository receipt: A document that proves ownership of an asset that is in a bank's depository and is issued to the original depositor of the asset by the bank.

discounting: A time value of money tool that is used to find the present value of an investment by dividing the future value by the compounded rate of return: $PV = (FV)/(1 + r)^n$.

disposition effect: An effect that describes the notion that people hate to sell losing investments—they'll hold on to them for years, hoping that some miracle will push the price back up to what they paid.

diversification: The practice of investing in several or many different assets rather than only one or a few assets.

dividend: The profit that a company pays out to its shareholders.

dividend discount model (DDM): A fundamentals-based stock-pricing model that is represented by $D/(r - g)$, where D is the next year's dividend, r is the expected return on the stock, and g is the growth rate of the dividend.

dividend policy: The way a company chooses to pay out dividends and how it changes these payouts over time

dividend reinvestment program (DRiP): A stockholding plan in which any dividends earned on the shares are automatically reinvested in the shares.

dividend yield: The annual dividend on a stock divided by its price.

dollar-cost averaging: A strategy that involves investing a certain amount of money each month and staying fully invested in the market at all times.

Dutch auction method: A method in which everyone who is interested in a particular IPO submits a bid for shares that tells what price they will pay and how many shares they'll buy at that price. The bids are then ranked by price offered, starting from the highest and running to the lowest.

earnings before interest and taxes (EBIT): Net sales minus the expenses of running a company.

efficient markets hypothesis (EMH): An economic theory that suggests that market prices fully incorporate information that is known now and that new information is incorporated very quickly into market prices.

equity: The difference between assets and liabilities, which tells you what a company is worth.

equity fund: A mutual fund that holds only stocks in its portfolio.

equity REIT: A type of REIT that invests directly in real estate—buildings and land.

exchange-traded fund (ETF): A fund that combines some of the features of a mutual funds with some of the features of individual stocks, including being listed and traded on an exchange.

expected return: The best guess of an investment's future return; represents the return that is truly expected to be delivered by the investment.

fallen angel: A bond that starts out highly rated but then gets downgraded to junk status.

financial asset: A document that entitles its owner to receive something of value, generally a set of cash payments, from someone else.

financial option: The right to buy or sell a particular asset at a preagreed price on or before a certain date.

financial statement analysis: The practice of forming ratios and other statistics using the numbers presented in a set of financial statements.

Fisher effect: A theory that states that the interest rate on any bond is the sum of the real rate of interest plus the expected annual inflation over the life of the bond.

foreign exchange: One of the largest and most active asset markets on the planet that involves betting on the direction of exchange rates.

foreign exchange risk: The risk that any capital gains or other returns on an investment in foreign assets will be offset by unfavorable changes in the exchange rate.

futures contract: A standardized agreement in which an investor pays a price now, called the futures price, to be entitled to receive an asset on a later date specified in the contract.

future value: The value of an investment, or a debt, at a future date n periods from the current time: $FV_n = (PV)(1 + r_p)^n$, where FV stands for future value at time n (that is, n periods from now) and PV stands for present value—which is what something is worth now, at time 0. The r_p is the periodic rate for whatever compounding period is used to calculate your returns.

global fund: A type of mutual fund that invests in American and foreign assets.

idiosyncratic risk: The type of risk in an unexpected return that is specific to each particular asset and doesn't share anything in common with any other assets; risk that you can reduce through diversification.

income fund: A type of equity fund whose focus is on earning high-dividend income.

indexed bond: The general term for a bond whose interest rate rises with inflation.

index option: Options on futures contracts on stock indexes.

inflation: A general increase in prices.

initial margin: A margin requirement that is the minimum ownership stake you have to take in order to start a leveraged investment.

initial public offering (IPO): A special sale in which a company first sells its shares to the public; marks the transition from being a privately held company that only 500 or fewer people can own to becoming a publicly held company that anyone can own a part of.

intangible asset: A type of real asset that is invisible but nonetheless real—such as ideas, knowledge, and skills.

international fund: A type of mutual fund that invests only in assets from outside the United States.

investing: Spending your money, time, or other resources to create or acquire assets.

investment plan: A set of decisions about how much to invest, which types of investments and strategies to try, and when to sell investments.

issuer: The party who promises to give the owner of a financial asset something of value, including a firm, the government, or a person.

junk bond: A bond that involves high-yield, or non-investment-grade, debt.

leverage: Determines how much a firm is borrowing and is often expressed as total assets divided by total equity.

liability: What a firm owes to other parties.

load: A sales fee that a mutual fund charges.

long-term capital gain: A trading profit that you make on an investment that you've held for longer than 1 year.

maintenance margin: A margin requirement that is the minimum level of equity that you have to maintain at all times after you make an initial leveraged purchase.

margin: The share of an asset owned by a leveraged investor; the value of an equity stake in an asset divided by the total value of the asset.

margin call: A request from your broker to deposit cash or securities into your brokerage account in order to bring your equity in the shares at least back up to the maintenance margin level.

margin requirement: A minimum required ownership stake.

material information: Highly desirable and profitable information that affects the market price of an asset when it's revealed to the market.

maturity: The length of time until the final payment on a bond.

medium-term note (MTN): A bond that typically matures in 1 to 5 years.

method of comparables: A valuation method that is based on using ratios to value stocks.

mortgage-backed security (MBS): A special type of bond that is issued by a special corporation that buys and holds hundreds or thousands of mortgages.

mortgage REIT: A type of REIT that invests in mortgages and mortgage-backed securities.

mutual fund: A package of stocks, bonds, and perhaps other instruments.

net asset value (NAV): The market value of a portfolio on a particular day minus any liabilities of the fund divided by the total number of units.

net income: EBIT minus interest and corporate income taxes.

net sales: Sales minus returns.

note: A bond that matures in 1 to 10 years.

open-end mutual fund: A type of mutual fund that is always ready to issue new shares by selling them to investors and to redeem shares from investors.

option: A contract that gives its buyer the right, but not the obligation, to take some action—which usually involves buying or selling something.

payout ratio: The fraction of earnings per share (EPS) that is paid out to a company's shareholders: D/EPS.

PEG ratio: A ratio found by taking a company's price-to-earnings (P/E) ratio and dividing by the growth rate of earnings.

periodic return: The return you earn for holding an investment for 1 period, where the period can be any length of time.

plowback ratio: The fraction of earnings per share (EPS) that is reinvested in a company: (EPS $-$ D)/EPS, or $1 - $ (D/EPS).

portfolio allocation: The way in which you divide your investments across different investment categories.

preferred share: A stock that has a higher priority claim on a company's profits than a common share does.

price-to-earnings (P/E) ratio: A ratio of a company's price to its earnings per share (EPS).

principal: The par value of a bond.

private information: Information that is known only to a few people and isn't widely distributed or shared.

prospectus: A document describing the objectives, operation, and risks of a mutual fund.

put option: The right to sell an asset.

rating agency: A company that specializes in evaluating bonds and that gives out ratings based on the likelihood of full and on-time repayment of interest and principal.

real asset: An asset that is used directly in the production of goods and services.

real estate investment trust (REIT): A company that sells shares to investors once, at the beginning of a fund, and then uses the proceeds to invest in a portfolio of real estate assets.

restrictive covenant: A large set of terms and conditions that the buyer of a bond can make the issuer of the bond agree to.

return on assets (ROA): (EBIT − taxes)/total assets.

return on equity (ROE): Net income divided by equity.

riding the yield curve: A strategy that involves making extra returns on bonds by buying longer maturity bonds than you actually intend to hold to maturity and selling them after a few years.

scenario analysis: A type of financial analysis in which a complex future is simplified to just a few possibilities that are regarded as the most likely ones.

sector fund: A type of equity fund that invests in the shares of companies that are in the same type of sector or industry.

secured: Refers to a bond that is backed up by specific collateral.

security: Written evidence of the extension of a loan.

share: An equal portion of a company's stock.

short-term capital gain: A trading profit that you make on an investment that you've held for 1 year or less.

socially responsible fund: A type of mutual fund that pursues high returns but avoids investing in companies that engage in activities that some people find objectionable.

standard deviation of returns: A useful concept that tries to measure the average size of an unexpected return, or in other words, how much the actual return could differ from the expected return on average.

stated annual rate of return: A special form of a return that contains 2 pieces of information if quoted properly: an annual rate of return and the number of times per year the rate is compounded.

stock: A form of ownership that a firm issues that divides the ownership of the company into thousands—if not millions—of equal parts, or shares.

stock buyback: A transaction in which a company goes into the stock market and repurchases, or buys back, some of its outstanding shares.

stock dividend: A common type of noncash dividend in which a company pays out part of a share instead of cash for each share that an investor holds.

stock exchange: An organized market where people can meet and trade shares.

stock option: The right to buy or sell shares of a particular company.

storable commodity: A type of real asset that can be stored and retain value, such as cotton or oil.

structured product: A product that combines different financial instruments into a new one or that slices the payments from a financial instrument in new ways.

systematic risk: The type of risk in an unexpected return that is common across assets; risk that you can't get rid of through diversification.

tax-advantaged savings plan: A plan that is issued by the government that encourages saving, especially for retirement, because income taxes are deferred on the contributions that are made. This type of plan includes traditional IRAs and employment-related savings plans such as 401(k)s, 403(b)s for employees of nonprofits, SIMPLEs for employees of small companies, and SEPs for the self-employed.

technical analysis: A type of analysis that uses information in prices as well as in the volume of trading to make predictions about future price movements.

trust: A legal vehicle for holding property on behalf of someone.

turnover rate: The fraction of the total value of a mutual fund that a portfolio manager trades, or turns over, during a year.

unit investment trust: A type of collective investment scheme that buys and then holds a fixed portfolio of assets.

uptick rule: A regulation that is aimed directly at limiting the practice of short selling.

valuation model: A model that helps us figure out what something is worth.

valuation multiple: The ratio of one asset's price to its value driver.

yield to maturity: The average yield earned by a bond investor who buys a bond at the current market price and holds the bond to maturity.

zero-coupon bond: A bond that makes a single payment and that gives no interest payments, or coupons, between the time the bond is bought and the time that the borrower makes the payment to the buyer.

Bibliography

Arends, Brett. "Timber Is Very Safe: If the Sun Shines and It Rains, the Trees Grow on Schedule." *SmartMoney* 20, October 2011: 27. This article discusses investing in timberland and timberland investment management organizations (TIMOs).

Ball, Ray. "The Theory of Stock Market Efficiency: Accomplishments and Limitations." *Journal of Applied Corporate Finance* 8, no. 1 (1995): 4–17. This article is an excellent review of the evidence for and against the efficient markets hypothesis.

Benveniste, Lawrence M., and William J. Wilhelm, Jr. "Initial Public Offerings: Going by the Book." *Journal of Applied Corporate Finance* 10, no. 10 (1997): 98–108. This article explains the book-building process of IPOs and the underpricing of IPOs.

Berk, Jonathan, and Peter DeMarzo. "The Time Value of Money." Chap. 4 in *Corporate Finance*. 2nd ed. New York: Pearson Education, 2011. This chapter and the entire text give an additional perspective on how to work with time value of money and several of the other issues raised in this course.

Bodie, Zvi, Alex Kane, and Alan J. Marcus. *Essentials of Investments*. 8th ed. New York: McGraw-Hill Irwin, 2010. The Bodie, Kane, and Marcus textbooks are considered the best ones on the subject of investments. This one is a less technical version of *Investments*.

———. *Investments*. 9th ed. New York: McGraw-Hill Irwin, 2010. If you would like more technical and detailed information on many of the topics covered in this course, this is a very good place to look.

Bogle, John C. *Common Sense on Mutual Funds*. 10th ed. Hoboken, NJ: John Wiley and Sons, 2009. Bogle has strong opinions about how to invest, but they're worth learning about because they are simple and effective. Bogle is the founder of Vanguard and, therefore, a big proponent of passive mutual fund investing; this book is an excellent introduction to, and critique of, mutual fund investing.

————. *The Little Book of Common Sense Investing*. Hoboken, NJ: Wiley and Sons, 2007. This is a less technical introduction to Bogle's views on investing. *The Little Book* series features many experts on investing writing about the areas of their expertise, and they are worth a look.

Brealey, Richard A., Stewart C. Myers, and Franklin Allen. *Principles of Corporate Finance*. 10th ed. New York: McGraw-Hill Irwin, 2011. This corporate finance text has one of the best discussions of time value of money tools, and it has some different perspectives on several of the investment issues covered in the course.

Browning, E. S. "A Long-Term Case for Stocks," *The Wall Street Journal*, September 12, 2011. This article describes the views of Richard Sylla, a famous business historian, and focuses on his view that long-term stock returns will be favorable to investors.

Damadoran, Aswath. *The Little Book of Valuation: How to Value a Company, Pick a Stock, and Profit*. Hoboken, NJ: John Wiley and Sons, 2011. Damadoran is acknowledged as one of the top scholars in valuation. This book is a gentle introduction to valuation, and you may be interested in his other texts on valuation as well.

English, James. *Applied Equity Analysis*. New York: McGraw-Hill, 2001. This book offers an excellent look at valuing a company, written by someone from the business who is now a business school professor.

Ensign, Rachel Louise. "How to Profit When the Dollar Falls." *The Wall Street Journal*, September 7, 2011. This article discusses mutual funds and ETFs that trade in currencies.

Faerber, Esme. *All about Bonds, Bond Mutual Funds, and Bond ETFs*. 3rd ed. New York: McGraw-Hill, 2009. The *All about* books from McGraw-Hill are simple and clear descriptions of investment instruments. This offers a comprehensive look at the types of bond investments available.

————. *All about Investing.* New York: McGraw-Hill, 2006. Another *All about* guide that is a good all-around introduction to investing.

Fasciocco, Leo. "Buying on Margin Is a Double-Edged Sword." *Investor's Business Daily*, November 27, 1998. This article describes the attractions and dangers of using margin.

Greene, Kelly. "Don't Join the Ostrich Generation." *The Wall Street Journal*, September 17, 2011. This article gives some statistics about who is doing retirement planning and serves as a good wake-up call about doing financial planning for retirement.

Hough, Jack. "Dividends: Collect, Reinvest, Repeat—for Decades." *The Wall Street Journal*, September 10, 2011. Jack Hough is a great investment columnist who writes primarily about picking stocks. His columns in *SmartMoney* magazine and on smartmoney.com are worth looking for. This article discusses the value of investing for dividends.

————. "Getting the Most from a Lame 401(k) Retirement Plan." *The Wall Street Journal*, October 8, 2011. This article delivers just what the title says—advice about how to live with a 401(k) that isn't that great.

————. "Peeling Back the Market's P/E." *The Wall Street Journal*, September 17, 2011. This article is about using the method of comparables to understand the value of the entire market.

————. "REITs, Don't Fail Me Now." *The Wall Street Journal*, October 1, 2011. This article is about some of the main aspects of REITs that investors need to keep in mind when they consider investing in REITs.

————. *Your Next Great Stock: How to Screen the Market for Tomorrow's Top Performers.* Hoboken, NJ: John Wiley and Sons, 2008. This is worth looking at if you plan to be an active stock investor who wants to manage your own portfolio; it offers good advice about how to sort through the hundreds of stocks that exist.

Bibliography

Hull, John C. "Properties of Stock Options." Chap. 10 in *Fundamentals of Futures and Options Markets*. 7th ed. Upper Saddle River, NJ: Pearson Education, 2011. This is an excellent text that will teach you more about options. It's challenging, but Hull is one of the main experts on option pricing, and his books set the standard.

Ittelson, Thomas R. *Financial Statements*. Rev. ed. Franklin Lakes, NJ: Career Press, 2009. This is an extremely user-friendly introduction to financial statements and their analysis. This is a good complement to the chapters on financial statement analysis in most investment and corporate finance textbooks.

Kansas, Dave. The Wall Street Journal *Complete Money and Investing Guidebook*. New York: Three Rivers Press, 2005. This book is a comprehensive but not very deep introduction to personal investing. It's a good starting place if you're completely new to investing.

Larimore, Taylor, Mel Lindauer, Richard A. Ferri, and Laura F. Dogu. *The Bogleheads' Guide to Retirement Planning*. Hoboken, NJ: John Wiley and Sons, 2009. Bogleheads are people who follow the ideas of John Bogle, who has several citations in this bibliography. This book offers a comprehensive look at the process of planning for retirement from a Bogle-like perspective.

Lee, Dwight R., and James A. Verbrugge. "The Efficient Market Theory Thrives on Criticism." *Journal of Applied Corporate Finance* 9, no. 1 (1996): 35–40. This article discusses how the efficient markets hypothesis implies that the markets fix their own inefficiencies.

Levinsohn, Ben. "It's Payback Time!" *The Wall Street Journal,* August 27, 2011. This article discusses the return of higher dividends and the strategy of investing for dividends.

Malkiel, Burton G. *A Random Walk down Wall Street: The Time-Tested Strategy for Successful Investing*. Rev. ed. New York: W. W. Norton and Company, 2011. This is one of the classics of investing. Even if you disagree with the argument that passive investing is best, you should still read this book.

————. "Don't Panic about the Stock Market." *The Wall Street Journal*, August 8, 2011. This article argues against market timing, especially during times when the market has fallen.

————. "Investors Shouldn't Fear 'Spiders.'" *The Wall Street Journal*, May 30, 2000. This is a clear and concise article about the way that ETFs work and how they are different from mutual funds.

Malkiel, Burton G., and Charles D. Ellis. *The Elements of Investing*. Hoboken, NJ: John Wiley and Sons, 2010. This is a short and less technical introduction to investing.

Motley Fool Staff. "Exchange-Traded Funds." *The Motley Fool*. http://www.fool.com/investing/etf/index.aspx. This is a brief introduction to ETFs and some of their advantages over mutual funds.

National Association of Real Estate Investment Trusts, Inc. "All about REITs." *REIT.com*. http://www.reit.com/AboutREITs/AllAboutREITs.aspx. This is a brief introduction to REITs, but it links to other pages that get into more details of REIT investing.

Pearlman, Russell. "Annuities Provide Shelter in a Storm but Come With Their Own Risks." *The Wall Street Journal*, August 16, 2011. This article discusses the pros and cons of annuities that investors should consider.

————. "Follow the (New) Signs." *SmartMoney* 20, January 2011: 64–67. This article discusses some of the economic indicators that professionals like to watch in order to get a jump on other investors.

Perkins, Anthony B. "IPOs Go Dutch, and Small Investors Gain." *The Wall Street Journal*, December 27, 1999. This article describes the Dutch auction IPO process and what its advantages may be relative to book-building IPOs.

Pleven, Liam. "The Case against Commodities." *The Wall Street Journal*, October 5, 2011. As the title suggests, this article argues that commodities don't really make great long-term investments.

Pollock, Michael. "When Funds Turn Cold, Do You Sell?" *The Wall Street Journal*, August 8, 2011. This article discusses when to sell off mutual funds that are not performing as well as expected.

Prior, Anna. "Costly Currency." *SmartMoney* 20, February 2011: 28. This article discusses the many costs that you incur by trading foreign currencies.

Ruffenach, Glenn. "Do-It-Yourself Annuities: A Blueprint." *SmartMoney*, August 4, 2011. http://www.smartmoney.com/retirement/planning/doityourself-annuities-a-blueprint-1312412609198/?mg=com-sm. This is a practical guide to managing your own investments and cashing them out after retirement so that you provide yourself with a steady stream of income.

Shefrin, Hersh. "Behavioral Foundations." Chap. 1 in *Behavioral Corporate Finance: Decisions That Create Value*. New York: McGraw-Hill Irwin, 2007. Shefrin is one of the top experts in behavioral economics. This is an excellent introduction to the ways that human nature interferes with investing success.

Stewart, James B. "Breaking Up Is Hard to Do." *SmartMoney* 19, September 2010: 34–35. Stewart is a very good personal finance columnist for *SmartMoney* magazine and is always worth reading; you can find his columns online at smartmoney.com. This article discusses when to sell your assets.

———. "How Would a Common Sense Investing Approach Work with Bonds?" *SmartMoney* 20, March 2011: 24–25. This article discusses when to sell bonds, according to Stewart's so-called common sense approach to investing, which is a mild market-timing strategy.

———. "When People Act like I'm Crazy, I Know I'm on the Right Track." *SmartMoney* 20, July 2011: 22–23. This article discusses Stewart's common sense strategy applied to stocks.

Swensen, David F. *Unconventional Success: A Fundamental Approach to Personal Investment*. New York: The Free Press, 2005. This book lays out a set of core investments that every individual investor should hold. It's a bit too restrictive, but the book nonetheless is comprehensive and informative.

U.S. Securities and Exchange Commission. "Exchange-Traded Funds (ETFs)." http://www.sec.gov/answers/etf.htm. This is a brief but solid introduction to what ETFs are and what they do.

Woolley, Suzanne. "Squeeze Your Portfolio Harder." *BusinessWeek* no. 3914 (2004–2005): 136. This article discusses what covered calls are and how to use them.

Zweig, Jason. "Is Gold Cheap? Who Knows? But Gold-Mining Stocks Are." *The Wall Street Journal*, September 17, 2011. Zweig's column, "The Intelligent Investor," in *The Wall Street Journal* is worth following. This article discusses when to buy commodity producers' stock rather than the commodity.

———. *The Little Book of Safe Money*. Hoboken, NJ: John Wiley and Sons, 2010. This book gives advice about how to manage your finances and investments safely.

———. "Why Buying on the Dips Isn't All It's Cracked Up to Be." *The Wall Street Journal*, September 24, 2011. This article argues that the market-timing strategy of buying on the dips doesn't actually work very well.

———. "Why We Can't Let Go of Our Losers." *The Wall Street Journal*, October 15, 2011. This article discusses the psychological reasons that people hold losing investments too long and what you can do about it.

———. *Your Money and Your Brain: How the New Science of Neuroeconomics Can Help Make You Rich*. New York: Simon and Schuster, 2007. This book is about how human psychology and physiology can interfere with investing—or create opportunities for investing.

Internet Resources

Investopedia: The Web's Largest Investing Resource. http://www. investopedia.com. This is a very comprehensive website that provides simple definitions as well as extensive articles about most investing topics. It is information focused—not sales driven.

SmartMoney. http://www.smartmoney.com. Several personal financial magazines have good websites; this one is from *SmartMoney*, which is *The Wall Street Journal*'s personal finance magazine. The columns and news are well written, and the advice and other tools are useful.

The Motley Fool: To Educate, Amuse, and Enrich. http://www.fool.com. This website has become a little too commercial, but it still provides solid investing information and advice.

U.S. Securities and Exchange Commission. http://www.sec.gov. One of the missions of the U.S. Securities and Exchange Commission is to protect and educate individual investors. There are many links to good resources on this site.

Notes

Notes

Notes

Notes

Notes

Notes

Notes